The Making of a Mental Patient

Editors

RICHARD H. PRICE
Indiana University

BRUCE DENNER
*Community Mental Health Program
at the Illinois Mental Health Institutes*

HOLT, RINEHART AND WINSTON, INC.
New York   Chicago   San Francisco   Atlanta   Dallas
Montreal   Toronto   London   Sydney

Preface

A fundamental premise of this book is that an understanding of how other people perceive, react to, and influence the person who becomes a mental patient is as important as an understanding of biological or intrapsychic influences on his behavior. In a sense, then, this book is as much about the other people in the life of a mental patient as it is about the mental patient himself.

We have chosen to examine the social circumstances of the mental patient by following the sequence of events he encounters as he moves from community to hospital. We begin at the point at which someone, perhaps a family member or employer, first notices something odd or unusual about his behavior. We follow him during contacts with various community resources, during commitment proceedings, to his entrance and stay in a mental hospital, and finally we observe his return to the community where he attempts to resume his life and work. The papers in this volume have been selected and arranged to reflect this chronology and to focus on the life situation a person confronts at various critical stages in becoming a mental patient.

Of course, there are as many different sequences of this kind as there are people who become mental patients. At the same time there has been a recent shift in approach toward community-based treatment for mental patients. Thus, the picture provided by these articles can only be considered tentative. Nevertheless, if we are finally to understand the social environment of the mental patient and how it shapes his behavior, this is at least a place to begin.

We would like to thank a number of people for their help in the preparation of this book. Mary Price and Loretta Denner provided invaluable comic relief, Dennis and Pat Bouffard helped greatly in various capacities, and Janet Peckinpaugh, Darlene Stuckey, and Donna Littrell carefully and patiently typed portions of the manuscript.

Bloomington, Indiana   R.H.P.
Chicago, Illinois   B.D.

Contents

WITHDRAWN

INTRODUCTION

Becoming a mental patient is not a simple matter of getting sick or having a "nervous breakdown" and going to a mental hospital. The process of becoming a mental patient can be thought of as the product of the complex interaction of biological, experiential, and social factors that we are only beginning to understand. In order to gain even a rudimentary idea of how a person becomes a mental patient we must begin by considering the distinction between *individual differences* in behavior and the *social reaction* to those individual differences.

There are, of course, a variety of individual differences that play an important part in the day-to-day functioning of people. Individual differences that immediately come to mind include intellectual ability, stress tolerance, and interpersonal skills. Broadly speaking, these differences are determined by a person's social learning history, as well as by constitutional and genetic factors. Furthermore, how any particular person may react in a given situation is determined by a complex interaction of these factors. To take a simple example, a person having low stress tolerance and meager interpersonal skills is likely to react very differently in a stressful situation from a person with greater tolerance for stress and more substantial interpersonal skills.

Whatever the person's reaction, *once the behavior is observed and reacted to by others* an entirely different set of factors come into play. It is the social reaction to the person's behavior that determines whether or not that behavior will be seen as "normal" on the one hand or "peculiar" on the other. The social reaction may also play an important role in determining whether the person will come to be considered a "mental case" or merely an "eccentric." Just as a complex interaction of the variables controlling individual differences determines what behavior a person is likely to display in a given situation, so does a complex interaction of the variables controlling the social reaction to the behavior determine how it will be seen by others.

1

A partial list of the factors that are important in determining the social reaction to individual differences might include: community norms for and tolerance of various forms of behavior, the social and economic status of the person displaying the behavior, and the prevailing attitude toward and availability of mental health facilities. For example, the same behavior may be tolerated or passed off as "a little strange" in one community and seen as a sign of severe mental disturbance in another.

Thus, we wish to distinguish clearly between those factors that determine individual differences on the one hand and those that determine whether or not a person will become a mental patient on the other. This distinction has seldom been preserved in theoretical accounts of abnormal behavior. There are a number of important reasons for the failure to appreciate this distinction. Perhaps the most important reason is that there is almost invariably an *interaction* between the variables controlling individual differences and those that determine whether the person will become a mental patient or not. The interaction may take a variety of forms. For example, as we have suggested, the same behavior may evoke very different reactions in others depending upon community norms or the social context in which it occurs. In one case the person displaying deviant behavior may be viewed as eccentric, in the other case as psychotic. Or on the other hand, the same social situation, particularly if it is stressful, may produce very different reactions in different individuals. One person may react with fear, withdrawal, and depression while another may respond by actively coping with the situation.

Once made, the distinction between individual differences and the social reaction to those differences seems self-evident. Nevertheless, the distinction is often blurred and its implications are not examined. There are at least three additional reasons for the failure to appreciate this distinction.

The first class of reasons may be roughly described as conceptual. Sociologists and other researchers principally concerned with the societal reaction to various forms of behavior have come to conceive of the problem of abnormal behavior in a very different way from psychologists and psychiatrists who have emphasized the role of individual differences. Thus, students of society have quite understandably come to assume that the variables with which they are most concerned (such as social power and status, community norms) are of great importance in the expression and maintenance of abnormal behavior. Similarly, psychiatrists and psychologists who typically are concerned with the experiential and genetic determinants of individual differences have come to consider these variables as the most important determinants of abnormal behavior. As Price (1972) has noted, proponents of each point of view have come to "see" the problem of abnormal behavior quite differently. At their worst, such differences in emphasis become a kind of "nothing-butism" in which proponents of each view simply reassert their belief in the preeminence of their own favorite set of determinants.

The second reason is ideological and revolves around the question of the rights of the individual as opposed to those of society. Strong proponents of the position for individual rights tend to argue that nearly any form of social intervention in response to the behavior of an individual represents a threat to the right of self-determination of that individual. Proponents of the position for the rights of society, on the other hand, argue that society has a right to protection and that treatment is merely for the person's "own good." Becker (1964) has described these ideological differences in terms of what he calls "conventional and unconventional sentimentality." These ideological positions are also often tied to preconceptions about the etiology of mental illness. Champions of individual rights tend to attribute the major causes of psychopathology to unjust or capricious social forces while supporters of the rights of society usually attribute abnormal behavior to individual failings.

The third reason for the failure to appreciate the distinction between individual differences and patienthood is methodological. We have said that abnormal behavior is a product of the interaction of individual differences and social variables. However, since both sets of variables are already in operation when the behavior is observed in the clinic or laboratory it is very difficult to disentangle the effects of one or the other. Thus, in our current state of relative ignorance it is all too easy for proponents of one view or another to practice a kind of theoretical imperialism in which the phenomena of abnormal behavior is the disputed territory.

In this volume we are concerned with understanding the career of the mental patient largely from the point of view of the social reaction to him and his behavior. This is not to deny the importance of learning, genetic, and other factors in the production of whatever behavior it is that provides the stimulus for social reaction. But if it is the case, as we have suggested, that the social reaction to individual differences is important in determining the fate of those who will spend a substantial portion of their lives in mental hospitals, then the study of that reaction requires no further justification.

Becoming a Mental Patient

What happens to a person who becomes a mental patient? Certainly, there are as many answers to this question as there are people who have undergone the experience. But there is a growing body of literature that can provide us with some tentative answers to this question.

In order to understand how the process of becoming a mental patient unfolds and how it affects the individual, let us consider a hypothetical "case history" based on findings documented in the articles in this volume. Our case history begins at the point when someone first notices his "odd" or "peculiar" behavior and reacts to it and it ends when he is finally viewed by himself and others as a chronic mental patient.

As the patient moves through this sequence of events, we will note various crucial choice points. These choice points and the contingencies associated with them are important in determining whether the person is able to return to normal life or will continue on the path of his career to its end point—that of the chronic mental patient. By the time our story is finished, we should be able to more fully appreciate Goffman's (1959) comment that, "one could say that mental patients *distinctively* suffer not from mental illness but from contingencies" (p. 127).

The career of our hypothetical person begins when people, perhaps his wife or employer first notice that his behavior seems strange or peculiar to them. At first they may deny or minimize this peculiarity, but if the behavior becomes public or especially frightening, they may tentatively conclude that he has a "mental problem" (Mechanic, 1962; Smith et al., 1963; Yarrow et al., 1955).

Those especially concerned with the person may then contact one or more of a variety of people: the family physician, the clergyman, the police, or a psychiatrist (Clauson & Yarrow, 1955). Depending on who is consulted, the person's path to the mental hospital may turn in one direction or another. If the police are called in, they may simply administer "psychiatric first aid" (Bittner, 1967) and leave the person to his own devices. If it is the clergy, perhaps assurances and moral support will be offered. If the family doctor or a psychiatrist is consulted, the person may be referred for psychiatric treatment.

But even the fact that a person has sought help from a psychiatrist may alter other people's reactions to him, as Phillips (1963) has shown. The very act of seeking help may lead others to react negatively to him.

If it is concluded that hospitalization is necessary, the person may then have to undergo commitment proceedings. In this case he will be examined in court where a judge will hear testimony from psychiatrists concerning his competence. Often these proceedings are brief and cursory. Although such hearings are presumably intended to evaluate the competence of the individual, they may proceed on the *presumption* that he is mentally ill (Scheff, 1964).

Of course, not all persons react similarly to sanity hearings, and the way they react may affect whether they are released or committed to a mental hospital (Miller & Schwartz, 1966). In addition, whether the person has a lawyer or not may significantly affect the outcome of the hearing, regardless of how disturbed he appears (Wenger & Fletcher, 1969).

Yet another significant turn in the person's career comes as he first encounters the mental hospital. If he is a voluntary patient, whether he is admitted to the hospital or not may depend more on whether he has been hospitalized before than on how disturbed he appears (Mendel & Rapport, 1969). Once he is admitted, the person may undergo a series of depersonalizing processes. Often, personal effects will be taken from him. He will then begin to be indoctrinated into the life of the mental hospital (Goffman, 1959).

The very fact of being hospitalized is unsettling and may produce anxiety, paranoid suspicion, and depression (Goldman, Bohr, & Steinberg, 1970). Thus, simply being placed in a mental hospital may elicit behavior from the person that, although it is largely a reaction to the hospital environment, may then be interpreted as part of the patient's problem.

At the point of hospitalization and once he is hospitalized, the patient is subject to medical decisions. These decisions are often strongly affected by the use of a "conservative" decision-making strategy by the examining physician or psychiatrist. That is, when in doubt about the patient's mental state, the psychiatrist may decide to hospitalize or retain the person in the hospital (Scheff, 1963). This is probably a perfectly reasonable decision to make in the case of physical illness, particularly if it is contagious. But in the case of psychiatric hospitalization it may do the patient more harm than good. In addition, Temerlin (1968) has shown that psychiatric diagnoses may be affected by a variety of extraneous factors, including the opinions of prestigeful colleagues, rather than the actual behavior of the patient, even when these opinions are incorrect.

Once in the mental hospital, treatment may be instituted and the patient may find himself in a therapeutic community. But Zeitlyn (1969) suggests that such communities may at times be characterized by a staff which has an authoritarian orientation toward the patients and is more concerned with the appearance than with the reality of a therapeutic program. Some staff members the patient may encounter may be "key jinglers" who are more concerned with looking helpful to patients than actually being helpful (Hartman, 1969).

But the mental patient is not just a passive recipient of institutional demands and pressures. He often finds his own way of "making it" in the mental hospital. In fact, some patients may actually use their symptoms as a means of managing the impressions that they make on the staff in order to pursue their own goals in the hospital setting (Braginsky, Grosse, & Ring, 1966).

However, despite their attempts to cope with the hospital setting, patients are inevitably affected by their stay, particularly if it has been lengthy. Some patients may give up any hope of discharge and make the institution their home, passively relinquishing their responsibilities and rights (Zusman, 1966). Such patients are usually described as "institutionalized" and will face grave problems in adjusting when they are released from the mental hospital —if, in fact, they are ever released (Paul, 1969).

Upon release the ex-mental patient finds himself a stigmatized and rejected individual (Lamy, 1966). The stigma he now carries —that is, the fact that he has been a patient in a mental hospital— will affect his interpersonal relations and in some cases he may suffer job discrimination (Miller & Dawson, 1965). But even if the ex-mental patient is able to get a job there is evidence (Farina & Ring, 1965) that co-workers who perceive him as mentally ill may reject him. He may be blamed for poor job performance even when there is no objective evidence to substantiate such a claim.

The case history we have just sketched is not a pleasant nor a hopeful one. And certainly not all persons who enter mental hospitals will follow precisely the path we have outlined. But more is needed than simply to give an account of some of the abuses encountered by persons who undergo psychiatric hospitalization. We must consider the implications of becoming a mental patient from the point of view of the human and civil rights of the individual. At the same time, the case history outlined above suggests a number of implications for research that may clarify the picture still further.

Some Implications of Becoming a Mental Patient

Human and Civil Rights It is somewhat ironic that the concept of mental illness originally gained much of its impetus in the name of humanitarian reform, and yet today we find there exists a great deal of criticism of the concept of mental illness, at least in part for humanitarian reasons. Although Pinel was able to remove the chains from the inmates of the Bicêtre by declaring that they were mentally ill, today many people lose a substantial portion of their human and civil rights when the same declaration is made about them. Commitment proceedings, the right to treatment, research on incarcerated populations, and job discrimination are all issues that arise when we consider the potential abuse of the rights of persons who become mental patients.

The commitment proceeding itself raises a number of questions about the rights of persons designated as mentally ill. Tolchin, Steinfeld and Suchotliff (1970) point out that normally we place limitations on liberty of others only as a form of punishment for breaking a law, and only after due process of law has been observed. But in the case of the mental patient often the only laws he violates are the laws of psychiatry.

The papers in this volume by Scheff (1963) and by Miller and Schwartz (1966) suggest that the commitment proceeding is often a cursory affair in which the person being examined has little opportunity to defend himself and his actions. In fact, in many cases, the person being examined is presumed to be mentally ill even before the proceeding starts. In addition, the defendant is not necessarily represented by counsel. Lindman and McIntyre (1961) indicate that less than half of the states have laws that require that the patient be provided with counsel in commitment proceedings.

If an individual is committed to a mental institution he suffers the loss of a large number of rights that the ordinary citizen takes for granted. Mezer and Rheingold (1962) list a number of them: making a will, making a contract or deed, being married or divorced, adopting a child, receiving property, making a gift, voting, operating a vehicle, giving valid consent, being a witness or juror, or managing or participating in a business as a director or stockholder. It is important to note that when an individual loses his civil rights as a result of commitment proceedings, the loss is not selective. That is, it is not assumed that his presumed disability affects some areas of competency and not others. Instead, the fact that he is adjudged "mentally ill" strips him of all of his civil rights regardless of his actual capacity to carry out his rights and duties in any specific area.

A second area of concern is the right to treatment. Birnbaum (1960) advocates "recognition and enforcement of the legal right of the mentally ill inmate of a public mental institution to adequate medical treatment for his mental illness." But most large mental institutions are not really treatment institutions but instead function as custodial institutions whose primary mission is to contain those who violate others' sense of decency or reality. Thus, it is not clear that being hospitalized insures the right to treatment.

In addition, Tolchin, Steinfeld, and Suchotliff (1970) point out that mental patients are generally the last persons to be consulted in the matter of treatment and seldom are given the option to select their own treatment.

Perhaps more important is the right to refuse treatment. Persons with legitimate physical diseases retain the right to refuse treatment even if such a refusal is clearly not in their own interests. The only exceptions are infectious diseases that might create a danger to public health. But what about the mental patient? As Tolchin et al. (1970) point out, "After a particular treatment has been decided upon, the patient is usually not given the option to refuse treatment. Many of the same types of coercion used against patients who try to leave against medical advice are applied to patients who attempt to refuse treatment, for example, threat of loss of privileges. These threats are violations of rights done in the name of helping the patient, protecting him from himself and others" (p. 215).

Yet another area of concern involves research on incarcerated populations. Until recently mental patients were experimented upon with little or no regard for their right to refuse such experimentation. Even in the case where informed consent is required of the patient before he participates in research, there still remains the subtle coercion based on the possibility of preferential treatment for those who volunteer as research subjects. As Beecher (1970) notes, no explicit promise of preferential treatment need be made for the "volunteer" to believe that it might be forthcoming if he does participate in the research program.

Finally, after the patient has left the mental hospital, the threat to his civil and human rights may continue. The very fact that a person has spent some time in a mental institution may have an important effect on his ability to obtain and retain a job regardless of his current psychological state. The paper in this volume by Miller and Dawson (1965) documents some of the effects of the stigma of mental illness on the reemployment of ex-mental patients.

The fact that ex-mental patients are often discriminated against in the job market raises a provocative question. Can we compare the social dilemma of the mental patient with that of other minority groups? Scheff (1967) points out that popular conceptions of mental illness are often oversimplified, and that:

> The causal assumption of simplicity is reminiscent of situations involving racial or class distinctions. The superordinate group often holds stereotypes about the members of the subordinate group: "Everybody knows" that Negroes are inferior or that the lower classes are incapable of governing themselves. In order to understand the situation of the mentally ill, this discussion suggests that one could profit by comparing their position with that of other subordinate minorities. Psychological processes such as stereotyping, projection, and stigmatization, and social processes such as rejection, segregation, and isolation characterize, to some degree, the orientation of the in-group toward the out-group regardless of the basis of the distinction. (pp. 3–4)

Involuntary hospitalization is often defended on the grounds that society has a right to protect itself against persons who may be dangerous. Such protection may be necessary at times, but we may ask, on what basis does society make decisions about which persons are "dangerous" and which persons are "not dangerous"? Dershowitz (1969) reports that his survey of the literature on the prediction of antisocial conduct suggests that the few empirical studies which do exist indicate that psychiatrists are rather inaccurate predictors of antisocial conduct.

> Even more significant for legal purposes, it seems that psychiatrists are particularly prone to one type of error—overprediction. They tend to predict anti-social conduct in many instances where it would not, in fact, occur. Indeed, our research suggests that for every correct psychiatric prediction of violence, there are numerous erroneous predictions. That is, among every group of inmates presently confined on the basis of psychiatric predictions of violence, there are only a few who would, and many more who would not, actually engage in such conduct if released. (p. 47)

In all of the areas which we have briefly mentioned, commitment proceedings, the right to treatment, research on incarcerated populations, job discrimination, and incarceration because of presumed "dangerousness," there exist potential if not always actual threats to the human and civil rights of the person designated as mentally ill. It is our belief that these abuses are not the result of evil intentions. More often they are the result of well-meaning ignorance. But whatever the reason, be it evil intent or mere ignorance, the abuses do appear to exist and one obvious remedy is their exposure.

Implications for Research   One clear implication of the papers in this volume is that what we call mental illness is not merely a property of the behavior of those who are designated as mentally ill. Nor is it simply a product of social forces and institutions. It is instead a complex interaction of the two. A comprehensive and detailed description of abnormal behavior cannot emerge from the study of the individual in a contextual vacuum any more than it will emerge from a description of the social institutions currently used to treat that behavior. With this general orientation in mind, it is possible to point to a number of research questions to which we badly need answers.

Three problems that immediately suggest themselves are (1) the nature of the career of mental patients, (2) the effects of total institutions on symptom expression and maintenance, and (3) the role of public attitudes in the perception, shaping, and maintenance of abnormal behavior.

The papers in this volume suggest that it may be useful to study the careers of mental patients from the point at which someone initially "recognizes" their behavior as abnormal through successive stages. We do not yet have an adequate idea of the contingencies in the career of the mental patient. What are the important choice points in his career when he may either return to society or continue on his career as a mental patient? What variables affect these contingencies?

In addition, the role of the patient himself has often been ignored. We may ask, who is able to exit from the career of mental patient and who is not? What variables are associated with the ability to avoid psychiatric hospitalization? Is it the case, as some observers contend, that the ability to avoid being hospitalized is largely due to the social power to avoid being labeled? Or, on the other hand, is it merely that those who avoid hospitalization are less disturbed and, therefore, not "a danger to themselves or others" as is conventionally argued?

Similarly, we may ask, to what degree do psychiatric institutions themselves create or perpetuate symptoms? It is possible that much of the behavior of mental patients whom we observe in psychiatric hospitals is a result, not of their presumed illness, but of the environment in which they are forced to live. Recent research by Wing and Brown (1970) makes clear what has long been suspected. The environment of psychiatric hospitals can have a profound effect upon the type and severity of symptoms displayed by schizophrenic patients. The problem is a complex one. Moos (1968) and his colleagues (Moos & Houts, 1968) have shown that individual differences, situational factors, and the interaction between the two all may substantially affect symptoms.

A recent paper by Sarbin (1969) raises a related question. He suggests that "Many of the language and thought defects noted in hospitalized schizophrenics are *products, resultants*, or *outcomes* of certain . . . social events associated with labeling a person as mentally ill and with the attendant instrumental acts and rituals carried out by medical, legal, and other professional personnel" (p. 192). Thus, as Sarbin (1969) and Mednick and McNeil (1968) have noted, it is possible that studies of thought disorder in schizophrenia, if carried out on institutionalized groups, reflect the effects of institutionalization as much as some underlying disease process.

Yet another area that needs considerably more study is the area of public attitudes toward mental illness. Nunnally (1961) has made one such pioneering effort to study popular conceptions of mental health and mental illness. A recent review of public attitudes toward mental illness by Sarbin and Mancuso (1970) suggests, somewhat surprisingly, that the mental illness paradigm as a formula for understanding and controlling deviant conduct has not been widely accepted by the public. Furthermore, they suggest that the mental health movement, with all of its attempts to regard mental illness with the same nonrejecting valuations as physical illness, has failed. Instead, the public tends to hold negative valuations toward persons diagnosed as mentally ill.

The work of Yarrow and her colleagues as well as the work of Smith and Mechanic all suggest that we know little about how a person comes to be "recognized" as mentally ill. What sorts of behavior lead an observer to conclude that a particular individual might be suffering from a mental problem? What values, attitudes, and standards of the observer make him more or less prone to judge a person as "mentally ill"?

The need to study public attitudes toward mental illness is important, not only because the public may reject individuals designated as mentally ill but also because such attitudes will inevitably affect public policy. Nunnally (1961) has suggested that many of the same attitudes which the public holds about mentally ill persons are held by mental health professionals as well. There is a need not only to study the attitudes of laymen toward the mentally ill but the attitudes of policy makers, legislators, and those people charged with the care of persons described as mentally ill.

REFERENCES

Becker, H. *Outsiders: Studies in the sociology of deviance.* New York: Free Press, 1964.

Beecher, H. K. *Research and the individual: Human studies.* Boston: Little, Brown & Co., 1970.

Birnbaum, M. The right to treatment. *American Bar Association Journal*, 1960, *46*, 499–505.

Bittner, E. Police discretion in emergency apprehension of mentally ill persons. *Social Problems*, 1967, *14*, 278–292.

Braginsky, B. M., Grosse, M., & Ring, K. Controlling outcomes through impression management: An experimental study of the manipulative tactics of mental patients. *Journal of Consulting Psychology*, 1966, *30*, 295–300.

Clausen, J. A., & Yarrow, Marian R. Paths to the mental hospital. *Journal of Social Issues*, 1955, *11* (4), 25–32.

Dershowitz, A. M. The psychiatrist's power in civil commitment: A knife that cuts both ways. *Psychology Today*, 1969, *2*, 42–47.

Farina, A., & Ring, K. The influence of perceived mental illness on interpersonal relations. *Journal of Abnormal Psychology*, 1965, *70*, 47–51.

Goffman, E. The moral career of the mental patient. *Psychiatry*, 1959, *22*, 123–131.

Goldman, A. R., Bohr, R. H., & Steinberg, T. A. On posing as mental patients: Reminiscences and recommendations. *Professional Psychology*, 1970, *1*, 427–434.

Hartman, C. The key jingler. *Community Mental Health Journal*, 1969, *5*, 199–205.

Lamy, R. E. Social consequences of mental illness. *Journal of Consulting Psychology*, 1966, *30*, 450–455.

Lindman, F. T., & McIntyre, D. M. *The mentally disabled and the law.* Chicago: University of Chicago Press, 1961.

Mechanic, D. Some factors in identifying and defining mental illness. *Mental Hygiene*, 1962, *46*, 66–74.

Mednick, S. A., & McNeil, T. F. Current methodology on the etiology of schizophrenia: Serious difficulties which suggest the use of the high-risk-group method. *Psychological Bulletin,* 1968, *70,* 681–693.

Mendel, W. M., & Rapport, S. Determinants of the decision for psychiatric hospitalization. *Archives of General Psychiatry,* 1969, *20,* 321–328.

Mezer, R. R., & Rheingold, P. D. Mental capacity and incompetency: A psycho-legal problem. *American Journal of Psychiatry,* 1962, *118,* 827–831.

Miller, D., & Dawson, W. H. Effects of stigma on re-employment of ex-mental patients. *Mental Hygiene,* 1965, *49,* 281–287.

Miller, Dorothy, & Schwartz, M. County Lunacy Commission Hearings: Some observations of commitments to a state mental hospital. *Social Problems,* 1966, *14,* 26–35.

Moos, R. H. Situational analysis of a therapeutic community milieu. *Journal of Abnormal Psychology,* 1968, *73,* 49–61.

Moos, R. H., & Houts, P. S. Assessment of the social atmospheres of psychiatric wards. *Journal of Abnormal Psychology,* 1968, *73,* 595–604.

Nunnally, J. *Popular conceptions of mental health: Their development and change.* New York: Holt, Rinehart and Winston, 1961.

Paul, G. L. The chronic mental patient: Current status—future directions. *Psychological Bulletin,* 1969, *71,* 81–92.

Phillips, D. L. Rejection: A possible consequence of seeking help for mental disorders. *American Sociological Review,* 1963, *28,* 963–972.

Price, R. H. *Abnormal behavior: Perspectives in conflict.* New York: Holt, Rinehart and Winston, 1972.

Sarbin, T. R. Schizophrenic thinking: A role-theoretical analysis. *Journal of Personality,* 1969, *37,* 190–206.

Sarbin, T. R., & Mancuso, J. C. Failure of a moral enterprise: Attitudes of the public toward mental illness. *Journal of Consulting and Clinical Psychology,* 1970, *35,* 159–173.

Scheff, T. J. Decision rules, types of error and their consequences in medical diagnosis. *Behavioral Science,* 1963, *7,* 97–108.

Scheff, T. J. The societal reaction to deviance: Ascriptive elements in the psychiatric screening of mental patients in a midwestern state. *Social Problems,* 1964, *11,* 401–413.

Scheff, T. J. (Ed.) *Mental illness and social processes.* New York: Harper & Row, 1967.

Smith, Kathleen, Pumphrey, Muriel W., & Hall, J. C. The "last straw": The decisive incident resulting in the request for hospitalization in 100 schizophrenic patients. *American Journal of Psychiatry,* 1963, *120,* 228–233.

Temerlin, M. K. Suggestion effects in psychiatric diagnosis. *Journal of Nervous and Mental Disease*, 1968, *147*, 349–353.

Tolchin, G., Steinfeld, G., & Suchotliff, L. The mental patient and civil rights: Some moral, legal, and ethical considerations. *Professional Psychology*, 1970, *1*, 212–216.

Wenger, D. L., & Fletcher, C. R. The effect of legal counsel on admissions to a state mental hospital: A confrontation of professions. *Journal of Health and Social Behavior*, 1969, *10*, 66–72.

Wing, J. K., & Brown, G. W. *Institutionalism and schizophrenia: A comparative study of three mental hospitals.* Cambridge: Cambridge University Press, 1970.

Yarrow, Marian R., Schwartz, Charlotte G., Murphy, Harriet S., & Deasy, Leila C. The psychological meaning of mental illness in the family. *Journal of Social Issues*, 1955, *11* (4), 12–24.

Zeitlyn, B. B. The therapeutic community—fact or fantasy? *International Journal of Psychiatry*, 1969, *7*, 195–200.

Zusman, J. Some explanations of the changing appearance of psychotic patients. In E. M. Gruenberg (Ed.), *Evaluating the effectiveness of community mental health services.* New York: Milbank, 1966.

PART ONE

Personal and Public Reactions to Abnormal Behavior

The papers in this first section consider the events that can occur in the life of a person before he ever reaches the psychiatric hospital. A variety of different people in the community—his family, the police, the clergy, and various mental health professionals—may all have dealings with him before any decision for hospitalization is made. How others view the behavior of the person who is to become a mental patient is crucial. For in the last analysis, it is how others view his behavior and how they react to him that are the deciding factors in whether he will begin on the path to the mental hospital or remain in the community.

The article by Mechanic offers a descriptive model of the process by which people in the community come to judge a person as mentally ill. He points out that family, friends, community, and psychiatric authorities all may be involved in this process of redefinition. Each of these groups may have slightly different standards for deciding whether or not the person is suffering from symptoms of mental illness. Nevertheless, the evaluator, whoever he may be, attempts to understand the motives of the person suspected of mental illness by imagining himself in the circumstances of that person. If the evaluator can not empathize with the behavior and motives of the person, he may judge the behavior as "queer," "strange," or "sick."

Mechanic points out that the basic decision as to whether or not a person is suffering from mental illness is made by community members and not mental health professionals. Once the person is referred to the professionals, it is often already assumed that he is in need of treatment.

The paper by Yarrow and her colleagues brings to life, through illustrative case histories, one aspect of the definitional process described by Mechanic. The authors show how the wife of a potential mental patient perceives, reacts to, and copes with the disturbing and sometimes incomprehensible behavior of her husband. She begins with the assumption that nothing is wrong, but as his behavior continues, she slowly begins to reorganize her percep-

16

tions of him. Ultimately she arrives at the conclusion that he is a victim of mental illness and is in need of hospitalization.

The process by which the wife changes her perceptions of her husband is a complex one filled with ambiguities and ambivalence. But Yarrow and her colleagues find several distinct patterns that may emerge as the wife goes through successive redefinitions of her husband's problem. She is in a kind of "perceptual tug of war" between the growing evidence that something is wrong with him and her extreme reluctance to conclude that he is mentally ill. Her attempts to deal with this conflict may be manifested in outright denial or in attempts to normalize his behavior or to "balance off" his appropriate behavior against the obviously peculiar and bizarre behavior he engages in.

Of course, the police often deal with people who behave peculiarly. As Bittner points out in his fascinating paper, the police have the discretionary freedom to apprehend and convey people to mental hospitals on an emergency basis. He argues that police use this discretionary power only when there are no other alternatives available to them. Thus, how the police deal with mentally ill persons appears not to be so much a question of legality, but a question of practical alternatives.

Bittner suggests that it is not enough for an individual to be psychotic for the police to act. The case must be one that produces a threat to life or to the public order. One of the most fascinating aspects of Bittner's account is his description of the nonofficial ways that the police have of dealing with mentally ill people. Their goal appears to be to keep the peace rather than to enforce the law. In some cases they may entrust the observation of people suspected of mental illness to bartenders or news vendors. At times they may apply "psychiatric first aid" in which they make no attempt to suppress or deny the bizarre beliefs of the people they deal with. In other instances they may find individuals in the community to provide continuing care to disturbed individuals.

The paper by Smith and Hall is concerned with the question of the types of incidents that lead to hospitalization. These incidents are often described by the family of the patient as the "last straw" that led to hospitalization. The authors studied 100 decisive incidents that resulted in the subsequent hospitalization of diagnosed schizophrenic patients. They found that the incidents were quite varied and had no systematic relationship to the age, sex, marital status, religion, or social class of the person. Instead, what appeared to make an incident "decisive" depended on the specific sensitivities of the family or community member observing the behavior. If the behavior elicited fear, shame, or disgust in the observer, it was likely to become a "last straw."

In his article, Phillips shows that even when a person sees himself as needing help and actively seeks it, he will not be able to avoid the negative reactions of others. Phillips studied the reactions of community members to hypothetical individuals who sought different help sources. When the help source was a clergyman, the community member's reaction was mild and little rejection was observed. But if he sought help from a psychiatrist or a mental hospital, the community reaction was much more severe and rejecting. Thus, ironically, even an attempt to seek psychiatric help may elicit rejection by others.

Some Factors in Identifying and Defining Mental Illness

David Mechanic

The procedures through which persons in need of psychiatric treatment are identified and treated are frequently unclear. On some occasions persons exhibiting relatively mild symptoms are identified as psychiatric problems and appear for treatment, while persons with more serious psychiatric symptoms go unrecognized and untreated.

Yet the routes taken by patients who are brought to or appear at the hospital, clinic, or office of the private psychiatrist, provide the sociologist with an opportunity to illuminate the processes of patient selection and treatment.

A number of studies along these lines[1] have contributed richly to our understanding of these processes. These studies have pointed to the varying definitions of illness that are made at various locations in the social structure.[2] For example, the patient

This is a revised version of a paper presented at the Annual Meeting of the American Sociological Association in New York City in August, 1960. Reprinted from *Mental Hygiene*, vol. 46, 1962, pp. 66–74. The impressions reported here stem, in part, from exploratory interviews and observations at two California hospitals. These observations were carried out with the assistance of Research Grant MF–8516 of the National Institute of Mental Health.

[1] Hollingshead, A. B. and R. C. Redlich, *Social Class and Mental Illness* (New York: John Wiley & Sons, 1958); Myers, J. K. and B. H. Roberts, *Family and Class Dynamics in Mental Illness* (New York: John Wiley & Sons, 1959); Clausen, J. A. and Marian R. Yarrow, eds., "The Impact of Mental Illness on the Family," *Journal of Social Issues*, 11 (December, 1955); Cumming, Elaine and John Cumming, *Closed Ranks* (Cambridge, Mass.: Harvard University Press, 1957).

For an excellent study of the relationship between social class status and mode of treatment received, see Myers, J. K. and L. Schaffer, "Social Stratification and Psychiatric Practice: A Study of an Outpatient Clinic," *American Sociological Review*, 19 (June, 1954), 307–310.

[2] For some reviews of the problems of definition, see Jahoda, Marie, *Current Concepts of Positive Mental Health* (New York: Basic Books, Inc., 1958); Redlich, F. C., "The Concept of Health in Psychiatry," in Leighton, A. H., J. Clausen and R. Wilson, eds., *Explorations in Social Psychiatry* (New York: Basic Books, Inc., 1957); and Cumming and Cumming, *op. cit.*

may view his own illness in terms of his feeling state; his employer might evaluate his symptoms in terms of his apparent deviation from group requirements; and his family may adjudge him "ill" on the basis of the attitude he professes or his situational behavior.

Yet definitions *are* made; patients *do* appear for treatment—although at times by rather devious routes—and psychiatric aid *is* administered. It is the major purpose of this paper to consider some of the definitions that are made, the conflicts that occur, the manner in which resolutions are attempted, and the effects of the definitional process on the eventual decisions as to who receives treatment.

In essence, I will draw a descriptive model of the definitional processes by which persons within a community are adjudged "mentally ill" by family, friends, community authorities and even by themselves, based on observations made at admission wards in two California mental hospitals and other reported research results.

The early definitions of mental illness, especially in middle-class populations, are likely to take place in the groups within which the person primarily operates; evaluations are made by family, fellow employees, friends, and employers. If symptoms appear and are not recognized as such by members of the individual's more primary groups, it is unlikely that he will become accessible to psychiatric personnel unless his symptoms become visible, and disturbing enough to lead to his commitment to some treatment center by external authorities.

On other occasions, it is the person himself, who, in comparing his feelings and behavior with how he thinks others feel and behave or with how he has felt and behaved in the past, defines himself as ill and seeks what he regards as competent help.

Finally, when patients appear for psychiatric treatment, either on their own volition or under pressure of significant others, the physician evaluates the symptoms and then comes to some decision about the "illness." These various evaluations by the person himself, by his social group, by community agencies, and by psychiatric experts may be more or less consistent. However, discrepancies often occur, and when they arise, adequate solutions for resolving these differences are not always readily available.

Problems of definition arise, in part, because all behaviors occur within specific group contexts, and the frames of reference of the evaluators are not always comparable. Also, since the evaluators may be located at different foci of interaction with the person, the behavior they see may differ significantly.

The behaviors defined as symptoms of "illness" may be as much characteristic of some particular situation or group setting as they are enduring attributes of persons. For example, even with purely physiological symptoms, social definitions are applied which have important consequences for the patient and the course of his illness. The symptom may be defined as a sign of "illness" and receive the usual considerations of the sick role, or it may be viewed as an unjustifiable attempt to seek relief from legitimate expectations. It may be evaluated as a symbol of high prestige and community status (as a battle wound) or it may be seen as a consequence of promiscuous and shameful activities (as might be the case with venereal disease). The symptom, in sum, may be worthy of group consideration, sympathy and support, or it may be punished, criticized, or ignored.

Persons with intangible neurotic symptoms which might be interpreted as signs of weakness and excessive self-concern are reacted to quite differently from, for example, persons who have difficulties during such stressful situations as bereavement.

Although seemingly obvious, it is important to state that what may be viewed as deviant in one social group may be tolerated in another, and rewarded in still other groups. How group members view a particular behavior is likely to influence both the frequency with which it occurs and the extent to which it is exhibited. In other words, all groups exercise considerable control over their members.

"Mental illness" and other forms of deviancy become visible when persons in the participant's group recognize his inability and reluctance to make the proper response in his network of interpersonal relations. How a particular deviant behavior is to be evaluated depends largely on the frame of reference the evaluators assume. Whether a deviant act is seen as evidence of "crime," "corruption," "illness," and so on, will be contingent on the criteria with which the evaluator operates and how he applies them.

It is hypothesized that the evaluator attempts to understand the motivation of the actor. In the language of Mead, he assumes the role of the other and attempts to empathize. If the empathy process is successful, the evaluator is likely to feel that he has some basis for labeling the deviant act as "delinquency," "undependability," or whatever.[3] It is primarily in those cases where the evaluator feels at a loss in adequately empathizing with the actor and where he finds it difficult to understand what contributed to the response that the behavior is more likely to be labeled "queer," "strange," "odd," or "sick."

There are behaviors, however, where the distinction is unclear; where, for example, an understandable crime is committed, but the expressed motive makes little sense; it thus becomes difficult to decide whether the actor is a "criminal," a potential "mental patient," or both.[4] In general, however, mental illness is regarded

---

[3] In an interesting experimental study, Jones and deCharms found that the degree to which a confederate is seen as responsible for his behavior when he causes the group to fail is a definite factor in evaluating his dependability. If he causes the group to fail, but is viewed as lacking the necessary ability to perform the necessary task, he is less likely to be defined as "undependable" than if he is viewed as lacking motivation.

See Jones, E. E. and R. deCharms, "Changes in Social Perception as a Function of the Personal Relevance of Behavior," *Sociometry,* 20 (March, 1957), 75–85. Kingsley Davis also presents an argument similar to the one offered in the text of this paper. *See* Davis, K., *Human Society* (New York: Macmillan Co., 1958), Chap. 10.

[4] Public health programs attempt, in some measure, to change the lay evaluation of what constitutes "mental illness." A study by Woodward, J. L., "Changing Ideas on Mental Illness and Its Treatment," *American Sociological Review,* 16 (August, 1951), 443–454, indicates that in at least one community persons are becoming more sensitive to what physicians regard as signs of "mental illness." However, more recently, Shirley Starr, in the analysis of data from a National Opinion Research Center survey, points out that for most people "mental illness" is associated with violent, unpredictable behavior.

The Cummings, *op. cit.,* found that persons in the community they studied had fairly simple notions about "mental illness," and that they were relatively immune to the influence of an educational mental health program. In their book they attempt to analyze why this program failed.

As the public image of "mental illness" slowly changes to conform more closely to that held by the professional psychiatrist, predictability and the ability to take the role of the other may become less important in the evaluation made by lay persons.

R. T. LaPiere, in *The Freudian Ethic* (New York, Duell, Sloan & Pearce,

usually as a residual category for deviant behavior having no clearly specified label.

Of course the physician trained in the treatment of the mentally ill applies different criteria to behavior than does the layman. The criteria he applies to deviant behavior are more closely related to the theory of pathology he holds than to his own ability or inability to take the role of the other. The criteria he holds, however, are at times indefinite and the physician who practices in large treatment centers often must assume the illness of the patient who appears before him and then proceed to prescribe treatment. Both the abstract nature of the physician's theories and the time limitations imposed upon him by the institutional structure of which he is a part make it impossible for him to make a rapid study of the patient's illness or even to ascertain if illness, in fact, exists. Instead, it becomes necessary for him to assume the illness of the patient and to apply some label to the alleged if not recognizable symptoms. The consequences are that the basic decision about illness usually occurs prior to the patient's admission to the hospital and this decision is more or less made by nonprofessional members of the community. It therefore becomes a matter of considerable interest to understand how these nonprofessional members of the community define "mental illness."

Before moving on to discuss the variables affecting community definitions of "mental illness," it is important to emphasize in more detail the preceding point: that the basic decision about illness is usually made by community members and *not professional personnel*. Although the very "sick" are usually found in mental hospitals, there are occasions when very "sick" persons go unattended while moderately "sick" persons receive treatment. This selection is clearly based on social criteria, not on psychiatric ones.

The layman usually assumes that his conception of "mental illness" is not the important definition since the psychiatrist is

---

Inc., 1959) argues that the therapeutic ethic has influenced many segments of social action and that the consequences are that deviant persons are absolved from responsibility for their actions regardless of the direction of deviancy and the abilities of the evaluators to understand the motivation for deviancy. From this, argues LaPiere, stems the ideology of permissive and nonpunishing prisons, therapeutic schools for delinquents, etc.

the expert and presumably makes the final decision. On the contrary, community persons are brought to the hospital on the basis of lay definitions, and once they arrive, their appearance alone is usually regarded as sufficient evidence of "illness."

In the crowded state or county hospitals, which is the most typical situation, the psychiatrist does not have sufficient time to make a very complete psychiatric diagnosis, nor do his psychiatric tools provide him with the equipment for an expeditious screening of the patient. If he is a psychiatrist trained in the more orthodox psychoanalytic notions, his belief system makes it impossible to determine the "sickness" or "wellness" of the patient, since the classical theories assume that all people have unconscious drives which interfere with optimal functioning, and no clear practical criteria are provided for judging the "sick" from the "well."

In the two mental hospitals studied over a period of three months, the investigator never observed a case where the psychiatrist advised the patient that he did not need treatment. Rather, all persons who appeared at the hospital were absorbed into the patient population regardless of their ability to function adequately outside the hospital.

In this regard, it is important to note that mental hospitals care for more than the mentally ill. The unwanted, the aged, the indigent, the lonely, and others often enter public mental hospitals voluntarily. For example, on an alcoholic ward in a hospital studied by the author, staff generally recognized that as weather became cold and as snow began falling, indigent alcoholics would enter the hospital voluntarily, only to return to their usual patterns of life when the weather improved.

Psychiatric hospitals filled well over capacity will attempt to control more carefully those they will accept for treatment. But should beds be available, as was the case with the hospitals studied, it is likely that they will absorb whoever appears, at least for a time. This suggests that the definition of "mental illness" made by the lay public is crucial with regard to who is treated, and comprehension of medical care programs requires an understanding of how such definitions are made.

Intervention in a situation of "assumed mental illness" by family, friends, and others in the community is highly dependent on the visibility of symptoms.[5] Persons recognized and treated may not be those most in need of treatment by psychiatric criteria. Rather, it is at the point at which deviancy is most easily and clearly recognized—and most disturbing to the group—that pressures of various sorts are brought to bear on the person. Intervention, then, is likely to occur only after the person becomes a problem to himself or others, or gives definite indications that he will soon be a problem.

In evaluating the criteria by which visible symptoms might be judged, one practical basis is the extent to which the person failed to fulfill expectations adequately in performing his primary social roles (especially his familial and occupational roles), and the extent to which he violated legal and moral norms and highly important values of the group.

Whether a definition of deviancy is made and acted upon will depend largely on how serious the consequences of this deviation are for the group.[6] Some deviant behaviors are rewarded and tolerated. Others have some idiosyncratic function for the group, as is often the case with the "comic." Perhaps the deviant may be thought of as "eccentric," "queer," or "strange" but not sufficiently so to merit a definition of illness. However, should the deviancy begin to have serious consequences, because it is damaging or harmful to the individual, a group, or both, or because it becomes so visible to external groups that the family suffers loss of status, it might be redefined as "mental illness" and the person sent for treatment.

In some groups, of course, the stigma attached to a definition

---

[5] Lemert has pointed out that when an "ill" person deviates from role expectancies, his social visibility increases and others are constrained to respond accordingly to his behavior. In cases of violence and disorderly conduct, police action more often is taken. Where less violent behaviors occur—delusion, hallucinations, restlessness—if action is to be taken at all, it is likely to be taken by more primary associates. See Lemert, E., "Legal Commitment and Social Control," *Sociology and Research*, 30 (May–June, 1946), 370–378.

[6] In this regard, Jones and deCharms, *op. cit.*, found that behavior does not appear to have a constant meaning, and that the attribution of stable characteristics to behavior is dependent on the significance of the behavior for the perceiver's own value-maintenance or goal attainment.

of mental illness is sufficiently great to bring about group resistance to such a definition.[7] However, other factors being constant, a definition of "mental illness" is more likely to be made as the serious consequences of the deviancy increase.[8]

The size and form of social structure characteristic of a community can affect the visibility of symptomatology, hence its consequences and definition. The data relevant to this area, however, are not very clear. It appears that in the autonomy of a large and impersonal network of relationships, the social visibility of persons lessens and symptoms may not be defined as readily as in more intimate communities. However, in the latter case, where the demands of social life may not be as rigorous and the deviant may not be as much of an inconvenience, the behavior is more likely to be ignored or tolerated, and the deviant can perform useful social roles more readily. In the larger and more impersonal structures, the abilities required to obtain sufficient life gratifications may be greater, and the person handicapped in his interpersonal responses may have a more difficult time making a satisfactory adjustment to life demands.[9]

---

[7] In his research Clausen, et al., *op. cit.*, reports large differences in the degrees to which primary group members are willing to support and tolerate persons displaying schizophrenic symptoms. For excellent general reviews of the sociological mental health literature, see Clausen, J. A., "The Sociology of Mental Health," in Merton, R. K., L. Broom, and L. S. Cottrell, Jr., eds., *Sociology Today*, (New York: Basic Books, Inc., 1959), 485–508; and Clausen, J. A., *Sociology and the Field of Mental Health*, (New York: Russell Sage Foundation, 1956).

[8] From time to time, situations do occur where the social group uses the label "mental illness" as an excuse to rid itself of one of its members, if his presence or behavior is becoming annoying. This seems to occur relatively frequently with aged members in our society.

The absence of a strong familial feeling of responsibility to the aged often leads to hospitalization, especially in cases where the person makes more than the usual demands for care and attention. Often it becomes convenient for the family to view increasing demands as symptoms of "mental illness."

[9] The data in this general area lead to difficult problems of interpretation. Clausen writes:

> To explain, in part, the differential distribution of rates of hospitalization found by Faris and Dunham, Owen suggested that mentally ill persons are perceived and dealt with differently in different settings. Thus far, no one has demonstrated that the areas of the city and segments of the population with the highest rates of hospitaliza-

The visibility and consequences of deviancy also increase as the deviant act increases in frequency. Others factors being equal, the frequency of a deviant act will affect how likely it is to be noticed, defined, and acted upon. Moreover, as the deviant act increases in frequency, it becomes more annoying to the group and some sanction is more likely to follow.

Depending upon life circumstances, groups—both family and community—differ in the kinds and degree of toleration they have for various behaviors. When the vulnerability of the group increases, its toleration for deviancy decreases.[10] During stress

---

tion are characterized by a higher rate of recognition of mental illness than are other areas. Several studies suggest that, if anything, the reverse is true. There is substantial documentation, however, of the fact that the social status of the mentally ill person tends to influence the perception by his family and others of the nature of his problem, their modes of dealing with him prior to his entering medical-psychiatric channels, and the kinds of services offered to him by psychiatric clinics or hospitals. (*Sociology Today, op. cit.*, 494–495.)

The difficulties with the available data stem from the fact that important effects work at cross-purposes, and the studies, thus far, have not adequately controlled for these effects. One such factor is the varying toleration levels in the different kinds of communities reported by Eaton, J. and R. J. Weil, *Culture and Mental Disorders: A Comparative Study of the Hutterites and Other Populations* (Glencoe, Ill.: The Free Press, 1955). They report that the Hutterite culture, which seemingly had little mental illness, in fact, had prevalance rates similar to those found in other groups, but that in this culture mental illness was handled differently from the way it was handled among other groups.

Thus, while there may be lesser visibility in larger social structures, group toleration or the ability to make use of the psychologically handicapped may be more limited. Further research is needed in this general area, with a clearer delineation and control of visibility, tolerance, and role variables.

[10] In this respect, the data reported by Glass are especially interesting. See Glass, A. J., "Psychotherapy in the Combat Zone," in *Symposium on Stress* (Washington, D.C.: Army Medical Service Graduate School, Walter Reed Army Medical Hospital, 1953). He reports that when psychiatry casualties were evacuated to psychiatric facilities during the North African and Sicilian campaigns, few patients were salvaged for combat duty.

The psychiatrist usually assumed the patient was "ill" and "sought to uncover basic emotional conflicts or attempted to relate current behavior and symptoms with past personality patterns," which seemingly provided patients with "rational" reasons for their combat failure. Both patient and therapist were often readily convinced that the limit of combat endurance had been reached.

On the other hand, when patients were subsequently treated in the com-

situations and crises, vulnerability increases, group solidarity becomes more essential, and deviation is treated more harshly, especially where the deviation exacerbates the crisis and further increases group vulnerability.

Moreover, during periods of family and community stress, deviancy may increase because already handicapped persons find themselves unable to cope with the new and rigorous demands made upon them.

There are occasions when a person's behaviors, while tolerated in the primary group, become visible to authorities in the person's secondary groups who may have different values and stand-

---

bat zone with such interpersonal devices as suggestion, influence, etc., a much higher percentage were returned to combat.

As Clausen points out, "maintaining ties with their outfits and preserving a conception of themselves as somehow being able to cope seem to have given many men the strength to do exactly that. . . . A good deal of research is needed to learn under what circumstances withholding the label 'mental illness' may lead to more effective coping than would combining labeling and therapy." (See Clausen, *Sociology Today, op. cit.,* 503.)

Clausen's comments are especially interesting because we have some evidence that during periods of stress—with increasing social, psychological, and physical demands—rates of psychotic breakdown increase. However, if group solidarity is essential and group vulnerability is high, the sick role is not easily accorded to persons with neurotic-type symptoms, and considerable pressure is placed upon them to continue in their social roles.

See, Mechanic, D., "Illness and Social Disability: Some Problems in Analysis," *Pacific Sociological Review,* 2 (Spring, 1959), 37–41; and Schneider, D. M., "Social Dynamics of Physical Disability in Army Basic Training," in Kluckhohn, C., H. A. Murray, and A. M. Schneider, eds, *Personality in Nature, Society, and Culture, second edition* (New York: Alfred A. Knopf, 1956), 386–392.

The observations by Groen, C., "Psychogenesis and Psychotherapy of Ulcerative Colitis, *Psychosomatic Medicine,* 9 (May–June, 1947), 151–174, that the ulcer symptoms of his patients disappeared during the stress conditions of concentration camp life and often reappeared after leaving the concentration camp, raises some interesting questions, as W. Caudill has observed. *See* Caudill, W., *Effects of Social and Cultural Systems in Reactions to Stress* (New York: Social Science Research Council, 1958).

Whether the change during incarceration is a reaction to the change in the stressors, or is tied with shifts in the physiological, psychological, and social systems accompanying camp life, is a question for further and better-controlled research. Also, Groen's observations that the wives were providing their husbands with more emotional support than formerly is an important variable.

ards. Hence there are different toleration levels for various behaviors, and those who define these behaviors as signs of "mental illness" may forcefully bring the patient to a treatment center.[11]

When this occurs, the primary group sometimes resists the definition placed upon its member by the secondary authorities; and it is not unusual for conflicting definitions to arise among the patient, his family, the courts, and the hospital physician. While the court is likely to accept the professional opinion of the physician, there are occasions when the psychiatrist—who by independent criteria has either assumed or decided that serious pathology exists—insists that a patient is ill, while the patient and his family strongly resist this definition. In such cases, the physician is often reluctant to press his definition and urge court commitment, since this requires him to argue in some states that the patient is dangerous to himself and others, a contention which is very difficult to support in many cases. In these state institutions, when the physician does decide to press such a petition for the commitment of an unwilling patient, his decision is usually made on the basis of whether there is sufficient evidence to convince the court that the patient should be lawfully detained, even when the family is reluctant.

Often the patient is released from the hospital without detailed judicial consideration, not because the psychiatrist finds him free of serious pathology, but rather because the psychiatrist has anticipated what the court decision would be. If the psychiatrist is to gain commitment of an unwilling patient, he must usually convince the family that the patient is indeed seriously ill and in need of treatment, and bring them around to support his definition of the situation.

In any case, the psychiatrist treating a patient implicitly, if not explicitly, recognizes that it is important to communicate his perception of pathology to the patient and to his family. He also realizes that he must convince the patient that he is indeed "sick" and in serious need of treatment. The necessity of having the patient accept the psychiatric definition of his case is especially

---

[11] The data collected by Hollingshead and Redlich, *op. cit.*, indicate that members of the lower strata are most likely to take this path to treatment centers.

apparent in the early hospital experience, where the patient must become socialized to a "patient-role," accepting the definition of his symptoms placed upon him by the hospital population, including staff and other patients. Should the patient refuse to accept the patient-role and deny his illness, this resistance is viewed as a further symptom of the "illness," and he is told that if he is to get well, he must recognize the fact that he is ill.

Should the patient continue to reject the psychiatric definition of his illness, the psychiatrist is likely to report that the patient is a poor treatment risk. Furthermore, ancillary hospital staff and other patients also apply similar definitions of illness to the patient and expect him to accept these definitions. The patient's denials create social difficulties for him within the hospital, difficulties of adaptation to ward life which can be further viewed as indications that the patient is seriously ill and which reinforce the original impressions and definitions placed upon him by physicians, aides and other patients. Unless the patient begins to see himself through the eyes of the psychiatrist, hospital personnel, and other patients, he will remain a problem to the ward,[12] and his therapy and progress are likely to be viewed as inconsequential.

The foregoing suggests that if we are to understand the "mentally ill" patient, we must understand the situation from which he comes and the circumstances that led to the definition that he needs treatment. If the patient is to be effectively treated in regard to his life situation, we must understand what demands were made upon him and why he failed to meet these demands. Was it because he was unable to perceive the expectations of others accurately? Was it because he was unable to make proper responses? Or were there other reasons for his failure to meet expectations? Furthermore, we should want to inquire about the expectations he faced, the conflicts he perceived, and the crosscurrents of expectations and behaviors that led to the societal response and definitions of mental illness.

From a theoretical point of view, what has been attempted is

---

[12] A similar argument has been presented by Goffman, E., "The Moral Career of the Mental Patient," *Psychiatry*, 22 (May, 1959), 123–142, and Erikson, K. T., "Patient Role and Social Uncertainty—a Dilemma of the Mentally Ill, in Cohen, Mabel B., ed., *Advances in Psychiatry* (New York: W. W. Norton Co., 1959), 102–123.

a descriptive model of the definitional processes by which persons within a community are adjudged as mentally ill. If we are to expand our understanding of definitions of deviancy and mental illness, a logical step is to move in the direction of axiomatic models, utilizing relevant variables and encouraging systematic empirical investigation. It is with the constant interplay of exploratory observations, systematic theory, and rigorous empirical tests that our knowledge will develop in a useful fashion.

The Psychological Meaning of Mental Illness in the Family

*Marian Radke Yarrow, Charlotte Green Schwartz,
Harriet S. Murphy, and Leila Calhoun Deasy*

The manifestations of mental illness are almost as varied as the spectrum of human behavior. Moreover, they are expressed not only in disturbance and functional impairment for the sick person but also in disruptive interactions with others. The mentally ill person is often, in his illness, a markedly deviant person, though certainly less so than the popular stereotype of the "insane." One wonders what were the initial phases of the impact of mental illness upon those within the ill person's social environment. How were the disorders of illness interpreted and tolerated? What did the patients, prior to hospitalization, communicate of their needs, and how did others—those closest to the ill persons—attempt, psychologically and behaviorally, to cope with the behavior? How did these persons come to be recognized by other family members as needing psychiatric help?

This paper presents an analysis of cognitive and emotional problems encountered by the wife in coping with the mental illness of the husband. It is concerned with the factors which lead to the reorganization of the wife's perceptions of her husband from a *well* man to a man who is mentally sick or in need of hospitalization in a mental hospital. The process whereby the wife attempts to understand and interpret her husband's manifestations of mental illness is best communicated by considering first the concrete details of a single wife's experiences. The findings

Reprinted from the *Journal of Social Issues*, vol. XI, no. 4, pp. 12–24.

and interpretations based on the total sample are presented following the case analysis.

Illustrative Case

Robert F., a 35-year-old cab driver, was admitted to Saint Elizabeth's Hospital with a diagnosis of schizophrenia. How did Mr. F. get to the mental hospital? Here is a very condensed version of what his wife told an interviewer a few weeks later.

Mrs. F. related certain events, swift and dramatic, which led directly to the hospitalization. The day before admission, Mr. F. went shopping with his wife, which he never had done before, and expressed worry lest he lose her. This was in her words, "rather strange." (*His behavior is not in keeping with her expectations for him.*) Later that day, Mr. F. thought a TV program was about him and that the set was "'after him." "Then I was getting worried." (*She recognizes the bizarre nature of his reactions. She becomes concerned.*)

That night, Mr. F. kept talking. He reproached himself for not working enough to give his wife surprises. Suddenly, he exclaimed he did have a surprise for her—he was going to kill her. "I was petrified and said to him, 'What do you mean?' Then, he began to cry and told me not to let him hurt me and to do for him what I would want him to do for me. I asked him what was wrong. He said he had cancer. . . . He began talking about his grandfather's mustache and said there was a worm growing out of it." She remembered his watching little worms in the fish bowl and thought his idea came from that. Mr. F. said he had killed his grandfather. He asked Mrs. F. to forgive him and wondered if she were his mother or God. She denied this. He vowed he was being punished for killing people during the war. "I thought maybe . . . worrying about the war so much . . . had gotten the best of him." (*She tries to understand his behavior. She stretches the range of normality to include it.*) "I thought he should see a psychiatrist . . . I don't know how to explain it. He was shaking. I knew it was beyond what I could do. . . . I was afraid of him. . . . I thought he was losing his normal mental attitude and mentality, but I wouldn't say that he was insane or crazy, because he had always bossed me around before. . . ." (*She shifts back and forth in thinking his problem is psychiatric and in feeling it is normal behavior*

that could be accounted for in terms of their own experience.)
Mr. F. talked on through the night. Sometime in the morning, he
"seemed to straighten out" and drove his wife to work. (*This
behavior tends to balance out the preceding disturbed activities.
She quickly returns to a normal referent.*)

At noon, Mr. F. walked into the store where his wife worked
as a clerk. "I couldn't make any sense of what he was saying. He
kept getting angry because I wouldn't talk to him. . . . Finally,
the boss' wife told me to go home." En route, Mr. F. said his male
organs were blown up and little seeds covered him. Mrs. F. denied seeing them and announced she planned to call his mother.
"He began crying and I had to promise not to. I said, . . . 'Don't
you think you should go to a psychiatrist?' and he said, 'No, there
is nothing wrong with me.' . . . Then we came home, and I went
to pay a bill. . . ." (*Again she considers, but is not fully committed
to, the idea that psychiatric help is needed.*)

Back at their apartment, Mr. F. talked of repairing his cab
while Mrs. F. thought of returning to work and getting someone
to call a doctor. Suddenly, he started chasing her around the
apartment and growling like a lion. Mrs. F. screamed, Mr. F. ran
out of the apartment, and Mrs. F. slammed and locked the door.
"When he started roaring and growling, then I thought he was
crazy. That wasn't a human sound. You couldn't say a thing to
him. . . ." Later, Mrs. F. learned that her husband went to a nearby
church, created a scene, and was taken to the hospital by the
police. (*Thoroughly threatened, she defines problem as psychiatric.*)

What occurred before these events which precipitated the hospitalization? Going back to their early married life, approximately
three years before hospitalization, Mrs. F. told of her husband's
irregular work habits and long-standing complaints of severe
headaches. "When we were first married, he didn't work much
and I didn't worry as long as we could pay the bills." Mrs. F.
figured they were just married and wanted to be together a lot.
(*Personal norms and expectations are built up.*)

At Thanksgiving, six months after marriage, Mr. F. "got sick
and stopped working." During the war he contracted malaria, he
explained, which always recurred at that time of year. "He
wouldn't get out of bed or eat. . . . He thought he was constipated
and he had nightmares. . . . What I noticed most was his perspir-

ing so much. He was crabby. You couldn't get him to go to a doctor. . . . I noticed he was nervous. He's always been a nervous person. . . . Any little thing that would go wrong would upset him—if I didn't get a drawer closed right. . . . His friends are nervous, too. . . . I came to the conclusion that maybe I was happy-go-lucky and everyone else was a bundle of nerves. . . . For a cab driver, he worked hard—most cab drivers loaf. When he felt good, he worked hard. He didn't work so hard when he didn't." (*She adapts to his behavior. The atypical is normalized as his type of personality and appropriate to his subculture.*)

As the months and years went by, Mrs. F. changed jobs frequently, but she worked more regularly than did her husband. He continued to work sporadically, get sick intermittently, appear "nervous and tense" and refrain from seeking medical care. Mrs. F. "couldn't say what was wrong." She had first one idea, then another, about his behavior. "I knew it wasn't right for him to be acting sick like he did." Then, "I was beginning to think he was getting lazy because there wasn't anything I could see." During one period, Mrs. F. surmised he was carrying on with another woman. "I was right on the verge of going, until he explained it wasn't anyone else." (*There is a building up of deviant behavior to a point near her tolerance limits. Her interpretations shift repeatedly.*)

About two and a half years before admission, Mrs. F. began talking to friends about her husband's actions and her lack of success in getting him to a doctor. "I got disgusted and said if he didn't go to a doctor, I would leave him. I got Bill (the owner of Mr. F.'s cab) to talk to him. . . . I begged, threatened, fussed . . ." After that, Mr. F. went to a VA doctor for one visit, overslept for his second appointment and never returned. He said the doctor told him nothing was wrong.

When Mr. F. was well and working, Mrs. F. "never stopped to think about it." "You live from day to day. . . . When something isn't nice, I don't think about it. If you stop to think about things, you can worry yourself sick. . . . He said he wished he could live in my world. He'd never seem to be able to put his thinking off the way I do. . . ." (*Her mode of operating permits her to tolerate his behavior.*)

Concurrently, other situations confronted Mrs. F. Off and on, Mr. F. talked of a coming revolution as a result of which Negroes and Jews would take over the world. If Mrs. F. argued that she didn't believe it, Mr. F. called her "dumb" and "stupid." "The best thing to do was to change the subject." Eighteen months before admission, Mr. F. began awakening his wife to tell of nightmares about wartime experiences, but she "didn't think about it." Three months later, he decided he wanted to do something besides drive a cab. He worked on an invention but discovered it was patented. Then, he began to write a book about his wartime experiences and science. "If you saw what he wrote, you couldn't see anything wrong with it. . . . He just wasn't making any money." Mrs. F. did think it was "silly" when Mr. F. went to talk to Einstein about his ideas and couldn't understand why he didn't talk to someone in town. Nevertheless, she accompanied him on the trip. (*With the further accumulation of deviant behavior, she becomes less and less able to tolerate it. The perceived seriousness of his condition is attenuated so long as she is able to find something acceptable or understandable in his behavior.*)

Three days before admission, Mr. F. stopped taking baths and changing clothes. Two nights before admission, he awakened his wife to tell her he had just figured out that the book he was writing had nothing to do with science or the world, only with himself. "He said he had been worrying about things for ten years and that writing a book solved what had been worrying him for ten years." Mrs. F. told him to burn his writings if they had nothing to do with science. It was the following morning that Mrs. F. first noticed her husband's behavior as "rather strange."

In the long prelude to Mr. F.'s hospitalization, one can see many of the difficulties which arise for the wife as the husband's behavior no longer conforms and as it strains the limits of the expectations for him. At some stage the wife defines the situation as one requiring help, eventually psychiatric help. Our analysis is concerned primarily with the process of the wife's getting to this stage in interpreting and responding to the husband's behavior. In the preceding case are many reactions which appear as general trends in the data group. These trends can be systematized in terms of the following focal aspects of the process:

1. The wife's threshold for initially discerning a problem depends on the accumulation of various kinds of behavior which are not readily understandable or acceptable to her.

2. This accumulation forces upon the wife the necessity for examining and adjusting expectations for herself and her husband which permit her to account for his behavior.
3. The wife is in an "overlapping" situation, of problem—not problem or of normal—not normal. Her interpretations shift back and forth.
4. Adaptations to the atypical behavior of the husband occur. There is testing and waiting for additional cues in coming to any given interpretation, as in most problem solving. The wife mobilizes strong defenses against the husband's deviant behavior. These defenses take form in such reactions as denying, attenuating, balancing and normalizing the husband's problem.
5. Eventually there is a threshold point at which the perception breaks, when the wife comes to the relatively stable conclusion that the problem is a psychiatric one and/or that she cannot alone cope with the husband's behavior.

These processes are elaborated in the following analysis of the wives' responses.

Method of Data Collection

Ideally, to study this problem one might like to interview the wives as they struggled with the developing illness. This is precluded, however, by the fact that the problem is not "visible" until psychiatric help is sought. The data, therefore, are the wives' reconstructions of their earlier experiences and accounts of their current reactions during the husband's hospitalization.

It is recognized that recollections of the prehospital period may well include systematic biases, such as distortions, omissions and increased organization and clarity. As a reliability check, a number of wives, just before the husband's discharge from the hospital, were asked again to describe the events and feelings of the prehospital period. In general, the two reports are markedly similar; often details are added and others are elaborated, but events tend to be substantially the same. While this check attests to the consistency of the wives' reporting, it has, of course, the contamination of overlearning which comes from many retellings of these events.

The Beginnings of the Wife's Concern

In the early interviews, the wife was asked to describe the beginnings of the problem which led to her husband's hospitalization. ("Could you tell me when you first noticed that your husband was different?") This question was intended to provide an orientation for the wife to reconstruct the sequence and details of events and feelings which characterized the period preceding hospitalization. The interviewer provided a minimum of structuring in order that the wife's emphases and organization could be obtained.

In retrospect, the wives usually cannot pinpoint the time the husband's problem emerged. Neither can they clearly carve it out from the contexts of the husband's personality and family expectations. The subjective beginnings are seldom localized in

TABLE 1   REPORTED PROBLEM BEHAVIOR AT TIME OF THE WIFE'S INITIAL
CONCERN AND AT TIME OF THE HUSBAND'S ADMISSION TO HOSPITAL

Problem Behavior	Initially		At Hospital Admission	
	PSYCHOTICS	PSYCHO-NEUROTICS	PSYCHOTICS	PSYCHO-NEUROTICS
	N	N	N	N
Physical problems, complaints, worries	12	5	7	5
Deviations from routines of behavior	17	9	13	9
Expressions of inadequacy or hopelessness	4	1	5	2
Nervous, irritable, worried	19	10	18	9
Withdrawal (verbal, physical)	5	1	6	1
Changes or accentuations in personality "traits" (slovenly, deceptive, forgetful)	5	6	7	6
Aggressive or assaultive and suicidal behavior	6	3	10	6
Strange or bizarre thoughts, delusions, hallucinations and strange behavior	11	1	15	2
Excessive drinking	4	7	3	4
Violation of codes of "decency"	3	1	3	2
Number of Respondents	23	10	23	10

a single strange or disturbing reaction on the husband's part but rather in the piling up of behavior and feelings. We have seen this process for Mrs. F. There is a similar accumulation for the majority of wives, although the time periods and kinds of reported behavior vary. Thus, Mrs. Q. verbalizes the impact of a concentration of changes which occur within a period of a few weeks. Her explicit recognition of a problem comes when she adds up this array: her husband stays out late, doesn't eat or sleep, has obscene thoughts, argues with her, hits her, talks continuously, "cannot appreciate the beautiful scene," and "cannot appreciate me or the baby."

The problem behaviors reported by the wives are given in Table 1. They are ordered roughly; the behaviors listed first occurred primarily, but not exclusively, within the family; those later occurred in the more public domain. Whether the behavior is public or private does not seem to be a very significant factor in determining the wife's threshold for perceiving a problem.

There are many indications that these behaviors, now organized as a problem, have occurred many times before. This is especially true where alcoholism, physical complaints or personality "weaknesses" enter the picture. The wives indicate how, earlier, they had assimilated these characteristics into their own expectations in a variety of ways: the characteristics were congruent with their image of their husbands, they fitted their differential standards for men and women (men being less able to stand up to troubles), they had social or environmental justifications, etc.

When and how behavior becomes defined as problematic appears to be a highly individual matter. In some instances, it is when the wife can no longer manage her husband (he will no longer respond to her usual prods); in others, when his behavior destroys the status quo (when her goals and living routines are disorganized); and, in still others, when she cannot explain his behavior. One can speculate that her level of tolerance for his behavior is a function of her specific personality needs and vulnerabilities, her personal and family value systems and the social supports and prohibitions regarding the husband's symptomatic behavior.

Initial Interpretations of the Husband's Problem

Once the behavior is organized as a problem, it tends also to be interpreted as some particular kind of problem. More often than not, however, the husband's difficulties are not seen initially as manifestations of mental illness or even as emotional problems (Table 2).

Early interpretations often tend to be organized around physical difficulties (18% of cases) or "character" problems (27%). To a very marked degree, these orientations grow out of the wives' long-standing appraisals of their husbands as weak and ineffective or physically sick men. These wives describe their husbands as spoiled, lacking will-power, exaggerating little complaints and acting like babies. This is especially marked where alcoholism complicates the husband's symptomatology. For example, Mrs. Y., whose husband was chronically alcoholic, aggressive and threatening to her, "raving," and who "chewed his nails until they almost bled," interprets his difficulty thus: "He was just spoiled rotten. He never outgrew it. He told me when he was a child he could get his own way if he insisted, and he is still that way." This quotation is the prototype of many of its kind.

Some wives, on the other hand, locate the problem in the environment. They expect the husband to change as the environmental crisis subsides. Several wives, while enumerating difficulties and concluding that there is a problem, in the same breath say it is really nothing to be concerned about.

TABLE 2   INITIAL INTERPRETATIONS OF THE HUSBAND'S BEHAVIOR

Interpretation	Psychotics N	Psychoneurotics N
Nothing really wrong	3	0
"Character" weakness and "controllable" behavior (lazy, mean, etc.)	6	3
Physical problem	6	0
Normal response to crisis	3	1
Mildly emotionally disturbed	1	2
"Something" seriously wrong	2	2
Serious emotional or mental problem	2	2
Number of Respondents	23	10

Where the wives interpret the husband's difficulty as emotional in nature, they tend to be inconsistently "judgmental" and "understanding." The psychoneurotics are more often perceived initially by their wives as having emotional problems or as being mentally ill than are the psychotics. This is true even though many more clinical signs (bizarre, confused, delusional, aggressive and disoriented behavior) are reported by the wives of the psychotics than of the psychoneurotics.

Initial interpretations, whatever their content, are seldom held with great confidence by the wives. Many recall their early reactions to their husbands' behaviors as full of puzzling confusion and uncertainty. Something is wrong, they know, but, in general, they stop short of a firm explanation. Thus, Mrs. M. reports, "He was kind of worried. He was kind of worried before, not exactly worried. . . ." She thought of his many physical complaints; she "racked" her "brain" and told her husband, "Of course, he didn't feel good." Finally, he stayed home from work with "no special complaints, just blah," and she "began to realize it was more deeply seated."

Changing Perceptions of the Husband's Problem

The fog and uneasiness in the wife's early attempts to understand and cope with the husband's difficulties are followed, typically, by painful psychological struggles to resolve the uncertainties and to change the current situation. Usually, the wife's perceptions of the husband's problems undergo a series of changes before hospitalization is sought or effected, irrespective of the length of time elapsing between the beginnings of concern and hospitalization.

Viewing these changes macroscopically, three relatively distinct patterns of successive redefinitions of the husband's problems are apparent. One sequence (slightly less than half the cases) is characterized by a progressive intensification; interpretations are altered in a definite direction—toward seeing the problem as mental illness. Mrs. O. illustrates this progression. Initially, she thought her husband was "unsure of himself." "He was worried, too, about getting old." These ideas moved to: "He'd drink to forget. . . . He just didn't have the confidence. . . . He'd forget little things. . . . He'd wear a suit weeks on end if I didn't take it away from him. . . . He'd say nasty things." Then, when Mr. O. seemed "so confused," "to forget all kinds of things . . . where he'd come from . . . to go to work," and made "nasty, cutting remarks all the time," she began to think in terms of a serious personality disturbance. "I did think he knew that something was wrong . . . that he was sick. He was never any different this last while and I couldn't stand it any more. . . . You don't know what a relief it was . . ." (when he was hospitalized). The husband's drinking, his failure to be tidy, his nastiness, etc., lose significance in their own right. They move from emphasis to relief and are recast as signs of "something deeper," something that brought "it" on.

Some wives whose interpretations move in the direction of seeing their husbands as mentally ill hold conceptions of mental illness and of personality that do not permit assigning the husband all aspects of the sick role. Frequently, they use the interpretation of mental illness as an angry epithet or as a threatening prediction for the husband. This is exemplified in such references as: "I told him he should have his head examined," "I called him a half-wit," "I told him if he's not careful, he'll be a mental case." To many of these wives, the hospital is regarded as the "end of the road."

Other wives showing this pattern of change hold conceptions of emotional disturbance which more easily permit them to assign to their husbands the role of patient as the signs of illness become more apparent. They do not as often regard hospitalization in a mental hospital as the "last step." Nevertheless, their feelings toward their husbands may contain components equally as angry and rejecting as those of the wives with the less sophisticated ideas regarding mental illness.

A somewhat different pattern of sequential changes in interpreting the husband's difficulties (about one-fifth of the cases) is to be found among wives who appear to cast around for situationally and momentarily adequate explanations. As the situation changes or as the husband's behavior changes, these wives find reasons and excuses but lack an underlying or synthesizing theory. Successive interpretations tend to bear little relation to one another. Situational factors tend to lead them to seeing their husbands as mentally ill. Immediate, serious and direct physical threats or the influence of others may be the deciding factor. For example, a friend or employer may insist that the husband see a psychiatrist, and the wife goes along with the decision.

A third pattern of successive redefinitions (slightly less than one-third of the cases) revolves around an orientation outside the framework of emotional problems or mental illness. In these cases, the wife's specific explanations change but pivot around a denial that the husband is mentally ill.

A few wives seem not to change their interpretations about their husband's difficulties. They maintain the same explanation throughout the development of his illness, some within the psychiatric framework, others rigidly outside that framework.

Despite the characteristic shiftings in interpretations, in the group as a whole, there tend to be persisting underlying themes in the individual wife's perceptions that remain essentially unaltered. These themes are a function of her systems of thinking about normality and abnormality and about valued and devalued behavior.

The Process of Recognizing the Husband's Problem as Mental Illness

In the total situation confronting the wife, there are a number of factors, apparent in our data, which make it difficult for the wife to recognize and accept the husband's behavior in a mental-emotional-psychiatric framework. Many cross-currents seem to influence the process.

The husband's behavior itself is a fluctuating stimulus. He is not worried and complaining all of the time. His delusions and hallucinations may not persist. His hostility toward the wife may be followed by warm attentiveness. She has, then, the problem of deciding whether his "strange" behavior is significant. The greater saliency of one or the other of his responses at any moment of time depends in some degree upon the behavior sequence which has occurred most recently.

The relationship between husband and wife also supplies a variety of images and contexts which can justify varied conclusions about the husband's current behavior. The wife is likely to adapt to behavior which occurs in their day to day relationships. Therefore, symptomatic reactions which are intensifications of long-standing response patterns become part of the fabric of life and are not easily disentangled as "symptomatic."

Communications between husband and wife regarding the husband's difficulties act sometimes to impede and sometimes to further the process of seeing the difficulties within a psychiatric framework. We have seen both kinds of influences in our data. Mr. and Mrs. F. were quite unable to communicate effectively about Mr. F.'s problems. On the one hand, he counters his wife's urging that he see a doctor with denials that anything is wrong. On the other hand, in his own way through his symptoms, he tries to communicate his problems (pp. 32 and 33), but she responds only to his verbalized statements, taking them at face value.

Mr. and Mrs. K. participate together quite differently, examining Mr. K.'s fears that he is being followed by the F.B.I., that their house has been wired and that he is going to be fired. His wife tentatively shares his suspicions. At the same time, they discuss the possibility of paranoid reactions.

The larger social context contributes, too, in the wife's perceptual tug of war. Others with whom she can compare her husband provide contrasts to his deviance, but others (Mr. F.'s nervous friends) also provide parallels to his problems. The "outsiders," seeing less of her husband, often discount the wife's alarm when she presses them for opinions. In other instances, the friend or employer, less adapted to or defended against the husband's symptoms, helps her to define his problem as psychiatric.

This task before the wife, of defining her husband's difficulties, can be conceptualized as an "overlapping" situation (in Lewin's terms), in which the relative potencies of the several effective influences fluctuate. The wife is responding to the various sets of forces simultaneously. Thus, several conclusions or interpretations of the problem are simultaneously "suspended in balance," and they shift back and forth in emphasis and relief. Seldom, however, does she seem to be balancing off clear-cut alternatives, such as physical versus mental. Her complex perceptions (even those of Mrs. F. who is extreme in misperceiving cues) are more "sophisticated" than the casual questioner might be led to conclude.

Thus far, we have ignored the personally threatening aspects of recognizing mental illness in one's spouse, and the defenses which are mobilized to meet this threat. It is assumed that it is threatening to the wife not only to realize that the husband is mentally ill but further to consider her own possible role in the development of the disorder, to give up modes of relating to her husband that may have had satisfactions for her and to see a future as the wife of a mental patient. Our data provide systematic information only on the first aspect of this problem, on the forms of defense against the recognition of the illness. One or more of the following defenses are manifested in three-fourths of our cases.

The most obvious form of defense in the wife's response is the tendency to *normalize* the husband's neurotic and psychotic symptoms. His behavior is explained, justified or made acceptable by seeing it also in herself or by assuring herself that the particular behavior occurs again and again among persons who are not ill. Illustrative of this reaction is the wife who reports her husband's hallucinations and assures herself that this is normal because she herself heard voices when she was in the menopause. Another wife responds to her husband's physical complaints, fears, worries, nightmares, and delusions with "A lot of normal people think there's something wrong when there isn't. I think men are that way; his father is that way."

When behavior cannot be normalized, it can be made to seem less severe or less important in a total picture than an outsider might see it. By finding some grounds for the behavior or something explainable about it, the wife achieves at least momentary *attenuation* of the seriousness of it. Thus, Mrs. F. is able to discount partly the strangeness of her husband's descriptions of the worms growing out of his grandfather's mustache when she recalls his watching the worms in the fish bowl. There may be attenuation, too, by seeing the behavior as "momentary" ("You could talk him out of his ideas.") or by rethinking the problem and seeing it in a different light.

By *balancing* acceptable with unacceptable behavior or "strange" with "normal" behavior, some wives can conclude that the husband is not seriously disturbed. Thus, it is very important to Mrs. R. that her husband kissed her goodbye before he left for the hospital. This response cancels out his hostile feelings toward her and the possibility that he is mentally ill. Similarly, Mrs. V. reasons that her husband cannot be "out of his mind" for he had reminded her of things she must not forget to do when he went to the hospital.

Defense sometimes amounts to a thorough-going *denial*. This takes the form of denying that the behavior perceived can be interpreted in an emotional or psychiatric framework. In some instances, the wife reports vividly on such behavior as repeated thoughts of suicide, efforts to harm her and the like and sums it up with "I thought it was just a whim." Other wives bend their efforts toward proving the implausibility of mental illness.

After the husband is hospitalized, it might be expected that these denials would decrease to a negligible level. This is not wholly the case, however. A breakdown of the wives' interpretations just following the husband's admission to the hospital shows that roughly a fifth still interpret the husband's behavior in another framework than that of a serious emotional problem or mental illness. Another fifth ambivalently and sporadically interpret the behavior as an emotional or mental problem. The remainder hold relatively stable interpretations within this framework.

After the husband has been hospitalized for some time, many wives reflect on their earlier tendencies to avoid a definition of mental illness. Such reactions are almost identically described by these wives: "I put it out of my mind—I didn't want to face it—anything but a mental illness." "Maybe I was aware of it. But you know you push things away from you and keep hoping." "Now you think maybe you should have known about it. Maybe you should have done more than you did and that worries me."

Discussion

The findings on the perceptions of mental illness by the wives of patients are in line with general findings in studies of perception. Behavior which is unfamiliar and incongruent and unlikely in terms of current expectations and needs will not be readily recognized, and stressful or threatening stimuli will tend to be misperceived or perceived with difficulty or delay.

We have attempted to describe the factors which help the wife maintain a picture of her husband as normal and those which push her in the direction of accepting a psychiatric definition of his problem. The kind and intensity of the symptomatic behavior, its persistence over time, the husband's interpretation of his problem, interpretations and defining actions of others, including professionals, all play a role. In addition, the wives come to this experience with different conceptions of psychological processes and of the nature of emotional illness, itself, as well as with different tolerances for emotional disturbance. As we have seen, there are also many supports in society for maintaining a picture of normality concerning the husband's behavior. Social pressures and expectations not only keep *behavior* in line but to great extent *perceptions* of behavior as well.

There are implications of these findings both for those who are working in the field of prevention of mental illness and early detection of emotional disturbance as well as for the rehabilitation worker. They suggest that to acquaint the public with the nature of mental illness by describing psychotic behavior and emphasizing its nonthreatening aspect is, after all, an intellectualization and not likely to be effective in dealing with the threatening aspects of recognizing mental illness which we have described. Further, it is not enough simply to recognize the fact that the rehabilitation of patients is affected by the attitudes and feelings of the family toward the patient and his illness. Perhaps a better acceptance of the patient can be developed if families who have been unable to deal with the problem of the illness are helped to work through this experience and to deal with their difficulties in accepting the illness and what remains of it after the patient leaves the hospital.

Police Discretion in Emergency Apprehension of Mentally Ill Persons

Egon Bittner

The official mandate of the police includes provisions for dealing with mentally ill persons. Since such dealings are defined in terms of civil law procedures, the mandate of the police is not lim-

Reprinted from *Social Problems*, vol. 14, no. 3, Winter, 1967, pp. 278–292, by permission from the Society for the Study of Social Problems and the author. This research was supported in part by Grant 64-1-35 from the California Department of Mental Hygiene. I gratefully acknowledge the help I have received from Sheldon L. Messinger in preparing this paper.

ited to persons who for reasons of illness fail to observe the law. Rather, in suitable circumstances the signs of mental illness, or a competent allegation of mental illness, are in themselves the proper business of the police and can lead to authorized intervention. The expressed legal norms governing police involvement specify two major alternatives. On the one hand, policemen may receive court orders directing them to locate, apprehend, and convey named persons to specified hospitals for psychiatric observation and/or sanity hearings. On the other hand, policemen are authorized by statute to apprehend and convey to hospitals persons whom they perceive as ill, on an emergency basis. The first form parallels the common procedures of serving court warrants, while the second form involves the exercise of discretionary freedom that is ordinarily associated with making arrests without a warrant.[1]

The study reported in this paper concerns the rules and considerations underlying the exercise of discretion in emergency apprehensions. The findings are based on ten months of field work with the uniformed police patrol of a large West Coast city, and on psychiatric records of the hospital receiving all police referrals.[2] We shall first consider certain attitudinal and organizational factors involved in making emergency apprehensions. Next, we shall discuss the manifest properties of cases in which emergency apprehensions are frequently made. Finally, we shall deal with procedures directed toward recognized mentally ill persons who are not referred to the hospital. In the conclusion, we shall argue that the decision to invoke the law governing emergency apprehension is not based on an appraisal of objective features of cases. Rather, the decision is a residual resource, the use of which is

---

[1] See, for example, *Welfare and Institutions Code*, State of California, Division 6, Part 1, Chapter 1.

[2] The city has a population of approximately three-quarters of a million inhabitants and is patrolled by a uniformed police force of approximately 1,000 men. The receiving hospital is a public institution. Its psychiatric inpatient service registered a demand population of 7,500 during the period of the study, July 1, 1963–June 30, 1964. Eighty-eight per cent of this population has been accepted for observation and such short-term care as is ordinarily associated with it. The average length of stay of patients is just short of five days, with a distribution that is heavily skewed toward shorter stays. The hospital also houses a department of the court that holds sanity hearings.

determined largely by the absence of other alternatives. The domain of alternatives is found in normal peace-keeping activities in which considerations of legality play a decidedly subordinate role. We shall also allude to the fact that our interpretation has important bearing on the problem of police discretion to invoke the law in general.[3]

Organizational and Attitudinal Factors Influencing Emergency Apprehensions

The statutory authorization under which apprehensions of the mentally ill are made provides that an officer may take steps to initiate confinement in a psychiatric hospital when he believes "as the result of his own observations, that the person is mentally ill and because of his illness is likely to injure himself or others if not immediately hospitalized."[4] It is fair to say that under ordinary circumstances police officers are quite reluctant to invoke this law. That is, in situations where, according to their own judgment, they are dealing with an apparently mentally ill person they will generally seek to employ other means to bring the existing problem under control. This does not mean that they attempt to deal with the problem as if it did not involve a mentally ill person, or as if this person's illness were none of their business. It merely means that they will try to avoid taking him to the hospital.

The avoidance of emergency apprehensions has a background that might be called doctrinal.[5] To take someone to the hospital means giving the facts of his illness formal recognition and using them as grounds for official action. The police, however, disavow

---

[3] The problem referred to is treated in Joseph Goldstein, "Police Discretion Not to Invoke the Criminal Process," *Yale Law Journal*, 69 (1960), pp. 543–594; W. R. LaFave, "The Police and Non-enforcement of the Law," *Wisconsin Law Review* (1962), pp. 104–137, 179–239; S. H. Kadish, "Legal Norms and Discretion in the Police and Sentencing Process," *Harvard Law Review*, 75 (1962), pp. 904–931; I. Piliavin and S. Scott, "Police Encounters with Juveniles," *American Journal of Sociology*, 70 (1964), pp. 206–214; Nial Osborough, "Police Discretion Not to Prosecute Students," *Journal of Criminal Law, Criminology and Police Science*, 56 (1965), pp. 241–245.

[4] *Welfare and Institutions Code, op. cit.*, Section 5050.3.

[5] The term "doctrinal" is perhaps too strong, but only in the sense that the scheme of reasoning and justification lacks explicit formulation.

all competence in matters pertaining to psychopathology and seek to remain within the lines of restraint that the disavowal imposes. Accordingly, the diagnosis they propose is not only emphatically provisional but also, in a sense, incidental. From their point of view it is not enough for a case to be serious in a "merely" psychiatric sense. To warrant official police action a case must also present a serious police problem. As a general rule, the elements that make a case a serious police matter are indications that if a referral is not made, external troubles will proliferate. Among these, danger to life, to physical health, to property, and to order in public places, are objects of prominent concern. Estimating the risk of internal deterioration of the psychiatric condition as such is perceived as lying outside of the scope of police competence and thus not an adequate basis for making emergency apprehensions.

While a narrow construction of the police mandate might have the consequence of eliminating certain cases from the purview of official police interest, it does not eliminate the possibility of liberal use of the authorization. Thus, it might be expected that officers would tend to refer relatively few persons who are "merely" very ill psychiatrically but many persons who are troublesome without being very ill. This expectation seems especially reasonable since the police recently have been denied the use of certain coercive means they have employed in the past to control troublesome persons.[6] On a practical level such procedures would simply follow considerations of expediency, with the law providing a particular method and justification for taking care of matters that need be taken care of.[7] Indeed, given the

---

[6] The literature on this topic is voluminous and heavily polemical. For a general overview, see Wayne R. LaFave, *Arrest*, Boston: Little, Brown & Co., 1965; W. T. Plumb, Jr., "Illegal Enforcement of the Law," *Cornell Law Quarterly*, 24 (1939), pp. 337–393; Jim Thompson, "Police Control Over Citizen Use of the Public Streets," *Journal of Criminal Law, Criminology and Police Science*, 49 (1959), pp. 562–568; R. C. Donnelly, "Police Authority and Practices," *Annals of the American Academy of Political and Social Science*, 339 (1962), pp. 90–110; Arthur H. Sherry, "Vagrants, Rogues and Vagabonds," *California Law Review*, 48 (1960), pp. 557–573.

[7] I have dealt with the practice of invoking official rules of procedure to legitimize various "necessary" activities, as a general problem in formal organizations, in "The Concept of Organization," *Social Research*, 32 (1965), pp. 239–255.

heavy emphasis that mental hygiene receives in police training, it would be scarcely appropriate to attribute devious motives to the police if they were to use the "narrow construction" of the law "widely," for in many instances of untoward, but not necessarily illegal, behavior, the evidence of more or less serious psychopathology is close to the surface.[8] In fact, however, policemen do not make such use of the law. Instead, they conform in practice very closely to the views they profess. To make an emergency apprehension they require that there be indications of serious external risk accompanied by signs of a serious psychological disorder. There exist several attitudinal and organizational factors that help to explain the reluctance of the police to take official steps on the basis of the assumption or allegation of mental illness.

First, the views and knowledge of the police about mental illness are in close agreement with the views and knowledge of the public in general. Policemen, like everyone else, appear to have a correct conception of the nature of mental illness, in terms of standards of modern psychiatry, but like everyone else they avail themselves of various forms of denial when it comes to doing something about it.[9] The facts come into consciousness, as it were, without implying practical consequences; or, at least, the import of the facts is set aside in view of other considerations. Since the police almost always act on fragmentary information, their reasons for not taking any official steps are posited, among others, in the undetermined aspects of the case that must be presumed to have some undefined relevance. For example, one of the possibilities that officers must always consider is the chance that their involvement could be exploited by unknown persons for unknown reasons. Since they are not expert in symptoms of psychopathology, their desire to avoid possible future embarrassment is quite strong.

Second, policemen confront perversion, disorientation, misery,

---

[8] The problem of the devious and exploitative use of the determination of mental illness in the administration of justice is dealt with by Thomas Szasz in a number of publications. See especially his latest book, *Psychiatric Justice,* New York: Macmillan, 1965.

[9] Shirley Star, "The Public's Ideas About Mental Illness," paper presented to the National Association of Mental Health, Indianapolis, 1955, (mimeo); "The Place of Psychiatry in Popular Thinking," paper presented to the American Association of Public Opinion Research, 1957 (mimeo).

irresoluteness, and incompetence much more often than any other social agent. They can readily point to a large number of persons who, to all appearances, are ready for the "booby hatch," but who nevertheless seem to lead such lives as they can without outside aid or intervention. Against this background the requirement that one should have a good brain and an even temper belong to the same category of wishes as that one should have a large and steady income. Thus, making emergency apprehensions is, among others, a matter of economy. Lower the standards somewhat and the number of apprehensions might be multiplied by a substantial factor. Similar considerations apply to making various types of arrests. Though the police could readily multiply the number of arrests for some petty offenses, they somehow manage to produce just the right number to keep the courts busy and the jails full. With the same uncanny instinct they burden the hospital just to the limit of its capacity.

Third, though policemen readily acknowledge that dealing with mentally ill persons is an integral part of their work, they hold that it is not a proper task for them. Not only do they lack training and competence in this area but such dealings are stylistically incompatible with the officially propounded conception of the policeman's principal vocation. It involves none of the skills, acumen, and prowess that characterize the ideal image of a first-rate officer. Given the value that is assigned to such traits in furthering a man's career, and as grounds for esteem among his co-workers, it is a foregone conclusion that conveying a "mental case" to the hospital will never take the place of catching Willie Sutton in the choice of worthwhile activities. The opportunities for making spectacular arrests are not so widely available to the uniformed patrolman as to compete for attention with the emergency apprehensions of mentally ill persons, but the established ways of collecting credits with one's superiors work against the development of voluntary interest with patients.

Fourth, officers complain that taking someone to the psychiatric service of the hospital is a tedious, cumbersome, and uncertain procedure. They must often wait a long time in the admitting office and are occasionally obliged to answer questions of the admitting psychiatrist that appear to place their own judgment in doubt. They must also reckon with the possibility of being turned down by the psychiatrist, in which case they are left with an aggravated problem on their hands. The complaints about the hospital must be understood in the light of a strong and widely respected rule of police procedure. The rule demands that an officer bring all cases assigned to him to some sort of closure within reasonable limits of time and effort. The ability to take care of things in a way that avoids protracted and complicated entanglements and does not cause repercussions is, in fact, a sign of accomplished craftsmanship in police work that runs a close second to the ability to make important arrests. Relative to this standard, contacts with the hospital and the attitudes of psychiatrists are a source of endless frustration. Policemen are often puzzled by the hospital's refusal to lend its resources to help in keeping life outside free of violence and disorder; and, though they are relatively rarely turned down by admitting psychiatrists, many officers can cite cases in which persons who were not accepted into the hospital brought grief upon themselves and others.

Fifth, in addition to these experiences, certain other facts about the hospital exercise a restraining influence upon the making of emergency apprehensions. All officers are explicitly aware that taking someone to the hospital is a civil rather than a criminal matter. They are continually reminded of this distinction, and they employ the appropriate linguistic conventions in referring to such cases and in talking with ill persons and their relatives. The actual situation belies all this euphemizing and officers are unavoidably aware of this, too. Ill persons are, indeed, arrested on account of being ill. They are not taken to the jail, to be sure, but they are nevertheless locked up. The knowledge that the mental hospital is a place in which to lock people up is inferentially prior to the making of emergency apprehensions. It is only natural that officers would infer from witnessed hospital procedures with mentally ill patients to the conditions that presumably warrant them. To think otherwise would impugn the whole system, which operates not only under medical supervision but also under the auspices of the courts. Thus, in making an emergency apprehension the officer has to consider whether the person in question presents risks of such magnitude as warrant his confinement together with the rest of the "crazy" people who apparently require this sort of treatment.[10]

---

[10] We propose that the degradation ceremony of the mental patient, to which Goffman refers in his work, presents itself to the policeman as a justified necessity with certain patients.

Conditions Surrounding Emergency Apprehensions

Despite the strong reluctance of the police, emergency apprehensions of mentally ill persons are quite frequent. Indeed, officers of the uniformed patrol make them about as often as they arrest persons for murder, all types of manslaughter, rape, robbery, aggravated assault, and grand theft, taken together; and more than one fifth of all referrals to the receiving psychiatric service of the public hospital come from this source.[11]

In only a very few instances does the emergency apprehension involve the use of physical coercion. In most cases patients are passively compliant or at least manageable by means of verbal influence. At times patients go willingly, or perhaps even voluntarily.[12] In approximately half of the cases policemen encounter the patient without any warning. This happens either when officers run into the person in the course of patrolling or when they are dispatched to some address by radio, without any indication of the nature of the problem they will have to deal with. In the other half, officers are informed that they will have to deal with a possible "mental case."[13] Though the observations on which this account is based do not permit a firm inference in this matter, it appears that prior labeling does not play a role in the formation of the policeman's decision to make an apprehension.

Five types of circumstances in which emergency apprehensions are made anywhere from often to virtually always can be isolated. It is important to define the nature of this inventory. Policemen typically do not reach the conclusion that an apprehension should be made by searching for, or finding, such features as we shall

---

[11] During the period of the study policemen apprehended and referred to the hospital approximately 1,600 patients. The total number of arrests for the mentioned offenses, by the uniformed patrol, was exactly 1,600, according to published statistics of the police department. However, the study covered the period from July 1, 1963, to June 30, 1964, while the published statistics of the department cover the calendar year of 1964.

[12] This observation is frankly judgmental; no one can estimate reliably the extent of covert coercion standing behind compliance. It is, however, not startlingly unusual for patients to ask policemen to take them to the hospital.

[13] The information comes to the officer through radio code. The code contains special designations to indicate that an assignment involves a mental case, a suicide attempt, or an assignment of unknown nature.

enumerate. Thus, these are not, in any real sense, criterion situations. Furthermore, each of the five types encompasses cases that are linked by the rule of analogy rather than by the rule of identity.[14] By this we do not mean merely that actual instances differ over a wide range of permissible variations. Rather, we propose that the membership of any particular case in a class, or in the scheme of classes in general, is based less on the presence or absence of specific characteristics than on the judgment that the case *amounts* to being of this or that class. If such a conclusion is to be reached, the case must not be allowed to dissolve into its particulars. Instead, the conclusion is reached as much by attending to the case as such, as it is reached by attending to its contextual background.

The following three horizons of context appear to matter in cases of referrible mental illness: First, the *scenic* horizon, consisting of all the more or less stable features of the background that can be brought into play as employable resources to handle the problem, or that may assume the character of added reasons for making the emergency apprehension. Second, the *temporal* horizon, including both the changing nature of the problem as it is being attended to and what can be known or surmised about its past and future. Third, the *manipulative* horizon, which consists of considerations of practicality from the standpoint of the police officer. For example, an officer may encounter a mentally ill person in some such circumstances as we shall presently describe. He may learn that the person is a member of a stable and resourceful kinship group and that relatives can be mobilized to take care of him. In addition, there is information that the person has been in a similar state before and that he received outpatient psychiatric attention at that time. Whether this person will be moved to the hospital might then depend on whether others can take over within the limits of time the officer can allocate to waiting for them to arrive on the scene. The manipulative horizon is of particular interest and we shall discuss it more extensively in

---

[14] Edward H. Levi has argued that reasoning by analogy prevails generally in the administration of justice; see his *Introduction to Legal Reasoning*, Chicago: University of Chicago Press, 1949. Since policemen must be attuned to the style of proof and inference that is used in courts, it would not be unreasonable to assume that they might assimilate some of this pattern of thinking.

the section of the paper dealing with persons who are not referred to the hospital.

One further explanation—our description of the five categories of cases does not imply that officers themselves employ subcategories to classify mentally ill persons when they refer them to the hospital on an emergency basis. Rather, we propose the inventory as a scheme of prototypes to which policemen analogize in practice when they are confronted with a mentally ill person.

(1) When there is evidence that a person has attempted, or is attempting, suicide he is virtually always taken to the hospital. Occasionally officers have doubts about the genuineness of the attempt, but such doubts do not seem to weigh significantly against making the apprehension. In some instances the evidence in support of the presumption that an attempt has been made, or is contemplated, is ambiguous. In such cases the prevailing practice is to act on the basis of positive indications. Furthermore, the information that an attempt has been made appears to be a sufficient indication in itself for an emergency apprehension. Not only is it not necessary for the victim to exhibit other signs of a mental disorder but there is no way in which a person can demonstrate that he is not in need of psychiatric attention, once the facts of the attempt have been adequately established. Both the most playful and the most rationally considered suicide attempts are treated as suggesting serious morbidity. The only circumstance under which officers can be dissuaded from taking a potential victim to the hospital is when a physician officially assumes responsibility for the case. Finally, when officers confront a person who shows patent signs of a mental disorder and they learn that this person has in the past attempted suicide, this information is apt to contribute significantly to the decision to make an emergency apprehension, even if the earlier attempts are not clearly connected with the present episode. In short, suicide presents the "ideal" combination of serious psychopathology and serious police business.

(2) When the signs of a serious psychological disorder, i.e., expressions of radically incongruous affect or thought, are accompanied by distortions of normal physical appearance, the person in question is usually taken to the hospital. Such things as injuries of unknown origin, seizures, urinary incontinence, odd posturing, nudity, extreme dirtiness, and so on, all tend to augment the

import of psychological indications. All such features are perceived as signifying loss of control over one's appearance and as
adequate grounds to expect a further proliferation of external
problems. An apprehension will not be made, however, if the
situation contains features indicating a mere momentary lapse of
control. For example, in a case in which the police were summoned to deal with a severely retarded person living with her
parents, the officers helped in restoring the normally functioning
restraint and supervision. Scenically, the home environment
offered a sufficient guarantee of control; historically, the situation
was known to have been managed adequately in the past; and,
manipulatively, the disruption could be remedied within reasonable time and with the cooperation of all parties who had a legitimate stake in the case.

(3) When the signs of serious psychological disorder are expressed in highly agitated forms, and especially when they are
accompanied by incipient or actual acts of violence, the person
is often taken to the hospital. Two further conditions must be
met, however, before the apprehension is seriously considered.
The violence or the threat of violence must be non-trivial. For
example, a feeble and senile old woman assaulting her normally
healthy son will not be taken to the hospital, but the son may be
advised about the availability of hospitalization. Furthermore, the
agitated person must be largely unresponsive to efforts to pacify
him.

(4) Persons who appear to be seriously disoriented, or who
by acting incongruously create a nuisance in a public place, are
often taken to the hospital. Ordinarily policemen will make an
effort to induce the person to leave the scene while helping him
on his way to his normal habitat. Only when it becomes clear
that such a person cannot be expediently returned to a sheltered
place, or remanded to some caretaker, and when he is in danger
of suffering injury due to accident or exposure, will he be taken
to the hospital.

(5) In the cases named so far the police act mainly on the
basis of firsthand observation. Though there is always a certain
amount of received information present, it plays a secondary role
in the decision-making. The fifth category, however, is based
primarily on received information. When requests for police aid
come from complainants who stand to the allegedly mentally ill

person in some sort of instrumental relationship, i.e., from physicians, lawyers, teachers, employers, landlords, and so on, the police generally, though by no means always, move the patient to the hospital.[15] It is usually assumed that the instrumentally related persons have exhausted their power and duty to help before calling the police and that there is little else left to do but to make an emergency apprehension. Interestingly, however, similar requests, in quite similar circumstances, made by family members, friends, roommates, or neighbors are usually not honored. Thus, for example, a severely depressed person may be taken to the hospital from his place of employment, on the urging of a doctor or his employer, both of whom presumably have already attempted alternative solutions, while he would be left in the care of his parent with the advice that the parent seek hospitalization for the patient.

The five types of circumstances in which emergency apprehensions are typically made are, of course, not mutually exclusive. Indeed, most actual cases are, in terms of their external circumstances, overdetermined. The general impression one gets from observing the police is that, except for cases of suicide attempts, the decision to take someone to the hospital is based on overwhelmingly conclusive evidence of illness. The very stringency of criteria would lead one to expect that the police often deal with persons who are also seriously ill but whom they do not take to the hospital. In our description of the five types we have already alluded to the fact that this is in fact so. We have also mentioned earlier that such persons do not fall outside the purview of police interest once it is decided that they need not be apprehended. We now turn to the description of alternative methods of handling mentally ill persons, about which no records are kept.

---

[15] In general, policemen insist on getting a fairly detailed story from the complainant and also on seeing the patient before they decided to make an emergency apprehension. One physician who was interviewed in the course of the study complained about this with a good deal of chagrin. From his point of view the police should take the word of a doctor without questioning him. Officers, however, maintain that the doctor's judgment would not protect them in the case of future complaints; they prefer making an "honest mistake." Policemen are generally acutely aware of the requirement of personal knowledge in finding "adequate grounds" for any action.

Non-official Ways of Dealing with Mentally Ill Persons

The following description of police dealings with mentally ill persons concerns cases in which formal emergency apprehensions are not made. We shall concentrate on encounters in which officers explicitly recognize signs of mental illness and in which they treat the illness as the primary and, in most instances, the only business at hand. That is, we will not be dealing with cases such as, for example, those involving an offender about whom policemen say, after they have arrested him, "What a nut!" Nor will we deal with cases involving various types of troublesome persons who are perceived to be, among other things, "slightly crazy." To be sure, in actual police work there exists no clear-cut dividing line segregating persons who are blatantly mentally ill from persons who are "slightly crazy." For clarity, however, we shall concentrate on extreme cases.

De Facto Emergency Apprehensions

To begin, we must consider certain types of police involvement that straddle the borderline between making and not making apprehensions. In such cases the patient usually ends up in the hospital but the police manage to avoid taking formal action. Insofar as the officers have no official part in the decision and thus no responsibilities, these cases might be considered *de facto* but not *de jure* emergency apprehensions. Occasionally policemen are summoned to aid in the move of a recalcitrant patient. The move is actually under way and the officers are merely expected, in their own words, to "do the dirty work." Though officers cannot readily avoid responding to such requests they typically do not employ coercive means. Instead, they remain in the background as a safety precaution against the possibility that the situation might get out of hand. Beyond that, they disperse curious onlookers, and at times provide help such as calling for an ambulance or a taxi. By and large they do nothing that will change the course of the ongoing development. They interpret their presence as having the value of making something that is already fully determined as peaceful and painless as possible. Insofar as they speak to the patient at all, they restrict their remarks to indicating that the move is legitimate and in his best interest. In fact, the officers are usually the only persons on the scene who listen attentively to the patient and who use the leverage of trust to facilitate the move. Though such cases do not involve police initiative and involve no police decisions, the successful accomplishment of these referrals actually does depend on the availability of police aid. The very fact that the person who made the decision solicited help is an indication that he could probably not have prevailed by himself, or at least not on that occasion. Generally, police officers do not accompany the patient to the hospital and their involvement is not a matter of record.

Another form of *de facto* apprehension occurs when officers transport a person whom they recognize as mentally ill to a medical emergency service. In such cases it is necessary, of course, that there be present some sort of physical complaint in addition to the psychiatric complaint. It is generally expected that the admitting physician will make the further referral to the psychiatric service. By this method policemen avoid taking formal action on account of mental illness and also, incidentally, avoid having to deal with psychiatric staff which they find much more cumbersome than dealing with medical staff. Only rarely are records kept of these cases; such records as do exist identify the interventions as aiding a sick person rather than making an emergency apprehension.

Restitution of Control

By far the larger number of police encounters with mentally ill persons results neither in *de jure* nor in *de facto* emergency apprehensions. Rather, the involvements begin and end in the field. No other social agency, either legal or medical, participates in these cases and the policeman acts as the terminal, all-purpose remedial agent.

While discussing typical emergency apprehension situations we mentioned that officers often try to find competent persons to whom they may relinquish the care of the patient, or they try to return the ill person to his normal habitat in which he presumably can manage his affairs with minimal adequacy. Only in rare instances is this a simple "lost persons" problem. In these relatively rare cases, persons with stable social ties and fixed positions in the community escape the normally functioning controls or suffer a breakdown away from home. Whenever circumstances indicate that this is the case, the police will bring their technical communication and transportation facilities into play to locate caretakers for the patient. Though this is by no means always easy, it is a relatively simple problem. It may not be possible to find the caretakers within the time that can be allocated to the search, but the problem at least has a solution. In fact, when the caretakers cannot be expediently located, and the ill person is taken to the hospital, the search for the caretakers continues for the sake of informing them where the patient is. As a last resort, the identity of the lost mentally ill person is entered in the lost persons record to make it possible to respond to inquiries of caretakers. In general, however, the police are ready to devote a good deal of effort to returning persons to circumstances in which they are sheltered. As might be expected, however, persons with stable social ties and fixed positions in the community only rarely depend on the aid of the police and in many such instances the fact that the person is abroad is known before he is located because of inquiries of frantic relatives.

Much more difficult are cases in which the ill person cannot be presumed to be someone's responsibility in a structured sense, and whose living arrangements are unstable. In such cases the high proficiency of the police in tracing leads and in locating viable support are noteworthy. To solve such problems the officer invokes his detailed knowledge of people and places in the district he patrols. This knowledge, as often as not, permits him to guess who the person is and where he normally belongs. Failing this, the officer will know where to look and whom to ask for information. Bits and fragments of evidence have high informational value because the officer can fill in the missing parts out of past experiences in the same locale and with related persons.

This informational advantage is useful not only in the search for caretakers but also functions as the context for the considered transfer of responsibility. For while it is true that officers generally welcome opportunities to be rid of a mentally ill person, they are not uncritical about whom they will yield to. In one observed instance, for example, a young woman in agitated distress was taken to the hospital in part because her fiancé arrived on the scene and proposed to take over. Prior to his arrival the officers were about ready to leave the patient in the care of her mother and a neighbor who appeared to have a soothing influence on her. The entry of the fiancé seemed quite innocuous to the observer, but the officers gathered from his remarks that the arrangements he had in mind were not only not feasible but even destructive. The evaluation was possible because the officers knew many factual details about the places, persons, and arrangements the man envisioned. It is important to emphasize that the critical approach is not pursued by deliberate inquiry and scrutiny of all aspects of cases and decisions. Rather, the informational advantage of the officers automatically raises the level of demand for plausibility. That is, they can judge whether some proposed solution is practical and acceptable with reference to empirical details of particular known places, at specified times, and in known social contexts. In the instance cited, this background information persuaded the officers that the patient could not be left safely unattended.

Among the types of persons to whom policemen most readily transfer responsibilities are family members and physicians. It is, however, not unusual to find neighbors, hotel clerks, landlords, bartenders, or shopkeepers entrusted with someone who is mentally ill. Especially in blighted parts of the city such persons are known to "keep an eye" on certain others. In such areas the policeman often stands in the midst of a referral and information system that is unstable and informally fluid, but the network of connections is so rich and ramified that an accredited member of the system is scarcely ever completely at a loss. For example, an officer might learn from a news vendor that a certain bartender might know someone who knows something about a senile old lady. If the bartender does not happen to be on duty, some patron in the bar, or the pawnbroker across the street might know. Here it is important to emphasize that news vendors and bartenders are not so much good sources of information, as that they become good sources of information, and incidentally also good resource persons, when the officer knows them personally and is personally known to them. The officer's superior competence is to a large extent dependent on the fact that he is accepted as a powerful and in certain ways uniquely authoritative member of a system of mutual aid.

Unfortunately, we know very little about the ways in which people in blighted areas of the city corroborate each others' identity and augment each others' feeble powers. But there is no doubt that the policeman is the only social agent who has some access to the functioning of this arrangement, and the only one who can employ it knowledgeably for the protection and aid of its members. The unique effectiveness of the officer as a quasi-member of this community hinges on the fact that he can invoke the powers of coercion; the effectiveness of this resource would be, however, drastically reduced if he were not also an insider who understands the dominant interests and attitudes of the denizens. It is the officer's grasp of the stable aspects of the social structure of life in slums, in rooming house sections, and in business districts—aspects that often elude the attention of outside observers—that permits him to find alternatives to the emergency hospitalization of mentally ill persons. In certain ways, dealing with persons who inhabit blighted parts of urban areas is an easier task for a seasoned foot patrolman than dealing with persons who have stable addresses and social ties, although, of course, once the latter are located a more permanent solution is guaranteed.

The relative stability of circumstances to which a mentally ill person can be returned is, of course, distributed on a continuum. At one extreme there are those patients who need only be conveyed to worried relatives, and at the other extreme there are those who can only be returned to a status of inconspicuous anonymity. With the latter, as with those who have some tenuous ties, the problem of letting the patient slip back into his normal groove is adumbrated with questions whether the normally working controls can be entrusted with "taking care of the problem." In terms of the policeman's own standards of proper procedure it is scarcely ever sufficient to remove the patient from sight. What is intended, instead, is the achievement of a solution of some degree of permanency. Although the officer's own altruism is the main acknowledged motivational impetus for this activity, the achievement of this goal is also a practical necessity. To settle for less than an adequate solution is apt to result in repeated calls and more work.

"Psychiatric First Aid"

The involvement of the police with mentally ill persons who are not taken to the hospital is not confined to finding responsible caretakers for them, or to taking them to their normally sheltered place. Nor is this always the problem at hand, for quite often the very person who is most eligible for this role is the one who solicited police intervention. In these cases officers always administer some sort of direct "psychiatric first aid," even though they repudiate this designation. It is extremely rare that officers encounter a patient who is too passive or too withdrawn for interaction of some sort. In fact, most of the patients the police encounter are in states of relatively high agitation and can be drawn into an exchange. From the officer's point of view, his task consists of monitoring the transition of a state of affairs from its dangerous phase to a phase of relative safety and normalcy.

Although police training and literature have come to include references to the handling of mentally ill persons, it is fair to say that officers are not instructed in anything that deserves to be called a technique. With no more to go on than the maxims of kindness and caution, officers tend to fall back on being formally correct policemen. To start, seasoned officers invariably remove the patient from the immediate context in which they find him. In this they merely follow good police practice in general, applicable to all types of persons who attract police attention. The object is to establish boundaries of control and to reduce the complexity of the problem.[16] When it is not feasible to move the patient, the context is altered by removing others. The result in either case is the envelopment of the subject by police attention.

In direct dealings with the patient the policeman tries to establish and maintain the pretense of a normal conversational situation. All of the patient's remarks, allegations, or complaints are treated in a matter-of-fact manner. Policemen do not attempt to suppress or eliminate the absurd and bizarre, but rather leave them aside while concentrating verbal exchanges on the ordinary aspects of things. By this method every situation acquires a certain sense of normalcy. For example, in one observed instance a middle-aged lady complained, in highly agitated panic, that she was pursued by neighbors with an unheard-of weapon. Without questioning the lady's beliefs about what is possible in the domain

---

[16] One police lieutenant explained that one of the major stresses of police work has to do with the fact that officers are often forced to reach difficult decisions under the critical eye of bystanders. Such situations contain the simple hazard of losing physical control of the case as well as the risk that the officer's decision will be governed by external influence or provocation.

of weaponry, or what might be reasonably assumed about the motives of angry neighbors, the officers went through the motions of dealing with the situation as if it involved a bona fide complaint. They searched the premises for nonexistent traces of impossible projectiles. They carefully took note of mundane particulars of events that could not have happened and advised the lady to be on the alert for suspicious occurrences in the future. The intervention, which lasted approximately one hour, terminated when the lady came to equate her predicament with the predicament of all other persons who were under some sort of threat and who apparently survive under police protection. She was visibly calmed and expressed the belief that the officers understood what she was facing and that it was within their capacity to ensure her safety. In the end, the conversation turned to such practical matters as how to summon the police quickly in situations of imminent danger and how to make doubly sure that locks on windows and doors were secure. Throughout the conversation the officers gave no hint that they doubted any part of the story. They did not challenge the statement that a projectile may travel through walls, furniture, and clothes without leaving any traces but be, nevertheless, fatal to persons. They also took pains to convince the lady that it would be tactically unwise and impractical to arrest or even interview suspected neighbors at this stage of the case.

Although the method of field work, as employed in this study, does not permit the formulation of reliable estimates of frequencies, it can be said that neither the observations nor the interviews with policemen suggested that the distribution of "psychiatric first aid" is anything but random, relative to social class. Furthermore, such interventions sometimes involve patients exhibiting signs of very serious psychopathology. In general, agitated patients receive much more careful and protracted attention than patients who are overtly passive, which accords with the fact that officers give high priority to risks of proliferation of external troubles. Finally, although the police occasionally encounter the same patient repeatedly, they tend to treat each confrontation as a separate emergency. Every precinct station has a fund of knowledge about persons who have been the subjects of past "psychiatric first aid," but there is no sustained concern for these persons. Whenever certain known persons come to the attention of officers, it is said that they are "acting up again." The avoidance of sustained concern and attention is part of the official posture of the police and an expression of the fact that the illness as such is of little interest and that it acquires relevance only through its unpredictable exacerbations.

The attitudes and procedures of "psychiatric first aid" are in a general sense representative of the overall involvement of the police with mental illness. The attitudes and procedures also play a role in cases in which emergency apprehensions are made. In the latter instances they provide, in part, the background for the decision, in the sense that if these measures do not succeed in reducing the potential of the external risk, the patient will be taken to the hospital. Thus, the practice of "psychiatric first aid" and the skill that it involves represent the core of what we earlier identified as the manipulative horizon of relevance in the decision-making process. The point to be emphasized about these interventions is that they involve no basic modification of police posture but rather its use for the particular purposes of dealing with patients. Though the officers are fully aware that they are dealing with mentally ill persons, they do not act in the manner of quasi-mental-health-specialists.

Continuing Care

After having placed proper emphasis on the generally prevalent pattern of the episodic, emergency, and ad hoc involvement of policemen with mentally ill persons, we turn to a significantly less frequent type of activity practiced by a limited number of patrolmen. In contrast with "psychiatric first aid," foot patrolmen, especially when they work in the slum, tenderloin, business, or rooming-house districts of the city, know some mentally ill persons with whom they have established a more or less regularized pattern of running into each other. Some of these persons are apparently chronic schizophrenics, others seem mentally defective, and others are senile. Many have a history of past hospitalization. Though the officers do not attempt to diagnose these persons, they recognize the presence of substantial psychological handicaps. Indeed, the officer's interaction with and interest in these people is basically structured by the consideration that they suffer from serious disorders.

The encounters are so highly routinized that they scarcely have an event-character of their own. It is part of the ordinary routine for a foot patrolman to meet people and to engage them in conversations. Each encounter is in its own way thematized. The themes occasionally are determined in terms of the prevailing contingencies of situations. For the most part, however, the exchanges are better understood, and often can only be understood, as episodes in long-standing relationships, with past exchanges furnishing the tacit background for presently exchanged remarks. This format of meetings holds also for the encounters with known mental patients, except that in these cases the encounters are thematized by the person's psychological handicap. Officers acknowledge that their approach and manipulation of the patient is deliberately organized around this concern.

In one observed instance a young man approached an officer in a deteriorating business district of the city. He voiced an almost textbook-type paranoid complaint. From the statements and the officer's responses it could be gathered that this was a part of a sequence of conversations. The two proceeded to walk away from an area of high traffic density to quieter parts of the neighborhood. In the ensuing stroll the officer inspected various premises, greeted passers-by, and generally showed a low level of attentiveness. After about twenty-five minutes the man bade the officer goodbye and indicated that he would be going home now. The officer stated that he runs into this man quite often and usually on the same spot. He always tried to lead the man away from the place that apparently excites his paranoid suspicions. The expressions of inattentiveness are calculated to impress the person that there is nothing to worry about, while, at the same time, the efforts the man must make to hold the officer's interest absorb his energies. This method presumably makes the thing talked about a casual matter and mere small-talk. Thus, the practices employed in sustained contacts involve, like the practices of "psychiatric first aid," the tendencies to confine, to disregard pathological material, and to reduce matters to their mundane aspects.

Conclusion

Certain structural and organizational restraints leading to an apparent reluctance on the part of the police to invoke the law governing emergency apprehensions of mentally ill persons were discussed. Next we described the external properties of situations in which the law is often invoked. This approach left a seemingly residual category of cases in which persons are judged to be mentally ill but are not taken to the hospital. The category is residual, however, only in conjunction with one particular conception of the nature of police work. According to this conception the police act with competence and authority only when their actions can be subsumed under the heading of some legal mandate. If the conditions for making an arrest or an emergency apprehension are not satisfied, then, presumably, an officer has no further legitimate business with the case. It is universally accepted that the police could not possibly conform fully to this rule. Not only is it inevitable, but it has been said to be desirable that officers use a variety of means in keeping the peace.

In real police work the provisions contained in the law represent a resource that can be invoked to handle certain problems. Beyond that, the law contains certain guidelines about the boundaries of legality. Within these boundaries, however, there is located a vast array of activities that are in no important sense determined by considerations of legality. In fact, in cases in which invoking the law is not a foregone conclusion, as for example in many minor offenses or in the apprehension of mentally ill persons, it is only speciously true to say that the law determined the act of apprehension, and much more correct to say that the law made the action possible. The effective reasons for the action are not located in the formulas of statutes but in considerations that are related to established practices of dealing informally with problems.[17]

---

[17] We are talking about practice, of course, but the problem stands in the midst of a debate in legal theory. If it is maintained that the substance of the law is that it contains a system of rules of conduct, informing people what they must not do, and providing sanctions for violations, then neither the policeman nor the judge has any legitimate powers to exculpate a violator. If, however, it is maintained that the substance of the law is that it contains a system of rules limiting the powers of the institutions of the polity with respect to certain offenders and offensive types of conduct, then alternative means of control are not out of order, provided that they are not explicitly forbidden. The former position is expressed in Jerome Hall, *General Principles of Criminal Law*, Indianapolis: Bobbs-Merrill, 1947; an exposition of the latter view is contained in Norberto Bobbio, "Law and Force," *The Monist*, 49 (1965), pp. 321–342.

The important point about the relevance of established practice is that it contains the means and considerations in terms of which judgments are made whether there is any need to invoke the law. The practices are, of course, responsive to influences from the courts, from prosecutors, and the public. They also stand in some relationship of correspondence to the intent of the law. Some problems are routinely handled by invoking the law, in other cases it is merely one of the available alternatives. In these latter cases it is possible that an officer who merely complies with the law may nevertheless be found to be an incompetent practitioner of his craft. About him it may be said that he should have been able to handle the problem in some other way. The other ways of handling are not explicitly codified and they undoubtedly depend on personal ingenuity on the part of the officer. Their foundation, however, is in a transmittable skill.

When one defines these established practices as the focal point of reference of police function, instead of ministerial law enforcement, then the cases of mentally ill persons who are not referred to hospitals do not constitute a residual category. Instead, "psychiatric first aid" appears as the standard practice that contains within the realms of its possibilities the emergency apprehension. In certain cases, as for example in cases involving suicide attempts, the apprehension is virtually a foregone conclusion, but in general it is viewed as merely one of several ways of solving problems. It happens to be the only visible alternative, but this is an artifact resulting from existing police recording systems that note only those actions that involve ministerial law enforcement. Indeed, it can safely be said that the proper understanding of recorded interventions hinges on the knowledge of cases for which there is no official record. When, for example, we say that one of the necessary conditions for the emergency apprehension is the discernment of the risk of proliferation of external troubles, then we must add that these are such perceived risks as cannot be controlled by the ordinarily available means contained in the standard practices. Thus, to understand the perception of risk it is necessary to know the structure of what can be, and is normally done to control it.

In this paper we have tried to describe briefly certain practices of dealing with mentally ill persons and we have argued that the structure and means contained in these practices determine who will be referred to the hospital on an emergency basis. The external characteristics of cases are not irrelevant to the decisions, but their import is always mediated by practical considerations of what can and need be done alternatively. We should like to propose that such procedures as finding responsible caretakers who will "look out" for the patient, or "psychiatric first aid," or the sustained interest in some patients by foot patrolmen, are part of a larger domain of police work. We further propose that this work, which has been called "keeping the peace,"[18] in differentiation from "enforcing the law," consists of occupational routines with particular procedures, skills, standards, and information, in short, of craft, that meets certain tacit public expectations.[19] Chances are that when police decisions are viewed from the perspective of the requirements of this craft, rather than with an interest in seeking to discover how well they correspond to the conventional formalities of the law, they may appear quite a bit less adventitious than they are generally perceived to be. To say, however, that there exists a body of methodically organized routines for keeping the peace, which in some sense influence police decisions to invoke the law, in no way settles the question whether the currently prevailing patterns of police discretion are desirable or not. It merely urges that the study of it will furnish a more realistic basis for appraisal.

---

[18] Michael Banton proposed and discussed the distinction between peacekeeping and law-enforcement functions in his book, *The Policeman in the Community*, New York: Basic Books, 1965.

[19] Elaine Cumming and her co-workers define the policeman engaged in activities that do not relate to "keeping the law from being broken and apprehending those who break it" as an "amateur social worker." They do not consider, however, that their conception of the role of the policeman, that is, as being limited to law enforcement and restrictive control, may have been correct only "by definition and by law," and not in reality. Our own contention is that keeping the peace contains elements of control *and* support in a unique combination and that its pursuit has nothing amateurish about it. See Elaine Cumming *et al.*, "Policeman as Philosopher, Guide and Friend," *Social Problems*, 12 (1965), pp. 276–286.

The "Last Straw": The Decisive Incident Resulting in the Request for Hospitalization in 100 Schizophrenic Patients

Kathleen Smith, Muriel W. Pumphrey, and Julian C. Hall

Since there is current interest in substantially reducing the amount of inpatient care required for the mentally ill, the question arose as to whether hospitalization might be prevented by immediate intensive medical and social work collaboration when a request for hospitalization was received. Attention was focused on the decisive incident which impelled the family, neighbors, or police to decide that a particular individual could no longer remain in the community and that hospitalization was essential. This critical incident preceding a request for hospitalization was often described by the family as the "last straw."

Method

Descriptive material concerning the events preceding a request for hospitalization was available in two systematic studies of patients with schizophrenic reaction (4). Thirty-three patients had been chosen for a biochemical and EEG study in 1954-55 (10). Sixty-seven patients had been selected for the NIMH-Collaborative Study of Phenothiazines in Acute Schizophrenia in 1961-62 (7). In the first study the circumstances of admission to the hospital were obtained by a psychiatric nurse during the course of a 2-hour interview with the relatives. In the second study one of the two social work authors secured an extensive account of the way in which hospitalization had taken place. The psychiatrist author had participated in both of these studies and had screened each of the patients for the two studies shortly after admission to the hospital. Characteristics of the sample are shown in Figure 1.

Read at the 119th annual meeting of the American Psychiatric Association, St. Louis, Mo., May 6–10, 1963. Supported by USPHS Grant MYP-4667 (Psychopharmacology Service Center-NIMH). Reprinted from *The American Journal of Psychiatry*, vol. 120, 1963, pp. 228–233. Copyright 1963, the American Psychiatric Association.

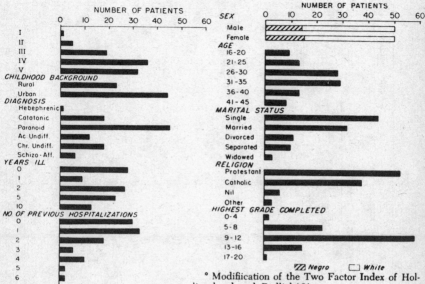

FIGURE 1 Characteristics of the Sample

° Modification of the Two Factor Index of Hollingshead and Redlich(6).

The 100 final decisive incidents were arranged into 25 types and classified into 3 categories according to the way in which the event had been perceived by the family or the community. Behavior was seen as (a) *actually or potentially harmful* to the patient or others, ("threatened to hit husband," "attacked mother with a gun," "choked a child," or "cut wrists in a suicidal attempt"); (b) *socially unacceptable* because of its embarrassing, disgusting, or puzzling nature, ("nude" in a public park, "ate raw chicken," "spit on the neighbors," or "irrational about radar"); and (c) *indicating mental illness and requiring treatment* in a mental hospital, ("thought he was losing his mind and begged his mother to take him to the hospital," "referred by her doctor because of hallucinations," or the husband knew she "was very ill when she accused a man in a car following her and misidentified the driver as Frank"). Comparable events which were tolerated without a request for hospitalization and which preceded the final event were tabulated in Table 1.

TABLE 1   INCIDENTS PRECEDING HOSPITALIZATION

Category	Decisive Incident			Prior Incident		
	NUMBER	AT HOME	COMMU-NITY	NUMBER	AT HOME	COMMU-NITY
I. Danger to Self or Others	53	43	10	61	51	10
1. Accidental injury	2	1	1	4	2	2
2. Suicidal threat or attempt	4	3	1	12	11	1
3. Refusing to eat	4	3	1	5	5	0
4. Harm to adult (family)	25	24	1	23	20	3
5. Harm to adult (not family)	2	0	2	3	1	2
6. Harm to child (family)	5	5	0	6	4	2
7. Harm to child (not family)	1	0	1	0	0	0
8. Destruction of property	6	6	0	7	7	0
9. Firesetting	2	1	1	1	1	0
10. Resisting arrest	2	0	2	0	0	0
II. Socially Unacceptable Behavior	38	10	28	155	111	44
11. Shouting	7	1	6	15	11	4
12. Nudity	5	0	5	2	1	1
13. Obscene words	3	0	3	5	5	0
14. Refusing to talk	1	1	0	15	13	2
15. Irrational talk	7	3	4	49	38	11
16. Inexplicable behavior	6	2	4	46	34	12
17. Poor judgment about money	2	1	1	5	1	5
18. Uncontrollable crying	2	1	1	1	1	0
19. Running away	1	0	1	0	0	0
20. Spitting on others	1	0	1	0	0	0
21. Wandering	1	0	1	8	0	8
22. Would not come out of room	2	1	1	9	8	1
III. Illness Requires Treatment	9	5	4	2	2	0
23. Patient request	4	4	0	1	1	0
24. Family request	1	1	0	1	1	0
25. Medical recommendation	4	0	4	0	0	0
Total	100	58	42	218	164	54

The 3 main categories were explored in relation to demographic, cultural, social and medical characteristics. The generalizability and validity of the data were compared across the dimensions of time, geographical location, hospital, race, socioeconomic group, three observers, and two professional disciplines.

Findings

The "last straws" were quite varied and bore no statistically significant relationship to age, sex, race, marital status, religion, education, occupation, social class, rural-urban rearing before age 12, subtype of schizophrenic reaction, number of years since the onset of psychosis, acuteness of onset, length of stay in the hospital, or whether the patient lived alone or with his family.

With a greater number of previous hospitalizations the type of "last straw" tended to shift from a mild behavioral problem to a fear of harm and then to actual assault. Harm to others involved family members and not outsiders in 30 of the 33 instances.

Nine types of events had been tolerated frequently without a request for hospitalization: suicidal threats, threats of harm to family members, destructiveness, shouting, obscene words, irrational talk, inexplicable behavior, wandering, and refusing to come out of a room. Suicidal attempts and actual harm to others were not tolerated. Fifty-eight final events occurred at home and 42 in the community. The community sought removal of patients with shouting, nudity, and obscene words, but was quite tolerant of those with irrational talk and inexplicable behavior. Among the 100 patients, there had been 17 previous efforts to obtain hospitalization. The family had reached a "last straw," but the police or the emergency room staff thought some alternative was possible, and the patient was not admitted. When the next attempt to obtain hospitalization occurred, the "last straw" was a different one in 13 of 17 instances and tended to be more serious.

When the "last straws" were grouped into the 3 major categories and compared across time (1954-55 and 1961-62), there were no significant differences. When dangerous behavior was subdivided into actual harm and threat of harm, there was less actual harm in the later period. In comparing the data from two field investigators in 1961-62, there was a significant difference

TABLE 2 CATEGORIES OF DECISIVE INCIDENTS COMPARED BY TIME AND OB-
SERVER

| Category | 1954-55 | | 1961-62 | | |
	TOTAL N = 100	NURSE N = 33	SOCIAL WORKER 1 N = 34	SOCIAL WORKER 2 N = 33	COMBINED N = 67
Dangerous behavior	53.0%	48.5%	47.0%	63.6%	55.2%
Actual harm	23.0	33.3	17.6	18.1	17.8
Threat of harm	30.0	15.2	29.4	45.5	37.3
Socially unaccept-able behavior	38.0	39.3	44.1	30.3	37.3
Illness requires treatment	9.0	12.1	8.8	6.1	7.5

between threat of harm and socially unacceptable behavior
(Table 2).

Data from 9 hospitals which varied in geographical location
and type of hospital[3] were available in somewhat different form
and are shown in Table 3. These results suggest that the factors
leading to hospitalization vary among the hospitals. It is noted
that Malcolm Bliss Mental Health Center tends to be higher on
assault, destructiveness, and family fear of the patient and lower
on patient's wish and medical recommendation. This may depend
on the varied referral sources and admission policies whereby
patients reach particular hospitals.

Discussion

Several authors have commented on the paucity of data concerning the ways in which people react to increasing psychotic
behavior outside the hospital (3, 12). Yarrow, *et al.* (3) have
written about the responses of wives to the disruptive behavior
of their psychotic husbands. Other authors have examined the
process in which care was sought only after the mentally ill per-

---

[3] Institute of Living, Hartford, Conn.; Payne Whitney Clinic, New York,
N.Y.; Mercy-Douglass Hospital, Philadelphia, Pa.; D.C. General Hospital,
Washington, D.C.; Malcolm Bliss Mental Health Center, St. Louis, Mo.;
Boston State Hospital, Boston, Mass.; Rochester State Hospital, Rochester,
N.Y.; Springfield State Hospital, Sykesville, Md.; and Kentucky State Hos-
pital, Danville, Ky.

TABLE 3 FACTORS LEADING DIRECTLY TO HOSPITALIZATION

Factor	Nine Hospitals (N = 374) Percent	Bliss Hospital (N = 67) Percent
Patient's wish	12.3	4.5
Medical recommendation	20.0	6.0
Patient's inability to care for self	7.7	3.0
Patient's assaultiveness	5.9	13.4
Patient's destructiveness of property	1.3	6.0
Patient's general unmanageability	23.5	17.9
Patient's self-destructiveness	1.1	4.5
Family's fear of patient	6.1	19.4
Patient's suicide attempt or serious threat of suicide	2.7	1.5
Male patient's cessation of paid work	1.3	1.5
Female patient's cessation of paid work	0.5	1.5
Female patient's cessation of housework	0.3	0.0
Female patient's cessation of child care	0.3	1.5
Other	16.8	19.4
	99.7%	100.1%

son gradually was perceived as sick and after frequent delays had ensued (1, 3, 8, 11, 13). In these studies the final and decisive incidents have been referred to occasionally and incidentally as a part of that process. The present study was concerned only with the final disruption that tipped the balance and resulted in hospitalization.

It was assumed that the behavior and feelings of both the patient and those interacting with him during a final recognized crisis would have to be taken into account in considering alternatives for hospitalization. Ordinarily, the act of hospitalization in any medical condition occurs after an individual is perceived as ill. According to Dr. Dorrian Apple, the perception of illness requires that the symptoms be presently active, acute and well-defined, and leading to an impairment of activity (1). Although these criteria were met, only 4 of the 100 schizophrenic patients saw themselves as ill with a need for hospitalization. In 96 instances someone other than the patient perceived the illness and made the decision to bring the patient to the hospital. If Dr. Apple's criteria were to be applied to the family or community member that made the decision, it might be reasoned that the patient's behavior had to be presently active, acute and well-defined, and must have led to impairment of the activity of the family or the community. Our data suggest that this impairment must be quite marked before action is taken, for example:

> A male patient hit his mother periodically, talked in a loud and hostile manner to the voices, used profane language, and masturbated openly at home for one year. The decision to seek hospitalization occurred promptly when he carved obscenities on the new grand piano. The mother acted because she was afraid that her spouse, the patient's step-father, would leave her, since the piano was a status symbol and the carvings would present tangible evidence to the neighbors that the family was indecent.

This mother's reaction also illustrates the specific nature of the "last straw" and shows how it is directly related to the value judgments and the internal conflicts of a particular family. In general, families were sensitive whenever behavior aroused feelings of fear, shame, or disgust. In 23 instances the patient was perceived as doing something actually dangerous and in 30 instances as about to commit such an act. This type of behavior elicited an immediate sense of fear and a conviction that protective custody and control were necessary. In most instances the patient harmed or threatened to harm family members at home rather than involving outsiders. Brown (2) also noted that threats of harm and actual harm to others almost always involved a family member. Some families could tolerate threats of harm to themselves but did not request hospitalization until the patient was about to involve outside community members.

In 23 cases the patient was doing something regarded as a flagrant violation of community norms of behavior, such as being nude or obscene. If unacceptable behavior occurred at home, it was frequently tolerated. Members of the community were less tolerant possibly because of uncertainty as to whether the patient might become dangerous, or to guard the community standards of decency and order.

Because of the serious nature of the final incidents and the strong feelings they evoked, it seemed mandatory that a hospital setting offer protection and support when the family and the community had had all the stress they could tolerate. Present collaborative methods include no other effective techniques for handling extreme fear when the possibility of genuine danger remains, or for relieving extreme emotional and physical exhaustion on the part of the family. Attempts by other investigators to provide alternatives to hospitalization in a mixed diagnostic group show that about half of the patients require admission. Friedman, *et al.* (5), found that after a crisis had already arisen with an outpatient that it was difficult for a collaborative team approach to prevent hospitalization. In his series of cases 40% required hospitalization. Moore, *et al.* (9), utilizing a clinical team and home visits, found that 51% had to be admitted. Our data suggest that this proportion is even higher when only psychotic patients are considered.

A reduction in the number of admissions to a mental hospital appears to depend on care reaching the patient before a severe "last straw" occurs. In most instances it is the family and the community member rather than the schizophrenic patient who will have to be encouraged to seek care earlier in the illness. Methods for this await further development. Before families in large numbers are motivated to consult medical opinion when the behavior is more easily tolerated, community resources will have to be made available for quick and appropriate response.

Summary

The decisive incident that forced a decision that a particular individual could no longer remain in the community and must be admitted to a mental hospital was studied from the point of view of the person making this decision. Descriptive data on 100 schizophrenic patients were analyzed to determine whether prompt medical and social work collaboration at the point of admission might prevent hospitalization.

Fifty-three patients actually committed or threatened to commit a dangerous act. Thirty-eight patients exhibited behavior that was socially unacceptable. Nine patients were perceived as needing treatment for illness. Only 4 patients requested hospitalization.

Demographic and social characteristics were not statistically significant in relation to the type of "last straw." As the number of hospitalizations mounted, the crucial event tended to progress from a mild behavioral change to threatening behavior, to actual assault. The final events were "family and community specific" and depended on particular standards and sensitivities.

Since many "last straws" are extreme and the family and the community have reached their limit of tolerance, the number of hospital admissions can be reduced only by extending care to the patient before his removal from the community is the only alternative.

Bibliography

1. Allport, G. W.: Personality and the Social Encounter. Boston: Beacon Press, 1960.
2. Brown, B. S.: Missouri Med., *60*: 253, 1963.
3. Clausen, J. A., and Yarrow, M. R. (Eds.): J. Social Issues, *11*: 6, 12, 25, 33, 1955.
4. Diagnostic and Statistical Manual, Mental Disorders. Washington, D.C.: APA, 1952.
5. Friedman, T. T., *et al.*: Am. J. Psychiat., *116*: 807, 1960.
6. Hollingshead, A., and Redlich, F.: Social Class and Mental Illness. New York: Wiley, 1958.
7. Klerman, G. L.: Psychopharmacol. Serv. Cent. Bull.: U.S. Dept. of Health, Education, and Welfare, Jan. 1961.
8. Lewis, V. S., and Zeichner, A. H.: Ment. Hyg., *44*: 503, 1960.
9. Moore, R. F., *et al.*: Am. J. Psychiat., *119*: 560, 1962.
10. Smith, K., *et al.*: Arch. Neurol. Psychiat., *77*: 528, 1957.
11. Warner, S. L.: Ment. Hyg., *45*: 122, 1961.
12. Wood, E. C., *et al.*: Arch. Gen. Psychiat., *3*: 632, 1960.
13. Wood, E. C., *et al.*: *Ibid.*, *6*: 39, 1962.

Rejection: A Possible Consequence of Seeking Help for Mental Disorders

Derek L. Phillips

The nonconformist, whether he be foreigner or 'odd ball,' intellectual or idiot, genius or jester, individualist or hobo, physically or mentally abnormal—pays a price for 'being different' unless his peculiarity is considered acceptable for his particular group, or unless he lives in a place or period of particularly high tolerance or enlightenment.[1]

The penalty that *mentally ill* persons pay for "being different" is often rejection by others in the community. Following the increased interest of social scientists in the public's attitudes toward the mentally ill,[2] this research investigates some of the factors involved in the rejection of mentally ill individuals.

Reprinted from the *American Sociological Review*, vol. 28, 1963, pp. 963–972, by permission of the American Sociological Association and the author. This investigation was carried out during the tenure of a Predoctoral Fellowship from the National Institute of Mental Health. The writer wishes to thank C. Richard Fletcher, Phillip S. Hammond, and Elton F. Jackson for their helpful suggestions.

[1] Joint Commission on Mental Illness and Health, *Action for Mental Health*, New York: Science Editions, 1961, p. 69.

[2] See, for example, John A. Clausen and Marian R. Yarrow, "Paths to the Mental Hospital," *The Journal of Social Issues*, 11 (November, 1955), pp. 25–32; Elaine and John Cumming, *Closed Ranks: An Experiment in Mental Health Education*, Cambridge: Harvard University Press, 1957; Bruce P. Dohrwend, Viola W. Bernard, and Lawrence C. Kolb, "The Orientations of Leaders in an Urban Area Toward Problems of Mental Illness," *The American Journal of Psychiatry*, 118 (February, 1962), pp. 683–691; Howard E. Freeman and Ozzie G. Simmons, "Mental Patients in the Community," *American Sociological Review*, 23 (April, 1958), pp. 147–154; Gerald Gurin, Joseph Veroff, and Sheila Feld, *Americans View Their Mental Health*, New York: Basic Books, 1960; E. Gartly Jaco, *The Social Epidemiology of Mental Disorders*, New York: Russell Sage Foundation, 1960; Paul V. Lemkau and Guido M. Crocetti, "An Urban Population's Opinion and Knowledge about Mental Illness," *The American Journal of Psychiatry*, 118 (February, 1962), pp. 692–700; Jum C. Nunnally, Jr., *Popular Conceptions of Mental Health*, New York: Holt, Rinehart and Winston, 1961; Glen V. Ramsey and Melita Seipp, "Public Opinions and Information Concerning Mental Health," *Jour-*

This paper presents the results of a controlled experiment in influencing people's attitudes toward individuals exhibiting symptoms of mental illness. The research attempts to determine the extent to which people's attitudes toward an individual exhibiting disturbed behavior are related to their knowledge of the particular help-source that the individual is using or has used. The term "help-source" here refers to such community resources as clergymen, physicians, pyschiatrists, marriage counselors, mental hygiene clinics, alcohol clinics, and mental hospitals, each of which is frequently concerned with persons having emotional problems.

Most studies concerned with attitudes toward the mentally ill have focused on the individual's behavior as the sole factor determining whether or not he is rejected by others. Other research has considered the importance of psychiatric treatment or hospitalization in *identifying* the individual as mentally ill and, subsequently, leading to his rejection.[3] But as far as could be determined, no study has been made of the importance of utilizing other help-sources in determining or influencing public attitudes toward individuals exhibiting disturbed behavior.

In a number of studies respondents have been asked whether they considered various *descriptions* to be those of mentally ill persons, and some respondents were found unable to recognize certain serious symptoms of disturbed behavior. Star, for example, asking 3500 respondents about six case abstracts of mentally ill persons, found that 17 per cent of the sample said that none of these imaginary persons was sufficiently deviant to represent what they meant by mental illness. Another 28 per cent limited their concept of mental illness to the paranoid, the only description where violence was a prominent feature of the behavior.[4] Elaine and John Cumming, asking questions about the same six

---

nal of Clinical Psychology, 4 (October, 1948), pp. 397–406; Charlotte Green Schwartz, "Perspectives on Deviance—Wives' Definitions of Their Husbands' Mental Illness," *Psychiatry*, 20 (August, 1957), pp. 275–291; Shirley Star, "The Place of Psychiatry in Popular Thinking," paper presented at the meeting of the American Association for Public Opinion Research, Washington, D.C., May 1957; Julian L. Woodward, "Changing Ideas on Mental Illness and Its Treatment," *American Sociological Review*, 16 (August, 1951), pp. 443–454.

[3] See Clausen and Yarrow, *op. cit.*, and Cumming and Cumming, *op. cit.*
[4] Star, *op. cit.*

descriptions of deviant behavior, found that the majority of people dismissed the descriptions, even when they were clinically grave, as normal, with such comments as "It's just a quirk, it's nothing serious."[5]

Sharply in disagreement with these findings, however, are the results of studies by Lemkau and Crocetti, and by Dohrenwend, Bernard and Kolb. Using three of the Star abstracts, Lemkau and Crocetti found that 91 per cent of their sample identified the paranoid as mentally ill, 78 per cent identified the simple schizophrenic, and 62 per cent identified the alcoholic.[6] Dohrenwend and his associates, interviewing "leaders in an urban area," used the six Star abstracts. They report that "all saw mental illness in the description of paranoid schizophrenia; 72 per cent saw it in the example of simple schizophrenia; 63 per cent in the alcoholic; about 50 per cent in the anxiety neurosis and in the juvenile character disorder; and 40 per cent in the compulsive-phobic."[7] These findings, although somewhat inconsistent, do indicate some public ignorance concerning the signs and symptoms of mental illness. More important here, they tell us nothing about how the public *feels* toward the individuals in these case abstracts.

Hospitalization is another cue that has been found to influence recognition of a person as mentally ill. The Cummings state, "Mental illness, it seems, is a condition which afflicts people who must go to a mental institution, but up until they go almost anything they do is fairly normal."[8]

Apparently some people can correctly identify symptoms of mental illness and others cannot, while for some the mentally ill are only those who have been in a mental hospital. But it seems equally important to ask whether people *reject* individuals displaying symptoms of mental illness or those who have been hospitalized. In part, the task of this research was to determine the extent to which people reject various descriptions of disturbed behavior. An additional cue—the *help-source* that the individual described is utilizing—was presented to the respondents in order

---

[5] Elaine and John Cumming, "Affective Symbolism, Social Norms, and Mental Illness," *Psychiatry*, 19 (February, 1956), pp. 77–85.

[6] Lemkau and Crocetti, *op. cit.*, p. 694.

[7] Dohrenwend, Bernard and Kolb, *op. cit.*, p. 685.

[8] Cumming and Cumming, *Closed Ranks, op. cit.*, p. 102.

to ascertain the importance of the help-source in determining rejection of mentally ill individuals. Four help-sources that people with mental disorders often consult[9]—the clergyman, the physician, the psychiatrist, and the mental hospital—were represented.

Several recent studies have been concerned with the help-sources that people suggest using for mental disorders, as well as the ones they actually have used.[10] Considerable evidence from these studies indicates that people have strong negative attitudes toward psychiatrists and mental hospitals and toward individuals using either of these help-sources.[11] But there seems to be no evidence of negative attitudes toward clergymen or physicians, or toward people consulting these two help-sources. Further, the fact that people with emotional problems are more likely to consult clergymen and physicians than psychiatrists and mental hospitals[12] suggests the absence of strong negative attitudes toward the latter and those utilizing them. Gurin points out that they ". . . are the areas most people turn to with their personal problems; they are the major 'gatekeepers' in the treatment process, either doing the treating themselves or referring to a more specialized professional resource."[13] Both the clergyman and the physician are professionally involved in what are usually defined as "the private affairs" of others. They have, what Naegele calls ". . . legitimate access to realms beyond public discussion."[14]

Although it is probably true that the public does not hold negative attitudes toward clergymen and physicians, I suggest that an individual consulting either of these help-sources may more often lose face, and more often be regarded as deviant, than an individual exhibiting the same behavior who does not consult one of these professional resources. How does this come to be so?

---

[9] See, for example, Gurin, *et al., op. cit.*

[10] Dohrenwend, *et al., op. cit.*; Gurin, *et al., op. cit.*; Ramsey and Seipp, *op. cit.*; Woodward, *op. cit.*

[11] Clausen and Yarrow, *op. cit.*; Cumming and Cumming, *op. cit.*; Frederick C. Redlich, "What the Citizen Knows About Psychiatry," *Mental Hygiene*, 34 (January, 1950), pp. 64–70; Star, *op. cit.*

[12] Gurin, *et al., op. cit.*, p. 307.

[13] *Ibid.*, p. 400.

[14] Kasper D. Naegele, "Clergymen, Teachers, and Psychiatrists: A Study in Roles and Socialization," *The Canadian Journal of Economic and Political Science*, 22 (February, 1956), p. 48.

As Clausen and Yarrow point out, "There is an ethic of being able to handle one's own problems by oneself, which applies not only to psychiatric problems."[15] Similarly, Ewalt says, "One value in American culture compatible with most approaches to a definition of positive mental health appears to be this: An individual should be able to stand on his own two feet without making undue demands or impositions on others."[16] In another statement of this view, Kadushin reports that, in answer to the question "Would you tell people in general that you came here?" (the Peale-Blanton Religio-Psychiatric Clinic), a respondent replied "... I wouldn't tell people in general. I know that there's still a stigma attached to people who seek psychiatric aid, and I guess I'm ashamed that I couldn't manage my own problem."[17]

Thus, an outside observer's knowledge that a person is consulting any of the four help-sources discussed may have at least two important consequences for the individual with a behavior problem: (1) He is defined as someone who *has* a problem. Moreover, the further along the continuum from clergyman to mental hospital the individual moves, the more his problem is seen as a serious one, and individuals consulting a psychiatrist or a mental hospital are very often defined as "mentally ill" or "insane." (2) The individual is defined as unable to handle his problem by himself.

I am suggesting that the reported inability of some persons to recognize certain serious symptoms of disturbed behavior is due to difficulty in evaluating an individual's behavior, and that knowledge about what help-source the individual is utilizing helps others decide whether he is "deviant" or has a problem that he cannot cope with himself. And an important social consequence for the person who, because of his behavior or choice of help-source, is defined as deviant may be *rejection*.

---

[15] Clausen and Yarrow, *op. cit.*, p. 63.

[16] Jack K. Ewalt, intro., Marie Jahoda, *Current Concepts of Positive Mental Health*, New York: Basic Books, 1958, p. xi.

[17] Charles Kadushin, "Individual Decisions to Undertake Psychotherapy," *Administrative Science Quarterly*, 3 (December, 1958), p. 389.

Gurin, *et al.*, report that 25 per cent of their respondents who had problems but did not utilize help tried to solve the problems by themselves, *op. cit.*, pp. 350–351.

These considerations led to formulation of the following hypothesis: Individuals exhibiting identical behavior will be increasingly rejected as they are described as not seeking any help, as utilizing a clergyman, a physician, a psychiatrist, or a mental hospital.

Method

To test this hypothesis, interviews were conducted with a systematic sample[18] of 300 married white females selected from the address section of the City Directory of Branford, a southern New England town of approximately 17,000 population.[19] The sample was so small that the need to control for a number of variables was obvious. Thus, males,[20] non-whites, and unmarried respondents were excluded from the sample.

The interviews took place in the respondents' homes and were of 20 to 40 minutes duration. Each respondent was given five cards, one at a time, describing different behaviors. The interviewer read each description aloud from the interview schedule as the respondent followed by reading the card.

Case abstract (A) was a description of a paranoid schizophrenic, (B) an individual suffering from simple schizophrenia, (C) an anxious-depressed person, (D) a phobic individual with

---

[18] The sample was drawn from the address section of the Directory, with every 15th address marked for interview. The first address was drawn randomly from the first 15 entries; thereafter every 15th address was included until the total sample of 300 was obtained.

[19] Twenty-eight of the households drawn in the original sample refused to be interviewed. In each of these cases, a substitution was made by selecting an address at random from the same street. Four of these substitutes refused to be interviewed, necessitating further substitution. Also requiring substitution were three addresses that could not be located and six wives of household heads who were divorced, separated, or widowed, rather than married. Selecting substitutes from the same neighborhood was done on the assumption that persons living in the same neighborhood would resemble one another in certain important ways; they were more likely, than people living in different neighborhoods, to be of similar socio-economic status. Although the possibility of bias still exists, so few substitutions were necessary that, hopefully, the effect is minimal.

[20] In a pre-test with a sample of 32 women and 28 men, no significant differences were found between the rejection rates of men and women.

compulsive features, and (E) a "normal" person. The first four abstracts were, in the main, the same as those developed by Shirley Star, formerly of the National Opinion Research Center in Chicago.[21] The fifth abstract, that of the "'normal'"[22] individual, was developed expressly for this research.[23]

The five case abstracts were presented in combination with information about what help-source an individual was utilizing, in the following manner:

(1) Nothing was added to the description of the behavior—this was, of course, the absence of any help.

(2) Affixed to the description was the statement: "He has been going to see his clergyman regularly about the way he is getting along."

(3) Affixed to the description was the statement: "He has been going to see his physician regularly about the way he is getting along."

(4) Affixed to the description was the statement: "He has been going to see his psychiatrist regularly about the way he is getting along."

(5) Affixed to the description was the statement: "He has been in a mental hospital because of the way he was getting along."

This research required an experimental design permitting classification of each of the two independent variables (behavior and help-source) in five categories.[24] Observations for all possible

---

[21] Star, *op. cit.*

[22] The normal person was described as follows: "Here is a description of a man. Imagine that he is a respectable person living in your neighborhood. He is happy and cheerful, has a good enough job and is fairly well satisfied with it. He is always busy and has quite a few friends who think he is easy to get along with most of the time. Within the next few months he plans to marry a nice young woman he is engaged to."

[23] My purpose was to determine (a) whether the rejection of the mentally ill descriptions might in part be accounted for by individuals who rejected everyone regardless of behavior; and (b) whether the utilization of a help-source alone could influence rejection, or whether it was the "combination" of deviant behavior and the use of a help-source that led to rejection.

[24] The advantages of including tests of different combinations of two or more variables within one experiment have been cited by several writers concerned with experimental design. For example, D. J. Finney, *The Theory of Experimental Design*, Chicago: The University of Chicago Press, 1960, p. 68, notes the following advantages: "(1) To broaden the basis of inferences relating to one factor by testing that factor under various conditions

combinations of the values of the two variables would have been desirable, but this clearly was not feasible. Hence the observations were arranged in the form of a Graeco-Latin Square[25] so as to obtain a large amount of information from a relatively small number of observations. Specifically, this type of design enables us to discover: (a) the influence of different types of behavior in determining rejection, and (b) the influence of different help-sources in determining rejection.

The 300 respondents were divided at random into five groups of 60 individuals each. Every individual in each group saw five combinations of behavior and help-source, but no group or individual saw any given behavior or any given help-source more than once. In order to assure that the rejection rates were not affected by the *order* in which individuals saw the combinations, the experiment was designed so that each behavior and each help-source was seen first by one group, second by another, third by another, fourth by another, and last by the remaining group.[26]

Thus, in the Graeco-Latin Square design, three variables were considered (behavior, help-source, and order). The data were classified in five categories on each of these variables. See Figure 1, where the letters in each cell indicate a description of behavior, and the numbers in each cell indicate the help-source utilized. In the top left-hand cell, for example, the letter A indi-

---

of others; (2) To assess the extent to which the effects of one factor are modified by the level of others; (3) To economize in experimental material by obtaining information on several factors without increasing the size of the experiment beyond what would be required for one or two factors alone."

[25] For two excellent explanations of the Graeco-Latin Square design see, Finney, *op. cit.*, and E. F. Lindquist, *Design of Experiments in Psychology and Education*, Boston: Houghton Mifflin, 1953.

[26] In addition, to 50 per cent of the respondents, the paranoid, the depressed individual, and the "normal" person were presented as males, with the simple schizophrenic and the phobic-compulsive individual presented as females. The other half of the sample saw a reversed order—the simple schizophrenic and the compulsive individuals as males, and the paranoid, depressed, and "normal" persons as females. Since both the male case abstracts and the female case abstracts were rejected in accordance with the pattern shown in Table 1, they will not be discussed further in this paper. The findings for the *differences* in the *absolute* rejection of males and females exhibiting a given behavior and utilizing the same help-source will be the subject of a forthcoming paper.

FIGURE 1   THE GRAECO-LATIN SQUARE DESIGN[a]

	Order				
	1	2	3	4	5
Group 1	A1	B2	C3	D4	E5
Group 2	B3	C4	D5	E1	A2
Group 3	C5	D1	E2	A3	B4
Group 4	D2	E3	A4	B5	C1
Group 5	E4	A5	B1	C2	D3

[a] N for each cell in the table is 60.

cates that the paranoid schizophrenic was the description seen first by Group 1, and that he was described as seeing help-source 1 (that is, he was not described as seeking any help). Similarly, in the bottom right-hand cell, the letter D indicates that the phobic-compulsive person was the abstract seen fifth by Group 5, and that he was described as consulting help-source 3 (a physician).

After reading each combination of behavior and help-source, the respondents were asked a uniform series of questions. These questions made up a social distance scale, indicating how close a relation the respondent was willing to tolerate with the individuals in the case abstracts. This scale was used as the measure of *rejection*, the dependent variable in the research.

The social distance scale consisted of the following items: (1) "Would you discourage your children from marrying someone like this?" (2) "If you had a room to rent in your home, would you be willing to rent it to someone like this?" (3) "Would you be willing to work on a job with someone like this?" (4) "Would you be willing to have someone like this join a favorite club or organization of yours?" (5) "Would you object to having a person like this as a neighbor?"[27]

The range of possible scores for each combination of help-source and behavior was from zero (when no items indicated rejection) through five (when all items indicated rejection). A test of reproducibility was applied and the resulting coefficient

---

[27] The above order duplicates the order of "closeness" represented by the scale. The items, however, were administered to each respondent in a random fashion.

TABLE 1   REJECTION SCORES[a] FOR EACH HELP-SOURCE AND BEHAVIOR COMBINATION[b]

Behavior	Help-Source Utilized					
	NO HELP	CLERGY-MAN	PHYSI-CIAN	PSYCHI-ATRIST	MENTAL HOSPITAL	TOTAL
Paranoid Schizophrenic	3.65	3.33	3.77	4.12	4.33	3.84
Simple Schizophrenic	1.10	1.57	1.83	2.85	3.68	2.21
Depressed-Neurotic	1.45	1.62	2.07	2.70	3.28	2.22
Phobic-Compulsive	.53	1.12	1.18	1.87	2.27	1.39
Normal Individual	.02	.22	.50	1.25	1.63	.72
Total	1.35	1.57	1.87	2.56	3.04	—

$$F = 23.53, p < .001$$

[a] Rejection scores are represented by the mean number of items rejected on the Social Distance Scale.
[b] N for each cell in the table is 60.

was .97, indicating that the scale met acceptable standards; i.e., was a unidimensional scale.

It should be emphasized that each combination of behavior and help-source was seen by 60 respondents. It also bears repeating that each respondent was presented with five combinations of behavior and help-source. Thus, each respondent contributed a rejection score (on the social distance scale) to each of five cells out of the 25 cells in Figure 1. An analysis of variance of the form generally applied to planned experiments was carried out.[28]

Results and Discussion

Table 1 presents the mean rejection rate for each combination of behavior and help-source. An individual exhibiting a given type of behavior is increasingly rejected as he is described as seeking no help, as seeing a clergyman, as seeing a physician, as seeing a psychiatrist, or as having been in a mental hospital. The relation between the independent variable (help-source) and the depend-

---

[28] See, for example, Lindquist, *op. cit.*, chs. 12 and 13.

ent variable (rejection) is statistically significant at the .001 level. Furthermore, the reversal in the "paranoid schizophrenic" row is the only one among 25 combinations.[29]

The relation between the other independent variable (behavior) and rejection is also significant at the .001 level. In fact, the F obtained for the relation between behavior and rejection ($F = 64.52$) is much higher than the F obtained for the relation between help-source and rejection ($F = 23.53$). In other words, when a respondent was confronted with a case abstract containing both a description of their individual's behavior and information about what help-source he was utilizing, the description of behavior played a greater part (i.e., accounted for more variance) than the help-source in determining how strongly she rejected the individual described.

As was indicated earlier, the main purpose of this presentation is to show the extent to which attitudes toward an individual exhibiting symptoms of mental illness are related to knowledge of the particular help-source that he is utilizing. The importance of the type of behavior is of secondary interest here; I have investigated the relation between behavior and rejection mainly to ascertain the *relative* importance of each of the two elements presented in the case abstracts. The relation between behavior and rejection will be fully treated in a future paper.

The totals at the bottom of Table 1 show that the largest increase in the rejection rates occurs when an individual sees a psychiatrist. That is, the rejection rate for individuals described as consulting a physician (1.87) differs from the rejection rate for individuals described as consulting a psychiatrist (2.56) to a degree greater than for any other comparison between two adjacent help-sources. The second largest over-all increase in rejection occurs when the individual is described as having been in a mental hospital, and the smallest net increase (.20) occurs when the individual sees a clergyman, compared to seeking no help at all.

Probably the most significant aspect of the effect of help-source on rejection rates is that, for four of the five case abstracts, the biggest increase in rejection occurs when the individual is described as consulting a psychiatrist, and in three of the five

---

[29] Following Lindquist, neither order nor interaction was found to be statistically significant at the .20 level. See Lindquist, *op. cit.*, pp. 273–281.

abstracts the second largest increase occurs when the individual is depicted as having been in a mental hospital. Not only are individuals increasingly rejected as they are described as seeking no help, as seeing a clergyman, a physician, a psychiatrist, or a mental hospital, but they are *disproportionately* rejected when described as utilizing the latter two help-sources. This supports the suggestion made earlier that individuals utilizing psychiatrists and mental hospitals may be rejected not only because they have a health problem, and because they are unable to handle the problem themselves, but also because contact with a psychiatrist or a mental hospital defines them as "mentally ill" or "insane."

Despite the fact that the "normal" person is more an "ideal type" than a normal person, when he is described as having been in a mental hospital he is rejected more than a psychotic individual described as not seeking help or as seeing a clergyman, and more than a depressed-neurotic seeing a clergyman. Even when the normal person is described as seeing a psychiatrist, he is rejected more than a simple schizophrenic who seeks no help, more than a phobic-compulsive individual seeking no help or seeing a clergyman or physician.

As was noted previously, there is one reversal in Table 1. The paranoid schizophrenic, unlike the other descriptions, was rejected more strongly when he was described as not utilizing any help-source than when he was described as utilizing a clergyman. The paranoid was described in the case abstract as suspicious, as picking fights with people who did not even know him, and as cursing his wife. His behavior may be so threatening and so obviously deviates from normal behavior, that the respondents feel that he is socially less objectionable when he takes a step to help himself. In other words, the individual *obviously* in need of professional help is in a sense "rewarded" for seeking at least one kind of help, that of the clergyman. And though the paranoid schizophrenic is increasingly rejected when he is described as utilizing a physician, a psychiatrist, and a mental hospital, the relative amount of increase is much less than for the other four case abstracts.

Mentally ill persons whose behavior does not deviate markedly from normal role-expectations may be assigned responsibility for their own behavior. If so, seeking any professional help is an admission of inability to meet this responsibility. An individual whose behavior is markedly abnormal (in this instance, the paranoid schizophrenic) may not, however, be considered responsible for his behavior or for his recovery, and is, therefore, rejected less than other individuals when he seeks professional help.

Controls

To determine whether the findings were spurious, the relation between help-source and rejection was observed under several different controls. The association was maintained within age groups, within religious affiliation groups, within educational attainment groups, and within groups occupying different positions in the status hierarchy.[30] The association was also maintained within groups differing in authoritarianism.[31]

But when (1) experience with someone who had sought help for emotional problems[32] and (2) attitude toward the norm of self-reliance,[33] were controlled, the relation between help-source and rejection was specified.

Table 2 presents the rejection rates for respondents reporting a relative who sought help, those reporting a friend who sought help, and those who knew no one who sought help for emotional problems. For ease of presentation and interpretation, the rejection rates for the five case abstracts have been combined.[34]

There are two points of interest in Table 2. One is the difference in rejection rates *among* the three groups of respondents. But because these interesting differences are peripheral to the central concern here, I will focus, instead, on the second point

---

[30] For details of the classification procedures, see pp. 82–88 of the author's doctoral dissertation, of which this research is a part: "Help-Sources and Rejection of the Mentally Ill," unpublished Ph.D. Dissertation, Yale University, 1962.

[31] For details of the authoritarian scale, see *ibid.*, p. 77.

[32] The question was: "We've been talking about people with worries and problems. Have any of your close friends or relatives had any psychiatric treatment or gone to a hospital or professional person, or community agency, regarding emotional problems?" If the respondent answered in the affirmative, she was asked who this person was.

[33] Attitude toward self-reliance was measured by the respondent's reaction to the following statement: "People should be expected to handle their own problems," with a choice of four responses—strongly agree, agree somewhat, disagree somewhat, and strongly disagree.

[34] Because our primary interest is in the effect of help-source rather than behavior, rejection rates will hereafter be presented in combined form only.

TABLE 2   REJECTION SCORES[a] FOR ALL CASES BY HELP-SOURCE AND ACQUAINT-
ANCE WITH HELP-SEEKERS

Help-Source Utilized	Acquaintance		
	RELATIVE ($N = 37$)	FRIEND ($N = 73$)	NO ONE ($N = 190$)
No help-source	2.35	1.45	1.12
Clergyman	2.06	1.45	1.51
Physician	1.30	1.58	2.09
Psychiatrist	2.08	2.53	2.66
Mental Hospital	2.38	2.82	3.25

[a] Rejection scores are represented by the mean number of items rejected
on the Social Distance Scale.

of interest. This is the consistent increase—*within* two of the three
groups of respondents—in rejection scores for persons not seeking
any help, utilizing a clergyman, a physician, a psychiatrist, or a
mental hospital.

Respondents *not* acquainted with a help-seeker as well as those
acquainted with a help-seeking *friend* adhere to the pattern of
rejection previously demonstrated in Table 1. But respondents
with a help-seeking *relative* deviate markedly from this pattern.
They reject persons not seeking help more than they do persons
consulting a clergyman, physician, or psychiatrist, and almost as
much as those utilizing a mental hospital. And they reject persons
consulting a clergyman more than those consulting a physician.

Perhaps respondents with help-seeking relatives are more able
to recognize the behavior in the abstracts as that of persons who
need help and therefore they reject them strongly when they do
not seek help. A similar explanation may apply to the rejection
of persons using a clergyman. That is, these respondents may see
the clergyman as not being what Parsons calls "technically competent help"[35] and equate seeing him with not seeking help. The

---

[35] Talcott Parsons, *The Social System*, Glencoe, Ill.: The Free Press, 1950,
p. 437. Parsons states that ". . . the fourth closely related element [in the
sick role] is the obligation—in proportion to the severity of the condition,
of course—to seek *technically competent* help, namely in the most usual case,
that of a physician and to *cooperate* with him in the process of trying to get
well." He makes this point again in "Definitions of Health and Illness in the
Light of American Values and Social Structure," in E. Gartly Jaco (ed.),
Patients, Physicians and Illness, Glencoe, Ill.: The Free Press, 1959, pp.
165–187.

TABLE 3 REJECTION SCORES[a] FOR ALL MENTALLY ILL CASES BY HELP-SOURCE
AND ACQUAINTANCE WITH HELP-SEEKERS

Help-Source Utilized	Acquaintance		
	RELATIVE ($n = 37$)	FRIEND ($n = 73$)	NO ONE ($n = 190$)
No help-source	2.81	1.64	1.16
Clergyman	2.20	1.65	1.86
Physician	1.51	1.91	2.46
Psychiatrist	2.45	2.88	2.90
Mental Hospital	3.04	3.14	3.51

[a] Rejection scores are represented by the mean number of items rejected on the Social Distance Scale.

comparatively low rejection of persons consulting a physician may reflect the respondents' belief that a physician is one of the professional resources that one *should* utilize for emotional problems, and that a physician brings the least stigma to the user; whereas the psychiatrist and the mental hospital, though both competent resources, tend to stigmatize the user much more.[36]

The reader will recall that one of the case abstracts presented to the respondents was that of a "normal" individual. Since respondents with a help-seeking relative may reject the non-help-seeking cases because they are recognized as needing help, including the description of the normal person may "distort" the findings. The rejection rates for the four mentally ill abstracts have, therefore, been separated from those for the normal person and presented in Table 3. Inspection of this table reveals the same pattern found in Table 2, except that the rejection rate for persons utilizing each help-source is somewhat higher than in Table 2.[37]

Turning now to the relation between adherence to the norm of self-reliance and rejection of persons described as using the various help-sources, the data in Table 4 indicate that the asso-

---

[36] We might expect those with help-seeking friends to reject in the same pattern as those with help-seeking relatives. Although both groups of respondents have had experience with someone who sought help, those whose experience was with friends probably were not so involved in the other's welfare and therefore had less intimate a knowledge of the help-sources people consult for emotional problems.

[37] This is not surprising in light of the generally low rejection of the "normal" person.

TABLE 4   REJECTION SCORES[a] FOR ALL CASES BY HELP-SOURCE AND ADHERENCE TO THE NORM OF SELF-RELIANCE

Help-Source Utilized	Adherence to Norm of Self-Reliance		
	DISAGREE (N = 28)	AGREE SOMEWHAT (N = 128)	AGREE STRONGLY (N = 144)
No help-source	1.79	1.39	1.22
Clergyman	1.68	1.56	1.52
Physician	1.67	1.87	2.00
Psychiatrist	2.43	2.52	2.65
Mental Hospital	2.64	3.09	3.23

[a] Rejection scores are represented by the mean number of items rejected on the Social Distance Scale.

ciation between help-source and rejection is maintained even among those who do not strongly adhere to the norm of self-reliance.[38] Among respondents agreeing either strongly or somewhat to the norm of self-reliance there is a consistent increase in rejection of persons as they moved from no help to the mental hospital. Respondents *not* adhering to the norm of self-reliance, however, reject persons not seeking help more than they do persons seeing a clergyman or a physician.[39]

This pattern is similar to the one followed by respondents who had help-seeking relatives (see Table 2),[40] and the same general interpretation may be appropriate. Respondents who do not agree that people should handle their own problems may view people seeing a clergyman as "handling their own problems." If this is true, then those not adhering to the norm of self-reliance would be expected to reject persons who see a clergyman, as well as those who seek no help.

[38] Only 9 per cent disagreed (either somewhat or strongly) with the statement about people handling their own problems. This finding lends support to the proposition that people in our society are expected to handle their own problems.

[39] Again we ignore differences *among* the various groups of respondents. Our primary interest is in determining whether the relation between help-source and rejection is maintained *within* each group.

[40] It should be recalled that the latter respondents also rejected persons not seeking help more than persons seeing a psychiatrist; the findings with respect to experience with a help-seeking relative and non-adherence to the norm of self-reliance are not entirely similar.

Thus, for the great majority of respondents, who either (1) have not had experience with a relative who sought help for emotional problems, or (2) adhere to the norm of self-reliance, help-source and rejection are strongly associated.[41]

On the other hand, respondents who have had experience with a help-seeking relative deviate quite sharply from the rejection pattern of the majority, as do those who do not adhere to the norm of self-reliance. Nevertheless, this deviant pattern appears to make sense theoretically. Those acquainted with a help-seeking relative, having had more exposure to sick-role prescriptions, may be highly rejecting of persons not seeking help because they feel that people should seek "technically competent help." Respondents not adhering to the norm of self-reliance may reject non-help-seekers for a similar reason. They too may feel that handling one's own problems is inappropriate, and that people should seek competent help. And, as suggested previously, both groups may equate help from a clergyman with no help at all.[42]

Conclusions and Implications

On the basis of these findings from a southern New England town, the source of help sought by mentally disturbed individuals appears to be strongly related to the degree to which others in the community reject them. Individuals are increasingly rejected as they are described as utilizing no help, as utilizing a clergyman, a physician, a psychiatrist, or a mental hospital.

Controls for age, religion, education, social class, and authoritarianism failed to diminish the relationship, but controls for experience with an emotionally disturbed help-seeker and for adherence to the norm of self-reliance tended to specify it. Respondents who had had experience with a help-seeking relative deviated markedly from the pattern followed by the rest of the sample, as did respondents not adhering to the norm of self-

---

[41] It would have been desirable to control for experience and attitude toward self-reliance simultaneously, but there were too few (13) respondents who reported experience with a help-seeking relative *and* did not adhere to the norm of self-reliance.

[42] The small number of respondents with a help-seeking relative (37), and the small number not adhering to the norm of self-reliance (28), make these findings, as well as their interpretation, highly tentative.

reliance. Both of these groups rejected people seeking no help more than they did those consulting a clergyman or a physician, and respondents with help-seeking relatives also reject non-help-seekers more than those consulting a psychiatrist. Both groups rejected persons seeing a clergyman more than those seeing a physician.

The evidence presented here suggests that a mentally ill person who seeks help may be rejected by others in the community. The findings also have implications for what Mechanic and Volkart call "the inclination to adopt the sick role."[43] We can easily imagine an individual who, because he fears the stigma attached to the help-seeker, does not utilize a professional resource for his problems. Avoiding the possibility of rejection, he also denies himself technically competent help.[44]

Thus the utilization of certain help-sources involves not only a *reward* (positive mental health), but also a *cost* (rejection by others and, consequently, a negative self-image);[45] we need to assess the net balance of gains and losses resulting from seeking help for problems of disturbed behavior.

The present analysis has been concerned with the rejection of help-seekers in hypothetical situations. Future research should be designed so that it would be possible to examine the rejection of help-seekers in "real" situations. Hopefully, the present research will provide some understanding and raise significant questions about the consequences of seeking help for problems of disturbed behavior in our society.

[43] David Mechanic and Edmund A. Volkart, "Stress, Illness, and the Sick Role," *American Sociological Review*, 26 (February, 1961), pp. 51–58.

[44] Jaco, *op. cit.*, points out that "If mental disease carries a stigma in a particular community, it is likely that many families will use extreme measures to conceal the fact that a member is mentally ill; even to the extent of preventing him from obtaining psychiatric treatment in that area." (p. 18)

[45] For an interesting presentation of cost and reward, see George C. Homans, *Social Behavior: Its Elementary Forms*, New York: Harcourt, Brace & World, 1961, ch. 5.

PART TWO
Commitment Proceedings

The commitment proceeding is an important turn on the path to the mental hospital. In the last analysis it is the court that determines whether an individual should be committed to a mental institution, but, as a rule, medical and civil authorities combine forces in making this decision. The procedure is designed to maximize fairness and rationality, but the papers included in this section make it clear that there may be a large gap between intent and practice.

Scheff's examination of the commitment proceeding shows that, typically, these hearings are extremely brief and cursory. This could be dismissed as a simple matter of neglect except that, according to Scheff, the decision to commit a person is based on the *presumption* of illness. That is, psychiatrists appear to presume that people brought by their families or others to such a hearing *must* be mentally ill or they would not be there in the first place.

Scheff's analysis of the motivation for such biased and cursory examinations is equally interesting. According to Scheff, psychiatrists involved in the commitment process subscribe to a number of beliefs that might be characterized as "psychiatric ideology." They are persuaded that persons who are mentally ill will deteriorate without treatment, that the treatment is generally effective, that there are no risks to the patient in involuntary hospitalization, and that extensive questioning can be damaging to the mental condition of the patient. Finally, they argue that since mentally ill persons may be dangerous to themselves or others, it is better to risk hospitalization than to risk the harm a patient might bring to himself or to other people.

Scheff also notes that the community attitudes concerning mental illness are converted into community pressure on the judge, because he is often an elected official. The judge, in turn, transmits this pressure to court psychiatrists since he appoints them. Scheff argues that it is not likely that the judge will reappoint a psychiatrist who releases a patient who might have the slightest chance of harming himself or other people. The judge simply will not risk the community repercussions.

The paper by Miller and Schwartz provides an answer to the question of who is committed and why. Although these authors make it clear that the commitment proceeding does not yield a simple pattern of results, they do confirm Scheff's finding that commitment proceedings often proceed on the presumption of the insanity of the defendant.

The authors also find that the likelihood of commitment depends heavily upon the interpersonal skills of that defendant. If he is able to present himself as being in control and interpersonally effective, he is likely to be released. At least two patterns emerge that result in commitment. If the person offers no objection to the proceeding and is generally passive, he is likely to be committed. On the other hand, if he objects violently, this may be taken as evidence of his unstable mental state and he will be committed.

But, as Miller and Schwartz point out, we should not conclude that relatives, who are often the complainants in such hearings, are necessarily eager to "railroad" the patient into the hospital. Relatives who testify against the defendant are often under considerable strain and are very much concerned about the breach of family loyalty that such a legal action may represent. To the relatives of the patient, the decision for hospitalization often appears to be the only solution to an intractable problem.

The paper by Wenger and Fletcher focuses on procedural variables and their effect on the probability of commitment. They find that when legal counsel for the defendant is present, hearings take nearly twice as long as when the defendant has no legal counsel. In addition, and much more important, when the patient does have a lawyer defending his interests, he is much less likely to be committed. One might expect that this finding is due to the fact that people who are actually less disturbed are the same people who are able to retain a lawyer, and, therefore, are less likely to be committed. But the authors find that the effect of legal counsel on commitment decisions persists regardless of the patient's condition.

These three papers suggest that a great many factors besides the psychiatric state of the patient may determine whether he is committer or not. Commitment appears also to be contingent on the presumption of illness, psychiatric ideology, community pressure, and whether or not the individual is represented by legal counsel.

The Societal Reaction to Deviance: Ascriptive Elements in the Psychiatric Screening of Mental Patients in a Midwestern State

Thomas J. Scheff (with the assistance of Daniel M. Culver)

The case for making the societal reaction to deviance a major independent variable in studies of deviant behavior has been succinctly stated by Kitsuse:

> A sociological theory of deviance must focus specifically upon the interactions which not only define behaviors as deviant but also organize and activate the application of sanctions by individuals, groups, or agencies. For in modern society, the socially significant differentiation of deviants from the non-deviant population is increasingly contingent upon circumstances of situation, place, social and personal biography, and the bureaucratically organized activities of agencies of control.[1]

In the case of mental disorder, psychiatric diagnosis is one of the crucial steps which "organizes and activates" the societal reaction, since the state is legally empowered to segregate and isolate those persons whom psychiatrists find to be committable because of mental illness.

Recently, however, it has been argued that mental illness may be more usefully considered to be a social status than a disease, since the symptoms of mental illness are vaguely defined and widely distributed, and the definition of behavior as symptomatic of mental illness is usually dependent upon social rather than medical contingencies.[2] Furthermore, the argument continues,

Reprinted from *Social Problems*, Vol. 11, No. 4, Spring, 1964, pp. 401–413, by permission from the Society for the Study of Social Problems and the author. This report is part of a larger study, made possible by a grant from The Advisory Mental Health Committee of Midwestern State. By prior agreement, the state in which the study was conducted is not identified in publications.

[1] John I. Kitsuse, "Societal Reaction to Deviant Behavior: Problems of Theory and Method," *Social Problems*, 9 (Winter, 1962), pp. 247–257.
[2] Edwin M. Lemert, *Social Pathology*, New York: McGraw-Hill, 1951; Erving Goffman, *Asylums*, Chicago: Aldine, 1962.

the status of the mental patient is more often an ascribed status, with conditions for status entry external to the patient, than an achieved status with conditions for status entry dependent upon the patient's own behavior. According to this argument, the societal reaction is a fundamentally important variable in all stages of a deviant career.

The actual usefulness of a theory of mental disorder based on the societal reaction is largely an empirical question: to what extent is entry to the status of mental patient independent of the behavior or "condition" of the patient? The present paper will explore this question for one phase of the societal reaction: the legal screening of persons alleged to be mentally ill. This screening represents the official phase of the societal reaction, which occurs after the alleged deviance has been called to the attention of the community by a complainant. This report will make no reference to the initial deviance or other situation which resulted in the complaint, but will deal entirely with procedures used by the courts after the complaint has occurred.

The purpose of the description that follows is to determine the extent of uncertainty that exists concerning new patients' qualifications for involuntary confinement in a mental hospital, and the reactions of the courts to this type of uncertainty. The data presented here indicate that, in the face of uncertainty, there is a strong presumption of illness by the court and the court psychiatrists.[3] In the discussion that follows the presentation of findings, some of the causes, consequences and implications of the presumption of illness are suggested.

The data upon which this report is based were drawn from psychiatrists' ratings of a sample of patients newly admitted to the public mental hospitals in a Midwestern state, official court records, interviews with court officials and psychiatrists, and our observations of psychiatric examinations in four courts. The psychiatrists' ratings of new patients will be considered first.

In order to obtain a rough measure of the incoming patient's qualifications for involuntary confinement, a survey of newly admitted patients was conducted with the cooperation of the

---

[3] For a more general discussion of the presumption of illness in medicine, and some of its possible causes and consequences, see the author's "Decision Rules, Types of Error and Their Consequences in Medical Diagnosis," *Behavioral Science*, 8 (April, 1963), pp. 97–107.

hospital psychiatrists. All psychiatrists who made admission examinations in the three large mental hospitals in the state filled out a questionnaire for the first ten consecutive patients they examined in the month of June, 1962. A total of 223 questionnaires were returned by the 25 admission psychiatrists. Although these returns do not constitute a probability sample of all new patients admitted during the year, there were no obvious biases in the drawing of the sample. For this reason, this group of patients will be taken to be typical of the newly admitted patients in Midwestern State.

The two principal legal grounds for involuntary confinement in the United States are the police power of the state (the state's right to protect itself from dangerous persons) and *parens patriae* (the State's right to assist those persons who, because of their own incapacity, may not be able to assist themselves.)[4] As a measure of the first ground, the potential dangerousness of the patient, the questionnaire contained this item: "In your opinion, if this patient were released at the present time, is it likely he would harm himself or others?" The psychiatrists were given six options, ranging from Very Likely to Very Unlikely. Their responses were: Very Likely, 5%; Likely, 4%; Somewhat Likely, 14%; Somewhat Unlikely, 20%; Unlikely, 37%; Very Unlikely, 18%. (Three patients were not rated [1%].)

As a measure of the second ground, *parens patriae*, the questionnaire contained the item: "Based on your observations of the patient's behavior, his present degree of mental impairment is: None . . . . . Minimal . . . . . Mild . . . . . Moderate . . . . . Severe . . . . . " The psychiatrists' responses were: None, 2%; Minimal, 12%; Mild, 25%; Moderate, 42%; Severe, 17%. (Three patients were not rated [1%].)

To be clearly qualified for involuntary confinement, a patient should be rated as likely to harm self or others (Very Likely, Likely, or Somewhat Likely) and/or as Severely Mentally Impaired. However, voluntary patients should be excluded from this analysis, since the court is not required to assess their qualifications for confinement. Excluding the 59 voluntary admissions (26% of the sample), leaves a sample of 164 involuntary confined

---

[4] Hugh Allen Ross, "Commitment of the Mentally Ill: Problems of Law and Policy," *Michigan Law Review*, 57 (May, 1959), pp. 945–1018.

patients. Of these patients, 10 were rated as meeting both qualifications for involuntary confinement, 21 were rated as being severely mentally impaired, but not dangerous, 28 were rated as
dangerous but not severely mentally impaired, and 102 were rated
as not dangerous nor as severely mentally impaired. (Three patients were not rated.)

According to these ratings, there is considerable uncertainty
connected with the screening of newly admitted involuntary patients in the state, since a substantial majority (63%) of the
patients did not clearly meet the statutory requirements for involuntary confinement. How does the agency responsible for
assessing the qualifications for confinement, the court, react in the
large numbers of cases involving uncertainty?

On the one hand, the legal rulings on this point by higher courts
are quite clear. They have repeatedly held that there should be
a presumption of sanity. The burden of proof of insanity is to be
on the petitioners, there must be a preponderance of evidence,
and the evidence should be of a "clear and unexceptionable"
nature.[5]

On the other hand, existing studies suggest that there is a presumption of illness by mental health officials. In a discussion of
the "discrediting" of patients by the hospital staff, based on observations at St. Elizabeth's Hospital, Washington, D.C., Goffman
states:

> [The patient's case record] is apparently not regularly used to
> record occasions when the patient showed capacity to cope hon-
> orably and effectively with difficult life situations. Nor is the case
> record typically used to provide a rough average or sampling of
> his past conduct. [Rather, it extracts] from his whole life course
> a list of those accidents that have or might have had "sympto-
> matic" significance. . . . I think that most of the information
> gathered in case records is quite true, although it might seem
> also to be true that almost anyone's life course could yield up
> enough denigrating facts to provide grounds for the record's
> justification of commitment.[6]

---

[5] This is the typical phrasing in cases in the *Dicennial Legal Digest*, found
under the heading "Mental Illness."

[6] Goffman, *op. cit.*, pp. 155, 159.

Mechanic makes a similar statement in his discussion of two large mental hospitals located in an urban area in California:

> In the crowded state or county hospitals, which is the most typical situation, the psychiatrist does not have sufficient time to make a very complete psychiatric diagnosis, nor do his psychiatric tools provide him with the equipment for an expeditious screening of the patient . . .
>
> In the two mental hospitals studied over a period of three months, the investigator never observed a case where the psychiatrist advised the patient that he did not need treatment. Rather, all persons who appeared at the hospital were absorbed into the patient population regardless of their ability to function adequately outside the hospital.[7]

A comment by Brown suggests that it is a fairly general understanding among mental health workers that state mental hospitals in the U.S. accept all comers.[8]

Kutner, describing commitment procedures in Chicago in 1962, also reports a strong presumption of illness by the staff of the Cook County Mental Health Clinic:

> Certificates are signed as a matter of course by staff physicians after little or no examination . . . The so-called examinations are made on an assembly-line basis, often being completed in two or three minutes, and never taking more than ten minutes. Although psychiatrists agree that it is practically impossible to determine a person's sanity on the basis of such a short and hurried interview, the doctors recommend confinement in 77% of the cases. It appears in practice that the alleged-mentally-ill is presumed to be insane and bears the burden of proving his sanity in the few minutes allotted to him . . .[9]

These citations suggest that mental health officials handle uncertainty by presuming illness. To ascertain if the presumption

---

[7] David Mechanic, "Some Factors in Identifying and Defining Mental Illness," *Mental Hygiene*, 46 (January, 1962), pp. 66–75.

[8] Esther Lucile Brown, *Newer Dimensions of Patient Care*, Part I, New York: Russell Sage, 1961, p. 60, fn.

[9] Luis Kutner, "The Illusion of Due Process in Commitment Proceedings," *Northwestern University Law Review*, 57 (Sept. 1962), pp. 383–399.

of illness occurred in Midwestern State, intensive observations of screening procedures were conducted in the four courts with the largest volume of mental cases in the state. These courts were located in the two most populous cities in the state. Before giving the results of these observations, it is necessary to describe the steps in the legal procedures for hospitalization and commitment.

Steps in the Screening of Persons Alleged To Be Mentally Ill

The process of screening can be visualized as containing five steps in Midwestern State:

1. The application for judicial inquiry, made by three citizens. This application is heard by deputy clerks in two of the courts (C and D), by a court reporter in the third court, and by a court commissioner in the fourth court.

2. The intake examination, conducted by a hospital psychiatrist.

3. The psychiatric examination, conducted by two psychiatrists appointed by the court.

4. The interview of the patient by the guardian *ad litem*, a lawyer appointed in three of the courts to represent the patient. (Court A did not use guardians *ad litem*.)

5. The judicial hearing, conducted by a judge.

These five steps take place roughly in the order listed, although in many cases (those cases designated as emergencies) step No. 2, the intake examination, may occur before step No. 1. Steps No. 1 and No. 2 usually take place on the same day or the day after hospitalization. Steps No. 3, No. 4, and No. 5 usually take place within a week of hospitalization. (In courts C and D, however, the judicial hearing is held only once a month.)

This series of steps would seem to provide ample opportunity for the presumption of health, and a thorough assessment, therefore, of the patient's qualifications for involuntary confinement, since there are five separate points at which discharge could occur. According to our findings, however, these procedures usually do not serve the function of screening out persons who do not meet statutory requirements. At most of these decision points, in most of the courts, retention of the patient in the hospital was virtually automatic. A notable exception to this pattern was found in one of the three state hospitals; this hospital attempted to use step No. 2, the intake examination, as a screening point to discharge patients that the superintendent described as "illegitimate," i.e., patients who do not qualify for involuntary confinement.[10] In the other two hospitals, however, this examination was perfunctory and virtually never resulted in a finding of health and a recommendation of discharge. In a similar manner, the other steps were largely ceremonial in character. For example, in court B, we observed twenty-two judicial hearings, all of which were conducted perfunctorily and with lightning rapidity. (The mean time of these hearings was 1.6 minutes.) The judge asked each patient two or three routine questions. Whatever the patient answered, however, the judge always ended the hearings and retained the patient in the hospital.

What appeared to be the key role in justifying these procedures was played by step No. 3, the examination by the court-appointed psychiatrists. In our informal discussions of screening with the judges and other court officials, these officials made it clear that although the statutes give the court the responsibility for the decision to confine or release persons alleged to be mentally ill, they would rarely if ever take the responsibility for releasing a mental patient without a medical recommendation to that effect. The question which is crucial, therefore, for the entire screening process is whether or not the court-appointed psychiatric examiners presume illness. The remainder of the paper will consider this question.

Our observations of 116 judicial hearings raised the question of the adequacy of the psychiatric examination. Eighty-six of the hearings failed to establish that the patients were "mentally ill" (according to the criteria stated by the judges in interviews).[11]

---

[10] Other exceptions occurred as follows: the deputy clerks in courts C and D appeared to exercise some discretion in turning away applications they considered improper or incomplete, at step No. 1; the judge in Court D appeared also to perform some screening at step No. 5. For further description of these exceptions see "Rural-Urban Differences in the Judicial Screening of the Mentally Ill in a Midwestern State." (In press)

[11] In interviews with the judges, the following criteria were named: Appropriateness of behavior and speech, understanding of the situation, and orientation.

Indeed, the behavior and responses of 48 of the patients at the hearings seemed completely unexceptionable. Yet the psychiatric examiners had not recommended the release of a single one of these patients. Examining the court records of 80 additional cases, there was still not a single recommendation for release.

Although the recommendation for treatment of 196 out of 196 consecutive cases strongly suggests that the psychiatric examiners were presuming illness, particularly when we observed 48 of these patients to be responding appropriately, it is conceivable that this is not the case. The observer for this study was not a psychiatrist (he was a first year graduate student in social work) and it is possible that he could have missed evidence of disorder which a psychiatrist might have seen. It was therefore arranged for the observer to be present at a series of psychiatric examinations, in order to determine whether the examinations appeared to be merely formalities or whether, on the other hand, through careful examination and interrogation, the psychiatrists were able to establish illness even in patients whose appearance and responses were not obviously disordered. The observer was instructed to note the examiner's procedures, the criteria they appeared to use in arriving at their decision, and their reaction to uncertainty.

Each of the courts discussed here employs the services of a panel of physicians as medical examiners. The physicians are paid a flat fee of ten dollars per examination, and are usually assigned from three to five patients for each trip to the hospital. In court A, most of the examinations are performed by two psychiatrists, who went to the hospital once a week, seeing from five to ten patients a trip. In court B, C and D, a panel of local physicians was used. These courts seek to arrange the examinations so that one of the examiners is a psychiatrist, the other a general practitioner. Court B has a list of four such pairs, and appoints each pair for a month at a time. Courts C and D have a similar list, apparently with some of the same names as court B.

To obtain physicians who were representative of the panel used in these courts, we arranged to observe the examinations of the two psychiatrists employed by court A, and one of the four pairs of physicians used in court B, one a psychiatrist, the other a general practitioner. We observed 13 examinations in court A and 13 examinations in court B. The judges in courts C and D refused to give us the names of the physicians on their panels, and we were unable to observe examinations in these courts. (The judge in court D stated that he did not want these physicians harassed in their work, since it was difficult to obtain their services even under the best of circumstances.) In addition to observing the examinations by four psychiatrists, three other psychiatrists used by these courts were interviewed.

The medical examiners followed two lines of questioning. One line was to inquire about the circumstances which led to the patient's hospitalization, the other was to ask standard questions to test the patient's orientation and his capacity for abstract thinking by asking him the date, the President, Governor, proverbs, and problems requiring arithmetic calculation. These questions were often asked very rapidly, and the patient was usually allowed only a very brief time to answer.

It should be noted that the psychiatrists in these courts had access to the patient's record (which usually contained the Application for Judicial Inquiry and the hospital chart notes on the patient's behavior), and that several of the psychiatrists stated that they almost always familiarized themselves with this record before making the examination. To the extent that they were familiar with the patient's circumstances from such outside information, it is possible that the psychiatrists were basing their diagnoses of illness less on the rapid and peremptory examination than on this other information. Although this was true to some extent, the importance of the record can easily be exaggerated, both because of the deficiencies in the typical record, and because the way it is usually utilized by the examiners.

The deficiencies of the typical record were easily discerned in the approximately one hundred applications and hospital charts which the author read. Both the applications and charts were extremely brief and sometimes garbled. Moreover, in some of the cases where the author and interviewer were familiar with the circumstances involved in the hospitalization, it was not clear that the complainant's testimony was any more accurate than the version presented by the patient. Ofter the original complaint was so paraphrased and condensed that the application seemed to have little meaning.

The attitude of the examiners toward the record was such that even in those cases where the record was ample, it often did not figure prominently in their decision. Disparaging remarks about the quality and usefulness of the record were made by several of the psychiatrists. One of the examiners was apologetic about his use of the record, giving us the impression that he thought that a good psychiatrist would not need to resort to any information outside his own personal examination of the patient. A casual attitude toward the record was openly displayed in 6 of the 26 examinations we observed. In these 6 examinations, the psychiatrist could not (or in 3 cases, did not bother to) locate the record and conducted the examination without it, with one psychiatrist making it a point of pride that he could easily diagnose most cases "blind."

In his observations of the examinations, the interviewer was instructed to rate how well the patient responded by noting his behavior during the interview, whether he answered the orientation and concept questions correctly, and whether he denied and explained the allegations which resulted in his hospitalization. If the patient's behavior during the interview obviously departed from conventional social standards (e.g., in one case the patient refused to speak), if he answered the orientation questions incorrectly, or if he did not deny and explain the petitioners' allegations, the case was rated as meeting the statutory requirements for hospitalization. Of the 26 examinations observed, eight were rated as Criteria Met.

If, on the other hand, the patient's behavior was appropriate, his answers correct, and he denied and explained the petitioners' allegations, the interviewer rated the case as not meeting the statutory criteria. Of the 26 cases, seven were rated as Criteria Not Met. Finally, if the examination was inconclusive, but the interviewer felt that more extensive investigation might have established that the criteria were met, he rated the cases as Criteria Possibly Met. Of the 26 examined, 11 were rated in this way. The interviewer's instructions were that whenever he was in doubt he should avoid using the rating Criteria Not Met.

Even giving the examiners the benefit of the doubt, the interviewer's ratings were that in a substantial majority of the cases he observed, the examination failed to establish that the statutory criteria were met. The relationship between the examiners' recommendations and the interviewer's ratings are shown in the following table.

TABLE 1   OBSERVER'S RATINGS AND EXAMINERS' RECOMMENDATIONS

Observer's Ratings		Criteria Met	Criteria Possibly Met	Criteria Not Met	Total
Examiners'	Commitment	7	9	2	18
Recommendations	30-day Observation	1	2	3	6
	Release	0	0	2	2
	Total	8	11	7	26

The interviewer's ratings suggest that the examinations established that the statutory criteria were met in only eight cases, but the examiners recommended that the patient be retained in the hospital in 24 cases, leaving 16 cases which the interviewer rated as uncertain, and in which retention was recommended by the examiners. The observer also rated the patient's expressed desires regarding staying in the hospital, and the time taken by the examination. The ratings of the patient's desire concerning staying or leaving the hospital were: Leave, 14 cases; Indifferent, 1 case; Stay, 9 cases; and Not Ascertained, 2 cases. In only one of the 14 cases in which the patient wished to leave was the interviewer's rating Criteria Met.

The interviewers ranged in length from five minutes to 17 minutes, with the mean time being 10.2 minutes. Most of the interviews were hurried, with the questions of the examiners coming so rapidly that the examiner often interrupted the patient, or one examiner interrupted the other. All of the examiners seemed quite hurried. One psychiatrist, after stating in an interview (before we observed his examinations) that he usually took about thirty minutes, stated:

> It's not remunerative. I'm taking a hell of a cut. I can't spend 45 minutes with a patient. I don't have the time, it doesn't pay.

In the examinations that we observed, this physician actually spent 8, 10, 5, 8, 8, 7, 17, and 11 minutes with the patients, or an average of 9.2 minutes.

In these short time periods, it is virtually impossible for the examiner to extend his investigation beyond the standard orientation questions, and a short discussion of the circumstances which brought the patient to the hospital. In those cases where the patient answered the orientation questions correctly, behaved appropriately, and explained his presence at the hospital satisfactorily, the examiners did not attempt to assess the reliability of the petitioner's complaints, or to probe further into the patient's answers. Given the fact that in most of these instances the examiners were faced with borderline cases, that they took little time in the examinations, and that they usually recommended commitment, we can only conclude that their decisions were based largely on a presumption of illness. Supplementary observations reported by the interviewer support this conclusion.

After each examination, the observer asked the examiner to explain the criteria he used in arriving at his decision. The observer also had access to the examiner's official report, so that he could compare what the examiner said about the case with the record of what actually occurred during the interview. This supplementary information supports the conclusion that the examiner's decisions are based on the presumption of illness, and sheds light on the manner in which these decisions are reached:

1. The "evidence" upon which the examiners based their decision to retain often seemed arbitrary.

2. In some cases, the decision to retain was made even when no evidence could be found.

3. Some of the psychiatrists' remarks suggest prejudgment of the cases.

4. Many of the examinations were characterized by carelessness and haste. The first question, concerning the arbitrariness of the psychiatric evidence, will now be considered.

In the weighing of the patient's responses during the interview, the physician appeared not to give the patient credit for the large number of correct answers he gave. In the typical interview, the examiner might ask the patient fifteen or twenty questions: the date, time, place, who is President, Governor, etc., what is 11x10, 11x11, etc., explain "Don't put all your eggs in one basket," "A rolling stone gathers no moss," etc. The examiners appeared to feel that a wrong answer established lack of orientation, even when it was preceded by a series of correct answers. In other words, the examiners do not establish any standard score on the orientation questions, which would give an objective picture of the degree to which the patient answered the questions correctly, but seem at times to search until they find an incorrect answer.

For those questions which were answered incorrectly, it was not always clear whether the incorrect answers were due to the patient's "mental illness," or to the time pressure in the interview, the patient's lack of education, or other causes. Some of the questions used to establish orientation were sufficiently difficult that persons not mentally ill might have difficulty with them. Thus one of the examiners always asked, in a rapid-fire manner: "What year is it? What year was it seven years ago? Seventeen years before that?" etc. Only two of the five patients who were asked this series of questions were able to answer it correctly. However, it is a moot question whether a higher percentage of persons in a household survey would be able to do any better. To my knowledge, none of the orientation questions that are used have been checked in a normal population.

Finally, the interpretations of some of the evidence as showing mental illness seemed capricious. Thus one of the patients, when asked, "In what way are a banana, an orange, and an apple alike?" answered, "They are all something to eat." This answer was used by the examiner in explaining his recommendation to commit. The observer had noted that the patient's behavior and responses seemed appropriate and asked why the recommendation to commit had been made. The doctor stated that her behavior had been bizarre (possibly referring to her alleged promiscuity), her affect inappropriate ("When she talked about being pregnant, it was without feeling,") and with regard to the question above:

> She wasn't able to say a banana and an orange were fruit. She couldn't take it one step further, she had to say it was something to eat.

In other words, this psychiatrist was suggesting that the patient manifested concreteness in her thinking, which is held to be a symptom of mental illness. Yet in her other answers to classification questions, and to proverb interpretations, concreteness was not apparent, suggesting that the examiner's application of this test was arbitrary. In another case, the physician stated that he thought the patient was suspicious and distrustful, because he had asked about the possibility of being represented by counsel at the judicial hearing. The observer felt that these and other similar interpretations might possibly be correct, but that further investigation of the supposedly incorrect responses would be needed to establish that they were manifestations of disorientation.

In several cases where even this type of evidence was not available, the examiners still recommend retention in the hospital. Thus, one examiner, employed by court A stated that he had recommended 30-day observation for a patient whom he had thought *not* to be mentally ill, on the grounds that the patient, a young man, could not get along with his parents, and "might get into trouble." This examiner went on to say:

> We always take the conservative side. [Commitment or observation] Suppose a patient should commit suicide. We always make the conservative decision. I had rather play it safe. There's no harm in doing it that way.

It appeared to the observer that "playing safe" meant that even in those cases where the examination established nothing, the psychiatrists did not consider recommending release. Thus in one case the examination had established that the patient had a very good memory, was oriented and spoke quietly and seriously. The observer recorded his discussion with the physician after the examination as follows:

> When the doctor told me he was recommending commitment for this patient too (he had also recommended commitment in the two examinations held earlier that day) he laughed because he could see what my next question was going to be. He said, "I already recommended the release of two patients this month." This sounded like it was the maximum amount the way he said it.

Apparently this examiner felt that he had a very limited quota on the number of patients he could recommend for release (less than two percent of those examined).

The language used by these physicians tends to intimate that mental illness was found, even when reporting the opposite. Thus in one case the recommendation stated: "No gross evidence of delusions or hallucinations." This statement is misleading, since not only was there no gross evidence, there was not any evidence, not even the slightest suggestion of delusions or hallucinations, brought out by the interview.

These remarks suggest that the examiners prejudge the cases they examine. Several further comments indicate prejudgment. One physician stated that he thought that most crimes of violence were committed by patients released too early from mental hospitals. (This is an erroneous belief.)[12] He went on to say that he thought that all mental patients should be kept in the hospital at least three months, indicating prejudgment concerning his examinations. Another physician, after a very short interview (8 minutes), told the observer:

> On the schizophrenics, I don't bother asking them more questions when I can see they're schizophrenic because *I know what they are going to say.* You could talk to them another half hour and not learn any more.

Another physician, finally, contrasted cases in which the patient's family or others initiated hospitalization ("petition cases," the great majority of cases) with those cases initiated by the court:

> The petition cases are pretty *automatic.* If the patient's own family wants to get rid of him you know there is something wrong.

The lack of care which characterized the examinations is evident in the forms on which the examiners make their recommendations. On most of these forms, whole sections have been left unanswered. Others are answered in a peremptory and uninformative way. For example, in the section entitled Physical Examination, the question is asked: "Have you made a physical examination of the patient? State fully what is the present physical condition.", a typical answer is "Yes. Fair.", or, "Is apparently in good health." Since in none of the examinations we observed was the patient actually physically examined, these answers ap-

---

[12] The rate of crimes of violence, or any crime, appears to be less among ex-mental patients than in the general population. Henry Brill and Benjamin Maltzberg, "Statistical Report Based on the Arrest Record of 5354 Ex-patients Released from New York State Mental Hospitals During the Period 1946–48." Mimeo available from the authors; Louis H. Cohen and Henry Freeman, "How Dangerous to the Community Are State Hospital Patients?", *Connecticut State Medical Journal*, 9 (Sept., 1945), pp. 697–700; Donald W. Hastings, "Follow-up Results in Psychiatric Illness," *Amer. Journal of Psychiatry*, 118 (June 1962), pp. 1078–1086.

pear to be mere guesses. One of the examiners used regularly in court B, to the question "On what subject or in what way is derangement now manifested?" always wrote in "Is mentally ill." The omissions, and the almost flippant brevity of these forms, together with the arbitrariness, lack of evidence, and prejudicial character of the examinations, discussed above, all support the observer's conclusion that, except in very unusual cases, the psychiatric examiner's recommendation to retain the patient is virtually automatic.

Lest it be thought that these results are unique to a particularly backward Midwestern State, it should be pointed out that this state is noted for its progressive psychiatric practices. It will be recalled that a number of the psychiatrists employed by the court as examiners had finished their psychiatric residencies, which is not always the case in many other states. A still common practice in other states is to employ, as members of the "Lunacy Panel," partially retired physicians with no psychiatric training whatever. This was the case in Stockton, California, in 1959, where the author observed hundreds of hearings at which these physicians were present. It may be indicative of some of the larger issues underlying the question of civil commitment that, in these hearings, the physicians played very little part; the judge controlled the questioning of the relatives and patients, and the hearings were often a model of impartial and thorough investigation.

Discussion

Ratings of the qualifications for involuntary confinement of patients newly admitted to the public mental hospitals in a Midwestern state, together with observations of judicial hearings and psychiatric examinations by the observer connected with the present study, both suggest that the decision as to the mental condition of a majority of the patients is an uncertain one. The fact that the courts seldom release patients, and the perfunctory manner in which the legal and medical procedures are carried out, suggest that the judicial decision to retain patients in the hospital for treatment is routine and largely based on the presumption of illness. Three reasons for this presumption will be discussed: financial, ideological, and political.

Our discussions with the examiners indicated that one reason that they perform biased "examinations" is that their rate of pay is determined by the length of time spent with the patient. In recommending retention, the examiners are refraining from interrupting the hospitalization and commitment procedures already in progress, and thereby allowing someone else, usually the hospital, to make the effective decision to release or commit. In order to recommend release, however, they would have to build a case showing why these procedures should be interrupted. Building such a case would take much more time than is presently expended by the examiners, thereby reducing their rate of pay.

A more fundamental reason for the presumption of illness by the examiners, and perhaps the reason why this practice is allowed by the courts, is the interpretation of current psychiatric doctrine by the examiners and court officials. These officials make a number of assumptions, which are now thought to be of doubtful validity:

1. The condition of mentally ill persons deteriorates rapidly without psychiatric assistance.
2. Effective psychiatric treatments exist for most mental illnesses.
3. Unlike surgery, there are no risks involved in involuntary psychiatric treatment: it either helps or is neutral, it can't hurt.
4. Exposing a prospective mental patient to questioning, cross-examination, and other screening procedures exposes him to the unnecessary stigma of trial-like procedures, and may do further damage to his mental condition.
5. There is an element of danger to self or others in most mental illness. It is better to risk unnecessary hospitalization than the harm the patient might do himself or others.

Many psychiatrists and others now argue that none of these assumptions are necessarily correct.

1. The assumption that psychiatric disorders usually get worse without treatment rests on very little other than evidence of an anecdotal character. There is just as much evidence that most acute psychological and emotional upsets are self-terminating.[13]

---

[13] For a review of epidemiological studies of mental disorder see Richard J. Plunkett and John E. Gordon, *Epidemiology and Mental Illness*, New

2. It is still not clear, according to systematic studies evaluating psychotherapy, drugs, etc., that most psychiatric interventions are any more effective, on the average, than no treatment at all.[14]

3. There is very good evidence that involuntary hospitalization and social isolation may affect the patient's life: his job, his family affairs, etc. There is some evidence that too hasty exposure to psychiatric treatment may convince the patient that he is "sick," prolonging what might have been an otherwise transitory episode.[15]

4. This assumption is correct, as far as it goes. But it is misleading because it fails to consider what occurs when the patient who does not wish to be hospitalized is forcibly treated. Such patients often become extremely indignant and angry, particularly in the case, as often happens, when they are deceived into coming to the hospital on some pretext.

5. The element of danger is usually exaggerated both in amount and degree. In the psychiatric survey of new patients in state mental hospitals, danger to self or others was mentioned in about a fourth of the cases. Furthermore, in those cases where danger is mentioned, it is not always clear that the risks involved are greater than those encountered in ordinary social life. This issue has been discussed by Ross, an attorney:

> A truck driver with a mild neurosis who is "accident prone" is probably a greater danger to society than most psychotics; yet, he will not be committed for treatment, even if he would be benefited. The community expects a certain amount of

---

York: Basic Books, 1960. Most of these studies suggest that at any given point in time, psychiatrists find a substantial proportion of persons in normal populations to be "mentally ill." One interpretation of this finding is that much of the deviance detected in these studies is self-limiting.

[14] For an assessment of the evidence regarding the effectiveness of electroshock, drugs, psychotherapy, and other psychiatric treatments, see H. J. Eysenck, *Handbook of Abnormal Psychology*, New York: Basic Books, 1961, Part III.

[15] For examples from military psychiatry, see Albert J. Glass, "Psychotherapy in the Combat Zone," in *Symposium on Stress*, Washington, D.C., Army Medical Service Graduate School, 1953, and B. L. Bushard, "The U.S. Army's Mental Hygiene Consultation Service," in *Symposium on Preventive and Social Psychiatry*, 15–17 (April 1957), Washington, D.C.: Walter Reed Army Institute of Research, pp. 431–443. For a discussion of essentially the same problem in the context of a civilian mental hospital, cf. Kai T. Erikson, "Patient Role and Social Uncertainty—A Dilemma of the Mentally Ill," *Psychiatry*, 20 (August 1957), pp. 263–275.

> dangerous activity. I suspect that as a class, drinking drivers
> are a greater danger than the mentally ill, and yet the drivers
> are tolerated or punished with small fines rather than inde-
> terminate imprisonment.[16]

From our observations of the medical examinations and other
commitment procedures, we formed a very strong impression that
the doctrines of danger to self or others, early treatment, and the
avoidance of stigma were invoked partly because the officials believed them to be true, and partly because they provided convenient justification for a pre-existing policy of summary action,
minimal investigation, avoidance of responsibility and, after the
patient is in the hospital, indecisiveness and delay.

The policy of presuming illness is probably both cause and
effect of political pressure on the court from the community. The
judge, an elected official, runs the risk of being more heavily
penalized for erroneously releasing than for erroneously retain-
ing patients. Since the judge personally appoints the panel of
psychiatrists to serve as examiners, he can easily transmit the
community pressure to them, by failing to reappoint a psychiatrist
whose examinations were inconveniently thorough.

Some of the implications of these findings for the sociology of
deviant behavior will be briefly summarized. The discussion
above, of the reasons that the psychiatrists tend to presume illness, suggests that the motivations of the key decision-makers in
the screening process may be significant in determining the extent
and direction of the societal reaction. In the case of psychiatric
screening of persons alleged to be mentally ill, the social differentiation of the deviant from the non-deviant population appears
to be materially affected by the financial, ideological, and political position of the psychiatrists, who are in this instance the key
agents of social control.

Under these circumstances, the character of the societal reaction appears to undergo a marked change from the pattern of
denial which occurs in the community. The official societal reaction appears to reverse the presumption of normality reported by
the Cummings as a characteristic of informal societal reaction, and

---

[16] Ross, *op. cit.*, p. 962.

instead exaggerates both the amount and degree of deviance.[17] Thus, one extremely important contingency influencing the severity of the societal reaction may be whether or not the original deviance comes to official notice. This paper suggests that in the area of mental disorder, perhaps in contrast to other areas of deviant behavior, if the official societal reaction is invoked, for whatever reason, social differentiation of the deviant from the non-deviant population will usually occur.

Conclusion

This paper has described the screening of patients who were admitted to public mental hospitals in early June, 1962, in a Midwestern state. The data presented here suggest that the screening is usually perfunctory, and that in the crucial screening examination by the court-appointed psychiatrists, there is a presumption of illness. Since most court decisions appear to hinge on the recommendation of these psychiatrists, there appears to be a large element of status ascription in the official societal reaction to persons alleged to be mentally ill, as exemplified by the court's actions. This finding points to the importance of lay definitions of mental illness in the community, since the "diagnosis" of mental illness by laymen in the community initiates the official societal reaction, and to the necessity of analyzing social processes connected with the recognition and reaction to the deviant behavior that is called mental illness in our society.

---

[17] Elaine Cumming and John Cumming, *Closed Ranks*, Cambridge, Mass.: Harvard University Press, 1957, 102; for further discussion of the bipolarization of the societal reaction into denial and labeling, see the author's "The Role of the Mentally Ill and the Dynamics of Mental Disorder: A Research Framework," *Sociometry*, 26 (December, 1963), pp. 436–453.

County Lunacy Commission Hearings: Some Observations of Commitments to a State Mental Hospital

Dorothy Miller and Michael Schwartz

Entrance into a mental hospital represents a major change in a person's social role and in his psychological self-image. This change is sometimes welcomed, but more often the patient is ambivalent or resistant. The decision to commit a person to the mental hospital is generally made by people other than the patient. The legal procedure of commitment is society's attempt to ensure maximum rationality and fairness in the decision.[1]

Who is committed and why? This paper attempts to examine the workings of one county lunacy commission in order to find what distinguishes those defendants who are committed from those who are not.[2] Legal procedures of commitment vary from state to state, but in most cases a medical commission and either a lawyer or a judge are required to decide upon the admission of a person to a state hospital, thus combining both medical and civil authority.

Before a person comes to a hearing before a lunacy commission, someone must file an affidavit containing "evidence" of mental illness. A court order is then issued, requiring the person named to enter a hospital or other facility for an observation period.

Reprinted from *Social Problems*, vol 14, no. 1, Summer, 1966, pp. 26–35, by permission from the Society for the Study of Social Problems and the authors.

[1] State hospitals are now admitting a growing number of patients on a "volunteer basis." Mental health education, via mass media and popular legend, has markedly affected the image of psychiatric treatment. However, many "volunteer patients" are only partially motivated by their own "insight into illness" and may actually be responding to social pressure brought to bear by their families. In some instances, state hospitals prefer the commitment, rather than the voluntary procedure, because they may need the power to hold the patient against his will. See Victor Goertzel, "Voluntary and Court Committed Patients," *California Mental Health Research Digest*, vol. 1, no. 4, 1963, pp. 25–27.

[2] The original study was done under the supervision of Erving Goffman, Professor of Sociology, University of California, Berkeley, California.

After this short period (suposedly seventy-two hours),[3] the complainants and the defendant appear at a committee hearing which decides whether the defendant shall be committed to a state mental hospital.

Since this report focuses upon face-to-face interaction at the hearing, only passing mention can be made to the process which preceded the appearance before the lunacy commission. The elements which enter into the family or community's decision to send a person into a mental hospital are little known, but it appears that such decisions are often made only after both a long period of mutually destructive interaction *and* the intervention of some outside person. This "outsider" offers a new definition for the situation, which may move the family to settle upon commitment as a resolution of the difficulty. The social censure that accompanies putting one's aged mother, or the father of one's children, into an "insane asylum" can be very severe. Further, the personal hatred and guilt which may erupt can make future cohesion within the family extremely difficult.

The typologies of hearings developed in this report do not refer to "personality types" but, rather, describe "interactional sets." Each hearing is seen as a social act, with each participant coming to the hearing with a purpose in mind. The transactions that occur during the hearing reflect the alignments of each participant to the situation as well as the previous actions taken. These "interactional sets" are typed, and each hearing is classified by one of four "types of alignment."

The Setting

We observed a total of fifty-eight individual hearings of a county lunacy commission. The commission members were two local doctors, one of whom was a psychiatrist, and a judge of the Superior Court. The judge, after hearing testimony from the complainants and the examining physicians, made one of three dispositions: (1) dismissed the defendant; (2) held the defendant

---

[3] The seventy-two-hour observation period is often continued for as long as a week or more, particularly in the smaller population centers where a commission meets only once a week. See Trudy Baum *et al.*, *The Marin County Mental Health Association Report*, 1963.

over for further observation until the next commission hearing; (3) committed the defendant to a state mental hospital.

The general pattern of procedure at these commission hearings was informal; most courtroom etiquette was discarded, although many of the structural formalities remained. Such relaxation of formality allowed the rigid rules governing the usual criteria for admissibility of evidence and assessment of the credibility of witnesses to be suspended temporarily. Presumably the informal legal procedure was intended to offer witnesses, both lay and professional, wide latitude in presenting their evidence and to show all possible humane concern to each patient and his family.

These hearings were held in a small auditorium. Seated around a long table were the judge, the two doctors, and a deputy sheriff in full uniform, complete with a gun.[4] At one end was the Clerk of the Court, who swore in all witnesses. A county court reporter was added after two observed hearings.

The judge introduced himself and the doctors in a very stylized manner to each patient as he came before the commission. He did not announce the purpose of the hearing to the pre-patient, nor did he inform him of his rights to counsel or a jury trial. In only one case, discussed at length later, was the defendant represented by counsel.

The hearing proceeded very rapidly, beginning with a brief report of the defendant's condition given by one or both of the examining medical doctors. The complainants were not always asked to speak. The pre-patient often was not spoken to. After the brief report the judge rendered his verdict and the pre-patient was ushered out the door through which he had entered. The witnesses were sent back up the aisle to the outside hall. Even in those hearings where the pre-patient was released, the same segregation of complainant and defendant occurred at the close of the hearing.

The judge then signed the necessary forms; the clerk took them away and placed the next patient's case record before the judge. On some occasions, post-hearing remarks were passed between

---

[4] Two Mexican patients who did not understand English were committed and thought they were being confined in a military prison. They later cited the presence of this uniformed officer as partial evidence for this definition of the situation.

TABLE 1   AVERAGE AND MEDIAN LENGTH OF TIME OF LUNACY COMMISSION
HEARING BY TYPE OF OUTCOME

Outcome	No.	%	Average (Min.)	Median (Min.)
Committed	39	68	3.8	3
Held-over	6	10	4.8	4.5
Released	13	22	5.5	4
Total	58	100	4.4	3

the judge and the medical doctors. No other person spoke—each held his assigned position throughout the hearing.

The defendants and the complainants did not have a structured frame of reference to offer them clues for their own behavior, while the commission members seemed to have developed a series of reactions for each type of situation. A general air of strain and anxiety was present throughout the hearings.

As Table 1 shows, the average length of the hearings was 4.1 minutes—the median length was less than three.

Such speed was possible because of the efficiency of the permanent commission and the confusion of the temporary participants. The doctors had examined the defendants prior to the hearing, so their "briefing of the case" enabled the judge to make his decision rapidly.

The medical doctors recommended commitment to the mental hospital in nearly all cases. In those few cases where they did not, they found the defendants to be "emotionally disturbed" and in need of out-patient psychiatric care. Thus, not one of the fifty-eight persons was given a clean bill of mental health by the examining professionals![5] Several defendants protested that the doctors had not really talked with them, or had done so for only a moment.

Throughout the series of observations it appeared that the rules of conduct were very clear to the commission, although not necessarily to the other participants. They were similar to all rules which operate between a superior and a subordinate in structured

---

[5] Thomas J. Scheff, "The Societal Reactions to Deviance," *Social Problems*, 2 (Spring, 1964), pp. 401–413. He reported also that he found a strong presumption of mental illness by the court and the court psychiatrists (p. 402). See pp. 100–119 above.

settings, such as those between adults and children.[6] Deviations from any or all of these basic rules of etiquette were viewed as a breach of conduct and treated in that way, even in those cases where the transgressor did not know he had erred. Such breaches were ignored, interpreted in other ways, turned aside with a cliché, or capped by an authoritative statement from the judge. (In three cases, the defendant exploded into anger and was taken away by the two orderlies who had been standing by.)

Types of Alignments to the Situation

We observed four types of responses in these fifty-eight cases, and we used these to develop interactional sets for the analysis of four alignments to the situation.

In each type of these four alignments we studied the accused's definition of the situation and his behavior; the reactions of the complainants, the psychiatrists, and the judge, as well as the over-all group feeling. The "types" were based on the interactional patterns which we observed occurring between the participants and were not meant to imply "personality types."

1. *Defiance Alignments:* Twenty-one (36 per cent) of the situations were distinguished by the defendants' pattern of resistance to the commitment procedure, the complainants, or the situation in general.

Such resistance was manifested in varying degrees of intensity, ranging from silent disdain to verbal protest on to assaultive violence. In general, the resisters appeared to be younger, more aware, more capable, more intelligent than defendants in other alignments. Patients who were defiant usually were concerned about their rights; they seemed to be aware that their liberty was in jeopardy and attempted to fight the "injustice" they felt was being done to them at the hearing.

Resisters provided the dramatic highlights of the hearings and held the interest of the professionals. Often, patterns of resistance were the subjects of pre- and post-hearing discussions between the professionals. The judge tended to take a personal interest in these resisters, often conducting his own brief "psychiatric examination," making his own "clinical diagnosis" of their cases, and

---

[6] Erving Goffman, *Behavior in Public Places*, Glencoe, Ill.: The Free Press, 1963.

TABLE 2   TYPE OF ALIGNMENT BY NUMBER RELEASED AND AVERAGE TIME
OF HEARING

Type	Number	Released No.	%	Average Time Minutes
Defiance	21	7	33	5.7
Bewilderment	16	3	19	3.8
Non-participation	8	1	13	2.9
Volunteer	13	2	18	3.8
Total	58	13	22	4.4

even collecting quite different data than the other professionals
had presented.

Many who resisted commitment elicited the judge's empathy
and special attention and, as a result, *one-half of those who resisted were either released or held over for further study.* (The
three who were held over, however, were later committed. See
Table 2.)

Resisters who were not committed differed from those who
were committed in that they were able to question the validity
of the complainants' case, rather than just the doctors' testimony.
All those who attacked the decision or recommendations of the
professionals were committed, often with some abrupt terminal
remark by the judge. However, the defendant who turned on his
complainants had the best of it and, in such cases, the tables were
turned. The complainants were then driven to elaborate their side
of the case, and only when the emotional level between them and
the defendants rose to a "boiling point" did the complainant appear to be justified. If the defendant "exploded" into some type
of violent language or action, the complainants considered themselves vindicated and sat back, as if to say, "There, see—I told
you so!"

These situations were dramatic, and at times it seemed as if the
professionals, too, toyed with the various elements of resentment,
recrimination, and rejection. They seemed to engage in a "preci-
pice-hanging" game, i.e., to attempt to permit the situation to go
so far but no further. Three times during the period of these
observations the hearings exploded into physical violence, which
ruptured the setting and caused considerable collective unrest
among the professionals.

An examination of the accused's family role position revealed that those who resisted were more likely to be members of a family group than were those who did not resist (Q = .59). Among those who were spouses, approximately 40 per cent were resisters, while only 25 per cent of those who lived outside a family group were resisters. Among the resisters, *spouses were likely to be released, while those who filled the family role position of a relative and those who were living outside the family were likely to be committed.* (Q = .71)

The significant others of those who were defiant were forced to accuse the pre-patient of rather serious or exaggerated anti-social acts, i.e., some type of violence or crimes against persons. They sometimes presented the pre-patient as a "clever" person who was privately violent and really needed "help," despite his public denials and objections.

In some cases it appeared that the relatives were afraid they were losing possession of the pre-patient. They often explained in great detail how they had tried in vain to control the pre-patient, carefully explaining that they were not discarding the accused; they only wanted him to be "taught a lesson" so he could then be returned to them as a more controlled, contrite, and obedient person after a period in the mental hospital. Often they indicated considerable fear of the defendant, indicating that they were afraid he would not forgive them after his release for taking such drastic action as committing him to a mental hospital. They sought assurances from the professionals that the defendant would, in fact, later accept and understand their good intentions which led them to having him confined in a mental hospital. Such reassurances were automatically given, generally by the psychiatrist on the commission.

The general feeling at these resisters' hearings was one of excitement and tension. Open conflict seemed to be only a breath away.

One case deserves mention because it was different from all of the other observed cases. It was the only case in which a defending attorney appeared, and which adhered to strict formal court procedure. One might say that this case approximated the "ideal" in that every action seemed focused on protecting the defendant from "injustice."

The defendant was a fifty-year-old woman, very well dressed, albeit obviously "hungover." She was accompanied by two nurses (who were especially solicitous of her), and a young attorney, eager and protective. The complainants, her husband and his two brothers, were well-dressed ranchers and appeared affluent.

In this case, the medical doctors gave no report, but merely asked the husband to present his story. Briefly, the husband's story focused on a possible divorce with the community property settlement after a twenty-three-year marriage. The husband wanted to prevent his wife from obtaining a divorce because of the resultant property division. He sought to have his rebellious spouse adjudged mentally ill because of her heavy drinking and her "illness" (manifested by long absences in Las Vegas where she gambled and went out with other men). He stated she needed "help" and he wanted to "get it for her." The brothers seconded his story. Her attorney presented his client as "upset" because of the marital conflict, and defended her civil rights. She was, of course, not committed to the mental hospital.

This special drama approached farcical limits. All present were "innocent" in appearance—pious, courteous, and correct. At the close of the hearing the defendant was released to "seek private psychiatric care" *and* a divorce. This exceptional hearing took seventeen minutes; all participants had their "day in court."

This incident afforded a good baseline for comparison with the other fifty-seven hearings. No other defendant was represented by an attorney: no other case was presented without a diagnosis of psychiatric illness or comment by the examining physicians; in no other case did all civilians testify fully without an interruption or termination of their stories by the judge; no other case involved so much solicitous concern from the professional staff; no other case focused on the protection of the defendant's property and civil rights; no other case was presented, heard, and disposed of in such a fully formal manner. This woman took full advantage of her civil rights and, by so doing, was released.

2. Bewilderment Alignments: Sixteen (28 per cent) of the accused were distinguished by their general air of bewilderment at the hearing. This alignment described settings where the accused patients were aged, physically incapacitated, or socially retarded.

Most of these bewildered persons were committed to the mental hospital. The single release in this category occurred when a daughter assured the commission that the patient would be committed when she got him to his home state. Two others were "released" to a nursing home. Most of these defendants plaintively asked not to be kept in the mental hospital. However, some did not seem aware of the nature of the occasion, and no one told them what the "trial" was all about, although several asked what was going on. Most had some inkling of danger and reacted to it with increased confusion and anxiety.

Many complainants were overtly distressed at testifying against an aged parent or a relative, who was hurt and shocked by their testimony. In response to the pathos inherent in such a situation, all concerned tended to skirt the issues, although they strongly pointed out to the commission that there was no other alternative to commitment. Often they spoke as though the defendant, although present, could not, in fact, understand what was being said. Often the complainants were adult sons who remained silent while their wives (the daughters-in-law) recited a long list of reasons why they could not care for the patient. Since the family could not afford private medical or custodial care, they were forced to commit their aged parent to a state hospital.

These hearings of the bewildered were conducted very rapidly; the average time was less than four minutes as compared to 5.7 minutes for "defiant" pre-patients. One of the techniques for managing the shamefaced interaction was to handle all discussions in a "jolly," superficial manner; another was to treat the hearing as a business-like, routine transaction.

Many of the defendants were aged persons who had been living alone and were unable physically to care for themselves. The physicians' evidence dwelt at length on the organic "senile" problems of the pre-patients and on their need for care and supervision. The judge showed concern in such cases, frequently questioning relatives as to why they could not take the aged person into their home.[7]

The group feeling in these hearings was often that of a child's game of "let's pretend." The professionals smoothed over the situation so that the central issue of confinement to a mental hospital never came into sharp focus. The use of clichés, combined with

---

[7] M. F. Lowenthal, *Lives in Distress: The Paths of the Elderly to the Psychiatric Ward*, New York: Basic Books, 1964. She presents an analysis of the ways in which aged persons are re-defined as psychiatric patients.

the speed of the transaction, accomplished a rapid disposition of these cases. The feeble objections of the accused, who were bewildered about the proceedings, were hushed, and vague reassurances were given that all would be well.

3. *Non-Participation Alignments:* Eight (14 per cent) of the observed cases remained mute throughout their hearing. These silent ones were frequently confined to a wheelchair, or were non-English speaking persons.[8]

All of the silent ones were committed, except for one who was sent to an available veterans home. They did not seem to pay close attention to the professionals and looked about the room or sat apathetically and did not speak even if spoken to (although they seldom were). They, in fact, for whatever reasons, did not enter into participation of the decision-making process about their own fate, but remained mute and aloof from the entire procedure.

In some of these cases there were no complainants and, when there were, they spoke of the defendant as though he were a "non-person," who could no longer be cared for outside the hospital. The physicians made very clear statements specifying that the accused was "sick." They usually spoke frankly about the psychiatric or organic symptoms (including venereal disease, etc.) or the poor prognosis, as though the accused were either deaf or absent. These hearings were the shortest of all, averaging 2.9 minutes, with six of the eight completed in two minutes or less.

The fate of the non-English speaking persons was a matter of special interest. Generally, a hospital attendant who spoke their language attempted to interpret for the defendant, often with unanticipated reactions. For example, one Mexican-American was obviously shocked and insulted by the woman attendant's translation given in the Spanish familiar form. He drew himself up in a stance of dignity and "withdrew" from the field insofar as he could. *Those who could not or would not defend themselves were not defended.*

In those cases where a complainant was present there seemed to be a working consensus between him and the examining doctors; they acted as partners performing a ritual. No question was raised

---

[8] Esther Blanc, a social psychiatry student at the University of California, School of Nursing, San Francisco, who is conducting a study of Spanish-American mental patients, contributed special insight into this group.

regarding the relative's "duty" or the pre-patient's type of "illness." The group feeling centered on and arose out of the transactions between the complainants and the professionals; the defendants did not and were not expected to participate.

4. *Volunteer Alignments: Type A:* In eleven (17 per cent) of the observed cases the accused patients behaved like obedient children. They said they realized they were "sick and needed help." They frequently spoke in psychiatric terms about their own behavior. They looked at the doctors with great admiration and solicitation. The physicians responded to them with smiles and agreement, affirming to these pre-patients that they did, indeed, need psychiatric help. The physicians often praised these patients and their families for carrying through and seeking help in an intelligent manner, i.e., by requesting and consenting to admission to the state mental hospital.

The complainant showed much affection to the defendants. The judge spoke in a paternal, courtly manner, and assured the patient that all would soon be resolved. There was an air of good fellowship and mutual admiration at these hearings. All of these "psychiatric converts" or their families had been former state hospital employees, nurses, rehabilitation workers, or prior mental hygiene clinic patients. They seemed to be comfortably aware of their proper place and carried out the commitment ritual with dispatch and decorum.

The group feeling was one of a stylized ritual rather than a moment of traumatic decision. These volunteers had prior experience with the psychiatric model and persuaded themselves, or had been persuaded by their significant others, that coming into the state mental hospital was going to help them in some real way.

Type B: Two of the observed cases (4 per cent) spoke in the same general manner as those who had been "converted" to the psychiatric perspective, but were refused admission to the state mental hospital. These volunteers were judged to be "alcoholics," hence, malingerers. One had been in the mental hospital before and had since "fallen off the wagon," and the other had relatives who did not think commitment was really required at this time, even though the pre-patient was asking for readmission. A middle-aged woman, who had previously been committed as an alcoholic, wanted to return to the hospital ward where she had made friends and where she had found some relief from the deadly boredom of living with a "dull" husband. She seemed to prefer the mental hospital to her daily "ordeal." The other was a man who was under indictment for writing bad checks and appeared to be seeking commitment in preference to going to jail.[9]

In these cases the physicians found that, while these subjects had "emotional problems," they were not likely to benefit from hospital care. The judge became very stern and berated these persons for their lack of control over their drinking or for their anti-social behavior. Even further, he threatened them with a sentence of six months in the county jail for drunkenness if they appeared before him again. In general, the professionals acted suspicious.[10]

Why did some of these self-defined "patients" elicit the good will and empathy of the commission, while the others aroused the ire and condemnation of the staff? The reaction of the group seemed affected by: (1) whether or not the pre-patients held jobs and retained vestiges of their occupational roles, or were unemployed, or were not in the labor market (i.e., if it was thought that they did not seem to show concern about "earning their way"); (2) whether they were older, with records of previous treatment failures or jail sentences, or were young and undergoing hospitalization for the first time;[11] (3) whether the defendants were in-

---

[9] This case seemed similar to the one described in Ken Kesey, *One Flew Over the Cuckoo's Nest*, New York: Viking, 1962, where Big Red chose the mental hospital in preference to jail.

[10] Certainly, this attitude by professionals has been present throughout society's treatment of the poor and socially incapable. The history of social welfare movements has been full of concern that the "unworthy poor" would somehow manage to get help. In fact, early professional training for social workers developed to prevent too much "unwise giving" to the poor and ill, lest they be encouraged to continue an indolent and immoral existence. Proper training was thought to be necessary to teach social workers to give short shift to such "connivers" and "chiselers." Such a history and set of attitudes reflect the reactions of professionals who classify behavior in terms of "sinfulness" or "sickness." The moral issue of "psychiatric cases" often poses such dispositional or administrative dilemmas.

[11] In this connection, note must be made of the influence of the available case record on each defendant. In those cases appearing at the hospital door for the first time, the judge had a folder before him containing the affidavit filed by the complainant which, aside from some "face sheet" data, described the type of behavior forming the basis for the charge of "insanity." It appears that this described behavior was sometimes taken by the judge with

gratiating, grateful, and able to verbalize their eagerness to "work on" their problems, or whether they were somehow unable to convince the professionals of their "sincerity" or their "motivation."

The harsh, rejecting attitude of the professionals transformed the interaction of these hearings, making it impossible for the two pre-patients to fill the "good patient" role. They reacted to the professionals' suspicion with a grin or a shrug of their shoulders.

Summary

These findings reveal that certain actions have a greater likelihood for one commitment outcome as against another. Those defendants who were able to defend their civil liberty by demonstrating interactional ability, i.e., those who were able to present themselves in a controlled and effective manner, were likely to be released. Those who either did not openly object, or objected in violent or abusive ways, were committed to the state hospital.

However, these findings, in themselves, illustrate a crude type of "justice" resulting from the legal hearings. One might suppose that those who, for whatever reason, reacted to stress and threat in ineffective or inappropriate ways, e.g., by sulking, by withdrawing, by violence, were not likely to be able to conduct themselves appropriately in other stressful or even routine social situations. They took the role of others poorly and, perhaps for this, they were hospitalized. One could argue this same lack of social acumen and awareness had been the basis of their social discomfort, whatever their psychiatric diagnosis might be.

Relatives were also under great strain by virtue of their appearance in the role of the complainant. Their reactions ranged from great shame to profound relief. To interpret these observations as showing that these relatives were engaged in "railroading" their unwanted family member into the mental hospital is to distort reality. The strain of breaking ties of loyalty and of facing up to

---

a "grain of salt"—at least he frequently asked about it and accepted a milder version of the behavior from the defendant. In the case of the former mental patient or the former criminal, however, the judge also had that person's official case record before him, with all the former aberrations preserved intact. The effect of a written record of former deviant behavior upon the face-to-face situation must not be underestimated. In these cases, it seemed to be a critical factor in the judge's decision.

the public ordeal of commitment was great indeed. Apparently the complainants took on this role with great distaste and, generally, only after they had experienced long periods of discomfort and dismay. They felt they were in a trap and, for them, the mental hospital seemed to be the only way out.

In general, commitment to a mental hospital had many meanings and many consequences for all concerned, depending upon the definitions which emerged from the interaction.

This observational study found that those persons who were able to approach the judge in a controlled manner, use proper eye contact, sentence structure, posture, etc., and who presented their stories without excessive emotional response or blandness and with proper demeanor, were able to obtain the decision they wanted—whether it was release or commitment—despite any "psychiatric symptomatology."

These hearings appear to be neither thorough nor careful. The short period of time spent on each pre-patient and the fact that there was often no one (including himself) to speak on his behalf contributed to a definite feeling that there was a presumption of insanity held by the commission members. Those who were not committed were released because they were able to "turn the tables" on their complainants and to change the impression of the judge.

Since the hearings were usually so perfunctory, one is tempted to conclude that the judgment about mental illness was made earlier in the commitment process, and that the hearing was a rubber stamp to this earlier decision. The data in this study suggested that, while the medical staff had decided on commitment, it was possible for the judge to reverse the medical recommendation of commitment, since he did so in nearly one-fourth of the cases.

A study of the pre-examinations was beyond the scope of the present endeavor, and we can make no conclusive statements about them.[12] There is, however, evidence to suggest that the medical examination is as summary as the hearing itself. We stated above that several pre-patients mentioned that the doctors

---

[12] Karl Kreplin, a doctoral candidate at the University of California, Berkeley, is currently studying this aspect, and his results should be available shortly.

had not seen them at all, while others claimed that the examination was brief and superficial. Thomas Scheff,[13] in a study of commitment procedures in another state, found the examinations were haphazard and superficial, noteworthy mainly for their presumption of insanity. Finally, the fact that in only a few of the fifty-eight cases did the doctors not recommend commitment suggests that their examinations did not discriminate among these patients.

The possibility exists, of course, that almost all patients brought before the commission were mentally incompetent. This implies, however, that the laymen who originally signed the commitment papers were unerring in their diagnosis. We find this hard to believe, considering the state of the public's knowledge of the nature of mental illness. Naturally, it is important to investigate this aspect of the commitment process to find exactly what motivates a family to send one of its members to a mental hospital. It is possible that they are only moved to such a drastic measure when the situation becomes so severe that the patient is clearly imbalanced.

If it seems from these observations that such lunacy commission hearings are painful or misdirected, what, then, are the suggested alternatives? How does one arrange to treat "mental illness" in which the basic symptoms are resistance, denial, and flight from the source of "help"? These questions can only be raised. Certainly, the professionals at these hearings struggled with their assignments—delicately balancing "justice" against "necessity." These professionals occupied a guilt-producing, anxious position. Perhaps out of such discomfort can come other ways of administering justice while offering care to the suffering.

---

[13] Thomas J. Scheff, "Decision Rules, Types of Error, and Their Consequences in Medical Diagnosis," *Behavioral Science*, 8 (April, 1963), pp. 97–107. See pp. 211–229 below.

The Effect of Legal Counsel on Admissions to a State Mental Hospital: A Confrontation of Professions

Dennis L. Wenger and C. Richard Fletcher

The field of forensic psychiatry may be conceptually divided into two areas of interaction centering in two social settings, the courtroom and the mental hospital, where the professions of law and psychiatry are found in confrontation. In the courtroom, what is viewed as a basically legal problem (guilt or innocence) has superimposed upon it a psychiatric qualification (insanity, incompetency, etc.). In the mental hospital, on the other hand, what is viewed as a basically psychiatric problem (the presence of mental illness and the need for hospitalization) has superimposed upon it a legal qualification (constitutional liberties, a trial by jury, etc.).

This study is concerned with the second area, with particular emphasis on the questions of relative authority of psychiatrists and lawyers in involuntary hospitalization of mental patients. The effect of legal counsel in the admission process will be empirically investigated.

Each year approximately 250,000 patients are committed to mental hospitals, most of them involuntarily. (Joint Commission, 1961:21) An individual in committed status suffers a loss of civil liberties, insofar as he is automatically considered legally incompetent, cannot vote, make a valid contract, marry, divorce, communicate freely with the outside, operate a motor vehicle, etc. In short, the mental patient is deprived of many civil rights. For these reasons lawyers as well as psychiatrists have taken an interest in the procedures concerning involuntary commitment. In this instance, however, a common interest does not mean a common viewpoint, for there is a debate between lawyers and doctors as to what should be the method for involuntary commitment and detention. The medical profession basically believes that the law must remain as informal as possible, arguing that excessive legal formality is harmful to the individual. The legal profession, on the other hand, states that the fundamental principles of justice

Reprinted from the *Journal of Health and Human Behavior*, vol. 10, 1969, pp. 66–72.

(presence at the hearing, the right to legal counsel and trial by jury, etc.) are guaranteed to all and must not be withheld from mental patients.[1] The present study will examine this professional confrontation.

Our empirical examination of this confrontation can be analyzed instructively as the competition of two professions over jurisdiction of an area of expert knowledge. A profession can be viewed as having acquired a body of expert knowledge over which it has legal monopoly and self-surveillance. In discussion of this professional control, Blau and Scott assert:

> Professionals in a given field constitute a colleague group of equals. Every member of the group, *but nobody else*, is assumed to be qualified to make professional judgements. (emphasis added) (Blau and Scott, 1962:63)

Psychiatric and legal professions compete in their claims to expertise and decision-making authority regarding hospital commitment. As Goode (1960) states, the intensity of conflicts about encroachment (i.e., arguments about professional mandate) are greatest when the occupation deals with an individual client, and cannot easily demonstrate its competence. Professionals admit that they need their client's cooperation for economic and social survival, (Freidson: 1966) because these clients will grant an effective monopoly to the profession through license only when it has shown that it is the sole master of its craft, and that its decisions are not reviewed by other professions. (Goode: 1960:903) Both the legal and medical professions believe that they should have ultimate authority in the area and, of course, should be held accountable only to their own professional peers.

There are several areas of disagreement between the two professions. (Davidson, 1965:282) First, the medical profession favors "easy" commitment procedures. The profession believes that the needs of the patient are best met by allowing for rapid placement in the mental hospital without legal qualifications. For example, the doctors believe that (1) rules of evidence exclude

---

[1] In fairness to the psychiatric profession, it should be pointed out that many psychiatrists are uneasy about the process of formal commitment and much prefer voluntary admission to the hospital. See, for example, Group for the Advancement of Psychiatry (1966).

much that is medically relevant, (2) the atmosphere of the court-room has a punitive aura, (3) the terminology of the law is traumatic to sensitive people, (4) excessive legalism discourages families from seeking early medical care, etc. The legal profession, on the other hand, favors "strict" commitment. Lawyers believe that the individual's civil liberties are best served if the due process of law is *not* removed. In the words of one legal authority, "We need the limited requirement of due process. Every man should be entitled to a fair hearing, on notice, should he be threatened with confinement." (Kutner, 1962: 383–399)

Second, there are many other controversial issues in this debate. Many questions center about (1) the merits of jury decisions, (2) the notification and presence of the patient at his hearing, (3) the patient's right to legal counsel, (4) railroading, (5) the need for a psychiatric "watchdog agency," and even (6) the correct definition of mental illness. The area of debate which best illustrates the controversy over the professional right to mandate and license, however, concerns the problem of ultimate authority. "It is the official position of the American Psychiatric Association that physicians should have unrestricted power to commit." (Szasz, 1963: 61) The medical profession believes "provisions should be made for involuntary hospitalization without the necessity of court proceedings." (Davidson, 1965:282) They argue that the question of commitment is a medical decision. Either the person is, or is not, mentally ill. If he is mentally ill, he must be committed and given treatment as rapidly as possible. The problem is simply one of diagnosis and treatment. Since diagnosis is part of the expert body of knowledge that lies within the domain of the medical profession, psychiatrists should have the ultimate authority in decisions on commitments.

Lawyers, on the other hand, argue that the situation is not that simple. They state that the problem is basically a legal one due to the loss of civil liberties which results from commitment. The legal profession appears to view the mental hospital as a " corrective institution," similar to a prison, whose main functions are incarceration, custodial care, and rehabilitation.[2] The due process of law must be served if anyone is committed to such an institu-

---

[2] See Levinson and Gallagher (1964:15–33) for a discussion of mental hospitals as therapeutic and corrective institutions.

tion. Furthermore, Ross states that there are two reasons, besides the obvious loss of civil liberties, why commitment is not a purely medical matter. First, mental illness is not a fact in the same sense as a broken leg: he believes it is a theory used to explain deviant behavior. Second, the psychiatrist is not the person necessarily most qualified to decide on commitment, because of the legal problems involved. Ultimate authority in decisions of commitment must reside in the courts; it is a legal problem. (Ross, 1959:945)

Representatives of these two professions confront each other in an admission hearing when the patient is represented by legal counsel. Legal counsel attempts to serve two functions for the client. First, the lawyer attempts to safeguard his client's civil liberties and the due process of law. Second, he "builds a case" which will convince the examining psychiatrists and court referee that his client is "sane" and should not be committed. This second function is directly related to the aforementioned problem of ultimate authority. If the problem is purely a medical and diagnostic one, the presence of legal counsel should have little effect in influencing the commitment decision of the examining commission. If, however, the problem is not simply a medical question, one would expect positive association between the presence of legal counsel and the admission decision. This relationship has not been empirically investigated previously.[3]

Research Procedures

The method of non-participant observation was employed in this study. The authors observed admission hearings to a state mental hospital for 81 persons. Random observations were made over a period of four and a half months. Notes were taken on the general patterns of interaction and the personal characteristics of the pre-patients and complainants, i.e., those individuals who had filled out the affidavit claiming that pre-patient was mentally ill. Discussions with various participants in the hearing system (the

---

[3] There have been two previous investigations of commitment hearings. Neither study, however, was concerned with legal counsel. Miller and Schwartz (1966) examined the relationship between interactional sets and the commitment decision. Scheff (1966:128–155) investigated the hypothesis that psychiatrists exhibit a preference for Type 2 errors (acceptance of the hypothesis of illness rather than of normality or health).

court referee, bailiff, psychiatrists, social workers, etc.) were recorded and further analyzed.

The commitment hearings were held in a room at a midwestern state mental hospital. These hearings were an adjunct of the Probate Court. In these hearings, a court referee presided, while two psychiatrists examined the alleged patients and issued opinions as to commitment.[4] Although not a judge, the referee had the final authority. However, in no instance did he decide in opposition to the psychiatrists' opinion. Therefore the doctors' decisions were, in effect, final. A court bailiff was also present. In these hearings, if the individual was found in "need of treatment," he was placed in the hospital for a period not to exceed ninety days, at which time a second or "ninety day hearing" was held to determine whether he would be released or committed for an indefinite period. The room in which the hearings were held was small, with seating on three sides for 25 people. The participants sat at a "T" shaped table in the center of the room. From a legal standpoint, the hearing was very informal. Most of the rules on admissible evidence, e.g., hearsay evidence, were relaxed, and both the legal and medical participants accepted this procedure. No oaths were taken, and although some lawyers attempted to "have their day in court," very little "courtroom drama" was involved. It was felt by the psychiatrists that these hearings should be informal so that no undue stigma be presented to the patient.

Briefly, the typical pattern of interaction would begin with the bailiff bringing the patient, complainant, and lawyers (if present) into the room. The referee would ask the complainant why he felt the patient was "ill." The complainant would present and build his case. The patient would then be interviewed by first the psychiatrist and then the referee. The psychiatrists then would present their recommendations to the referee who made the final decision on commitment based upon their opinions.[5]

---

[4] The Ohio Penal Code (n.d.: Sections 16–22) only requires that one doctor, not necessarily a psychiatrist, examine the patient.

[5] The psychiatrists performed a preliminary psychiatric examination on all of the pre-patients the evening before the hearing. During the hearing the psychiatrists appeared to be familiar with the patients and often seemed to have already made their decision before the hearing began. It was not possible to observe this first examination. However, one patient had escaped the previous afternoon and had not been seen by the psychiatrist prior to the hearing. His hearing took 4½ minutes.

TABLE 1   THE EFFECT OF LEGAL COUNSEL UPON THE LENGTH OF THE HEAR-
            ING

Condition	Number	Percentage	Mean (min.)	Median (min.)	Range (min.)
Legal Counsel	15	18.5	16.84	10.08	.45–43.00
No Legal Counsel	66	81.5	6.15	4.50	1.42–10.00
Total	81	100.0	8.13	5.03	.45–43.00

Findings

Of the 81 cases observed, 65 (80.3%) were placed in the hospital for the 90-day period. Sixty-six (81.5%) of the pre-patients were not represented by legal counsel.[6] The average length of time for each case was 8.13 minutes; the median was 5.03 minutes, and the range was from .45 to 45 minutes. There was, however, a striking difference between the length of those hearings in which legal counsel was present and those without legal counsel. The hearings with legal counsel were over twice as long as those without legal counsel (See Table 1).

Miller and Schwartz report similar findings with respect to the relative length of the hearings resulting in admission and release. (Miller and Schwartz, 1966:28)

The major interest of the investigation, however, was to determine the association between the presence of legal counsel and the commitment decision. The relationship is shown in Table 2. First, it can be noted that 61 (91%) of those without legal counsel were admitted, but only 4 (26%) of those with legal counsel were admitted. Eleven (74%) of those with legal counsel were not admitted as opposed to only 5 (8.9%) of the patients without legal counsel. The findings are statistically significant, and the Q of .942 shows a high positive association between the presence of legal counsel and the decision not to hospitalize the patient.

While the above data appear to substantiate the effect of legal

---

[6] Legal counsel is allowed, but is not mandatory or provided in these hearings. Free legal counsel is available in the area through the Legal Aid Society, the American Civil Liberties Union, and the like. It is not known to what extent the pre-patient is informed of his rights to legal counsel or is urged to secure this aid. One pre-patient, however, on being told that she would have to be kept for 90 days, became indignant. She had desired to have legal counsel, but the social workers had told her that she wouldn't need it because "the hearing board is fair."

TABLE 2   THE EFFECT OF LEGAL COUNSEL UPON THE ADMISSION DECISION

	Admitted	Not Admitted	Total
Legal Counsel	4	11	15
No Legal Counsel	61	5	66
Total	65	16	81

$$x^2 = 33.35 \quad df = 1, \quad P < .001 \quad Q = .942$$

counsel upon the commitment decision, it appeared plausible that this high correlation was merely masking a more crucial antecedent determinant. Conceivably the individuals who were "sane" (i.e., did not meet the legal requirements for commitment in the State of Ohio) were more likely to acquire legal counsel than those who were "insane."[7] Perhaps the decision to release the patient was made on the basis of his condition, not his legal representation. If so, the relationship between legal counsel and the committment decision observed in Table 2 would be spurious, for it masks the more crucial antecedent determinant of the patient's condition.

In order to control for the condition of the patient, each pre-patient was categorized by the observers as to whether or not he met the legal criteria for commitment in the state.[8] At the time of the hearing, if the pre-patient is not suffering from a mental illness which lessens his capacity to use judgment, self-control; is

[7] In the State of Ohio, "mental illness is an illness which so lessens the capacity of the person to use self-control, judgment, and discretion in the conduct of his affairs and social relations as to make it necessary or advisable for him to be under care, supervision, guidance, or control." Also, the patient must show danger "to himself or others" in certain involuntary cases. (Ohio Penal Code, n.d.: Section 16–20).

[8] See Miller and Schwartz (1966:28) for the legal criteria for commitment. The authors observed each patient and compared their observable condition with the legal criteria for commitment. The patient was categorized as either (1) meeting the legal criteria, (2) being a "borderline case," or (3) not meeting the legal criteria. The observer's decision was made *before* the psychitrists presented their recommendation to the court referee. The patients who definitely met the legal criteria were often quite psychotic, suffered from delusions, were confused or irrational, were not able to care for themselves, etc. This category included a few extremely senile and advanced arteriosclerotic patients, a number of extreme mentally retarded individuals, and a few schizophrenic persons. Those classified as "borderline" or as not meeting the criteria included many neurotics, alcoholics, elderly individuals who had no one to take care of them and were being "dumped"

TABLE 3   RELATIONSHIP BETWEEN LEGAL COUNSEL AND THE PATIENT'S CONDITION[a]

Condition	Criteria Met		Borderline		Criteria Not Met	
	NO.	PER CENT	NO.	PER CENT	NO.	PER CENT
Legal Counsel	1	5	6	20.7	8	34.8
No Legal Counsel	19	95	23	79.3	15	65.2
Total	20	100	29	100.0	23	100.0

$x^2 = 8.163$ df = 2. P < .02
C = .319   C max = .816

[a] Nine patients were not present at their hearings and data are not available.

not in need of guidance or control; is not dangerous to himself or others, etc., his condition has not met the legal criteria for commitment and he should therefore not be hospitalized. Nine of the patients were not present at their hearings and could not be classified by the observers. Of the remaining 72 cases, however, 20 (27.7%) definitely met the criteria, 29 (42.7%) were classified as "borderline," and 23 (29.6%) were judged as *not* meeting the legal criteria for commitment.

The three categories of pre-patients were then cross-tabulated with the presence of legal counsel. The results are presented in Table 3. The percentage of patients with legal counsel increases

---

in the hospital, husbands or wives whose spouse had tried to commit them during a domestic quarrel, etc. This method is similar to that employed by Scheff (1966:151–153). The authors realize the problems involved with this methodology. Not being psychiatrists they are not "qualified" to make psychiatric diagnoses. However, diagnostic labels were of relatively little interest to them compared to the question of whether the patient met the legal criteria for admission. The classification was made at the time of the hearing because according to law the patient was to be committed or released depending on his condition *at that time*. There was no reason for "bias" in the classification process since the basic results of the study depended neither upon the number of patients classified in any category, nor upon a high level of precision in classifying them. Indeed, bias would probably have been increased by bringing a psychiatrist in to assist in the classification, since he would probably have distorted the customary social process of the hearing and generally contaminated the findings. Another potential bias was avoided by making the classification before the admitting psychiatrists had made their decisions whether or not to admit the patient to the hospital.

steadily as one moves from the "criteria met" to the "criteria not met" category.

After this analysis had been completed, we asked one of the examining psychiatrists if there were any distinguishing characteristics of patients with legal counsel, such as type or severity of condition, social class, I.Q., etc. His response was, "These factors have nothing to do with the case. There is no difference in severity or income or social class or I.Q. It's purely an individual matter, just a quirk of the individual. They've heard it from somebody somewhere along the line." His impression is not supported by our data. The results obtained are shown in Table 4. These results suggest that legal counsel affects the admission of patients within each condition category. Looking first at the borderline cases, all 23 of the patients without legal counsel were admitted. Of the 6 patients with legal counsel, however, three were not admitted. Turning to those not meeting the legal criteria of mental illness, 10 of 15 patients without legal counsel were admitted, but none of those with legal counsel were admitted. Patients with legal counsel were much less likely to be hospitalized than those without legal counsel.

From the above data it appears that the inverse relationship between the presence of legal counsel and mental hospital admission is not spurious. Lawyers do appear to lessen the likelihood of their clients being admitted.

TABLE 4 RELATIONSHIP BETWEEN LEGAL COUNSEL AND THE ADMISSION DECISION, BY PATIENT'S CONDITION

Condition:	*Criteria Met*		*Borderline*		*Criteria Not Met*	
DECISION:	AD-MITTED	NOT AD-MITTED	AD-MITTED	NOT AD-MITTED	AD-MITTED	NOT AD-MITTED
Legal Counsel	1	0	3	3	0	8
No Legal Counsel	19	0	23	0	10	5
Total	20	0	26	3	10	13
	Significance not computed		Fischer's Exact Probability $< .005$ $C = .567$ C max $= .707$		Fischer's Exact Probability $< .003$ $C = .541$ C max $= .707$	

Discussion and Summary

The effect of legal counsel on the decision to admit patients to a midwestern mental hospital has been shown. There appears to be a high association (.942) between the presence of legal counsel and the decision not to admit the person to the hospital. This association remains even when the patient's condition as evaluated by an observer is held constant. The patients classified as borderline or as criteria-not-met, and who had legal counsel, were more likely to be released than similar patients not represented by a lawyer. Lawyers, with their knowledge of the state legal statutes and its "loopholes," appear to be fairly successful at influencing the commitment decision and securing the release of their clients.

These findings are related to the previous discussion of the medical-legal debate as a confrontation of professions over a body of expert knowledge and the question of ultimate authority. If the admission decision is a purely medical problem based upon expert diagnosis, then the presence of legal counsel should not affect the decision; the person is or is not mentally ill and should correspondingly be committed or released. As we have seen, however, legal counsel does affect this decision.

Following the completion of this analysis, we asked one of the examining psychiatrists whether, in his impression, the presence of legal counsel had any effect upon the decision to release a patient he represented. He responded, "There is no correlation between them. Legal counsel doesn't make a particle of difference to the psychiatrist, not one iota of difference. If a patient is sick, he's *sick*, that's all. If he's got a broken arm, he's got a broken arm. It's not a legal type of thing. He's been brought to the attention of the court because he's sick. His lawyer can't make any new evidence. I've been around 25 years and I know what goes on. No, the proof of the pudding is in the eating, isn't it? And in all my experience of 15,000 admissions we have never had a writ of habeas corpus that was upheld in court. And you know darn well if there's a man who's there who should not be there, there'd be a successful writ." When we asked what his response would be to a future study which showed a .9 correlation between the presence of legal counsel and release, his response was, "I don't care what your study shows, I know my *facts*, so stop wasting your time and efforts."

This clinical impression, notwithstanding the number of years over which it was formed, is brought into serious question by our findings. In this particular hospital, at least, psychiatrists possess something less than ultimate authority in the decision to admit patients, particularly the patients who appeared not to meet the legal criteria for mental illness, or were borderline in this respect. More than psychiatrists might care to perceive, lawyers influence their decisions. We suggest that in this competition for authority there exists not necessarily an overt quarrel, but an uneasy peace which is sustained between the two professions, partly on the basis of the psychiatrists' unintended and unwitting trade-off of effective authority to the lawyers, in exchange for the privilege of ostensible authority in the carefully staged setting of the admission hearings. Some suggestive support for this speculation is provided by the manner in which one of the participating psychiatrists in our setting anxiously defended the contrary clinical impression, even to the extent of advising against our empirical examination of the question.

References

Blau, Peter M. and W. Richard Scott, 1962, Formal Organizations: A Comparative Approach. San Francisco: Chandler Publishing Co.

Davidson, Henry A., 1965, Forensic Psychiatry. New York: Ronald Press and Co.

Freidson, Eliot, 1966, "Client control and medical practice," in Scott, W. Richard and Edmund Volkart (eds.). Medical Care. New York: John Wiley and Sons.

Goode, William J., 1960, "Encroachment, charlatanism, and the emerging profession: psychology, sociology, and medicine." American Sociological Review 25 (December):902–914.

Group for the Advancement of Psychiatry, 1966, Laws Governing the Hospitalization of the Mentally Ill. Report No. 161.

Joint Commission on Mental Illness and Health, 1961, Action for Mental Health. New York: Basic Books.

Kutner, Luis, 1962, "The illusion of due process in commitment proceedings." Northwestern Law Review 57 (September):383–399.

Levinson, Daniel and Eugene Gallagher, 1964, Patienthood in the Mental Hospital. Boston: Houghton-Mifflin.

Miller, Dorothy and Michael Schwartz, 1966, "County lunacy commission hearings: some observations of commitments to a state mental hospital." Social Problems 14 (Summer):25–36.

Ohio Penal Code n.d. R. C. No. 5123.44.

Ross, Henry A., 1959, "Commitment of the mentally ill, problems of law policy." Michigan Law Review 57 (May):945–1018.

Scheff, Thomas J., 1966, Being Mentally Ill. Chicago: Aldine Publishing Company.

Szasz, Thomas, 1963, Law, Liberty and Psychiatry. New York: The Macmillan Company.

PART THREE

The Mental Hospital: Early Processing and Psychiatric Decisions

The first article by Goffman, in itself, provides an introduction to this section. Goffman's evocative description of the "moral career of the mental patient" summarizes the prehospital events in the life of the mental patient. In addition, it allows us to anticipate some of the events discussed in later sections as he describes how patients, once they enter the hospital, adjust to and cope with the hospital setting.

Goffman argues that the career of the prepatient can be seen as a process of extrusion from the community. The prepatient begins with the rights and relationships most of us possess, and by the time he enters the hospital, he is left with little of either. Goffman suggests that the career of the mental patient begins with a circuit of agents and agencies that participate in his passage from civilian life to that of a mental patient. These agents and agencies—which may include relatives, mental health professionals, and others—move him along what Goffman describes as a "betrayal funnel." The patient is passed from hand to hand and from relative to mental health professional until he ultimately finds himself in the psychiatric hospital. Goffman suggests that as he proceeds along the path, what is actually happening to him is subtly denied by everyone concerned as he moves ever closer to psychiatric hospitalization. Once in the mental hospital, the mental patient embarks on a new way of life, dictated to a large degree by the subculture of the hospital itself.

The paper by Goldman and his colleagues describes the experiences of two psychologists who, disguised as mental patients, had themselves admitted to a large state psychiatric hospital. One of the two psychologists was assigned to a treatment and the other to a custodial ward. Both experienced intense feelings of fear of being forgotten in the mental hospital or of being betrayed by their friends, and both suffered from intense boredom. They also found that minor events took on disproportionate significance. In addition, the lack of information about events in the outside world created considerable disorientation and confusion. Clearly, these effects were the result of the situation into which they placed themselves. It is possible that mental status examinations administered by psychiatrists may reveal disorientation, attributed to the patient's disorder rather than to the situation in which he finds himself.

The authors note that, from the perspective of the patient, the staff is divided into two groups. Professional personnel work a conventional eight-hour day and are seen as remote from the patient. On the other hand, the attendants who work around the clock in shifts are forced into closer relationships with the patients. These investigators found that in the acute treatment ward, an exchange system developed between the attendants and the patients. The attendants rewarded patients for help with minor duties which the attendants themselves did not have time to perform. This system of mutual reward placed the patients in a dependent position with respect to the attendants, and the authors feel that this dependency may have a great deal to do with the development of chronicity and institutionalization among the patients. The mutual-exchange system was much less obvious on the custodial ward where negative sanctions for noncooperation seemed to be the typical method of control. Goldman and his colleagues make it clear that the attendant is forced into a controlling role and forced to make the patients dependent on him. The demands of the attendants' jobs, understaffing, and other difficulties force them to utilize the patients in this way.

If a person is brought directly to the psychiatric hospital, he will be interviewed by the admitting staff who serve as the "gate keepers." What are the criteria for deciding whether or not to admit a person to a psychiatric hospital? The most obvious answer to this question is that those persons who are most severely disturbed will be admitted.

The paper by Mendel and Rapport suggests that this is not necessarily the case. They studied consecutive decisions made by social workers, psychologists, and psychiatrists to admit psychiatric patients to a large psychiatric facility. In examining the basis on which decisions were made, they found that it was not the severity of symptoms but whether or not the person had been previously hospitalized that determined whether he would be hospitalized. However, it is of interest to note that the decision-makers themselves believed that they were making decisions on the basis of severity of symptoms even though it could be shown that they were not doing so.

The study by Mendel and Rapport thus suggests that the decision to hospitalize a person is influenced by previously made decisions to hospitalize him and not his apparent need for hospitalization. One implication of this finding is that there may be a kind of "spiral effect" operating in the career of mental patients. The simple fact that they have been hospitalized before markedly increases the possibility that they will be hospitalized again, because previous hospitalization operates as an implicit criterion for future hospitalization.

The paper by Scheff examines the decision rules used in medicine to determine whether a person should receive treatment or not. Scheff concludes that the operative decision rule in medical practice takes the form: "Better to treat an individual who is not sick than to fail to treat a person who might be ill." The psychiatrist's implicit rule is "when in doubt, continue to suspect and treat illness."

In the case of physical diseases, this sort of bias may benefit the patient, but in the case of abnormal behavior, the application of this decision rule may have very different effects. Scheff suggests that it is possible that physicians may actually be "creating" cases of mental illness by applying this medical decision rule to psychiatric practice.

Once the patient has been admitted to the hospital, it is very likely that he will be examined by a psychiatrist or psychologist and a decision will be made about his diagnosis. Often the final decision about an individual's diagnosis will be made in a large staff meeting attended by psychiatrists, psychologists, and social workers.

The usual assumption is that the patient's psychological history, his current behavior, and possibly psychological test results will form the basis for diagnosis. This may often be the case, but the article by Temerlin shows that the mere suggestion by a prestigeful psychiatric colleague can markedly bias the diagnosis. Temerlin presented a recorded interview by a trained actor carefully designed to portray a psychologically healthy man to psychiatrists, clinical psychologists, and graduate students in clinical psychology. When a prestigeful psychiatrist suggested that the individual might actually be psychotic, Temerlin found that this suggestion had a marked effect on the diagnosis produced by all three groups.

Temerlin has uncovered yet another variable that may contribute to the "pathological bias" manifested in mental health professionals' diagnoses. It is quite possible that this pathological bias, whatever its source, may actually contribute to the longer hospital stay or custodial treatment of many patients who might benefit from early release from the hospital. Again we see that the patient's career can be affected by a variety of factors which have little to do with his psychological condition.

The Moral Career of the Mental Patient

Erving Goffman

Traditionally the term *career* has been reserved for those who expect to enjoy the rises laid out within a respectable profession. The term is coming to be used, however, in a broadened sense to refer to any social strand of any person's course through life. The perspective of natural history is taken: unique outcomes are neglected in favor of such changes over time as are basic and common to the members of a social category, although occurring independently to each of them. Such a career is not a thing that can be brilliant or disappointing; it can no more be a success than a failure. In this light, I want to consider the mental patient.

One value of the concept of career is its two-sidedness. One side is linked to internal matters held dearly and closely, such as image of self and felt identity; the other side concerns official position, jural relations, and style of life, and is part of a publicly accessible institutional complex. The concept of career, then, allows one to move back and forth between the personal and the public, between the self and its significant society, without having to rely overly for data upon what the person says he thinks he imagines himself to be.

This paper, then, is an exercise in the institutional approach to the study of self. The main concern will be with the *moral* aspects of career—that is, the regular sequence of changes that career entails in the person's self and in his framework of imagery for judging himself and others.[1]

Reprinted from *Psychiatry*, 1959, Vol. 22, 123–142. The study was conducted during 1955–56 under the auspices of the Laboratory of Socio-environmental Studies of the National Institute of Mental Health. I am grateful to the Laboratory Chief, John A. Clausen, and to Dr. Winifred Overholser, Superintendent, and the late Dr. Jay Hoffman, then First Assistant Physician of St. Elizabeth's Hospital, Washington, D.C., for the ideal cooperation they freely provided. A preliminary report is contained in Goffman, "Interpersonal Persuasion," pp. 117–193. In *Group Processes: Transactions of the Third Conference*, edited by Bertram Schaffner, New York, Josiah Macy, Jr., Foundation, 1957. A shorter version of this paper was presented at the Annual Meeting of the American Sociological Society, Washington, D.C., August, 1957.

[1] Material on moral career can be found in early social anthropological work on ceremonies of status, transition, and in classic social psychological

The category "mental patient" itself will be understood in one strictly sociological sense. In this perspective, the psychiatric view of a person becomes significant only in so far as this view itself alters his social fate—an alteration which seems to become fundamental in our society when, and only when, the person is put through the process of hospitalization.[2] I therefore exclude certain neighboring categories: the undiscovered candidates who would be judged "sick" by psychiatric standards but who never come to be viewed as such by themselves or others, although they may cause everyone a great deal of trouble;[3] the office patient whom a psychiatrist feels he can handle with drugs or shock on the outside; the mental client who engages in psychotherapeutic relationships. And I include anyone, however robust in temperament, who somehow gets caught up in the heavy machinery of mental hospital servicing. In this way the effects of being treated as a mental patient can be kept quite distinct from the effects upon a person's life of traits a clinician would view as psychopathological.[4] Persons who become mental hospital

---

descriptions of those spectacular changes in one's view of self that can accompany participation in social movements and sects. Recently new kinds of relevant data have been suggested by psychiatric interest in the problem of "identity" and sociological studies of work careers and "adult socialization."

[2] This point has recently been made by Elaine and John Cumming, *Closed Ranks:* Cambridge, Commonwealth Fund, Harvard Univ. Press, 1957; pp. 101–102: "Clinical experience supports the impression that many people define mental illness as 'That condition for which a person is treated in a mental hospital.' . . . Mental illness, it seems, is a condition which afflicts people who must go to a mental institution, but until they do almost anything they do is normal." Leila Deasy has pointed out to me the correspondence here with the situation in white collar crime. Of those who are detected in this activity, only the ones who do not manage to avoid going to prison find themselves accorded the social role of the criminal.

[3] Case records in mental hospitals are just now coming to be exploited to show the incredible amount of trouble a person may cause for himself and others before anyone begins to think about him psychiatrically, let alone take psychiatric action against him. See John A. Clausen and Marian Radke Yarrow, "Paths to the Mental Hospital," *J. Social Issues* (1955) 11:25–32; August B. Hollingshead and Frederick C. Redlich, *Social Class and Mental Illness*; New York, Wiley, 1958; pp. 173–174.

[4] An illustration of how this perspective may be taken to all forms of deviancy may be found in Edwin Lemert, *Social Pathology*; New York, McGraw-Hill, 1951: see especially pp. 74–76. A specific application to mental

patients vary widely in the kind and degree of illness that a psychiatrist would impute to them, and in the attributes by which laymen would describe them. But once started on the way, they are confronted by some importantly similar circumstances and respond to these in some importantly similar ways. Since these similarities do not come from mental illness, they would seem to occur in spite of it. It is thus a tribute to the power of social forces that the uniform status of mental patient can not only assure an aggregate of persons a common fate and eventually, because of this, a common character, but that this social reworking can be done upon what is perhaps the most obstinate diversity of human materials that can be brought together by society. Here there lacks only the frequent forming of a protective group-life by ex-patients to illustrate in full the classic cycle of response by which deviant sub-groupings are psychodynamically formed in society.

This general sociological perspective is heavily reinforced by one key finding of sociologically oriented students in mental-hospital research. As has been repeatedly shown in the study of non-literate societies, the awesomeness, distastefulness, and barbarity of a foreign culture can decrease to the degree that the student becomes familiar with the point of view to life that is taken by his subjects. Similarly, the student of mental hospitals can discover that the craziness or "sick behavior" claimed for the mental patient is by and large a product of the claimant's social distance from the situation that the patient is in, and is not primarily a product of mental illness. Whatever the refinements of the various patients' psychiatric diagnoses, and whatever the special ways in which social life on the "inside" is unique, the researcher can find that he is participating in a community not significantly different from any other he has studied.[5] Of course, while restricting himself to the off-ward grounds community of paroled patients, he may feel, as some patients do, that life in the locked wards is bizarre; and while on a locked admissions or con-

---

defectives may be found in Stewart E. Perry, "Some Theoretic Problems of Mental Deficiency and Their Action Implications," *Psychiatry* (1954) 17: 45–73; see especially p. 68.

[5] Conscientious objectors who voluntarily went to jail sometimes arrived at the same conclusion regarding criminal inmates. See, for example, Alfred Hassler, *Diary of a Self-made Convict*; Chicago, Regnery, 1954; p. 74.

valescent ward, he may feel that chronic "back" wards are socially crazy places. But he need only move his spheres of sympathetic participation to the "worst" ward in the hospital, and this, too, can come into social focus as a place with a livable and continuously meaningful social world. This in no way denies that he will find a minority in any ward or patient group that continues to seem quite beyond the capacity to follow rules of social organization, or that the orderly fulfillment of normative expectations in patient society is partly made possible by strategic measures that have somehow come to be institutionalized in mental hospitals.

The career of the mental patient falls popularly and naturalistically into three main phases: the period prior to entering the hospital, which I shall call the *prepatient phase*; the period in the hopsital, the *inpatient phase*; the period after discharge from the hospital, should this occur, namely, the *ex-patient phase*.[6] This paper will deal only with the first two phases.

The Prepatient Phase

A relatively small group of prepatients come into the mental hospital willingly, because of their own idea of what will be good for them, or because of wholehearted agreement with the relevant members of their family. Presumably these recruits have found themselves acting in a way which is evidence to them that they are losing their minds or losing control of themselves. This view of oneself would seem to be one of the most pervasively threatening things that can happen to the self in our society, especially since it is likely to occur at a time when the person is in any case sufficiently troubled to exhibit the kind of symptom which he himself can see. As Sullivan described it,

> What we discover in the self-system of a person undergoing schizophrenic change or schizophrenic processes, is then, in its simplest form, an extremely fear-marked puzzlement, consisting of the use of rather generalized and anything but exquisitely refined referential processes in an attempt to cope with what is

---

[6] This simple picture is complicated by the somewhat special experience of roughly a third of ex-patients—namely, readmission to the hospital, this being the recidivist or "repatient" phase.

essentially a failure at being human—a failure at being anything that one could respect as worth being.[7]

Coupled with the person's disintegrative re-evaluation of himself will be the new, almost equally pervasive circumstance of attempting to conceal from others what he takes to be the new fundamental facts about himself, and attempting to discover whether others, too, have discovered them.[8] Here I want to stress that perception of losing one's mind is based on culturally derived and socially engrained stereotypes as to the significance of symptoms such as hearing voices, losing temporal and spatial orientation, and sensing that one is being followed, and that many of the most spectacular and convincing of these symptoms in some instances psychiatrically signify merely a temporary emotional upset in a stressful situation, however terrifying to the person at the time. Similarly, the anxiety consequent upon this perception of oneself, and the strategies devised to reduce this anxiety, are not a product of abnormal psychology, but would be exhibited by any person socialized into our culture who came to conceive of himself as someone losing his mind. Interestingly, subcultures in American society apparently differ in the amount of ready imagery and encouragement they supply for such self-views, leading to differential rates of *self-referral*; the capacity to take this disintegrative view of oneself without psychiatric prompting seems to be one of the questionable cultural privileges of the upper classes.[9]

For the person who has come to see himself—with whatever justification—as mentally unbalanced, entrance to the mental hospital can sometimes bring relief, perhaps in part because of the sudden transformation in the structure of his basic social situa-

---

[7] Harry Stack Sullivan, *Clinical Studies in Psychiatry*, edited by Helen Swick Perry, Mary Ladd Gawel, and Martha Gibbon (New York: Norton, 1956), pp. 184–185.

[8] This moral experience can be contrasted with that of a person learning to become a marihuana addict, whose discovery that he can be "high" and still "op" effectively without being detected apparently leads to a new level of use. See Howard S. Becker, "Marihuana Use and Social Control," *Social Problems*, III (1955), pp. 35–44; see especially pp. 40–41.

[9] See Hollingshead and Redlich, *op. cit.*, p. 187, Table 6, where relative frequency is given of self-referral by social class grouping.

tion; instead of being to himself a questionable person trying to maintain a role as a full one, he can become an officially questioned person known to himself to be not so questionable as that. In other cases, hospitalization can make matters worse for the willing patient, confirming by the objective situation what has theretofore been a matter of the private experience of self.

Once the willing prepatient enters the hospital, he may go through the same routine of experiences as do those who enter unwillingly. In any case, it is the latter that I mainly want to consider, since in America at present these are by far the more numerous kind.[10] Their approach to the institution takes one of three classic forms: they come because they have been implored by their family or threatened with the abrogation of family ties unless they go "willingly"; they come by force under police escort; they come under misapprehension purposely induced by others, this last restricted mainly to youthful prepatients.

The prepatient's career may be seen in terms of an extrusory model; he starts out with relationships and rights, and ends up, at the beginning of his hospital stay, with hardly any of either. The moral aspects of this career, then, typically begin with the experience of abandonment, disloyalty, and embitterment. This is the case even though to others it may be obvious that he was in need of treatment, and even though in the hospital he may soon come to agree.

The case histories of most mental patients document offenses against some arrangement for face-to-face living—a domestic establishment, a work place, a semi-public organization such as a church or store, a public region such as a street or park. Often there is also a record of some *complainant*, some figure who takes that action against the offender which eventually leads to his hospitalization. This may not be the person who makes the first move, but it is the person who makes what turns out to be the first effective move. Here is the *social* beginning of the patient's career, regardless of where one might locate the psychological beginning of his mental illness.

---

[10] The distinction employed here between willing and unwilling patients cuts across the legal one of voluntary and committed, since some persons who are glad to come to the mental hospital may be legally committed, and of those who come only because of strong familial pressure, some may sign themselves in as voluntary patients.

The kinds of offenses which lead to hospitalization are felt to differ in nature from those which lead to other extrusory consequences—to imprisonment, divorce, loss of job, disownment, regional exile, non-institutional psychiatric treatment, and so forth. But little seems known about these differentiating factors; and when one studies actual commitments, alternate outcomes frequently appear to have been possible. It seems true, moreover, that for every offense that leads to an effective complaint, there are many psychiatrically similar ones that never do. No action is taken; or action is taken which leads to other extrusory outcomes; or ineffective action is taken, leading to the mere pacifying or putting off of the person who complains. Thus, as Clausen and Yarrow have nicely shown, even offenders who are eventually hospitalized are likely to have had a long series of ineffective actions taken against them.[11]

Separating those offenses which could have been used as grounds for hospitalizing the offender from those that are so used, one finds a vast number of what students of occupation call career contingencies.[12] Some of these contingencies in the mental patient's career have been suggested, if not explored, such as socio-economic status, visibility of the offense, proximity to a mental hospital, amount of treatment facilities available, community regard for the type of treatment given in available hospitals, and so on.[13] For information about other contingencies one must rely on atrocity tales: a psychotic man is tolerated by his wife until she finds herself a boy friend, or by his adult children until they move from a house to an apartment; an alcoholic is sent to a mental hospital because the jail is full, and a drug addict because he declines to avail himself of psychiatric treatment on the outside; a rebellious adolescent daughter can no longer be managed at home because she now threatens to have an open

---

[11] Clausen and Yarrow, *op. cit.*

[12] An explicit application of this notion to the field of mental health may be found in Edwin Lemert, "Legal Commitment and Social Control," *Sociology and Social Research*, XXX (1946), pp. 370–378.

[13] For example, Jerome K. Meyers and Leslie Schaffer, "Social Stratification and Psychiatric Practice: A Study of an Outpatient Clinic," *American Sociological Review*, XIX (1954), pp. 307–310; Lemert, *op. cit.*, pp. 402–403; *Patients in Mental Institutions, 1941* (Washington, D.C.: Department of Commerce, Bureau of the Census, 1941), p. 2.

affair with an unsuitable companion; and so on. Correspondingly there is an equally important set of contingencies causing the person to by-pass this fate. And should the person enter the hospital, still another set of contingencies will help determine when he is to obtain a discharge—such as the desire of his family for his return, the availability of a "manageable" job, and so on. The society's official view is that inmates of mental hospitals are there primarily because they are suffering from mental illness. However, in the degree that the "mentally ill" outside hospitals numerically approach or surpass those inside hospitals, one could say that mental patients *distinctively* suffer not from mental illness, but from contingencies.

Career contingencies occur in conjunction with a second feature of the prepatient's career—the *circuit of agents*—and agencies—that participate fatefully in his passage from civilian to patient status.[14] Here is an instance of that increasingly important class of social system whose elements are agents and agencies which are brought into systemic connection through having to take up and send on the same persons. Some of these agent roles will be cited now, with the understanding that in any concrete circuit a role may be filled more than once, and that the same person may fill more than one of them.

First is the *next-of-relation*—the person whom the prepatient sees as the most available of those upon whom he should be able to depend most in times of trouble, in this instance the last to doubt his sanity and the first to have done everything to save him from the fate which, it transpires, he has been approaching. The patient's next-of-relation is usually his next of kin; the special term is introduced because he need not be. Second is the *complainant*, the person who retrospectively appears to have started the person on his way to the hospital. Third are the *mediators*—the sequence of agents and agencies to which the prepatient is referred and through which he is relayed and processed on his way to the hospital. Here are included police, clergy, general medical practitioners, office psychiatrists, personnel in public clinics, lawyers, social service workers, schoolteachers, and so on.

---

[14] For one circuit of agents and its bearing on career contingencies, see Oswald Hall, "The Stages of a Medical Career," *American Journal of Sociology*, LIII (1948), pp. 327–336.

One of these agents will have the legal mandate to sanction commitment and will exercise it, and so those agents who precede him in the process will be involved in something whose outcome is not yet settled. When the mediators retire from the scene, the prepatient has become an inpatient, and the significant agent has become the hospital administrator.

While the complainant usually takes action in a lay capacity as a citizen, an employer, a neighbor, or a kinsman, mediators tend to be specialists and differ from those they serve in significant ways. They have experience in handling trouble, and some professional distance from what they handle. Except in the case of policemen, and perhaps some clergy, they tend to be more psychiatrically oriented than the lay public, and will see the need for treatment at times when the public does not.[15]

An interesting feature of these roles is the functional effects of their interdigitation. For example, the feelings of the patient will be influenced by whether or not the person who fills the role of complainant also has the role of next-of-relation—an embarrassing combination more prevalent, apparently, in the higher classes than in the lower.[16] Some of these emergent effects will be considered now.[17]

In the prepatient's progress from home to the hospital he may participate as a third person in what he may come to experience as a kind of *alienative coalition.* His next-of-relation presses him into coming to "talk things over" with a medical practitioner, an office psychiatrist, or some other counselor. Disinclination on his part may be met by threatening him with desertion, disownment, or other legal action, or by stressing the joint and exploratory nature of the interview. But typically the next-of-relation will have set the interview up, in the sense of selecting the profes-

---

[15] See Cumming and Cumming, *op. cit.*, p. 92.

[16] Hollingshead and Redlich, *op. cit.*, p. 187.

[17] For an analysis of some of these circuit implications for the inpatient, see Leila Deasy and Olive W. Quinn, "The Wife of the Mental Patient and the Hospital Psychiatrist," *Journal of Social Issues,* XI (1955), pp. 49–60. An interesting illustration of this kind of analysis may also be found in Alan G. Gowman, "Blindness and the Role of the Companion," *Social Problems,* IV (1956), pp. 68–75. A general statement may be found in Robert Merton, "The Role Set: Problems in Sociological Theory," *British Journal of Sociology,* VIII (1957), pp. 106–120.

sional, arranging for time, telling the professional something about the case, and so on. This move effectively tends to establish the next-of-relation as the responsible person to whom pertinent findings can be divulged, while effectively establishing the other as the patient. The prepatient often goes to the interview with the understanding that he is going as an equal of someone who is so bound together with him that a third person could not come between them in fundamental matters; this, after all, is one way in which close relationships are defined in our society. Upon arrival at the office the prepatient suddenly finds that he and his next-of-relation have not been accorded the same roles, and apparently that a prior understanding between the professional and the next-of-relation has been put in operation against him. In the extreme but common case, the professional first sees the prepatient alone, in the role of examiner and diagnostician, and then sees the next-of-relation alone, in the role of adviser, while carefully avoiding talking things over seriously with them both together.[18] And even in those non-consultative cases where public officials must forcibly extract a person from a family that wants to tolerate him, the next-of-relation is likely to be induced to "go along" with the official action, so that even here the prepatient may feel that an alienative coalition has been formed against him.

The moral experience of being a third man in such a coalition is likely to embitter the prepatient, especially since his troubles have already probably led to some estrangement from his next-of-relation. After he enters the hospital, continued visits by his next-of-relation can give the patient the "insight" that his own best interests were being served. But the initial visits may temporarily strengthen his feeling of abandonment; he is likely to beg his visitor to get him out or at least to get him more privileges and to sympathize with the monstrousness of his plight—to which the visitor ordinarily can respond only by trying to maintain a hopeful note, by not "hearing" the requests, or by assuring the patient that the medical authorities know about these things and are doing what is medically best. The visitor then nonchalantly goes back into a world that the patient has learned is incredibly

---

[18] I have one case record of a man who claims he thought *he* was taking his wife to see the psychiatrist, not realizing until too late that his wife had made the arrangements.

thick with freedom and privileges, causing the patient to feel that his next-of-relation is merely adding a pious gloss to a clear case of traitorous desertion.

The depth to which the patient may feel betrayed by his next-of-relation seems to be increased by the fact that another witnesses his betrayal—a factor which is apparently significant in many three-party situations. An offended person may well act forbearantly and accommodatively toward an offender when the two are alone, choosing peace ahead of justice. The presence of a witness, however, seems to add something to the implications of the offense. For then it is beyond the power of the offended and offender to forget about, erase, or suppress what has happened; the offense has become a public social fact.[19] When the witness is a mental health commission, as is sometimes the case, the witnessed betrayal can verge on a "degradation ceremony."[20] In such circumstances, the offended patient may feel that some kind of extensive reparative action is required before witnesses, if his honor and social weight are to be restored.

Two other aspects of sensed betrayal should be mentioned. First, those who suggest the possibility of another's entering a mental hospital are not likely to provide a realistic picture of how in fact it may strike him when he arrives. Often he is told that he will get required medical treatment and a rest, and may well be out in a few months or so. In some cases they may thus be concealing what they know, but I think, in general, they will be telling what they see as the truth. For here there is quite relevant difference between patients and mediating professionals; mediators, more so than the public at large, may conceive of mental hospitals as short-term medical establishments where required rest and attention can be voluntarily obtained, and not as places of coerced exile. When the prepatient finally arrives he is likely to learn quite quickly, quite differently. He then finds that the information given him about life in the hospital has had the effect of his having put up less resistance to entering than he now sees he would have put up had he known the facts. Whatever the

---

[19] A paraphrase from Kurt Riezler, "Comment on the Social Psychology of Shame," *American Journal of Sociology*, XLVIII (1943), p. 458.

[20] See Harold Garfinkel, "Conditions of Successful Degradation Ceremonies," *American Journal of Sociology*, LXI (1956), pp. 420–424.

intentions of those who participated in his transition from person to patient, he may sense they have in effect "conned" him into his present predicament.

I am suggesting that the prepatient starts out with at least a portion of the rights, liberties, and satisfactions of the civilian and ends up on a psychiatric ward stripped of almost everything. The question here is *how* this stripping is managed. This is the second aspect of betrayal I want to consider.

As the prepatient may see it, the circuit of significant figures can function as a kind of *betrayal funnel*. Passage from person to patient may be effected through a series of linked stages, each managed by a different agent. While each stage tends to bring a sharp decrease in adult free status, each agent may try to maintain the fiction that no further decrease will occur: He may even manage to turn the prepatient over to the next agent while sustaining this note. Further, through words, cues, and gestures, the prepatient is implicitly asked by the current agent to join with him in sustaining a running line of polite small talk that tactfully avoids the administrative facts of the situation, becoming, with each stage, progressively more at odds with these facts. The spouse would rather not have to try to get the prepatient to visit a psychiatrist; psychiatrists would rather not have a scene when the prepatient learns that he and his spouse are being seen separately and in different ways; the police infrequently bring a prepatient to the hospital in a strait jacket, finding it much easier all around to give him a cigarette, some kindly words, and freedom to relax in the back seat of the patrol car; and finally, the admitting psychiatrist finds he can do his work better in the relative quiet and luxury of the "admission suite" where, as an incidental consequence, the notion can survive that a mental hospital is indeed a comforting place. If the prepatient heeds all of these implied requests and is reasonably decent about the whole thing, he can travel the whole circuit from home to hospital without forcing anyone to look directly at what is happening or to deal with the raw emotion that his situation might well cause him to express. His showing consideration for those who are moving him toward the hospital allows them to show consideration for him, with the joint result that these interactions can be sustained with some of the protective harmony characteristic of ordinary face-to-face dealings. But should the new patient cast his mind back over the sequence of steps leading to hospitalization, he may feel that everyone's *current* comfort was being busily sustained while his long-range welfare was being undermined. This realization may constitute a moral experience that further separates him for the time from the people on the outside.[21]

I would now like to look at the circuit of career agents from the point of view of the agents themselves. Mediators in the person's transition from civil to patient status—as well as his keepers, once he is in the hospital—have an interest in establishing a responsible next-of-relation as the patient's deputy or *guardian*; should there be no obvious candidate for the role, someone may be sought out and pressed into it. Thus while a person is gradually being transformed into a patient, a next-of-relation is gradually being transformed into a guardian. With a guardian on the scene, the whole transition process can be kept tidy. He is likely to be familiar with the prepatient's civil involvements and business, and can tie up loose ends that might otherwise be left to entangle the hospital. Some of the prepatient's abrogated civil rights can be transferred to him, thus helping to sustain the legal fiction that while the prepatient does not actually have his rights he somehow actually has not lost them.

Inpatients commonly sense, at least for a time, that hospitalization is a massive unjust deprivation, and sometimes succeed in convincing a few persons on the outside that this is the case. It often turns out to be useful, then, for those identified with inflicting these deprivations, however justifiably, to be able to point to the co-operation and agreement of someone whose relationship

---

[21] Concentration-camp practices provide a good example of the function of the betrayal funnel in inducing co-operation and reducing struggle and fuss, although here the mediators could not be said to be acting in the best interests of the inmates. Police picking up persons from their homes would sometimes joke good-naturedly and offer to wait while coffee was being served. Gas chambers were fitted out like delousing rooms, and victims taking off their clothes were told to note where they were leaving them. The sick, aged, weak, or insane who were selected for extermination were sometimes driven away in Red Cross ambulances to camps referred to by terms such as "observation hospital." See David Boder, *I Did Not Interview the Dead* (Urbana: University of Illinois Press, 1949), p. 81; and Ellie A. Cohen, *Human Behavior in the Concentration Camp* (London: Jonathan Cape, 1954), pp. 32, 37, 107.

to the patient places him above suspicion, firmly defining him as the person most likely to have the patient's personal interest at heart. If the guardian is satisfied with what is happening to the new inpatient, the world ought to be.[22]

Now it would seem that the greater the legitimate personal stake one party has in another, the better he can take the role of guardian to the other. But the structural arrangements in society which lead to the acknowledged merging of two persons' interests lead to additional consequences. For the person to whom the patient turns for help—for protection against such threats as involuntary commitment—is just the person to whom the mediators and hospital administrators logically turn for authorization. It is understandable, then, that some patients will come to sense, at least for a time, that the closeness of a relationship tells nothing of its trustworthiness.

There are still other functional effects emerging from this complement of roles. If and when the next-of-relation appeals to mediators for help in the trouble he is having with the prepatient, hospitalization may not, in fact, be in his mind. He may not even perceive the prepatient as mentally sick, or, if he does, he may not consistently hold to this view.[23] It is the circuit of mediators, with their greater psychiatric sophistication and their belief in the medical character of mental hospitals, that will often define the situation for the next-of-relation, assuring him that hospitalization is a possible solution and a good one, that it involves no betrayal, but is rather a medical action taken in the best interests of the prepatient. Here the next-of-relation may learn that doing his duty to the prepatient may cause the prepatient to distrust and even hate him for the time. But the fact that this course of action may have had to be pointed out and prescribed by pro-

---

[22] Interviews collected by the Clausen group at NIMH suggest that when a wife comes to be a guardian, the responsibility may disrupt previous distance from in-laws, leading either to a new supportive coalition with them or to a marked withdrawal from them.

[23] For an analysis of these nonpsychiatric kinds of perception, see Marian Radke Yarrow, Charlotte Green Schwartz, Harriet S. Murphy, and Leila Deasy, "The Psychological Meaning of Mental Illness in the Family," *Journal of Social Issues,* XI (1955), pp. 12–24; Charlotte Green Schwartz, "Perspectives on Deviance—Wives' Definitions of their Husbands' Mental Illness," *Psychiatry,* XX (1957), pp. 275–291.

fessionals, and be defined by them as a moral duty, relieves the next-of-relation of some of the guilt he may feel.[24] It is a poignant fact that an adult son or daughter may be pressed into the role of mediator, so that the hostility that might otherwise be directed against the spouse is passed on to the child.[25]

Once the prepatient is in the hospital, the same guilt-carrying function may become a significant part of the staff's job in regard to the next-of-relation.[26] These reasons for feeling that he himself has not betrayed the patient, even though the patient may then think so, can later provide the next-of-relation with a defensible line to take when visiting the patient in the hospital and a basis for hoping that the relationship can be re-established after its hospital moratorium. And of course this position, when sensed by the patient, can provide him with excuses for the next-of-relation, when and if he comes to look for them.[27]

Thus while the next-of-relation can perform important functions for the mediators and hospital administrators, they in turn can perform important functions for him. One finds, then, an emergent unintended exchange or reciprocation of functions, these functions themselves being often unintended.

The final point I want to consider about the prepatient's moral career is its peculiarly *retroactive* character. Until a person actually arrives at the hospital there usually seems no way of knowing for sure that he is destined to do so, given the determinative role

---

[24] This guilt-carrying function is found, of course, in other role complexes. Thus, when a middle-class couple engages in the process of legal separation or divorce, each of their lawyers usually takes the position that his job is to acquaint his client with all of the potential claims and rights, pressing his client into demanding these, in spite of any nicety of feelings about the rights and honorableness of the ex-partner. The client, in all good faith, can then say to self and to the ex-partner that the demands are being made only because the lawyer insists it is best to do so.

[25] Recorded in the Clausen data.

[26] This point is made by Cumming and Cumming, *op. cit.*, p. 129.

[27] There is an interesting contrast here with the moral career of the tuberculosis patient. I am told by Julius Roth that tuberculosis patients are likely to come to the hospital willingly, agreeing with their next-of-relation about treatment. Later in their hospital career, when they learn how long they yet have to stay and how depriving and irrational some of the hospital rulings are, they may seek to leave, be advised against this by the staff and by relatives, and only then begin to feel betrayed.

of career contingencies. And until the point of hospitalization is reached, he or others may not conceive of him as a person who is becoming a mental patient. However, since he will be held against his will in the hospital, his next-of-relation and the hospital staff will be in great need of a rationale for the hardships they are sponsoring. The medical elements of the staff will also need evidence that they are still in the trade they were trained for. These problems are eased, no doubt unintentionally, by the case-history construction that is placed on the patient's past life, this having the effect of demonstrating that all along he had been becoming sick, that he finally became very sick, and that if he had not been hospitalized much worse things would have happened to him—all of which, of course, may be true. Incidentally, if the patient wants to make sense out of his stay in the hospital, and, as already suggested, keep alive the possibility of once again conceiving of his next-of-relation as a decent, well-meaning person, then he, too, will have reason to believe some of this psychiatric work-up of his past.

Here is a very ticklish point for the sociology of careers. An important aspect of every career is the view the person constructs when he looks backward over his progress; in a sense, however, the whole of the prepatient career derives from this reconstruction. The fact of having had a prepatient career, starting with an effective complaint, becomes an important part of the mental patient's orientation, but this part can begin to be played only after hospitalization proves that what he had been having, but no longer has, is a career as a prepatient.

The Inpatient Phase

The last step in the prepatient's career can involve his realization—justified or not—that he has been deserted by society and turned out of relationships by those closest to him. Interestingly enough, the patient, especially a first admission, may manage to keep himself from coming to the end of this trail, even though in fact he is now in a locked mental-hospital ward. On entering the hospital, he may very strongly feel the desire not to be known to anyone as a person who could possibly be reduced to these present circumstances, or as a person who conducted himself in the way he did prior to commitment. Consequently, he may avoid talking to anyone, may stay by himself when possible, and may even be "out of contact" or "manic" so as to avoid ratifying any interaction that presses a politely reciprocal role upon him and opens him up to what he has become in the eyes of others. When the next-of-relation makes an effort to visit, he may be rejected by mutism, or by the patient's refusal to enter the visiting room, these strategies sometimes suggesting that the patient still clings to a remnant of relatedness to those who made up his past, and is protecting this remnant from the final destructiveness of dealing with the new people that they have become.[28]

Usually the patient comes to give up this taxing effort at anonymity, at not-hereness, and begins to present himself for conventional social interaction to the hospital community. Thereafter he withdraws only in special ways—by always using his nickname, by signing his contribution to the patient weekly with his initial only, or by using the innocuous "cover" address tactfully provided by some hospitals; or he withdraws only at special times, when, say, a flock of nursing students makes a passing tour of the ward, or when, paroled to the hospital grounds, he suddenly sees he is about to cross the path of a civilian he happens to know from home. Sometimes this making of oneself available is called "settling down" by the attendants. It marks a new stand openly taken and supported by the patient, and resembles the "coming-out" process that occurs in other groupings.[29]

---

[28] The inmate's initial strategy of holding himself aloof from ratifying contact may partly account for the relative lack of group formation among inmates in public mental hospitals, a connection that has been suggested to me by William R. Smith. The desire to avoid personal bonds that would give licence to the asking of biographical questions could also be a factor. In mental hospitals, of course, as in prisoner camps, the staff may consciously break up incipient group formation in order to avoid collective rebellious action and other ward disturbances.

[29] A comparable coming out occurs in the homosexual world, when a person finally comes frankly to present himself to a "gay" gathering not as a tourist but as someone who is "available." See Evelyn Hooker, "A Preliminary Analysis of Group Behavior of Homosexuals," *Journal of Psychology*, XLII (1956), pp. 217–225; see especially p. 221. A good fictionalized treatment may be found in James Baldwin's *Giovanni's Room* (New York: Dial, 1956), pp. 41–57. A familiar instance of the coming-out process is no

Once the prepatient begins to settle down, the main outlines of his fate tend to follow those of a whole class of segregated establishments—jails, concentration camps, monasteries, work camps, and so on—in which the inmate spends the whole round of life on the grounds, and marches through his regimented day in the immediate company of a group of persons of his own institutional status.[30]

Like the neophyte in many of these total institutions, the new inpatient finds himself cleanly stripped of many of his accustomed affirmations, satisfactions, and defenses, and is subjected to a rather full set of mortifying experiences: restriction of free movement, communal living, diffuse authority of a whole echelon of people, and so on. Here one begins to learn about the limited extent to which a conception of oneself can be sustained when the usual setting of supports for it are suddenly removed.

While undergoing these humbling moral experiences, the inpatient learns to orient himself in terms of the "ward system."[31] In public mental hospitals this usually consists of a series of graded living arrangements built around wards, administrative units called services, and parole status. The "worst" level involves nothing but wooden benches to sit on, some quite indifferent food, and a small piece of room to sleep in. The "best" level may involve a room of one's own, ground and town privileges, contacts with staff that are relatively undamaging, and what is seen as good food and ample recreational facilities. For disobeying the pervasive house rules, the inmate will receive stringent punishments expressed in terms of loss of privileges; for obedience he

---

doubt to be found among prepubertal children at the moment one of these actors sidles *back* into a room that had been left in an angered huff and injured *amour propre*. The phrase itself presumably derives from a *rite-de-passage* ceremony once arranged by upper-class mothers for their daughters. Interestingly enough, in large mental hospitals the patient sometimes symbolizes a complete coming out by his first active participation in the hospital-wide patient dance.

[30] See Goffman, "Characteristics of Total Institutions," pp. 43–84; in *Proceedings of the Symposium of Preventive and Social Psychiatry*; Washington, D.C., Walter Reed Army Institute of Research, 1958.

[31] A good description of the ward system may be found in Ivan Belknap, *Human Problems of a State Mental Hospital* (New York: McGraw-Hill, 1956), ch. ix, especially p. 164.

will eventually be allowed to reacquire some of the minor satisfactions he took for granted on the outside.

The institutionalization of these radically different levels of living throws light on the implications for self of social settings. And this in turn affirms that the self arises not merely out of its possessor's interactions with significant others, but also out of the arrangements that are evolved in an organization for its members.

There are some settings that the person easily discounts as an expression or extension of him. When a tourist goes slumming, he may take pleasure in the situation not because it is a reflection of him but because it so assuredly is not. There are other settings, such as living rooms, which the person manages on his own and employs to influence in a favorable direction other persons' views of him. And there are still other settings, such as a work place, which express the employee's occupational status, but over which he has no final control, this being exerted, however tactfully, by his employer. Mental hospitals provide an extreme instance of this latter possibility. And this is due not merely to their uniquely degraded living levels, but also to the unique way in which significance for self is made explicit to the patient, piercingly, persistently, and thoroughly. Once lodged on a given ward, the patient is firmly instructed that the restrictions and deprivations he encounters are not due to such blind forces as tradition or economy—and hence dissociable from self—but are intentional parts of his treatment, part of his need at the time, and therefore an expression of the state that his self has fallen to. Having every reason to initiate requests for better conditions, he is told that when the staff feel he is "able to manage" or will be "comfortable with" a higher ward level, then appropriate action will be taken. In short, assignment to a given ward is presented not as a reward or punishment, but as an expression of his general level of social functioning, his status as a person. Given the fact that the worst ward levels provide a round of life that inpatients with organic brain damage can easily manage, and that these quite limited human beings are present to prove it, one can appreciate some of the mirroring effects of the hospital.[32]

---

[32] Here is one way in which mental hospitals can be worse than concentration camps and prisons as places in which to "do" time; in the latter, self-insulation from the symbolic implications of the settings may be easier.

The ward system, then, is an extreme instance of how the physical facts of an establishment can be explicitly employed to frame the conception a person takes of himself. In addition, the official psychiatric mandate of mental hospitals gives rise to even more direct, even more blatant, attacks upon the inmate's view of himself. The more "medical" and the more progressive a mental hospital is—the more it attempts to be therapeutic and not merely custodial—the more he may be confronted by high-ranking staff arguing that his past has been a failure, that the cause of this has been within himself, that his attitude to life is wrong, and that if he wants to be a person he will have to change his way of dealing with people and his conceptions of himself. Often the moral value of these verbal assaults will be brought home to him by requiring him to practice taking this psychiatric view of himself in arranged confessional periods, whether in private sessions or group psychotherapy.

Now a general point may be made about the moral career of inpatients which has bearing on many moral careers. Given the stage that any person has reached in a career, one typically finds that he constructs an image of his life course—past, present, and future—which selects, abstracts, and distorts in such a way as to provide him with a view of himself that he can usefully expound in current situations. Quite generally, the person's line concerning self defensively brings him into appropriate alignment with the basic values of his society, and so may be called an *apologia*. If the person can manage to present a view of his current situation which shows the operation of favorable personal qualities in the past and a favorable destiny awaiting him, it may be called a *success story*. If the facts of a person's past and present are extremely dismal, then about the best he can do is to show that he is not responsible for what has become of him, and the term *sad tale* is appropriate. Interestingly enough, the more the person's past forces him out of apparent alignment with central moral values, the more often he seems compelled to tell his sad tale in any company in which he finds himself. Perhaps he partly responds to the need he feels in others of not having their sense of proper life courses affronted. In any case, it is among convicts, "winos," and prostitutes that one seems to obtain sad tales the

---

In fact, self-insulation from hospital settings may be so difficult that patients have to employ devices for this which staff interpret as psychotic symptoms.

most readily.[33] It is the vicissitudes of the mental patient's sad tale that I want to consider now.

In the mental hospital, the setting and the house rules press home to the patient that he is, after all, a mental case who has suffered some kind of social collapse on the outside, having failed in some over-all way, and that here he is of little social weight, being hardly capable of acting like a full-fledged person at all. These humiliations are likely to be most keenly felt by middle-class patients, since their previous condition of life little immunizes them against such affronts, but all patients feel some downgrading. Just as any normal behavior of his outside subculture would do, the patient often responds to this situation by attempting to assert a sad tale proving that he is not "sick," that the "little trouble" he did get into was really somebody else's fault, that his past life course had some honor and rectitude, and that the hospital is therefore unjust in forcing the status of mental patient upon him. This self-respecting tendency is heavily institutionalized within the patient society where opening social contacts typically involve the participants' volunteering information about their current ward location and length of stay so far, but not the reasons for their stay—such interaction being conducted

---

[33] In regard to convicts, see Anthony Heckstall-Smith, *Eighteen Months* (London: Allan Wingate, 1954), pp. 52–53. For "winos" see the discussion in Howard G. Bain, "A Sociological Analysis of the Chicago Skid-Row Lifeway" (Unpublished M.A. thesis, Department of Sociology, University of Chicago, September 1950), especially "The Rationale of the Skid-Row Drinking Group," pp. 141–146. Bain's neglected thesis is a useful source of material on moral careers.

Apparently one of the occupational hazards of prostitution is that clients and other professional contacts sometimes persist in expressing sympathy by asking for a defensible dramatic explanation for the fall from grace. In having to bother to have a sad tale ready, perhaps the prostitute is more to be pitied than damned. Good examples of prostitutes sad tales may be found in Henry Mahew, *London Labour and the London Poor*, Vol. IV, *Those That Will Not Work* (London: Charles Griffin and Co., 1862), pp. 210–272. For a contemporary source, see *Women of the Streets*, edited by C. H. Rolph (London: Secker and Warburg, 1955), especially p. 6: *"Almost always, however, after a few comments on the police, the girl would begin to explain how it was that she was in the life, usually in terms of self-justification. . . ."* Lately, of course, the psychological expert has helped out the profession in the construction of wholly remarkable sad tales. See, for example, Harold Greenwald, *The Call Girl* (New York: Ballantine Books, 1958).

in the manner of small talk on the outside.[34] With greater famil-
iarity, each patient usually volunteers relatively acceptable reasons for his hospitalization, at the same time accepting without
open immediate question the lines offered by other patients. Such
stories as the following are given and overtly accepted.

> I was going to night school to get a M.A. degree, and holding
> down a job in addition, and the load got too much for me.

> The others here are sick mentally but I'm suffering from a bad
> nervous system and that is what is giving me these phobias.

> I got here by mistake because of a diabetes diagnosis, and I'll
> leave in a couple of days. [The patient had been in seven weeks.]

> I failed as a child, and later with my wife I reached out for
> dependency.

> My trouble is that I can't work. That's what I'm in for. I had two
> jobs with a good home and all the money I wanted.[35]

The patient sometimes reinforces these stories by an optimistic
definition of his occupational status. A man who managed to obtain an audition as a radio announcer styles himself a radio announcer; another who worked for some months as a copy boy
and was then given a job as a reporter on a large trade journal,
but fired after three weeks, defines himself as a reporter.

A whole social role in the patient community may be constructed on the basis of these reciprocally sustained fictions. For
these face-to-face niceties tend to be qualified by behind-the-back
gossip that comes only a degree closer to the "objective" facts.
Here, of course, one can see a classic social function of informal
networks of equals: they serve as one another's audience for self-
supporting tales—tales that are somewhat more solid than pure
fantasy and somewhat thinner than the facts.

---

[34] A similar self-protecting rule has been observed in prisons. Thus, Alfred
Hassler, *Diary of a Self-Made Convict* (Chicago: Regnery, 1954), p. 76, in
describing a conversation with a fellow prisoner: *"He didn't say much about
why he was sentenced, and I didn't ask him, that being the accepted behavior in prison."* A novelistic version for the mental hospital may be found
in J. Kerkhoff, *How Thin the Veil: A Newspaperman's Story of His Own
Mental Crack-up and Recovery* (New York: Greenberg, 1952), p. 27.

[35] From the writer's field notes of informal interaction with patients, tran-
scribed as nearly verbatim as he was able.

But the patient's *apologia* is called forth in a unique setting, for few settings could be so destructive of self-stories except, of course, those stories already constructed along psychiatric lines. And this destructiveness rests on more than the official sheet of paper which attests that the patient is of unsound mind, a danger to himself and others—an attestation, incidentally, which seems to cut deeply into the patient's pride, and into the possibility of his having any.

Certainly the degrading conditions of the hospital setting belie many of the self-stories that are presented by patients, and the very fact of being in the mental hospital is evidence against these tales. And of course there is not always sufficient patient solidarity to prevent patient discrediting patient, just as there is not always a sufficient number of "professionalized" attendants to prevent attendant discrediting patient. As one patient informant repeatedly suggested to a fellow patient: "If you're so smart, how come you got your ass in here?"

The mental-hospital setting, however, is more treacherous still. Staff have much to gain through discreditings of the patient's story—whatever the felt reason for such discreditings. If the custodial faction in the hospital is to succeed in managing his daily round without complaint or trouble from him, then it will prove useful to be able to point out to him that the claims about himself upon which he rationalizes his demands are false, that he is not what he is claiming to be, and that in fact he is a failure as a person. If the psychiatric faction is to impress upon him its views about his personal make-up, then they must be able to show in detail how their version of his past and their version of his character hold up much better than his own.[36] If both the custodial and psychiatric factions are to get him to co-operate in

---

[36] The process of examining a person psychiatrically and then altering or reducing his status in consequence is known in hospital and prison parlance as bugging, the assumption being that once you come to the attention of the testers you either will automatically be labeled crazy or the process of testing itself will make you crazy. Thus psychiatric staff are sometimes seen not as discovering whether you are sick, but as making you sick; and "Don't bug me, man" can mean, "Don't pester me to the point where I'll get upset." Sheldon Messinger has suggested to me that this meaning of bugging is related to the other colloquial meaning, of wiring a room with a secret microphone to collect information usable for discrediting the speaker.

the various psychiatric treatments, then it will prove useful to disabuse him of his view of their purposes, and cause him to appreciate that they know what they are doing, and are doing what is best for him. In brief, the difficulties caused by a patient are closely tied to his version of what has been happening to him, and if co-operation is to be secured, it helps if this version is discredited. The patient must "insightfully" come to take, or affect to take, the hospital's view of himself.

The staff also have ideal means—in addition to the mirroring effect of the setting—for denying the inmate's rationalizations. Current psychiatric doctrine defines mental disorder as something that can have its roots in the patient's earliest years, show its signs throughout the course of his life, and invade almost every sector of his current activity. No segment of his past or present need be defined, then, as beyond the jurisdiction and mandate of psychiatric assessment. Mental hospitals bureaucratically institutionalize this extremely wide mandate by formally basing their treatment of the patient upon his diagnosis and hence upon the psychiatric view of his past.

The case record is an important expression of this mandate. This dossier is apparently not regularly used, however, to record occasions when the patient showed capacity to cope honorably and effectively with difficult life situations. Nor is the case record typically used to provide a rough average or sampling of his past conduct. One of its purposes is to show the ways in which the patient is "sick" and the reasons why it was right to commit him and is right currently to keep him committed; and this is done by extracting from his whole life course a list of those incidents that have or might have had "symptomatic" significance.[37] The

---

[37] While many kinds of organization maintain records of their members, in almost all of these some socially significant attributes can only be included indirectly, being officially irrelevant. But since mental hospitals have a legitimate claim to deal with the "whole" person, they need officially recognize no limits to what they consider relevant, a sociologically interesting licence. It is an odd historical fact that persons concerned with promoting civil liberties in other areas of life tend to favor giving the psychiatrist complete discretionary power over the patient. Apparently it is felt that the more power possessed by medically qualified administrators and therapists, the better the interests of the patients will be served. Patients, to my knowledge, have not been polled on this matter.

misadventures of his parents or siblings that might suggest a "taint" may be cited. Early acts in which the patient appeared to have shown bad judgment or emotional disturbance will be recorded. Occasions when he acted in a way which the layman would consider immoral, sexually perverted, weak-willed, childish, ill-considered, impulsive, and crazy may be described. Misbehaviors which someone saw as the last straw, as cause for immediate action, are likely to be reported in detail. In addition, the record will describe his state on arrival at the hospital—and this is not likely to be a time of tranquillity and ease for him. The record may also report the false line taken by the patient in answering embarrassing questions, showing him as someone who makes claims that are obviously contrary to the facts:

> Claims she lives with oldest daughter or with sisters only when sick and in need of care; otherwise with husband, he himself says not for twelve years.
> Contrary to the reports from the personnel, he says he no longer bangs on the floor or cries in the morning.
> . . . conceals fact that she had her organs removed, claims she is still menstruating.
> At first she denied having had premarital sexual experience, but when asked about Jim she said she had forgotten about it 'cause it had been unpleasant.[38]

Where contrary facts are not known by the recorder, their presence is often left scrupulously an open question:

> The patient denied any heterosexual experiences nor could one trick her into admitting that she had ever been pregnant or into any kind of sexual indulgence, denying masturbation as well.
> Even with considerable pressure she was unwilling to engage in any projection of paranoid mechanisms.
> No psychotic content could be elicited at this time.[39]

And if in no more factual way, discrediting statements often appear in descriptions given of the patient's general social manner in the hospital:

---

[38] Verbatim transcriptions of hospital case record material.
[39] Verbatim transcriptions of hospital case record material.

When interviewed, he was bland, apparently self-assured, and sprinkled high-sounding generalizations freely throughout his verbal productions.

Armed with a rather neat appearance and natty little Hitlerian mustache this 45 year old man who has spent the last five or more years of his life in the hospital, is making a very successful hospital adjustment living within the role of a rather gay liver and jim-dandy type of fellow who is not only quite superior to his fellow patients in intellectual respects but who is also quite a man with women. His speech is sprayed with many multi-syllabled words which he generally uses in good context, but if he talks long enough on any subject it soon becomes apparent that he is so completely lost in this verbal diarrhea as to make what he says almost completely worthless.[40]

The events recorded in the case history are, then, just the sort that a layman would consider scandalous, defamatory, and discrediting. I think it is fair to say that all levels of mental-hospital staff fail, in general, to deal with this material with the moral neutrality claimed for medical statements and psychiatric diagnosis, but instead participate, by intonation and gesture if by no other means, in the lay reaction to these acts. This will occur in staff-patient encounters as well as in staff encounters at which no patient is present.

In some mental hospitals, access to the case record is technically restricted to medical and higher nursing levels, but even here informal access or relayed information is often available to lower staff levels.[41] In addition, ward personnel are felt to have

---

[40] Verbatim transcriptions of hospital case record material.

[41] However, some mental hospitals do have a "hot file" of selected records which can be taken out only by special permission. These may be records of patients who work as administration-office messengers and might otherwise snatch glances at their own files; of inmates who had elite status in the environing community; and of inmates who may take legal action against the hospital and hence have a special reason to maneuver access to their records. Some hospitals even have a "hot-hot file," kept in the superintendent's office. In addition, the patient's professional title, especially if it is a medical one, is sometimes purposely omitted from his file card. All of these exceptions to the general rule for handling information show, of course, the institution's realization of some of the implications of keeping mental-hospital records. For a further example, see Harold Taxel, "Authority Structure in a Mental Hospital Ward" (Unpublished M.A. thesis, Department of Sociology, University of Chicago, 1953), pp. 11–12.

a right to know those aspects of the patient's past conduct which, embedded in the reputation he develops, purportedly make it possible to manage him with greater benefit to himself and less risk to others. Further, all staff levels typically have access to the nursing notes kept on the ward, which chart the daily course of each patient's disease, and hence his conduct, providing for the near present the sort of information the case record supplies for his past.

I think that most of the information gathered in case records is quite true, although it might seem also to be true that almost anyone's life course could yield up enough denigrating facts to provide grounds for the record's justification of commitment. In any case, I am not concerned here with questioning the desirability of maintaining case records, or the motives of staff in keeping them. The point is that, these facts about him being true, the patient is certainly not relieved from the normal cultural pressure to conceal them, and is perhaps all the more threatened by knowing that they are neatly available, and that he has no control over who gets to learn them.[42] A manly looking youth who responds

---

[42] This is the problem of "information control" that many groups suffer from in varying degrees. See Goffman, "Discrepant Roles," in *The Presentation of Self in Everyday Life* (New York: Anchor Books, 1959), ch. iv, pp. 141–166. A suggestion of this problem in relation to case records in prisons is given by James Peck in his story, "The Ship that Never Hit Port," in *Prison Etiquette*, edited by Holley Cantine and Dachine Rainer (Bearsville, N.Y.: Retort Press, 1950), p. 66.

"The hacks of course hold all the aces in dealing with any prisoner because they can always write him up for inevitable punishment. Every infraction of the rules is noted in the prisoner's jacket, a folder which records all the details of the man's life before and during imprisonment. There are general reports written by the work detail screw, the cell block screw, or some other screw who may have overheard a conversation. Tales pumped from stool pigeons are also included.

"Any letter which interests the authorities goes into the jacket. The mail censor may make a photostatic copy of a prisoner's entire letter, or merely copy a passage. Or he may pass the letter on to the warden. Often an inmate called out by the warden or parole officer is confronted with something he wrote so long ago he had forgot all about it. It might be about his personal life or his political views—a fragment of thought that the prison authorities felt was dangerous and filed for later use."

to military induction by running away from the barracks and hiding himself in a hotel-room clothes closet, to be found there, crying, by his mother; a woman who travels from Utah to Washington to warn the President of impending doom; a man who disrobes before three young girls; a boy who locks his sister out of the house, striking out two of her teeth when she tries to come back in through the window—each of these persons has done something he will have very obvious reason to conceal from others, and very good reason to tell lies about.

The formal and informal patterns of communication linking staff members tend to amplify the disclosive work done by the case record. A discreditable act that the patient performs during one part of the day's routine in one part of the hospital community is likely to be reported back to those who supervise other areas of his life where he implicitly takes the stand that he is not the sort of person who could act that way.

Of significance here, as in some other social establishments, is the increasingly common practice of all-level staff conferences, where staff air their views of patients and develop collective agreement concerning the line that the patient is trying to take and the line that should be taken to him. A patient who develops a "personal" relation with an attendant, or manages to make an attendant anxious by eloquent and persistent accusations of malpractice, can be put back into his place by means of the staff meeting, where the attendant is given warning or assurance that the patient is "sick." Since the differential image of himself that a person usually meets from those of various levels around him comes here to be unified behind the scenes into a common approach, the patient may find himself faced with a kind of collusion against him—albeit one sincerely thought to be for his own ultimate welfare.

In addition, the formal transfer of the patient from one ward or service to another is likely to be accompanied by an informal description of his characteristics, this being felt to facilitate the work of the employee who is newly responsible for him.

Finally, at the most informal of levels, the lunchtime and coffee-break small talk of staff often turns upon the latest doings of the patient, the gossip level of any social establishment being here intensified by the assumption that everything about him is in some way the proper business of the hospital employee. Theoretically there seems to be no reason why such gossip should not build up the subject instead of tear him down, unless one claims that talk about those not present will always tend to be critical in order to maintain the integrity and prestige of the circle in which the talking occurs. And so, even when the impulse of the speakers seems kindly and generous, the implication of their talk is typically that the patient is not a complete person. For example, a conscientious group therapist, sympathetic with patients, once admitted to his coffee companions:

> I've had about three group disrupters, one man in particular—a lawyer [sotto voce] James Wilson—very bright—who just made things miserable for me, but I would always tell him to get on the stage and do something. Well, I was getting desperate and then I bumped into his therapist, who said that right now behind the man's bluff and front he needed the group very much and that it probably meant more to him than anything else he was getting out of the hospital—he just needed the support. Well, that made me feel altogether different about him. He's out now.

In general, then, mental hospitals systematically provide for circulation about each patient the kind of information that the patient is likely to try to hide. And in various degrees of detail this information is used daily to puncture his claims. At the admission and diagnostic conferences, he will be asked questions to which he must give wrong answers in order to maintain his self-respect, and then the true answer may be shot back at him. An attendant whom he tells a version of his past and his reason for being in the hospital may smile disbelievingly, or say, "That's not the way I heard it," in line with the practical psychiatry of bringing the patient down to reality. When he accosts a physician or nurse on the ward and presents his claims for more privileges or for discharge, this may be countered by a question which he cannot answer truthfully without calling up a time in his past when he acted disgracefully. When he gives his view of his situation during group psychotherapy, the therapist, taking the role of interrogator, may attempt to disabuse him of his face-saving interpretations and encourage an interpretation suggesting that it is he himself who is to blame and who must change. When he claims to staff or fellow patients that he is well and has never been really sick, someone may give him graphic details of how, only one month ago, he was prancing around like a girl, or claiming that he was God, or declining to talk or eat, or putting gum in his hair.

Each time the staff deflates the patient's claims, his sense of what a person ought to be and the rules of peer-group social intercourse press him to reconstruct his stories; and each time he does this, the custodial and psychiatric interests of the staff may lead them to discredit these tales again.

Behind these verbally instigated ups and downs of the self is an institutional base that rocks just as precariously. Contrary to popular opinion, the "ward system" insures a great amount of internal social mobility in mental hospitals, especially during the inmate's first year. During that time he is likely to have altered his service once, his ward three or four times, and his parole status several times; and he is likely to have experienced moves in bad as well as good directions. Each of these moves involves a very drastic alteration in level of living and in available materials out of which to build a self-confirming round of activities, an alteration equivalent in scope, say, to a move up or down a class in the wider class system. Moreover, fellow inmates with whom he has partially identified himself will similarly be moving, but in different directions and at different rates, thus reflecting feelings of social change to the person even when he does not experience them directly.

As previously implied, the doctrines of psychiatry can reinforce the social fluctuations of the ward system. Thus there is a current psychiatric view that the ward system is a kind of social hothouse in which patients start as social infants and end up, within the year, on convalescent wards as resocialized adults. This view adds considerably to the weight and pride that staff can attach to their work, and necessitates a certain amount of blindness, especially at higher staff levels, to other ways of viewing the ward system, such as a method for disciplining unruly persons through punishment and reward. In any case, this resocialization perspective tends to overstress the extent to which those on the worst wards are incapable of socialized conduct and the extent to which those on the best wards are ready and willing to play the social game. Because the ward system is something more than a resocialization chamber, inmates find many reasons for "messing up" or getting into trouble, and many occasions, then, for demotion to less privileged ward positions. These demotions may be officially interpreted as psychiatric relapses or moral backsliding, thus protecting the resocialization view of the hospital; these interpretations, by implication, translate a mere infraction of rules and consequent demotion into a fundamental expression of the status of the culprit's self. Correspondingly, promotions, which may come about because of ward population pressure, the need for a "working patient," or for other psychiatrically irrelevant reasons, may be built up into something claimed to be profoundly expressive of the patient's whole self. The patient himself may be expected by staff to make a personal effort to "get well," in something less than a year, and hence may be constantly reminded to think in terms of the self's success and failure.[43]

In such contexts inmates can discover that deflations in moral status are not so bad as they had imagined. After all, infractions which lead to these demotions cannot be accompanied by legal sanctions or by reduction to the status of mental patient, since these conditions already prevail. Further, no past or current delict seems to be horrendous enough in itself to excommunicate a patient from the patient community, and hence failures at right living lose some of their stigmatizing meaning.[44] And finally, in accepting the hospital's version of his fall from grace, the patient can set himself up in the business of "straightening up," and make claims of sympathy, privileges, and indulgence from the staff in order to foster this.

Learning to live under conditions of imminent exposure and wide fluctuation in regard, with little control over the granting or withholding of this regard, is an important step in the socialization of the patient, a step that tells something important about what it is like to be an inmate in a mental hospital. Having one's past mistakes and present progress under constant moral review seems to make for a special adaptation consisting of a less than moral attitude to ego ideals. One's shortcomings and successes

---

[43] For this and other suggestions, I am indebted to Charlotte Green Schwartz.

[44] In the hospital I studied there did not seem to be a kangaroo court, and so, for example, an engaging alcoholic, who managed to get two very well-liked student nurses sent home for drinking with him, did not apparently suffer much for his betrayal of the desires of the peer group.

become too central and fluctuating an issue in life to allow the usual commitment of concern for other persons' views of them. It is not very practicable to try to sustain solid claims about oneself. The inmate tends to learn that degradations and reconstructions of the self need not be given too much weight, at the same time learning that staff and inmates are ready to view an inflation or deflation of a self with some indifference. He learns that a defensible picture of self can be seen as something outside oneself that can be constructed, lost, and rebuilt, all with great speed and some equanimity. He learns about the viability of taking up a standpoint—and hence a self—that is outside the one which the hospital can give and take away from him.

The setting, then, seems to engender a kind of cosmopolitan sophistication, a kind of civic apathy. In this unserious yet oddly exaggerated moral context, building up a self or having it destroyed becomes something of a shameless game, and learning to view this process as a game seems to make for some demoralization, the game being such a fundamental one. In the hospital, then, the inmate can learn that the self is not a fortress, but rather a small open city; he can become weary of having to show pleasure when held by troops of his own, and weary of having to show displeasure when held by the enemy. Once he learns what it is like to be defined by society as not having a viable self, this threatening definition—the threat that helps attach people to the self society accords them—is weakened. The patient seems to gain a new plateau when he learns that he can survive while acting in a way that society sees as destructive of him.

A few illustrations of this moral loosening and moral fatigue might be given. In state mental hospitals currently a kind of "marriage moratorium" appears to be accepted by patients and more or less condoned by staff. Some informal peer-group pressure may be brought against a patient who "plays around" with more than one hospital partner at a time, but little negative sanction seems to be attached to taking up, in a temporarily steady way, with a member of the opposite sex, even though both partners are known to be married, to have children, and even to be regularly visited by these outsiders. In short, there is license in mental hospitals to begin courting all over again, with the understanding, however, that nothing very permanent or serious can come of this. Like shipboard or vacation romances, these entanglements attest to the way in which the hospital is cut off from the outside community, becoming a world of its own, operated for the benefit of its own citizens. And certainly this moratorium is an expression of the alienation and hostility that patients feel for those on the outside to whom they were closely related. But, in addition, one has evidence of the loosening effects of living in a world within a world, under conditions which make it difficult to give full seriousness to either of them.

The second illustration concerns the ward system. On the worst ward level, discreditings seem to occur the most frequently, in part because of lack of facilities, in part through the mockery and sarcasm that seem to be the occupational norm of social control for the attendants and nurses who administer these places. At the same time, the paucity of equipment and rights means that not much self can be built up. The patient finds himself constantly toppled, therefore, but with very little distance to fall. A kind of jaunty gallows humor seems to develop in some of these wards, with considerable freedom to stand up to the staff and return insult for insult. While these patients can be punished, they cannot, for example, be easily slighted, for they are accorded as a matter of course few of the niceties that people must enjoy before they can suffer subtle abuse. Like prostitutes in connection with sex, inmates on these wards have very little reputation or rights to lose and can therefore take certain liberties. As the person moves up the ward system, he can manage more and more to avoid incidents which discredit his claim to be a human being, and acquire more and more of the varied ingredients of self-respect; yet when eventually he does get toppled—and he does —there is a much farther distance to fall. For instance, the privileged patient lives in a world wider than the ward, containing recreation workers who, on request, can dole out cake, cards, table-tennis balls, tickets to the movies, and writing materials. But in the absence of the social control of payment which is typically exerted by a recipient on the outside, the patient runs the risk that even a warmhearted functionary may, on occasion, tell him to wait until she has finished an informal chat, or teasingly ask why he wants what he has asked for, or respond with a dead pause and a cold look of appraisal.

Moving up and down the ward system means, then, not only a shift in self-constructive equipment, a shift in reflected status, but also a change in the calculus of risks. Appreciation of risks to his self-conception is part of everyone's moral experience, but an appreciation that a given risk level is itself merely a social arrangement is a rarer kind of experience, and one that seems to help to disenchant the person who undergoes it.

A third instance of moral loosening has to do with the conditions that are often associated with the release of the inpatient. Often he leaves under the supervision and jurisdiction of his next-of-relation or of a specially selected and specially watchful employer. If he misbehaves while under their auspices, they can quickly obtain his readmission. He therefore finds himself under the special power of persons who ordinarily would not have this kind of power over him, and about whom, moreover, he may have had prior cause to feel quite bitter. In order to get out of the hospital, however, he may conceal his displeasure in this arrangement, and, at least until safely off the hospital rolls, act out a willingness to accept this kind of custody. These discharge procedures, then, provide a built-in lesson in overtly taking a role without the usual covert commitments, and seem further to separate the person from the worlds that others take seriously.

The moral career of a person of a given social category involves a standard sequence of changes in his way of conceiving of selves, including, importantly, his own. These half-buried lines of development can be followed by studying his moral experiences—that is, happenings which mark a turning point in the way in which the person views the world—although the particularities of this view may be difficult to establish. And note can be taken of overt tacks or strategies—that is, stands that he effectively takes before specifiable others, whatever the hidden and variable nature of his inward attachment to these presentations. By taking note of moral experiences and overt personal stands, one can obtain a relatively objective tracing of relatively subjective matters.

Each moral career, and behind this, each self, occurs within the confines of an institutional system, whether a social establishment such as a mental hospital or a complex of personal and professional relationships. The self, then, can be seen as something that resides in the arrangements prevailing in a social system for its members. The self in this sense is not a property of the person to whom it is attributed, but dwells rather in the pattern of social control that is exerted in connection with the person by himself and those around him. This special kind of institutional arrangement does not so much support the self as constitute it.

In this paper, two of these institutional arrangements have been considered, by pointing to what happens to the person when these rulings are weakened. The first concerns the felt loyalty of his next-of-relation. The prepatient's self is described as a function of the way in which three roles are related, arising and declining in the kinds of affiliation that occur between the next-of-relation and the mediators. The second concerns the protection required by the person for the version of himself which he presents to others, and the way in which the withdrawal of this protection can form a systematic, if unintended, aspect of the working of an establishment. I want to stress that these are only two kinds of institutional rulings from which a self emerges for the participant; others, not considered in this paper, are equally important.

In the usual cycle of adult socialization one expects to find alienation and mortification followed by a new set of beliefs about the world and a new way of conceiving of selves. In the case of the mental-hospital patient, this rebirth does sometimes occur, taking the form of a strong belief in the psychiatric perspective, or, briefly at least, a devotion to the social cause of better treatment for mental patients. The moral career of the mental patient has unique interest, however; it can illustrate the possibility that in casting off the raiments of the old self—or in having this cover torn away—the person need not seek a new robe and a new audience before which to cower. Instead he can learn, at least for a time, to practise before all groups the amoral arts of shamelessness.

On Posing as Mental Patients: Reminiscences and Recommendations

*Arnold R. Goldman, Ronald H. Bohr, and
Thomas A. Steinberg*

This paper is based on the firsthand experiences of two investigators who served as disguised observers in a large metropolitan state mental hospital. The second author, a social psychologist, posed as an acute depressed patient on an admissions ward for one week; the third author, a clinical research psychologist, lived the role of a long-term psychotic for 51 hours on a continued-treatment ward for chronic patients. Throughout the entire period of their observations, both investigators were fully believed to be mental patients; indeed, neither ward personnel nor patients were ever aware of the investigators' identities. This report represents the combined views of the observers and of the senior author who conceived and organized the project.

Purpose and Rationale

Despite their responsibility for the care and treatment of the mentally ill, mental health professionals seem to lack an existential awareness of what it means to be a hospitalized patient. The present investigators believed that enacting the patient role, and being reacted to by others as mentally ill, could provide such an awareness. As has been discussed more fully elsewhere (Goldman & Bohr, 1968), enacting a given role can provide different information from what can be gained either by direct observation or even by engaging in conventional role-playing. Moreover, despite the serious ethical questions which have been raised about disguised observation (Caudill, 1958; Erikson, 1967), this technique

Reprinted from *Professional Psychology*, vol. 1, 1970, pp. 427–434. Copyright 1970, by the American Psychological Association, and reproduced by permission. A version of part of this paper was presented at the annual meeting of the Society for the Study of Social Problems, Boston, August 1968. Thanks are extended to Richard Sanders, Daniel Blain, Franklyn R. Clarke, Anthony Dunfield, Jane Perrine, and Louis H. Muzekari for their valuable assistance in conducting the project described in this paper.

has been used in the past to enhance mental health workers' understanding of the realities of patienthood (Caudill, Redlich, Gilmore, & Brody, 1952; Deane, 1961; Ishiyama, Batman, & Hewitt, 1967).

In brief, it was thought that disguised observation of the patient role could be of considerable value in the training of mental health professionals on the staff of the hospital under study. Because there were so many apparent risks to committing observers into a hospital as patients, however, the present project was designed as an exploratory study. Hence, the hospitalization of the two psychologists would serve to determine the risks, feasibility, and utility of posing as a patient in a state hospital. If disguised observation did show potential heuristic value, it was intended that students in various hospital traineeship programs (e.g., psychiatric aides, resident physicians, psychologists) would eventually undergo the procedure as an adjunct to their formal training.

A second reason for the present project arose from the intention of the new administration of the hospital under study to seek out and eliminate antitherapeutic ward practices. Because ward personnel might themselves be "too close" to the situation or "too defensive" to identify practices inimical to patient care, the disguised observers were charged with the responsibility of providing recommendations for ward improvement.[1]

---

[1] While the results reported in this paper suggest the applied and theoretical value of this endeavor, it is unfortunate that few of the original goals have been achieved. It has not proved possible to train numbers of hospital workers by having them adopt the patient role. However, the perspective gained in the present project has influenced subsequent training efforts. For example, trainees in social interaction therapy have recently received part of their instruction by serving in the role of assistants to psychiatric aides for short periods of time, performing typical aide duties, and discussing their responses to the experience with one another and with the aides with whom they worked (Bohr, 1969; Bohr & Offenberg, 1969). Furthermore, although some specific changes in ward procedures have been instituted since this project (e.g., changes in hour of waking up patients, new methods for distributing tobacco, candy, and magazines on various wards), the general lack of innovation bears witness to the difficulty of reforming institutional care.

Setting

At the time of the investigation, the institution studied embodied a great many of the undesirable features of a large public mental hospital. The facility, which was designed originally for 3,000 patients, housed a population of about 6,000; the degree of understaffing had long reached emergency levels, with the complement of professional personnel in some services falling 90% below acceptable staff requirements. Moreover, the hospital's discharge ratio was distressingly low, with the result that over 80% of the population had been in residence over two years (Steinberg, Goldman, & Sanders, 1968). Finally, like many state institutions, it evolved over the years into two virtually distinct hospitals: a very small but dynamic rehabilitation facility for schizophrenic patients in remission, and a very large but quiescent custodial hospital for organics and hard-core, refractory chronic psychotics (Sanders, Smith, & Weinman, 1967). In order to sample both types of facilities, as well as to test the administrative problems of "planting" observers, one author was "admitted" directly from the community into the admissions ward and the other was transferred from the rehabilitation unit to a chronic "back ward."

The male admissions ward entered by one observer housed approximately 60 patients and was located in a building constructed in 1950 which has remained in fair condition. The ward was comprised of seven nine-bed dormitory rooms and two dayrooms—one appealing and one not. The latter dayroom, which was referred to by some patients as the "dungeon" or "alley," contained only hard, stiff-backed chairs; the principal diversion in this barren room was an old television set. Ordinarily, the "dungeon" was the assignment for brand-new admissions as well as for patients judged "unable to leave the ward unescorted." The other dayroom was reserved for use by the "better" patients and was rather attractively furnished with drapes, comfortable chairs, books, games, and a large-screen television set.

The 80-bed "back ward" for chronic patients was located on a large, dilapidated (insect- and rodent-infested) and subsequently condemned building. As might be expected, physical conditions on the ward approached the ignominious. The ward housed primarily "good chronics" who were allowed to leave the ward unaccompanied.

The Experience of Hospitalization

For both observers the hospitalization experience aroused two painfully insistent feelings: agitated boredom and, quite unexpectedly, the fear of betrayal.

Betrayal

Immediately upon admission and throughout the course of their hospitalization, both researchers experienced a fear that they had been betrayed by their colleagues. Each was remarkably concerned about whether he would be left in the hospital indefinitely, only to be forgotten by friends and relatives. One observer in particular was so alarmed by the prospect that by the end of the week he had planned an escape route. Although no one connected with this project had anticipated the arousal of this feeling, it was interesting to find it foremost in the minds of laymen. Indeed, up to the present, the question invariably asked of the observers by staff, by journalists, and by lay audiences is usually along the lines of "Weren't you afraid they'd leave you in there?" That a fear of betrayal may be a common apprehension under such circumstances is further suggested in the findings of Ishiyama, who reports that, among the psychiatric attendants who experienced only one-half hour in a seclusion room, many became extremely anxious over the possibility of their being forgotten and left in the room (Ishiyama & Hewitt, 1966).

If a fear of betrayal can readily be evoked in "normals," it is likely that similar apprehensions and suspicions are aroused in mentally ill persons upon their initiation into a mental hospital. Certainly, many patients, as Goffman (1961, pp. 131–146) indicates, have just cause for "feeling betrayed," especially after having been told that they were "going for a ride in the country" or given some other subterfuge to get them into the hospital.

Since one obvious reaction to involuntary confinement is escape, certain flight responses might well be expected, particularly during the very first stages of a patient's hospitalization. In this context, it is useful to recall one observer's tentative escape plan and relate it to the results of a 36-month cohort study of escapes from the hospital under study. The investigation indicated that escape is an early occurring phenomenon, with more than half of all escapes having occurred between the first and eighth week following admission (Goldman & Offenberg, 1969).

Although fear of betrayal has long been a central theme in the autobiographical accounts of mental patienthood (e.g., Beers, 1956), hospital personnel have been sensitive neither to its occurrence nor to its possible consequences. The personal experiences of the two observers suggest that many of the suspicions harbored by patients may be situationally induced and, therefore, not always classically paranoid reactions. Perhaps the impersonalization as well as the ambiguity of hospital admission procedures—at least as they would appear to new patients—might be dealt with directly by clinicians and administrators. Indeed, much symptomatic behavior, including fear of betrayal, could be allayed or even precluded by better orientation procedures for new admissions and by clear structuring of the patients' initial hospital experiences.

Agitated Boredom

An immediate and overwhelming reaction in both observers to hospital life was boredom. More important, and contrary to the views of many of the hospital staff, mental patients themselves were not at all oblivious to the barrenness and emptiness of their physical surroundings.

Many patients with whom the observers interacted were painfully bored and sought something meaningful to occupy their time. As a consequence, at least for the observers themselves, relatively minor events quickly began to take on disproportionate significance. For example, a different dessert at dinnertime became the "event of the day," and success in obtaining change for a quarter became an accomplishment to be remembered. Closely related to this psychological magnification of minor events was a subjective change in the observers' time perspectives. Thus, once minor events were subjectively transformed into major occasions, they assumed the status of chronological landmarks, and it was by these landmarks that the observers and other patients marked the passage of hospital time. As one articulate patient on the admissions ward reported,

> Little things become very important around here. You don't use the days of the week to tell time, but you say, "Oh, that was the day we waited in the hall for the floor to dry after breakfast instead of going right into the dayroom." Or "That was the day we had ice cream." You start to think just about what happens in here, and any change in the routine becomes tremendously important.

It was noteworthy to find on both wards studied, and presumably throughout the hospital, that patients did not have easy access to newspapers or calendars. While it was the hospital's policy to deliver one newspaper daily to every ward, these periodicals were seldom if ever available to the majority of patients. The primary medium for current events was television, but television programs of an informational nature were generally vetoed by the patients in favor of the popular, bland situation comedies and variety shows. In the opinion of the observers, the impoverished environment of the ward fostered in patients an apathy toward the world outside.

In light of the scarcity of information available in the custodial psychiatric ward, it seems unrealistic to measure a mental patient's progress, degree of pathology, or readiness for release by his awareness of the date, of the names of various governmental leaders, or of other topical items of information.

The Exchange System: A Consequence of Deprivation

From the perspective of the patient, the hospital ward was divided into two distinct social worlds. On the one hand, there was the remote realm of nurses, mental health professionals, and all those persons on the other side of the locked ward door who wore shirts, ties, and were present weekdays from 8:30 A.M. to 4:30 P.M. On the other hand, there was the immediate domain of patients and attendants. In this domain there existed between patients and attendants an elaborate informal system of exchange (see Homans, 1961). This system existed, in part, because the parties involved had something of value to offer one another. An examination of the existing roles of attendants and patients makes abundantly clear the necessity of an exchange and reveals the tradable commodities each group possessed.

Since the size of the attendant staff was insufficient to allow them to fulfill all of their responsibilities (i.e., patient care *and* ward maintenance), attendants were in great need of assistance. And the patients met this need. Indeed, it has been often asserted (e.g., Bartlett, 1967) that most state hospitals could not operate without patient labor. However, what could attendants, low-echelon workers with little formal authority, offer to patients in return?

Mental patients, who are characteristically restricted to such a degree that they are extremely dependent on others for even the most minor amenities of life, could "win back" some of these apparently minor rights by assisting attendants. Since attendants had at their disposal few resources for rewarding patients, the abridgment of many rights served a utilitarian purpose. The attendants could trade small privileges (e.g., extra food, cigarettes, coffee, permission to carry matches, and violation of other hospital rules) for patient cooperation. Therefore, because of the nature of these two interacting social roles (i.e., mental patient and hospital attendant), there was established a basis for a system of mutual rewards.

This exchange was viewed as "just," and both parties felt that patients should be rewarded for assisting aides in their work. Failure to reward patients for cooperation was generally viewed as a violation of ward mores—even when this failure resulted from an attendant's strict adherence to hospital rules. To cite just one example, it was usual for "helpful" patients to be permitted to use the more desirable "front" dayroom despite the fact that some of them did not have ground privileges (i.e., permission to leave the ward unattended). Indeed, as one helpful patient without ground privileges explained when he was sent to the back dayroom, "It isn't fair—you work but they send you back here to the dungeon."

In the hierarchy of the hospital, attendants are the intermediaries between patients and other staff members. To enhance their own position, aides reinterpreted the actions of upper-echelon medical personnel in terms of the exchange system. Thus, decisions by professionals which were intended to have therapeutic utility were eventually communicated to patients by their attendants as rewards for cooperation. Typically, patients were given the distinct impression that it was the attendants themselves who were responsible for granting these rewards. For example, while physicians prescribed ground privileges for therapeutic reasons, attendants always passed them on to patients as a reward for cooperation in ward maintenance, with the implication that continued cooperation was expected if the patient wanted to keep his ground privileges.

This system of exchange may also play an indirect role in the process by which new patients are transformed into chronic ones. Part of the socialization of the new patient seems to involve his accepting a new image of himself, that of a mentally ill person who must be totally dependent upon others for even the most minor gratuities. The second author's initial introductions to the exchange system were most humbling. In one instance, a number of patients were being given dimes for having helped an attendant mop a floor. The observer had just arrived on the scene and was told by the attendant, "I'll buy you some coffee too when you've helped us clean up this utility room." At another time, the observer helped another attendant mop a floor and was told, "Go get something to eat—you helped us." The strong sense of humiliation experienced by the observer did not seem to be a reaction limited to middle class professionals; even working class patients, comparing this compensation with wages in industry, realized its inadequacy. It is of interest to note that within the course of just one week, however, these meager rewards came to be expected as payoffs for services rendered.

On the custodial ward, as far as the third author could see, there was no explicit exchange system; ward life seemed to go on automatically. With virtually no cues from attendants, patients would leave the building at the proper time to go to their assigned jobs, carry out routine ward chores, or assist the staff during special events in a seemingly spontaneous manner.

Some events occurred, however, which raised the question as to whether the absence of overt exchange behavior was more apparent than real. While patients were not positively reinforced for compliance on the custodial ward, uncooperative behavior was met with negative reinforcement. Any patient disrupting the harmony of ward life would quickly receive negative sanctions. Indeed, one attendant was observed telling a recalcitrant patient, "You know this floor is for patients who work—if you don't, we'll have to move you up to the third floor." Such proscriptions on the custodial ward, in contrast to direct positive reinforcements on the admissions ward, suggest the possibility that the mode of re-inforcement—positive or negative—is not the same for the novice and for the veteran patient, or possibly not the same for the acute and the chronic. In other words, one might speculate that new patients are initiated into the hospital system through the dis-tribution of postive rewards and, once having been incorporated into the system, these patients are controlled by the threatened loss of such rewards.

While the nature of the differences between the admissions ward and other settings remains equivocal, interviews with vari-ous personnel throughout the hospital suggested that exchange between patients and attendants was widespread. For example, it was reported that aides often gave ground privileges to "deserv-ing" patients without the approval of ward physicians, and with-drew ground privileges without the approval of ward physicians if they felt a patient was not working to capacity. Also, on various wards, state-issued tobacco and cigarette paper, the privilege of watching television in the evening, and coffee were employed as rewards. At one staff meeting, it was reported, an attendant com-plained that, because he could not obtain state coffee to "reward good patients," he had had to purchase coffee himself.

Implications

Knowledge of the hospital system of exchange seems to be of value in understanding several aspects of the behavior of patients and staff in psychiatric facilities. Parenthetically, it is of consider-able interest to note that, long before the advent of behavior therapy, psychiatric attendants had evolved their own form of "token economy" by which to mold patient behavior.

In terms of staff behavior, the present analysis suggests the possibility that severe restriction of patient behavior has an im-portant latent function, in addition to the manifest one of "pro-tecting patients from themselves and others." In effect, restriction provides lower echelon staff members with the means by which patient behavior can be rewarded. Seen from this perspective, the many ward restrictions placed upon patients become more comprehensible.

In contrast with interpretations of attendant behavior which stress the role of class-linked individual characteristics (e.g., educational background, beliefs about mental illness) as determinants of "antitherapeutic" job performance, the present paper emphasizes the possible significance of other variables. Notably, it seems quite possible that the organizational structure of the attendant role and the realities of his job (i.e., understaffing, responsibilities for both patient care and building maintenance) give him a vested interest in restricting the self-determination of patients. Viewing past investigations of mental health ideology (e.g., Cohen & Struening, 1962; Gilbert & Levinson, 1956), it is conceivable that custodial, "authoritarian" beliefs may be influenced in some measure by hospital structure and functioning—not only by the typical personality and social class characteristics of attendants. Certainly, just as the hospital as a social system elicits certain behaviors in patients, it can also elicit certain behaviors in staff members. These considerations raise the possibility that attendant attitudes may be changed through job restructuring, as well as through traditional educational attempts. Indeed, some research (see Colarelli & Siegel, 1966) indicates that psychiatric attendants do adopt considerably more therapeutic attitudes and behaviors when given greater autonomy of job performance and more authority in making decisions about patient treatment.

Conclusion

It is hoped that this account of the experiences of two trained observers posing as mental patients in a large state hospital has raised some significant questions about the effects of the institutional environment upon the behavior of mental patients. Specifically, reflecting the interests of both the clinical and social psychologists involved in this project, the issues focused on here suggest the intimate relationship between individual behavior and the immediate social environment. The experiences reported here hint at the relationship which exists between the reaction of the mental patient to boredom, poverty, and loss of status and responsibility, on the one hand, and the characteristics of hospitals which elicit these reactions, on the other. Enhanced awareness of this relationship may suggest experimental reforms aimed at correcting the environmental conditions which elicit "chronic" behavior in psychiatric patients.

References

Bartlett, F.L. Present-day requirements for state hospitals joining the community. *New England Journal of Medicine*, 1967, *267*, 90–94.

Beers, C. W. *A mind that found itself*. Garden City, N.Y.: Doubleday, 1956.

Bohr, R. H. Instruction in organizational psychology: A "survival kit" for new workers in a state hospital. *American Psychologist*, 1969, *24*, 765–766.

Bohr, R. H., & Offenberg, R. M. A factor analytic study of job perceptions in a state psychiatric hospital. *Psychological Reports*, 1969, *24*, 899–902.

Caudill, W. *The psychiatric hospital as a small society*. Cambridge: Harvard University Press, 1958.

Caudill, W., Redlich, F. C., Gilmore, H. R., & Brody, E. B. Social structure and interaction processes on a psychiatric ward. *American Journal of Orthopsychiatry*, 1952, *22*, 314–334.

Cohen, J., & Struening, E. L. Opinions about mental health in the personnel of two large mental hospitals. *Journal of Abnormal and Social Psychology*, 1962, *64*, 349–360.

Colarelli, N. J., & Siegel, S. M. *Ward H: An adventure in innovation*. New York: Van Nostrand, 1966.

Deane, W. N. The reactions of a nonpatient to a stay on a mental hospital ward. *Psychiatry*, 1961, *24*, 61–68.

Erikson, K. T. A comment on disguised observation in sociology. *Social Problems*, 1967, *14*, 366–372

Gilbert, D. C., & Levinson, D. J. Ideology, personality, and institutional policy in the mental hospital. *Journal of Abnormal and Social Psychology*, 1956, *53*, 263–271.

Goffman, E. *Asylums*. Garden City, N.Y.: Doubleday, 1961.

Goldman, A. R., & Bohr, R. H. Methods of observation: Implications for research and training. Paper presented at the meeting of the Pennsylvania Sociological Society, Villanova University, October 1968.

Goldman, A. R., & Offenberg, R. M. Escape from the mental hospital: A cohort analysis. Unpublished manuscript, Philadelphia State Hospital, 1969.

Homans, G. C. *Social behavior: Its elementary forms.* New York: Harcourt, Brace & World, 1961.

Ishiyama, T., Batman, R., & Hewitt, E. B. Let's be patients. *American Journal of Nursing,* 1967, *67,* 569–571.

Ishiyama, T., & Hewitt, E. B. Seclusion: A lesson for aides. *Journal of Psychiatric Nursing,* 1966, *4,* 563–570.

Sanders, R., Smith, R. S., & Weinman, B. S. *Chronic psychoses and recovery.* San Francisco: Jossey-Bass, 1967.

Steinberg, T. A., Goldman, A. R., & Sanders, R. Demographic factors associated with release from Philadelphia State Hospital: A preliminary report. *Pennsylvania Psychiatric Quarterly,* 1968, *8,* 38–47.

Determinants of the Decision for Psychiatric Hospitalization

Werner M. Mendel and Samuel Rapport

In the recent history of American psychiatry, the use of the hospital as a therapeutic intervention in the treatment of mental illness has been seriously questioned. Studies by Lafave,[1] Mendel,[2] and Pasamanick[3] have shown that patients who are treated without the use of the hospital in the management of their acute and chronic illness tend to display less morbidity and make more satisfactory extramural adjustment than those who have been hospitalized. As a result of these studies and the general recognition of the antitherapeutic effects of prolonged and inappropriate hospitalization, much emphasis has been placed on the clarification of the indications for hospitalization. It is generally agreed, even by the most conservative thinkers in psychiatry, that the patient should not be hospitalized simply because he is mentally ill or because the decision maker does not know what else to do with him. The criteria for psychiatric hospitalization outlined in the book *Therapeutic Management of Psychological Illness*[4] provide the basic guidelines for hospital admission for the staff and trainees of the Los Angeles County-University of Southern California Medical Center.

Our growing recognition that factors other than those related to patient's needs influenced the decision about hospitalization

Read before the American Psychiatric Association, Boston, May 17, 1968. Reprinted from *The Archives of General Psychiatry,* vol. 20, March, 1969, pp. 321–328. Copyright 1969, American Medical Association.

was greatly increased when we observed that the percentage of hospital admissions was consistently higher (doubled) during weekends and evening than during weekdays. This observation had been explained on the basis of the difference in the severity of psychopathy of the patients who were requesting admission during the night and on weekends. It was also observed that the staff social workers' decisions in favor of admission to the hospital were significantly less than the medical staff's. This had been explained by the assumption that the patients assigned to social workers had less severe symptoms than those evaluated by medical staff. Neither one of these factors, however, could be documented on the basis of the data obtained in this study. It became obvious that decisions about hospital admission were decisively influenced by personal, administrative, and other nonclinical psychiatric considerations.

Thus, we decided to do a detailed analysis of 33 decision makers who over a period of eight days made 269 separate decisions. We examined the decisions they made in an attempt to identify the relevant determinants they used in reaching their decision.

Method

During an eight-day period in August 1967, 269 individuals applied to the Psychiatric Division of the Los Angeles County-University of Southern California Medical Center for admission. Thirty-three professionals, including social workers, psychologists, resident psychiatrists, and staff psychiatrists, made 269 consecutive decisions for or against hospital admission after examining the patients seeking admission to the psychiatric hospital. Of the 269 consecutive decisions, 110, or 40.9%, resulted in hospitalization, while 159, or 59.1%, were not hospitalized.

Decision Makers and Results

| | PSW | PSYCHOL-OGISTS | PSYCHI-ATRISTS | *Residents* | | |
				1ST YR	2ND YR	3RD YR
Total = 33	5	2	6	6	10	4

	HOSPITALIZED	NOT HOSPITALIZED
Total = 269	110 = 40.9%	159 = 59.1%

TABLE 1 DECISION FOR HOSPITALIZATION

1. Patient's Name: 2. Date:
3. Hospitalized Today: Yes_____ No_____
4. Previous Hospitalization: Yes_____ No_____
5. Why did patient come today? (Not yesterday or tomorrow)
6. Official Diagnosis:
7. Severity of Pathology: 1___ 2___ 3___ 4___ 5___

1 - Minimal symptoms:	Never require hospitalization under ordinary circumstances.
2 - Moderate symptoms:	On occasion require hospitalization.
3 - Major symptoms:	Often require hospitalization under usual circumstances.
4 - Severe symptoms:	Usually require hospitalization under ordinary circumstances.
5 - Overwhelming symptoms:	Always require hospitalization under ordinary circumstances.

8. If social situation were different, would you hospitalize this patient at this time? Yes___ No___
9. What are patient's resources for support during this crisis?
    1) Parents;   2) Spouse;   3) Children;   4) Siblings;
    5) Friends;   6) Work;   7) School;   8) Religious Group;
    9) Political Group;   10) Club.
10. Name of Evaluator:
11. Discipline:

Since the hospital evaluation clinic and admission suite are in operation 24 hours each day and seven days each week, the decisions were made throughout a 168-hour week. At the time the decision was made, a clinical data form (Table 1) was filled out by the decision maker describing his assessment of the patient applicant for hospitalization. This assessment included the severity of symptoms, the social resources available to the patient, the attitude of the family, etc. Also noted at the same time was the hour of the day, the census of the hospital, the decision maker's profession, and the length of his clinical experience.

Four weeks after the eight-day period of observation during which the 269 consecutive decisions were studied, the 33 decision makers were asked to fill out a questionnaire (Table 2) in which they were asked to summarize their attitudes about the decision for hospitalization and to describe what they thought the relevant determinants were in making the decision. Three months later,

TABLE 2   RESEARCH QUESTIONNAIRE

1. Name   Profession
2. Education (after B.A. degree)   Degrees
3. Length of Clinical Training as of 8/15/67.
4. Length of Clinical Experience after formal training as of 8/15/67.
5. Length of Experience in doing psychiatric evaluations on admitting service as of 8/15/67.
6. Do you feel that inpatient treatment in this hospital is effective in relieving patients' distress? (Check one.)
   1) Always;   2) Generally;   3) On occasion;
   4) Rarely;   5) Never
7. If you were running your own hospital with ideal inpatient treatment facilities and staff, would you hospitalize the same, more, or fewer patients than you did during the week of the study?
8. If you could make your own policies and had unlimited time with each patient in the evaluation clinic, would you tend to hospitalize more, fewer, or the same number of patients you did during the period of the study?
9. On what basis do you think you make your decision to hospitalize or not to hospitalize? (Describe in brief paragraph.)
10. Please rate in order of importance (1 = most important) the factors in your decision about the advisability of hospitalizing the patient.

   1. Diagnosis   7. Attitude of people who bring patient
   2. Patient's discomfort
   3. Nature of patient's symptoms   8. Patient's educational level
   4. Attitude of relatives   9. Whether you like patient
   5. History of previous hospital-   10. Hospital census
      ization   11. Patient's social situation
   6. Your tiredness   12. Patient's social class
                                           13. Your training

each decision maker was interviewed individually to ascertain his description of the experience of making decisions for hospitalization. All of the decision makers observed in the study are routinely involved in making these decisions as part of their regular work. On the average, 1,200 to 1,400 patients apply for admission to the hospital each month. These decision makers are responsible for evaluating these patients and deciding about the admission request. At the time of the study, each of the 33 decision makers had at least one month's experience making such decisions. Many of the decision makers had several years' experience in these clinical tasks.

Results

Influence of Profession and Experience on Decisions

		Profession		Residents		
TOTAL = 33	PSW	PSY- CHOL	PSY- CHIAT	1ST YR	2ND YR	3RD YR
Hospitalized	25%	50%	37%	48%	49%	48%
Not hospitalized	75%	50%	63%	52%	51%	52%

	Experience*			
TOTAL = 269	0- 6 MO	6 MO- 1 YR	1 YR- 3 YR	3 YR +
Hospitalized	49%	43%	41%	32%
Not Hospitalized	51%	57%	59%	68%

* After degree and internship.

The outcome of the decisions for hospitalization was influenced by both the profession of the decision maker and the clinical experience of the decision maker.

Social workers tended to hospitalize significantly fewer applicants than did psychologists and psychiatrists. The more clinically experienced the decision maker was, the less he tended to hospitalize patients (see material above). The difference in decision outcome is statistically significant between the decision maker with less than six months' experience and those with over three years' experience.

The decision for hospitalization was not related to severity of symptoms of the patient at the time of decision. That is, the group

TABLE 3   SEVERITY OF SYMPTOMS

Total = 269 Severity of Symptoms*	1	2	3	4	5
Hospitalized	5%	8%	14%	33%	40%
Not hospitalized	6%	5%	17%	30%	42%

Decision Making and Severity of Symptoms		
Total = 269 Severity of Symptoms	1 & 2	3, 4, & 5
Hospitalized	13%	87%
Not hospitalized	11%	89%

* See Table 1, part 7.

Decision and Previous Psychiatric Hospitalization

Total = 269	*Hospitalization Previous*	*Not Previously Hospitalized*
n 110—Decision to hospitalize	77%	23%
n 159—Decision not to hospitalize	34%	66%

Previous Hospitalization and Severity of Symptoms

	Severity of Symptoms	
Previously Hospitalized	1* & 2	3, 4, 5
Yes	17%	83%
No	14%	86%

* See Table 1, part 7.

of patients who were hospitalized could not be distinguished from those who were not hospitalized on the basis of the decision maker's estimate of the severity of symptoms (Table 3).

The decision for hospitalization during the period of this study seemed definitely related to the patient's history of prior hospitalization. That is, if the patient had been hospitalized previously, his chance for being hospitalized at the time of this study was more than doubled.

The history of previous hospitalization was not, however, related to severity of symptoms. The two groups of patients, those previously hospitalized and those not previously hospitalized, were indistinguishable on the basis of severity of symptoms.

Although the number of decisions for hospitalization varied considerably from day to day, the rate of hospitalization did not seem to be related to hospital census. It should be noted, however, that the hospital census did not vary widely during the eight days of study. At other times, the census has been known to go 20% to 30% over capacity (Table 4).

The time of day and type of day made an important difference to the outcome of the decision. Almost twice as many people tended to be hospitalized between 5:00 PM and 9:00 AM on weekdays, and all day Saturday and Sunday (Table 5).

The population of applicants for hospitalization seen during weekdays from 9:00 AM to 5:00 PM was not, however, distinguishable from the population seen between 5:00 PM and 9:00 AM and weekends on the basis of severity of symptoms (Table 6).

TABLE 4 DECISION AND HOSPITAL CENSUS

Day of Study	Hospital Census % of Capacity	Decision for Hospitalization of Applicants
1 Friday	79%	38%
2 Saturday	85%	62%
3 Sunday	93%	59%
4 Monday	90%	41%
5 Tuesday	93%	34%
6 Wednesday	91%	51%
7 Thursday	93%	44%
8 Friday	87%	37%

The decision to hospitalize a patient was significantly influenced by the number of support resources available to the patient at the time the decision was made (Table 7). For purposes of this study, the patient's family and community resources were identified and appraised. The availability of resources to the patient significantly decreased the number of decisions for hospitalization.

Of the 110 patients hospitalized during the period of study, 84% would not have been hospitalized according to the decision maker if the social situation had been different.

TABLE 5 DECISION MAKING AND TIME OF DAY

	9:00 AM to 5:00 PM Monday-Friday (Total = 181)		5:00 PM to 9:00 AM Monday-Friday/All Day Saturday & Sunday (Total = 88)	
	HOSPITALIZED	NOT HOSPITALIZED	HOSPITALIZED	NOT HOSPITALIZED
Total = 269	32%	68%	61%	39%

TABLE 6 SEVERITY OF SYMPTOMS AND TIME OF DAY

Severity of Symptoms*	9:00 AM to 5:00 PM Monday-Friday (Total = 181)	5:00 PM to 9:00 AM Monday-Friday/All Day Saturday & Sunday (Total = 88)
1 & 2	18%	16%
3, 4, 5	82%	84%

* See Table 1, part 7.

TABLE 7   DECISION AND RESOURCES AVAILABLE TO PATIENT

Number of Resources	0	1	2	3+
Total = 269				
Hospitalized	63%	48%	41%	35%
Not hospitalized	37%	52%	59%	65%

Four weeks after the 269 decisions were made, a questionnaire was administered to the 32 decision makers in order to assess their attitudes about the decisions for or against hospitalization. (One of the first-year residents left the program and was not available for the follow-up study.)

All 32 decision makers reported on the follow-up questionnaire that they thought the severity of symptoms of the patient was a major factor in their decision for or against hospitalization. This is in striking contrast to the direct observation of decisions which showed that the patient population hospitalized was indistinguishable from the patient population not hospitalized on the basis of severity of symptoms (Table 8). On the basis of responses to the follow-up questionnaire, none of the decision makers felt that his decision for or against hospitalization was influenced by the history of previous hospitalization. Again, this is in sharp contrast to the data obtained at the time the actual clinical decision, which showed marked influence by the history of previous hospitalization on the outcome of the decision, was made.

The staff social workers who were those decision makers who hospitalized the fewest patients were also the group who thought they would like to have hospitalized the fewest patients as shown in the follow-up questionnaire. The staff psychiatrists seemed surest of their decisions by expressing the feeling that 68% of the decisions were in line with their ideals.

The 32 decision makers were interviewed four months after the observed decision-making period. The results from these interviews were as shown in Table 9.

The results show that on interview, in comparison to the self-administered questionnaire, significantly fewer decision makers were willing to say that severity of symptoms was the major factor in the decision for or against hospitalization. Many more were willing to say that they based it on patient discomfort (Table 9). Still, none of the decision makers thought that a history of pre-

TABLE 8 ATTITUDES OF DECISION MAKER: QUESTIONNAIRE RESULTS

	Residents			Staff		
	1ST YR	2ND YR	3RD YR	PSYCHIAT	PSYCHOL	PSW
TOTAL = 32	5	10	4	6	2	5
Major factor in decision						
Severity of symptoms	80%	90%	50%	84%	100%	40%
Patient's discomfort	20%	10%	25%	16%	—	20%
Social situation	—	—	25%	—	—	20%
Attitude of family	—	—	—	—	—	20%
Previous hospitalization	—	—	—	—	—	—
Least important factor						
Your tiredness	60%	50%	25%	51%	50%	40%
Patient's education level	20%	40%	25%	33%	—	20%
Diagnosis	20%	10%	50%	16%	50%	40%
Would like to hospitalize						
Fewer patients	20%	50%	75%	16%	50%	80%
Same number of patients	40%	40%	25%	68%	50%	20%
More patients	40%	10%	—	16%	—	—

vious hospitalization had any influence on their decision. A number of decision makers thought that their own tiredness was a factor in the decision when they were interviewed, while none chose this factor on the questionnaire. Differences in the results obtained from the questionnaire and from the interview were most marked in the resident groups and least marked among the staff psychiatrists and staff social workers.

TABLE 9   RESULTS OF INTERVIEW

	Residents			Staff		
	1ST YR	2ND YR	3RD YR	PSYCHIAT	PSYCHOL	PSW
TOTAL = 32	5	10	4	6	2	5
Major factor in decision						
Severity of symptoms	20%	20%	25%	16%	100%	—
Patient's discomfort	40%	60%	75%	68%	—	40%
Social situation	20%	20%	—	16%	—	60%
Attitude of family	20%	—	—	—	—	—
Previous hospitalization	—	—	—	—	—	—
Least important factor						
Examiner's tiredness	20%	30%	—	16%	—	20%
Patient's education level	—	10%	25%	52%	50%	40%
Diagnosis	80%	60%	75%	16%	—	40%
Other	—	—	—	16%	50%	—
Would like to hospitalize						
Fewer patients	80%	90%	75%	16%	100%	80%
Same amount of patients	20%	10%	25%	68%	—	20%
More patients	—	—	—	16%	—	—

Comment

It is interesting to note that the social workers hospitalized the fewest patients. There are three possible reasons for this. First, by virtue of their training and experience, they are more aware of family and community resources available to patients and rely more heavily on these factors in formulating their plans for effective intervention. They are, therefore, less influenced by the medical model of treatment. Secondly, in this setting, they work only during daytime hours and not on Saturdays and Sundays. Perhaps the increased rate of hospital admissions during nights and weekends in part may be the result of the unavailability of social workers or inaccessibility of social resources. Thirdly, decisions for admission made by nonphysician professionals have to be approved by the staff psychiatrist. This tends to have the decision maker consider more carefully his decision for hospitalization.

The number of years of clinical experience seemed to make a significant difference in the percentage of patients hospitalized. Those decision makers who had less than six months of clinical experience hospitalized a significantly larger group of patients than did those who had more than three years of clinical experience. This finding would confirm the observation that the inexperienced clinician will hospitalize patients to be "safe" because he is unsure of his evaluation and is far less resourceful in planning and implementing an alternative to hospitalization. Hospitalizing a patient is a way of avoiding immediate consequences of the decision. It allows the decision maker to avoid the final total responsibility.

A particularly surprising finding was that the decision for or against hospitalization was in fact not based on severity of symptoms. This was an unexpected outcome, particularly in view of the fact that the decision makers themselves thought that their decisions were based on this factor. It should be noted that generally the population of patients who apply for hospitalization at the Psychiatric Unit of the Los Angeles County-University of Southern California Medical Center represent the most severely ill population in the cachement basin of seven million people which the hospital serves. Perhaps this explains in part the lack of relation of severity of symptoms to the decision for hospitalization. Everyone who comes applying for admission is severely ill, and in the vast majority of cases, some aspect of this mental illness has become a social irritant.

Similarly surprising was the item of history of previous hospitalization. Our data indicated that there was a very high correlation between previous hospitalization and the decision to rehospitalize. The decision makers did not report that they were aware of being influenced by history of previous hospitalization, even though this was one of the most important factors in the decision-making process. Yet, patients previously hospitalized could not be distinguished from those not previously hospitalized on the basis of severity of symptoms at the time of application for admission.

The number of patients hospitalized during evening, nights, and weekends was markedly increased. This, again, was not related to the severity of symptoms. The applicant patient population during evenings, nights, and weekends was not distinguishable on the basis of severity of symptoms. This difference was probably related to two factors: (1) Many of the family and community resources could not be mobilized to aid the patient during the night and on weekends. (2) The decision makers during these times were less experienced since they are residents rather than staff psychiatrists. As a result of this finding, the hospital established an area in which all patients who are admitted to the hospital between 5:00 PM and 8:00 AM are kept and reevaluated in the morning by more experienced staff and when community and family resources are accessible. It was discovered that under these circumstances approximately 33% of the patients admitted to the holding area could be discharged in the morning, while the other 67% could not. Thus, this new service seems to offer support to our speculation in regard to the influence of unavailability of community resources on decision for hospitalization during nights and weekends and tends to support even further the contention that inexperienced personnel tend to rely more heavily on the hospital as a way of coping with crises. This view is further supported by the evidence from the study that the number of support resources available to the patient at the time he comes for hospitalization definitely influences the outcome of the decision.[5] Also, the reported feeling of the decision makers was that most of the 110 patients who were hospitalized would not have been hospitalized (84%) if more adequate family and community resources had been available.[6,7]

The questionnaire administered four weeks after the actual decisions were made showed that the decision makers had very different ideas about the factors influencing their decisions from those which actually were observed to influence them at the time the decision was made. For example, decision makers thought that the severity of the patient's symptoms was a most important factor. In fact, our observations showed that the severity of symptoms played no measurable part in the decision.

That group of decision makers who had hospitalized the most patients indicated on the questionnaire that under ideal circumstances they would have hospitalized an even larger percentage of the patients they saw. Those decision makers (primarily the social workers) who hospitalized the fewest felt that they would have hospitalized an even smaller percentage of the patients under ideal circumstances.

When they were again interviewed three months later, the results were somewhat different. Since the interview was conducted by a senior member of the teaching staff, it is understandable that the residents' replies were influenced by what they knew about the attitudes of the interviewer. Residents changed their minds the most. They were quite unwilling to admit to the interviewer that they would have liked to hospitalize more patients. The staff psychiatrists were most certain about their answers and least influenced by the interviewer. Thus, the results in the interview differed from those on the questionnaire.

It is interesting to note that none of the decision makers admitted, either on the questionnaire or to the interviewer, that the history of previous hospitalization had any influence on their decision. Yet, the data obtained at the time the decision was made shows that history of previous hospitalization, in fact, did influence their decision. Thus, the decision makers maintained an attitude of independence in regard to their decision when in fact their decisions were influenced by previous decisions about the patient. This observation is further evidence for the conclusion that to hospitalize a patient is a major decision which forever after changes the attitude of both the patient and those who care for the patient.

In the interview, a number of the clinicians stated that they were influenced by their liking or disliking of the patient. Although this factor was not mentioned as either the most important or least important in their decision, the tradition of being concerned with countertransference attitudes made the decision makers aware of the possibility of influence by this factor. Some decision makers reported that they tended to hospitalize patients they liked more than those they did not like, while others reported just the opposite effect of their feelings about the patient. From the observations made both on the questionnaire and during the interview, it becomes quite clear that the attitudes of the decision makers towards the hospital, the patients as people, and the illness have a profound, albeit covert, influence on their decision for or against hospitalization.

Conclusion

This study questions the traditional criteria for psychiatric hospitalization.

Administrative and organizational factors as well as personal attitudes and professional background are significant influences on the decision for or against hospitalization in the treatment of the mentally ill patient population.

The decision to hospitalize, particularly the first such decision in the history of the patient, changes the destiny of the individual forever after.

The decision to hospitalize was not based on the severity of the patient's symptoms or the magnitude of his distress in our sample of 269 decisions made by 33 decision makers. Yet, a large number of the decision makers thought that this factor played an important part in their decisions.

The existence or absence of social support resources played a critically important part in the decision as to whether a patient was hospitalized for treatment of his mental illness.

This study presented data which provides further evidence for the point of view that hospitalization is not a necessary or even useful approach to the treatment of mental illness if adequate community resources are available, experienced personnel has sufficient time to evaluate crisis, and service can be offered immediately to the patient when he needs it.

In this study the decision for or against hospitalization does not seem to be based on clinical psychiatric factors but rather on social and attitudinal factors, some of which influenced the decision makers even though they were unaware of such influences.

References

1. Herjanic, M., and LaFave, H. G.: "Two Years' Follow-up of 81 Chronic Hospitalized Patients," read before the American Psychiatric Association, May 12, 1966, Atlantic City, N.J.
2. Mendel, W.: Effect of Length of Hospitalization on Rate and Quality of Remission From Acute Psychotic Episodes, *J Nerv Ment Dis* *143*:226–233 (Sept) 1966.
3. Pasamanick, B.; Scarpitti, F. R.; and Dinitz, S.: *Schizophrenics in the Community*, New York: Appleton-Century-Crofts, 1967.
4. Mendel, W., and Green, G.: *The Therapeutic Management of Psychological Illness*, New York: Basic Books, Inc., Publishers, 1967.
5. Hollingshead, A. D., and Redlich, F.: *Social Class and Mental Illness*, New York: John Wiley & Sons, Inc., 1958.
6. Myers, J. K., and Roberts, B. H.: *Family and Class Dynamics in Mental Illness*, New York: John Wiley & Sons, Inc., 1959.
7. Freeman, H. E., and Simmons, O. G.: *The Mental Patient Comes Home*, New York: John Wiley & Sons, Inc., 1963.

Decision Rules, Types of Error, and Their Consequences in Medical Diagnosis

Thomas J. Scheff

Members of professions such as law and medicine frequently are confronted with uncertainty in the course of their routine duties. In these circumstances, informal norms have developed for handling uncertainty so that paralyzing hesitation is avoided. These norms are based upon assumptions that some types of error are more to be avoided than others; assumptions so basic that they

Reprinted from *Behavioral Science*, Vol. 8, No. 2, 1963, by permission of James G. Miller, M.D., Ph.D., Editor. Copyright 1963, *Behavioral Science*. This paper was written with the financial support of the Graduate Research Committee of the University of Wisconsin. Colleagues too numerous to list here made useful suggestions. David Mechanic was particularly helpful. An earlier version was presented at the Conference on Mathematical Models in the Behavioral and Social Sciences, sponsored by the Western Management Science Institute, University of California at Los Angeles, Cambria, California, November 3–5, 1961.

are usually taken for granted, are seldom discussed, and are therefore slow to change.

The purpose of this paper is to describe one important norm for handling uncertainty in medical diagnosis, that judging a sick person well is more to be avoided than judging a well person sick, and to suggest some of the consequences of the application of this norm in medical practice. Apparently this norm, like many important cultural norms, "goes without saying" in the subculture of the medical profession; in form, however, it resembles any decision rule for guiding behavior under conditions of uncertainty. In the discussion that follows, decision rules in law, statistics, and medicine are compared, in order to indicate the types of error that are thought to be the more important to avoid and the assumptions underlying this preference. On the basis of recent findings of the widespread distribution of elements of disease and deviance in normal populations, the assumption of a uniform relationship between disease signs and impairment is criticized. Finally, it is suggested that to the extent that physicians are guided by this medical decision rule, they too often place patients in the "sick role" who could otherwise have continued in their normal pursuits.

Decision Rules

To the extent that physicians and the public are biased toward treatment, the "creation" of illness, i.e., the production of unnecessary impairment, may go hand in hand with the prevention and treatment of disease in modern medicine. The magnitude of the bias toward treatment in any single case may be quite small, since there are probably other medical decision rules ("When in doubt, delay your decision") which counteract the rule discussed here. Even a small bias, however, if it is relatively constant throughout Western society, can have effects of large magnitude. Since this argument is based largely on fragmentary evidence, it is intended merely to stimulate further discussion and research, rather than to demonstrate the validity of a point of view. The discussion will begin with the consideration of a decision rule in law.

In criminal trials in England and the United States, there is an explicit rule for arriving at decisions in the face of uncertainty: "A man is innocent until proven guilty." The meaning of this rule is made clear by the English common-law definition of the phrase "proven guilty," which according to tradition is that the judge or jury must find the evidence of guilt compelling *beyond a reasonable doubt*. The basic legal rule for arriving at a decision in the face of uncertainty may be briefly stated: "When in doubt, acquit." That is, the jury or judge must not be equally wary of erroneously convicting or acquitting: the error that is most important to avoid is to erroneously convict. This concept is expressed in the maxim, "Better a thousand guilty men go free, than one innocent man be convicted."

The reasons underlying this rule seem clear. It is assumed that in most cases, a conviction will do irreversible harm to an individual by damaging his reputation in the eyes of his fellows. The individual is seen as weak and defenseless, relative to society, and therefore in no position to sustain the consequences of an erroneous decision. An erroneous acquittal, on the other hand, damages society. If an individual who has actually committed a crime is not punished, he may commit the crime again, or more important, the deterrent effect of punishment for the violation of this crime may be diminished for others. Although these are serious outcomes they are generally thought not to be as serious as the consequences of erroneous conviction for the innocent individual, since society is able to sustain an indefinite number of such errors without serious consequences. For these and perhaps other reasons, the decision rule to assume innocence exerts a powerful influence on legal proceedings.

Type 1 and Type 2 Errors

Deciding on guilt or innocence is a special case of a problem to which statisticians have given considerable attention, the testing of hypotheses. Since most scientific work is done with samples, statisticians have developed techniques to guard against results which are due to chance sampling fluctuations. The problem, however, is that one might reject a finding as due to sampling fluctuations which was actually correct. There are, therefore, two kinds of errors: rejecting a hypothesis which is true, and accepting one which is false. Usually the hypothesis is stated so that the former error (rejecting a hypothesis which is true) is the error that is thought to be the more important to avoid. This type of error is called an "error of the first kind," or a Type 1 error. The latter error (accepting a hypothesis which is false) is the less important error to avoid, and is called an "error of the second kind," or a Type 2 error (Neyman, 1950, pp. 265–266).

To guard against chance fluctuations in sampling, statisticians test the probability that findings could have arisen by chance. At some predetermined probability (called the alpha level), usually .05 or less, the possibility that the findings arose by chance is rejected. This level means that there are five chances in a hundred that one will reject a hypothesis which is true. Although these five chances indicate a real risk of error, it is not common to set the level much lower (say .001) because this raises the probability of making an error of the second kind.

A similar dilemma faces the judge or jury in deciding whether to convict or acquit in the face of uncertainty. Particularly in the adversary system of law, where professional attorneys seek to advance their arguments and refute those of their opponents, there is often considerable uncertainty even as to the facts of the case, let alone intangibles like intent. The maxim, "Better a thousand guilty men should go free, than one innocent man be convicted," would mean, if taken literally rather than as a rhetorical flourish, that the alpha level for legal decisions is set quite low.

Although the legal decision rule is not expressed in as precise a form as a statistical decision rule, it represents a very similar procedure for dealing with uncertainty. There is one respect, however, in which it is quite different. Statistical decision procedures are recognized by those who use them as mere conveniences, which can be varied according to the circumstances. The legal decision rule, in contrast, is an inflexible and binding moral rule, which carries with it the force of long sanction and tradition. The assumption of innocence is a part of the social institution of law in Western society; it is explicitly stated in legal codes, and is accepted as legitimate by jurists and usually by the general populace, with only occasional grumbling, e.g., a criminal is seen as "getting off" because of "legal technicalities."

Decision Rules in Medicine

Although the analogous rule for decisions in medicine is not as explicitly stated as the rule in law and probably is considerably less rigid, it would seem that there is such a rule in medicine which is as imperative in its operation as its analogue in law. Do physicians and the general public consider that rejecting the hypothesis of illness when it is true, or accepting it when it is false, is the error that is most important to avoid? It seems fairly clear that the rule in medicine may be stated as: "When in doubt, continue to suspect illness." That is, for a physician to dismiss a patient when he is actually ill is a Type 1 error, and to retain a patient when he is not ill is a Type 2 error.

Most physicians learn early in their training that it is far more culpable to dismiss a sick patient than to retain a well one. This rule is so pervasive and fundamental that it goes unstated in textbooks on diagnosis. It is occasionally mentioned explicitly in other contexts, however. Neyman, for example, in his discussion of X-ray screening for tuberculosis, states:

> "[If the patient is actually well, but the hypothesis that he is sick is accepted, a Type 2 error], then the patient will suffer some unjustified anxiety and, perhaps, will be put to some unnecessary expense until further studies of his health will establish that any alarm about the state of his chest is unfounded. Also, the unjustified precautions ordered by the clinic may somewhat affect its reputation. On the other hand, should the hypothesis [of sickness] be true and yet the accepted hypothesis be [that he is well, a Type 1 error], then the patient will be in danger of losing the precious opportunity of treating the incipient disease in its beginning stages when the cure is not so difficult. Furthermore, the oversight by the clinic's specialist of the dangerous condition would affect the clinic's reputation even more than the unnecessary alarm. From this point of view, it appears that the error of rejecting the hypothesis [of sickness] when it is true is *far more important* to avoid than the error of accepting the hypothesis [of illness] when it is false" (1950, p. 270, italics added).

Although this particular discussion pertains to tuberculosis, it is pertinent to many other diseases also. From casual conversations with physicians, the impression one gains is that this moral lesson is deeply ingrained in the physician's personal code.

It is not only physicians who feel this way, however. This rule is grounded both in legal proceedings and in popular sentiment. Although there is some sentiment against Type 2 errors (unnecessary surgery, for instance), it has nothing like the force and urgency of the sentiment against Type 1 errors. A physician who dismisses a patient who subsequently dies of a disease that should have been detected is not only subject to legal action for negligence and possible loss of license for incompetence, but also to moral condemnation from his colleagues and from his own conscience for his delinquency. Nothing remotely resembling this amount of moral and legal suasion is brought to bear for committing a Type 2 error. Indeed, this error is sometimes seen as sound clinical practice, indicating a healthy conservative approach to medicine.

The discussion to this point suggests that physicians follow a decision rule which may be stated, "When in doubt, diagnose illness." If physicians are actually influenced by this rule, then studies of the validity of diagnosis should demonstrate the operation of the rule. That is, we should expect that objective studies of diagnostic errors should show that Type 1 and Type 2 errors do not occur with equal frequency, but in fact, that Type 2 errors far outnumber Type 1 errors. Unfortunately for our purposes, however, there are apparently only a few studies which provide the type of data which would adequately test the hypothesis. Although studies of the reliability of diagnosis abound (Garland, 1959), showing that physicians disagree with each other in their diagnoses of the same patients, these studies do not report the validity of diagnosis, or the types of error which are made, with the following exceptions.

We can infer that Type 2 errors outnumber Type 1 errors from Bakwin's study of physicians' judgments regarding the advisability of tonsillectomy for 1,000 school children.

> Of these, some 611 had had their tonsils removed. The remaining 389 were then examined by other physicians, and 174 were selected for tonsillectomy. This left 215 children whose tonsils were apparently normal. Another group of doctors was put to work examining these 215 children, and 99 of them were adjudged in need of tonsillectomy. Still another group of doctors was then employed to examine the remaining children, and nearly one-half were recommended for operation (Bakwin, 1945, p. 693).

Almost half of each group of children were judged to be in need of the operation. Even assuming that a small proportion of children needing tonsillectomy were missed in each examination (Type 1 error), the number of Type 2 errors in this study far exceeded the number of Type 1 errors.

In the field of roentgenology, studies of diagnostic error are apparently more highly developed than in other areas of medicine. Garland (1959, p. 31) summarizes these findings, reporting that in a study of 14,867 films for tuberculosis signs, there were 1,216 positive readings which turned out to be clinically negative (Type 2 error) and only 24 negative readings which turned out to be clinically active (Type 1 error)! This ratio is apparently a fairly typical finding in roentgenographic studies. Since physicians are well aware of the provisional nature of radiological findings, this great discrepancy between the frequency of the types of error in film screening is not too alarming. On the other hand, it does provide objective evidence of the operation of the decision rule "Better safe than sorry."

Basic Assumptions

The logic of this decision rule rests on two assumptions:

1. Disease is usually a determinate, inevitably unfolding process, which, if undetected and untreated, will grow to a point where it endangers the life or limb of the individual, and in the case of contagious diseases, the lives of others. This is not to say, of course, that physicians think of all diseases as determinate: witness the concept of the "benign" condition. The point here is that the imagery of disease which the physician uses in attempting to reach a decision, his working hypothesis, is *usually* based on the deterministic model of disease.

2. Medical diagnosis of illness, unlike legal judgment, is not an irreversible act which does untold damage to the status and reputation of the patient. A physician may search for illness for an indefinitely long time, causing inconvenience for the patient, perhaps, but in the typical case doing the patient no irradicable harm. Obviously, again, physicians do not *always* make this assumption. A physician who suspects epilepsy in a truck driver knows full well that his patient will probably never drive a truck again if the diagnosis is made, and the physician will go to great lengths to avoid a Type 2 error in this situation. Similarly, if a

physician suspects that a particular patient has hypochondriacal trends, the physician will lean in the direction of a Type 1 error in a situation of uncertainty. These and other similar situations are exceptions, however. The physician's *usual* working assumption is that medical observation and diagnosis, in itself, is neutral and innocuous, relative to the dangers resulting from disease.[1]

In the light of these two assumptions, therefore, it is seen as far better for the physician to chance a Type 2 error than a Type 1 error. These two assumptions will be examined and criticized in the remainder of the paper. The assumption that Type 2 errors are relatively harmless will be considered first.

In recent discussions it is increasingly recognized that in one area of medicine, psychiatry, the assumption that medical diagnosis can cause no irreversible harm to the patient's status is dubious. Psychiatric treatment, in many segments of the population and for many occupations, raises a question about the person's social status. It could be argued that in making a medical diagnosis the psychiatrist comes very close to making a legal decision, with its ensuing consequences for the person's reputation. One might argue that the Type 2 error in psychiatry, of judging a well person sick, is at least as much to be avoided as the Type 1 error, of judging the sick person well. Yet the psychiatrist's moral orientation, since he is first and foremost a physician, is guided by the medical, rather than the legal, decision rule.[2] The psychiatrist continues to be more willing to err on the conservative side, to diagnose as ill when the person is healthy, even though it is no longer clear that this error is any more desirable than its opposite.[3]

---

[1] Even though this assumption is widely held, it has been vigorously criticized within the medical profession. See, for example, Darley (1959). For a witty criticism of both assumptions, see Ratner (1962).

[2] Many authorities believe that psychiatrists seldom turn away a patient without finding an illness. See, for example, the statement about large state mental hospitals in Brown (1961, fn. p. 60), and Mechanic (1962). For a study demonstrating the presumption of illness in psychiatric examinations, see Scheff (1963).

[3] "The sociologist must point out that whenever a psychiatrist makes the clinical diagnosis of an existing need for treatment, society makes the social diagnosis of a changed status for one of its members" (Erikson, 1957, p. 123).

There is a more fundamental question about this decision rule, however, which concerns both physical illness and mental disorder. This question primarily concerns the first assumption, that disease is a determinate process. It also implicates the second assumption, that medical treatment does not have irreversible effects.

In recent years physicians and social scientists have reported finding disease signs and deviant behavior prevalent in normal, noninstitutionalized populations. It has been shown, for instance, that deviant acts, some of a serious nature, are widely admitted by persons in random samples of normal populations (Wallerstein & Wyle, 1947; Porterfield, 1946; Kinsey, Pomeroy, & Martin, 1948). There is some evidence which suggests that grossly deviant, "psychotic" behavior has at least temporarily existed in relatively large proportions of a normal population (Clausen & Yarrow, 1955; Plunkett & Gordon, 1961). Finally, there is a growing body of evidence that many signs of physical disease are distributed quite widely in normal populations. A recent survey of simple high blood pressure indicated that the prevalance ranged from 11.4 to 37.2 per cent in the various subgroups studied (Rautahargu, Karvonen, & Keys, 1961; cf. Stokes & Dawber, 1959; Dunn & Etter, 1962).

It can be argued that physical defects and "psychiatric" deviancy exist in an uncrystallized form in large segments of the population. Lemert (1951, p. 75) calls this type of behavior, which is often transitory, *primary deviation.* Balint (1957, p. 18), in his discussion of the doctor-patient relationship, speaks of similar behavior as the "unorganized phase of illness." Balint seems to take for granted, however, that patients will eventually "settle down" to an "organized" illness. Yet it is possible that other outcomes may occur. A person in this stage might change jobs or wives instead, or merely continue in the primary deviation stage indefinitely, without getting better or worse.

This discussion suggests that in order to know the probability that a person with a disease sign would become incapacitated because of the development of disease, investigations quite unlike existing studies would need to be conducted. These would be longitudinal studies of outcomes in persons having signs of disease in a random sample of a normal population, in which no attempt was made to arrest the disease. It is true that there are a number of longitudinal studies in which the effects of treatment are compared with the effects of nontreatment. These studies, however, have always been conducted with clinical groups, rather than with persons with disease signs who were located in field studies.[4] Even clinical trials appear to offer many difficulties, both from the ethical and scientific points of view (Hill, 1960). These difficulties would be increased many times in controlled field trials, as would the problems which concern the amount of time and money necessary. Without such studies, nevertheless, the meaning of many common disease signs remains somewhat equivocal.

Given the relatively small amount of knowledge about the distributions and natural outcomes of many diseases, it is possible that our conceptions of the danger of disease are exaggerated. For example, until the late 1940's, histoplasmosis was thought to be a rare tropical disease, with a uniform fatal outcome. Recently, however, it was discovered that it is widely prevalent, and with fatal outcome or impairment extremely rare (Schwartz & Baum, 1957). It is conceivable that other diseases, such as some types of heart disease and mental disorder, may prove to be similar in character. Although no actuarial studies have been made which would yield the true probabilities of impairment, physicians usually set the Type 1 level quite high, because they believe that the probability of impairment from making a Type 2 error is quite low. Let us now examine that assumption.

The "Sick Role"

If, as has been argued here, much illness goes unattended without serious consequences, the assumption that medical diagnosis has no irreversible effects on the patient seems questionable. "The patient's attitude to his illness is usually considerably changed during and by, the series of physical examinations. These changes, which may profoundly influence the course of a chronic illness, are not taken seriously by the medical profession and, though

---

[4] The Framingham study is an exception to this statement. Even in this study, however, experimental procedures (random assignment to treatment and nontreatment groups) were not used (Dawber, Moore, & Mann, 1957, p. 5).

occasionally mentioned, they have never been the subject of a proper scientific investigation" (Balint, 1957, p. 43).

There are grounds for believing that persons who avail themselves of professional services are under considerable strain and tension (if the problem could have been easily solved, they would probably have used more informal means of handling it). Social-psychological principles indicate that persons under strain are highly suggestible, particularly to suggestions from a prestigeful source, such as a physician.

It can be argued that the Type 2 error involves the danger of having a person enter the "sick role" (Parsons, 1950) in circumstances where no serious result would ensue if the illness were unattended. Perhaps the combination of a physician determined to find disease *signs*, if they are to be found, and the suggestible patient, searching for subjective *symptoms* among the many amorphous and usually unattended bodily impulses, is often sufficient to unearth a disease which changes the patient's status from that of well to sick, and may also have effects on his familial and occupational status. (In Lemert's terms [1951], the illness would be *secondary deviation* after the person has entered the sick role.)

There is a considerable body of evidence in the medical literature concerning the process in which the physician unnecessarily causes the patient to enter the sick role. Thus, in a discussion of "iatrogenic" (physician-induced) heart disease, this point is made:

> The physician, by calling attention to a murmur or some cardiovascular abnormality, even though functionally insignificant, may precipitate [symptoms of heart disease]. The experience of the work classification units of cardiac-in-industry programs, where patients with cardiovascular disease are evaluated as to work capacity, gives impressive evidence regarding the high incidence of such functional manifestations in persons with the diagnosis of cardiac lesion (Warren & Wolter, 1954, p. 78).

Although there is a tendency in medicine to dismiss this process as due to quirks of particular patients, e.g., as malingering, hypochondriasis, or as "merely functional disease" (that is, functional for the patient), causation probably lies not in the patient, but in medical procedures. Most people, perhaps, if they actually have the disease signs and are told by an authority, the physician, that they are ill, will obligingly come up with appropriate symptoms.

A case history will illustrate this process. Under the heading "It may be well to let sleeping dogs lie," a physician recounts the following case:

> Here is a woman, aged 40 years, who is admitted with symptoms of congestive cardiac failure, valvular disease, mitral stenosis and auricular fibrillation. She tells us that she did not know that there was anything wrong with her heart and that she had had no symptoms up to 5 years ago when her chest was x-rayed in the course of a mass radiography examination for tuberculosis. She was not suspected and this was only done in the course of routine at the factory. Her lungs were pronounced clear but she was told that she had an enlarged heart and was advised to go to a hospital for investigation and treatment. From that time she began to suffer from symptoms—breathlessness on exertion—and has been in the hospital 4 or 5 times since. Now she is here with congestive heart failure. She cannot understand why, from the time that her enlarged heart was discovered, she began to get symptoms (Gardiner-Hill, 1958, p. 158).

What makes this kind of "role-taking" extremely important is that it can occur even when the diagnostic label is kept from the patient. By the way he is handled, the patient can usually infer the nature of the diagnosis, since in his uncertainty and anxiety he is extremely sensitive to subtleties in the physician's behavior. An interesting example of this process is found in reports on treatment of battle fatigue. Speaking of psychiatric patients in the Sicilian campaign during World War II, a psychiatrist notes:

> Although patients were received at this hospital within 24 to 48 hours after their breakdown, a disappointing number, approximately 15 per cent, were salvaged for combat duty . . . any therapy, including usual interview methods that sought to uncover basic emotional conflicts or attempted to relate current behavior and symptoms with past personality patterns seemingly provided patients with logical reasons for their combat failure. The insights obtained by even such mild depth therapy readily convinced the patient and often his therapist that the limit of combat endurance had been reached as proved by vulnerable personality traits. Patients were obligingly cooperative in supplying details of their neurotic childhood, previous emotional difficulties, lack of aggressiveness and other dependency traits. . . (Glass, 1953, p. 288; cf. Kardiner & Spiegel, 1947, Ch. 3,4).

Glass goes on to say that removal of the soldier from his unit for treatment of any kind usually resulted in long-term neurosis. In contrast, if the soldier was given only superficial psychiatric attention and *kept with his unit*, chronic impairment was usually avoided. The implication is that removal from the military unit and psychiatric treatment symbolizes to the soldier, behaviorally rather than with verbal labels, the "fact" that he is a mental case.

The traditional way of interpreting these reactions of the soldiers, and perhaps the civilian cases, is in terms of malingering or feigning illness. The process of taking roles, however, as it is conceived of here, is not completely or even largely voluntary. (For a sophisticated discussion of role-playing, see Goffman [1959, pp. 17–22].) Vaguely defined impulses become "real" to the participants when they are organized under any one of a number of more or less interchangeable social roles. It can be argued that when a person is in a confused and suggestible state, when he organizes his feelings and behavior by using the sick role, and when his choice of roles is validated by a physician and/or others, that he is "hooked," and will proceed on a career of chronic illness.[5]

Implications for Research

The hypothesis suggested by the preceding discussion is that physicians and the public typically overvalue medical treatment relative to nontreatment as a course of action in the face of uncertainty, and that this overvaluation results in the creation as well as the prevention of impairment. This hypothesis, since it is based on scattered observations, is put forward only to point out several areas where systematic research is needed.

From the point of view of assessing the effectiveness of medical practice, this hypothesis is probably too general to be used directly. Needed for such a task are hypotheses concerning the conditions under which error is likely to occur, the type of error that is likely, and the consequences of each type of error. Sig-

---

[5] Some of the findings of the Purdue Farm Cardiac Project support the position taken in this paper. It was found, for example, that "iatrogenics" took more health precautions than "hidden cardiacs," suggesting that entry into the sick role can cause more social incapacity than the actual disease does (Eichorn & Andersen, 1962, pp. 11–15).

nificant dimensions of the amount and type of error and its consequences would appear to be characteristics of the disease, the physician, the patient, and the organizational setting in which diagnosis takes place. Thus for diseases such as pneumonia which produce almost certain impairment unless attended, and for which a quick and highly effective cure is available, the hypothesis is probably largely irrelevant. On the other hand, the hypothesis may be of considerable importance for diseases which have a less certain outcome, and for which existing treatments are protracted and of uncertain value. Mental disorders and some types of heart disease are cases in point.

The working philosophy of the physician is probably relevant to the predominant type of errors made. Physicians who generally favor active intervention probably make more Type 2 errors than physicians who view their treatments only as assistance for natural bodily reactions to disease. The physician's perception of the personality of the patient may also be relevant; Type 2 errors are less likely if the physician defines the patient as a "crock," a person overly sensitive to discomfort, rather than as a person who ignores or denies disease.

Finally, the organizational setting is relevant to the extent that it influences the relationship between the doctor and the patient. In some contexts, as in medical practice in organizations such as the military or industrial setting, the physician is not as likely to feel personal responsibility for the patient as he would in others, such as private practice. This may be due in part to the conditions of financial remuneration, and perhaps equally important, the sheer volume of patients dependent on the doctor's time. Cultural or class differences may also affect the amount of social distance between doctor and patient, and therefore the amount of responsibility which the doctor feels for the patient. Whatever the sources, the more the physician feels personally responsible for the patient, the more likely he is to make a Type 2 error.

To the extent that future research can indicate the conditions which influence the amount, type, and consequences of error, such research can make direct contributions to medical practice. Three types of research seem necessary. First, in order to establish the true risks of impairment associated with common disease signs, controlled field trials of treated and untreated outcomes in a normal population would be needed. Second, perhaps in conjunction with these field trials, experimental studies of the effect of suggestion of illness by physicians and others would be necessary to determine the risks of unnecessary entry into the sick role.

Finally, studies of a mathematical nature seem to be called for. Suppose that physicians were provided with the results of the studies suggested above. How could these findings be introduced into medical practice as a corrective to cultural and professional biases in decision-making procedures? One promising approach is the strategy of evaluating the relative utility of alternative courses of action, based upon decision theory or game theory.[6]

Ledley and Lusted (1959) reviewed a number of mathematical techniques which might be applicable to medical decision-making, one of these techniques being the use of the "expected value" equation, which is derived from game theory. Although their discussion pertains to the relative value of two treatment procedures, it is also relevant, with only slight changes in wording, to determining the expected values of treatment relative to nontreatment. The expected values of two treatments, they say, may be calculated from a simple expression involving only two kinds of terms: the probability that the diagnosis is correct, and the absolute value of the treatment (at its simplest, the absolute value is the rate of cure for persons known to have the disease).

The "expected value" of a treatment is:

$$E_t = p_s \, v_s{}^s + (1 - p_s) \, v_h{}^s.$$

(The superscript refers to the way the patient is treated, the subscript refers to his actual condition, s signifies sick, h, healthy.) That is, the expected value of a treatment is the probability p that the patient has the disease, multiplied by the value of the treatment for patients who actually have the disease, plus the probability that the patient does not have the disease $(1 - p)$, multiplied by the value (or "cost") of the treatment for patients who do not have the disease.

Similarly, the expected value of nontreatment is:

$$E_n = p_s \, v_s{}^h + (1 - p_s) \, v_h{}^h.$$

That is, the expected value of nontreatment is the probability that the patient has the disease multiplied by the value (or "cost")

---

[6] For an introductory text, see Chernoff and Moses (1959).

of treating a person as healthy who is actually sick, plus the probability that the patient does not have the disease, multiplied by the value of not treating a healthy person.

The best course of action is indicated by comparing the magnitude of E_t and E_n. If E_t is larger, treatment is indicated. If E_n is larger, nontreatment is indicated. Evaluating these equations involves estimating the probability of correct diagnosis and constructing a payoff matrix for the values of $v_s{}^s$ (proportion of patients who actually had the disease who were cured by the treatment), $v_h{}^s$ (the cost of treating a healthy person as sick: inconvenience, working days lost, surgical risks, unnecessary entry into sick role), $v_s{}^h$ (cost of treating a sick person as well: a question involving the proportions of persons who spontaneously recover, and the seriousness of results when the disease goes unchecked), and finally, $v_h{}^h$ (the value of not treating a healthy person: medical expenses saved, working days, etc.).

To illustrate the use of the equation, Ledley and Lusted assign *arbitrary* absolute values in a case, because, as they say, "The decision of value problems frequently involves intangibles such as moral and ethical standards which must, in the last analysis, be left to the physician's judgment" (1959, p. 8). One might argue, however, that it is better to develop a technique for systematically determining the absolute values of treatment and nontreatment, crude though the technique might be, than to leave the problem to the perhaps refined, but nevertheless obscure, judgment processes of the physician. Particularly in a matter of comparing the value of treatment and nontreatment, the problem is to avoid biases in the physician's judgment due to the kind of moral orientation discussed above.

It is possible, moreover, that the difficulty met by Ledley and Lusted is not that the factors to be evaluated are "intangibles," but that they are expressed in seemingly incommensurate units. How does one weigh the risk of death against the monetary cost of treatment? How does one weigh the risk of physical or social disability against the risk of death? Although these are difficult questions to answer, the idea of leaving them to the physician's judgment is probably not conducive to an understanding of the problem.

Following the lead of the economists in their studies of utility, it may be feasible to reduce the various factors to be weighed to a common unit. How could the benefits, costs, and risks of alternative acts in medical practice be expressed in monetary units? One solution might be to use payment rates in disability and life insurance, which offer a comparative evaluation of the "cost" of death, and permanent and temporary disability of various degrees. Although this approach does not include everything which physicians weigh in reaching decisions (pain and suffering cannot be weighed in this framework), it does include many of the major factors. It therefore would provide the opportunity of constructing a fairly realistic payoff matrix of absolute values, which would then allow for the determination of the relative value of treatment and nontreatment using the expected value equation.[7]

Gathering data for the payoff matrix might make it possible to explore an otherwise almost inaccessible problem: the sometimes subtle conflicts of interest between the physician and the patient. Although it is fairly clear that medical intervention was unnecessary in particular cases, and that it was probably done for financial gain (Trussel, Ehrlich, & Morehead, 1962), the evaluation of the influence of remuneration on diagnosis and treatment is probably in most cases a fairly intricate matter, requiring precise techniques of investigation. If the payoff were calculated in terms of values to the patient *and* values to the physician, such problems could be explored. Less tangible values such as convenience and work satisfactions could be introduced into the matrix. The following statements by psychiatrists were taken from Hollingshead and Redlich's study of social class and mental disorder:

"Seeing him every morning was a chore; I had to put him on my back and carry him for an hour." "He had to get attention in large doses, and this was hard to do." "The patient was not interesting or attractive; I had to repeat, repeat, repeat." "She was a poor unhappy, miserable woman—we were worlds apart" (1958, p. 344).

This study strongly suggests that psychiatric diagnosis and

---

[7] It is possible that more sophisticated techniques may be applicable to the problem of constructing medical payoff matrices (Churchman, Ackoff, & Arnoff, 1957, Ch. 6 & 11). The possibility of applying these techniques to the present problem was suggested to the author by James G. March.

treatment are influenced by the payoff for the psychiatrist as well as for the patient. In any type of medical decision, the use of the expected value equation might show the extent of the conflict of interest between physician and patient, and thereby shed light on the complex process of medical decision making.

References

Bakwin, H. Pseudocia pediatricia. *New England J. Med.*, 1945, 232, 691–697.

Balint, M. *The doctor, his patient, and the illness.* New York: International Universities Press, 1957.

Brown, Esther L. *Newer dimensions of patient care.* New York: Russell Sage, 1961.

Chernoff, H., & Moses, L. E. *Elementary decision theory.* New York: Wiley, 1959.

Clausen, J. A., & Yarrow, M. R. Paths to the mental hospital. *J. soc. Issues*, 1955, 11, 25–32.

Churchman, C. W., Ackoff, R. L., & Arnoff, E. L. *Introduction to operations research.* New York: Wiley, 1957.

Darley, W. What is the next step in preventive medicine? *Assoc. Teachers prevent. Med. Newsletter*, 1959, 6.

Dawber, T. R., Moore, F. E., & Mann, G. V. Coronary heart disease in the Framingham study. *Amer. J. pub. Health*, 1957, 47 Part 2, 4–24.

Dunn, J. P., & Etter, L. E. Inadequacy of the medical history in the diagnosis of duodenal ulcer. *New England J. Med.*, 1962, 266, 68–72.

Eichorn, R. L., & Andersen, R. M. Changes in personal adjustment to perceived and medically established heart disease: a panel study. Paper read at American Sociological Association Meeting, Washington, D.C., 1962.

Erickson, K. T. Patient role and social uncertainty—a dilemma of the mentally ill. *Psychiatry*, 1957, 20, 263–274.

Gardiner-Hill, H. *Clinical involvements.* London: Butterworth, 1958.

Garland, L. H. Studies of the accuracy of diagnostic procedures. *Amer. J. Roentgenol., radium Therapy, nuclear Med.*, 1959, 82, 25–38.

Glass, A. J. Psychotherapy in the combat zone. *Symposium on stress.* Washington, D.C.: Army Medical Service Graduate School, 1953.

Goffman, E. *The presentation of self in everyday life.* Garden City, N.Y.: Doubleday Anchor, 1959.

Hill, A. B. (Ed.). *Controlled clinical trails.* Springfield, Ill.: Charles C Thomas, 1960.

Hollingshead, A. B., & Redlich, F. C. *Social class and mental illness.* New York: Wiley, 1958.

Kardiner, A., & Spiegel, H. *War stress and neurotic illness.* New York: Hoeber, 1947.

Kinsey, A. C., Pomeroy, W. B., & Martin, C. E. *Sexual behavior in the human male.* Philadelphia and London: W. B. Saunders, 1948.

Ledley, R. S., & Lusted, L. B. Reasoning foundations of medical diagnosis. *Science*, 1959, 130, 9–21.

Lemert, E. M. *Social pathology.* New York: McGraw-Hill, 1951.

Mechanic, D. Some factors in identifying and defining mental illness. *Ment. Hygiene*, 1962, 46, 66–74.

Neyman, J. *First course in statistics and probability.* New York: Holt, 1950.

* Parsons, T. Illness and the role of the physician. *Amer. J. Orthopsychiat.*, 1950, 21, 452–460.

Plunkett, R. J., & Gordon, J. E. *Epidemiology and mental illness.* New York: Basic Books, 1961.

Porterfield, A. L. *Youth in trouble.* Fort Worth, Tex.: Leo Potishman Foundation, 1946.

Rautahargu, P. M., Karvonen, M. J., & Keys, A. The frequency of arteriosclerotic and hypertensive heart disease in ostensibly healthy working populations in Finland. *J. chron. Diseases*, 1961, 13, 426–439.

Ratner, H. Medicine. *Interviews on the American character.* Santa Barbara: Center for the Study of Democratic Institutions, 1962.

Scheff, T. J. The presumption of illness in psychiatric screening. Paper read at Midwest Sociological Society Convention, Milwaukee, 1963.

Schwartz, J., & Baum, G. L. The history of histoplasmosis. *New England J. Med.*, 1957, 256, 253–258.

Stokes, J., & Dawber, T. R. The "silent coronary": the frequency and clinical characteristics of unrecognized myocardial infarction in the Framingham study. *Ann. internal Med.*, 1959, 50, 1359–1369.

Trussel, R. E., Ehrlich, June, & Morehead, Mildred. *The quantity, quality and costs of medical and hospital care secured by a sample of teamster families in the New York area.* New York: Columbia Univ. School of Public Health and Administrative Medicine, 1962.

Wallerstein, J. S., & Wyle, C. J. Our law-abiding law-breakers. *Probation*, 1947, 25, 107–112.

Warren, J. V., & Wolter, Janet. Symptoms and diseases induced by the physician. *Gen. Practitioner*, 1954, 9, 77–84.

Suggestion Effects in Psychiatric Diagnosis

Maurice K. Temerlin

In order to explore interpersonal influences which might affect psychiatric diagnosis, psychiatrists, clinical psychologists and graduate students in clinical psychology diagnosed a sound-recorded interview with a normal, healthy man. Just before listening to the interview, they heard a professional person of high prestige, acting as a confederate of the experimenter, say that the individual to be diagnosed was "a very interesting man because he looked neurotic but actually was quite psychotic."

Criteria of Mental Health

Since people are not perfect and any imperfection could be considered evidence of mental illness, a professional actor was trained to portray a mentally healthy man by these criteria: he was happy and effective in his work; he established a warm, gracious and satisfying relationship with the interviewer; he was self-confident and secure, but without being arrogant, competitive or grandiose. He was identified with the parent of the same sex, was happily married and in love with his wife and consistently enjoyed sexual intercourse. He felt that sex was fun, unrelated to anxiety, social-role conflict or status striving. This was built into his role because mental patients allegedly are sexually anhedonic. He was also defined as an empirically oriented agnostic, because mental patients so often are committed to religion, mysticism, extrasensory perception or occult phenomenon; he also had a benign, self-reflexive sense of humor to counteract the common impression that mental patients are humorless people who lack insight. He had no hallucinations, delusions or psychosomatic symptoms, and he also was provided with a happy childhood.

Reprinted from the *Journal of Nervous and Mental Disease*, vol. 147, copyright 1968, The Williams & Wilkins Co., Baltimore, Md. 21202, U.S.A., pp. 349–353. By permission of the Williams & Wilkins Company. This study was supported in part by the faculty research fund of the University of Oklahoma. Mr. William Trousdale helped gather the data for this study, and Jane Chapman, William Lemmon, Ruth Mansfield and Robert Ragland read the manuscript and made many helpful suggestions.

Since even the healthiest people presumably have anxieties related to difficult life situations, the actor expressed mild concern over Viet Nam, had occasional disagreements with his wife over whether to go to church or to stay in bed on Sunday morning and did not always know precisely how best to raise his children. To give him a reason for being in a clinical setting which would not automatically classify him as sick, the script defined him as a successful and productive physical scientist and mathematician (a profession as far away from psychiatry as possible) who had read a book on psychotherapy and wanted to talk about it.

Procedure

The actor memorized a script in which he described himself and his life. The context of the script and the relaxed way in which he portrayed it met the above criteria, as judged by three clinical psychologists (evaluating the interview without prior suggestion) and the control groups to be described later. He then was interviewed by the author as if he were a prospective patient. The actor knew the interview was being sound-recorded, but he did not know the purpose of the experiment or that the recording would be diagnosed by 45 graduate students in clinical psychology, 25 practicing clinical psychologists, and 25 psychiatrists. (A transcription of the interview is available upon request.) Psychologists and psychiatrists were selected from three cities on a stratified random basis to represent employment in clinics, state mental hospitals, Veterans hospitals and private practice. Graduate students were enrolled in APA-approved doctoral programs in clinical psychology at two Midwestern state universities.

The sound-recorded interview was played for the staff, interns, residents and consultants of the participating hospitals and clinics, ostensibly as part of a regular staff meeting, practicum meeting, research seminar or in-service training program in diagnostic interviewing. Shortly before the tape was played, the prestige confederate remarked that the patient on the tape was "a very interesting man because he looks neurotic, but actually is quite psychotic." For clinical psychologists and graduate students, the confederate was a well known psychologist with many professional honors. Psychiatrists were told that "two board-certified psychiatrists, one also a psychoanalyst, had found the recording interesting because the patient looked neurotic but actually was quite psychotic. However, two diagnostic opinions are not enough for a criterial diagnosis against which test scores can be correlated in a test construction project."

After listening to the interview, the subjects indicated their diagnosis on a data sheet which listed, in counterbalanced order, 10 psychoses, 10 neuroses, and 10 miscellaneous personality types, one of which was "normal or healthy personality." After encircling the category which best fits the patient, the subjects were asked to:

> Write a brief description of the patient to indicate the behavioral basis of your diagnosis. Be as descriptive as you can. Use no technical terms, and make as few inferences as possible. Just write what you heard the patient say that lead you to diagnose him as you did.

After they wrote the clinical report, the subjects were asked to change their original diagnosis if they wished, the prediction being that initial diagnoses would be corrected after observations and inferences were separated in the task of writing the clinical report.

Acting as confederates, other "subjects" conducted an informal "grapevine" debriefing to see if compliance with the suggestion had been conscious, to check on subject naivete (harder to control as the experiment progressed) and to see if the subjects had been suspicious of the procedure. After all data were collected, formal debriefings were conducted; those subjects whose diagnoses were correct were interviewed at length.

Controls

Four control groups were used. Three matched groups, stratified for professional identity, diagnosed the same recorded interview under different conditions. One diagnosed it with no prior suggestion; another diagnosed it with the prestige suggestion reversed. To control that a clinical setting alone might predispose a diagnostician to expect pathology, one group evaluated the interview as part of a project for selecting scientists to work in industrial research. These subjects were asked to listen to a sound recording of a "new kind of personnel interview, designed to obtain personal information related to scientific productivity," and then to evaluate a candidate for employment on 10 employment-relevant scales, such as responsibility, probable scientific productivity, relationships with colleagues and supervisors. Embedded among these distractor scales was a mental health scale with health and psychosis at the extremes and neurosis in the center. The first 30 seconds of the recording were changed to delete curiosity about psychotherapy and to substitute a personnel manager for a clinician; otherwise, the interview remained unchanged.

As a fourth control, a mock sanity hearing was conducted in a county courthouse with lay jurors randomly selected from a regular jury wheel.[1] Jurors judged the same interview after being told that the court was experimenting with a new procedure for conducting sanity hearings, with the jury listening to a recording of the diagnostic interview itself, rather than relying exclusively on psychiatric testimony.

Results

Control data are presented in Table 1. The diagnoses of experimental subjects are presented in Table 2. All differences between

TABLE 1   DIAGNOSES OF CONTROL SUBJECTS

	Mental Illness		
	PSYCHOSIS	NEUROSIS AND CHARACTER DISORDER	*Mental Health*
No prestige suggestion ($N = 21^*$)	0	9	12
Suggestion of mental health ($N = 20^*$)	0	0	20
Employment interview ($N = 24^*$)	0	7	17
Sanity hearing† ($N = 12$)	0	—‡	12

* Totals after a replication, grouped together when no differences were found on replication.

† Jurors voted individually, then after discussion, with the same results.

‡ In the sanity hearing jurors voted "sane" or "insane" to follow legal procedures as closely as possible.

---

[1] For this control group, I am grateful to Dr. Helen Klein, who conducted the mock sanity hearing.

TABLE 2   DIAGNOSES OF EXPERIMENTAL SUBJECTS

| | *Mental Illness* | | |
	PSYCHOSIS	NEUROSES AND CHARACTER DISORDERS	*Mental Health*
Psychiatrists ($N = 25$)	15	10	0
Clinical psychologists ($N = 25$)	7	15	3
Graduate students in clinical psychology ($N = 45$)	5	35	5

$x^2 = 20.21$, $df = 4$, $p < .001$.

experimental and control groups are significant at the .01 level, whether comparisons are made between specific groups or combined groups. For example, no control subject ever diagnosed psychosis, while in the experimental groups, diagnoses of psychosis were made by 60 per cent of the psychiatrists, 28 per cent of the clinical psychologists, and 11 per cent of the graduate students.

Differences between experimental groups are significant at the .001 level, indicating a relationship between the effect of prestige suggestion and professional identity. Prestige suggestion had most effect upon psychiatrists, biasing them in the direction of psychosis, least effect upon graduate students; clinical psychologists fell between these extremes, and both of these groups made significantly more diagnoses of neurosis and health than did psychiatrists. That this finding is a relationship between prestige suggestion and professional identity, rather than exclusively an occupational hazard of psychiatry, seems logical because psychologists and psychiatrists in the control groups did not diagnose differently. For example, when the prestige confederate of control group 2 said, "You know, I think this is a very rare person, a perfectly healthy man," psychologists, psychiatrists, and graduate students agreed unanimously. That professional identity, rather than length of training or experience, is the relevant variable is illustrated by a within-group analysis: no relationship was found between diagnosis and length of training for any experimental group.

The most common diagnoses of psychosis were, in order, these subclassifications of schizophrenia: pseudoneurotic, ambulatory, paranoid and hebephrenic. The most common diagnoses of neurosis were, in order, obsessive-compulsive neurosis, hysteria and passive-aggressive character disorder.

When asked to report the observations on which their diagnosis was based, the only subjects who even approximated doing so were those whose diagnoses were correct. Most subjects either mixed inferences and observations or reported inferences exclusively; some subjects reported inferences labled as observations. In other words, in spite of explicit instructions to avoid inferences and to be descriptive, only the few subjects who diagnosed health reported such observations as "the patient said that he was enjoying life, said that he was happily married, said that he was effective and productive in his work, and that he had had a happy childhood." And, to illustrate an appropriate connection of inference to observation, only the accurate diagnosticians added such inferences as "he also *seemed* to talk logically, coherently, and in a relaxed manner, and to establish a warm, friendly relationship with the clinician." It therefore was not surprising that no subject changed his diagnosis to one of health after writing a clinical report, although changes between categories of pathology were numerous.

The problem of obtaining consistent agreement between different observers is one of the oldest and most difficult problems of psychological research. This chronic difficulty probably was exacerbated by both the prestige suggestion and the nature of the concept of mental illness itself. That is, mental illness is a mentalistic concept; neurosis and psychosis are never directly observable but must be inferred from behavioral symptoms. This characteristic of the concept may have biased subjects to be inferential rather than descriptive. One psychiatrist illustrated this point by defending his diagnosis of psychosis with the comment, "Of course he looked healthy, but hell, most people are a little neurotic, and who can accept appearances at face value anyway?"

Discussion

While psychiatriac categories may be useful in clinical practice, numerous studies have found them to be unreliable statistically. Different psychiatrists frequently classify the same person within different categories, and the behavioral characteristics of the person may not be predicted from a knowledge of his psychiatric category (5). Furthermore, the same behavior may be considered evidence of mental illness when it occurs in a member of the lower socioeconomic classes and personal idiosyncrasy in a member of the upper class (2). This study suggests that suggestion effects may contribute to the unreliability of psychiatric diagnosis; no control subject ever diagnosed psychosis, for example, though 60 per cent of the psychiatrists diagnosed psychosis when this suggestion was present. The following factors may have contributed to the increased effect of the prestige suggestion upon psychiatrists.

1) Psychiatrists are, first and foremost, physicians. It is characteristic of physicians in diagnostically uncertain situations to follow the implicit rule "when in doubt, diagnose illness" because this is a less dangerous error than diagnosing health when illness is, in fact, present (3).

2) Psychiatry, as a division of organized medicine, has highly differentiated status and role hierarchies, and the system may reward conformity with prestige figures. Psychologists, with historical origins in philosophy and current identifications as social scientists, are more critical and skeptical, even to the point of divisiveness (1), as illustrated by the heterogeneous divisions of the American Psychological Association. The joke "wherever there are two psychologists, there are three opinions" is less descriptive of psychiatrists.

3) In their daily work psychiatrists probably encountered more psychotics than did clinical psychologists or graduate students, and thus they may have expected a psychotic even before the prestige suggestion.

The demonstrated susceptibility of psychiatric diagnosis to distortion through prestige suggestion could be determined in part by the nature of the concept of mental illness itself. It is doubtful that prestige suggestion could bias medical diagnosis so dramatically, on the theory that the substantive reality of physical illness would counterbalance the distorting effects of prestige suggestion. Such substantive realities are absent in mental illness, according to the provocative reasoning of Szasz (4).

Szasz maintains that psychiatric categories are not classifications of diseases, but instead are labels applied to disorganized social behavior. In other words, there is no such natural phe-

nomenon as a disease of the mind; people who exhibit unacceptable social behavior are simply labeled mentally ill. If Szasz is
correct, pyschiatric diagnosis is inherently unreliable because, instead of classifying observable diseases which exist "out there,"
it would be a process of labeling social behavior in terms of the
ethical and social norms of society and psychiatry. Since such
norms are vague, vary with culture and socioeconomic class and
usually are not explicit, diagnosis *as labeling* would have to vary
with the personal values and perceptual consistencies of the individual diagnostician. From Szasz's viewpoint, diagnosis would be
a process of understanding a unique person in a particular life
situation, in order to be of help; and psychotherapy is not treatment for disease but a process of learning more effective means
of relating to oneself and to other people.

Although most studies demonstrate the low reliability of psychiatric diagnosis (5), Szasz's point of view lacks general acceptance among mental health professionals. As one subject put it
during the debriefing, "Goddammit, the people are in the mental
hospitals, and you can't get them out by logic." Such reasoning,
however pragmatic, attributes more validity to diagnostic procedures than may be warranted, because sensory or social isolation
may produce the symptoms commonly attributed to mental illness. The problems raised by Szasz's provocative reasoning thus
remain unsolved. The basic problem in testing Szasz's position
experimentally is the difficulty of separating *diagnoses* of mental
illness from mental illness itself, if it exists, because there is no
operational criterion of mental illness which is independent of
psychiatric diagnosis, and with which psychiatric diagnosis might
be correlated in a validity study.

This study demonstrates that psychiatric diagnosis may be
studied *as if* it were a process of labeling social behavior by
manipulating the interpersonal context in which diagnoses are
made and by observing changes in the diagnostic labels applied
to a person of standard stimulus value. Through such studies the
interpersonal influences which affect psychiatric diagnosis may
be better understood, and this increased awareness can only enhance the accuracy and helpfulness of clinical judgment.

References

1. Chein, I. Some sources of divisiveness among psychologists. Amer. Psychol., *22*: 333–342, 1966.
2. Hollinghead, A. and Redlich, F. *Social Class and Mental Illness: A Community Study.* Wiley, New York, 1958.
3. Scheff, T. *Being Mentally Ill: A Sociological Theory.* Aldine, Chicago, 1966.
4. Szasz, T. *The Myth of Mental Illness.* Hoeber-Harper, New York, 1961.
5. Zigler, E. and Phillips, L. Psychiatric diagnosis and symptomatology. In Milton, O., ed. *Behavior Disorders*, pp. 61–74. Lippincott, New York, 1965.

PART FOUR

The Mental Hospital: Patient Strategies for Coping

After reading the articles in the preceding section, one might be tempted to conclude that the mental patient is a helpless person controlled by the social forces and pressures of the mental hospital. But the articles in this section suggest that some mental patients may have their own form of "counterpower." Braginsky and his colleagues suggest that mental patients may actually express or withhold the expression of their symptoms as a way of managing the impression they make on the treatment staff. By managing these staff impressions, the authors argue, the patient may be able to convince the staff that he is ready for discharge if that is what he wishes, or perhaps that he should remain in the hospital if that is what he desires.

The article by Braginsky, Grosse, and Ring suggests that not all patients wish to leave the mental hospital. Some patients ("old-timers") appear to prefer the hospital setting to the outside world and will behave in any way that assures them their place in the hospital. Other patients ("short-timers") seem anxious to leave the hospital and will also report their symptoms in whatever way seems appropriate to gain their freedom.

The second article, by Braginsky and Braginsky, tests their impression-management hypothesis in the context of the psychiatric interview. Their findings suggest that mental patients will respond according to their beliefs about the purpose of the interview. If they believe that the purpose of the interview is to decide whether they should be placed on a less desirable closed ward, they will suppress complaints to demonstrate that they are capable of remaining in the open ward setting. If, on the other hand, they believe that they may be discharged, and do not wish to be, they will present themselves as "sick" and ineligible for discharge. This research suggests that mental patients are not necessarily the ineffective, passive people that they are usually thought to be. Their behavior can be purposeful and goal-directed.

Of course, the mental patient's skill in impression management will vary, just as it does for people in everyday life, and will depend on how severely disturbed he is, as the article by Price clearly demonstrates. After reviewing the evidence for impression management, Price concludes that impression management may be important in the maintenance of symptoms of hospitalized patients but is unlikely to tell us anything important about the etiology of severe disorders such as schizophrenia.

Controlling Outcomes through Impression-Management: An Experimental Study of the Manipulative Tactics of Mental Patients

Benjamin M. Braginsky, Martin Grosse, and Kenneth Ring

The present investigation addresses itself to the following questions: Do mental patients attempt control of the outcome of the mental hospital's decisions as to which patients stay or leave, and are their attempts successful? It is clear that any conceptual or empirical attempt to answer these questions will be dependent upon the assumptions one holds about the nature of the mental patient, the nature of the mental hospital, and, of course, the nature of the marriage of both. At present there are two commonly held sets of assumptions about the nature of the mental hospital and the nature of mental patients which are relevant to the above problem.

One point of view is exemplified by Goffman (1961), who presents mental patients as not uniquely ineffective people but who, when caught in the massive and debilitating pressures of institutional life, become powerless and impotent. The mental patient is perceived as having little or no control over the hospital's decisions.

The other commonly held set of assumptions presents the mental patient as an individual who for most of his life has been an inert, helpless, frightened, and acquiescent individual (e.g., Downing, 1958; Fairweather, 1964; Gordon, 1961) whose mode of adaptation to the hospital is one of passive and helpless clinging to a benign and nurturant institution. For proponents of this point of view, patients remain in the hospital out of default; their pathological status, fused with fears of community life and coupled with a benign and accepting hospital, gives them no choice but to remain. This position views the prime determinants of staying or leaving the hospital as residing both in the hospital's decision-making apparatus and in the patient's pathological status.

These conceptualizations of the mental patient have in common two important implications. One, the patient is viewed as less than an active and effective organism, who can significantly affect the kinds of adaptations he makes to the hospital. Two, the hospital, whether it is seen as benign or oppressive, is conceived of as the most effective determinant of the patient's behavior and consequently of the subsequent discharge or chronicity of the patient.

These two sets of assumptions or points of view become suspect if we investigate and find, for example, that an important outcome of hospitalization such as staying or leaving is directly related to patient motives and manipulative strategies rather than being solely a product of hospital decision-making processes. Although results of this kind would in no way be definitive in either supporting or rejecting the above assumptions, they would increase the plausibility of a third point of view. That is, patients are by no means helpless and can be more effective in manipulating the hospital milieu to satisfy their own needs than is commonly observed. This position is implied by Levinson and Gallagher (1964) when they state that ". . . the mental patient is to be perceived as a responsible participant in organizational life. He is not primarily an object of social manipulation, nor is he completely a free agent."

The present investigators hold to this latter viewpoint. Specifically, we state that most patients have strong desires to either remain in or to leave the mental hospital and will attempt to maximize the satisfaction of these desires by the use of a variety of manipulative strategies. The particular manipulative strategy focused on in this study is the patient's use of impression management (Goffman, 1959). Goffman defines this particular form of manipulative behavior as the ability to control the impressions others form of you. In the context of the mental hospital it is the mental patient's ability to present an image or impression of himself as either being "ill" (if he wishes to remain in the hospital) or "healthy" (if he desires to leave the hospital).

If patients engage in and are effective in controlling the impressions staff form about them, one would expect to find a relationship between discharge rates and patient motives or desires.

If patients are not effective or do not engage in manipulative strategies, then no relationship should exist between patient desires and discharge rates, or even a negative one.

In this conceptual context, two groups of patients were chosen for study. One group we term "old-timers." These are open-ward patients who had been in the hospital for 3 months or longer at the time of this investigation and who had the lowest discharge rate in the hospital (17% of this group gets discharged during any 1 year). The large majority of patients in this group had been in the hospital for 3 years or longer. The second group focused on is what we term "short-timers." They were newly admitted patients who had been in the hospital less than 3 months and who were experiencing their first hospitalization. As a group they have the highest discharge rate in the hospital (80% are discharged within their first 3 months of hospitalization). With respect to these groups, we predicted the following:

1. Old-timers should be positively motivated to stay in the hospital and therefore should attempt to present themselves to the hospital staff as being "ill," thus maximizing their chances of remaining in the hospital.

2. Short-timers should be positively motivated to leave the hospital and therefore should attempt to present themselves to the hospital staff as being "healthy," thus maximizing their chances of leaving the hospital.

Method

A number of investigators have demonstrated the sensitivity of personality inventories to the selective censoring of responses by subjects in order to portray themselves in a socially desirable light (Crowne, 1960; Davids, 1964; Edwards, 1957; Getzel, 1954). In addition, these studies have demonstrated the usefulness of this phenomenon both in examining and understanding "impression management" in test-taking behavior, and in measuring the motives of the subjects, e.g., Marlowe-Crowne scale (1960) as a measure of need for social approval.

In the same vein, the present investigators devised a combined experimental induction and paper-and-pencil test procedure for determining (*a*) whether a particular group of patients will engage in impression management on a "mental status" test, (*b*) the kinds of performances they will engage in, that is, presenting themselves as "ill" or "healthy," and (*c*) the motivational structure of the group, that is, desires to remain or leave the hospital. This was accomplished by designing an experimental situation in which differences in patient responses to a "mental status" test were not a function of the content of the items but rather a function of the patient's desires to remain or leave the hospital and their use of the strategy of impression management.

Thirty Minnesota Multiphasic Personality Inventory (MMPI) items were selected as the experimental items for the "mental status" tests. They were chosen for their midpoint value on a social desirability scale (Dahlstrom & Welsh, 1960). We hopefully assumed that this would reduce the social desirability "pull" on test responses in either a true or false direction, thereby allowing for an optimum experimental induction effect on the subject's test responses.

Two test forms were then constructed. One form consisting of these 30 items was titled the Mental Illness Test. A second form containing the identical thirty items was titled the Self-Insight Test. Two sets of inductions were then devised, each induction being relevant only to its corresponding test form. The inductions were as follows:

Mental Illness Test Induction. Subjects assigned to this condition prior to taking the Mental Illness Test were told by the experimenter the following:

> This test is designed to measure how severely mentally ill a patient is. We have found that the more items answered True by a patient the more severely ill a patient is and the greater are his chances of remaining in the hospital for a long period of time. Patients who answer many of the items as False are less severely mentally ill and will probably remain in the hospital for a short period of time. We would like to find out how ill you are.

Self-Insight Test Induction. Subjects assigned to this condition were told by the experimenter the following:

> This test is designed to measure how much knowledge a patient has about himself. We have found that the more items answered True by a patient the more he knows about himself, the less

severely ill he is and the greater are his chances of remaining in the hospital for a short period of time. Patients who answer many of the items as False know less about themselves, are more mentally ill and will probably remain in the hospital for a long period of time. We would like to find out how much you know about yourself.

The instructions were designed to (*a*) increase the saliency of the patient's motives for either staying or leaving the hospital while in the testing situation, (*b*) offer the patient a "script" for what is the appropriate performance on the test if one wishes to leave or stay, and if one wishes to engage in impression management.

Using a stratified random sampling procedure 40 male, open-ward patients were selected as subjects: 20 old-timers and 20 short-timers. The 20 subjects in each group were randomly assigned to either one of the two experimental conditions. Therefore, 10 old-timers were randomly selected for the Mental Illness Test Induction condition, and 10 old-timers were randomly selected for the Self-Insight Test Induction condition. The identical procedure was followed for the short-timer group. In summary, we have a 2×2 analysis of variance design with 10 subjects per cell.

In addition, a control group of 20 old-timers was selected in the above fashion. They received the tests in the same manner as the above groups except without the inductions. The purpose of this group was to ascertain the effects of the experimenter's oral induction or "script" as compared to the effects of the printed titles of the tests and/or the general test-taking set the patient brings to the testing situation. Due to the difficulty in getting short-timers (most patients are readmissions), we decided not to run a control group with short-timers.

The experimenter (who tested all 60 subjects) used the standard operational procedures for contacting and testing patients. The subjects were in no way given the orientation of being involved in an experimental procedure but rather quite oppositely were given the orientation of being in a standard clinical evaluation situation.

Operational hypotheses. We assumed that if the old-timers were motivated to remain in the hospital and if they engage in impression management, they should score significantly higher (endorse more items as being true) on the Mental Illness Test than on the Self-Insight Test. Conversely, we assumed that if the short-timers were motivated to leave the hospital and if they also engaged in impression management, they should show a significant reversal of the above pattern of scores. Namely, short-timers should score significantly higher (endorse more items as being true) on the Self-Insight Test than on the Mental Illness Test. In other words, old-timers should engage in a test-taking performance or act designed to elicit the impression of being mentally ill while short-timers should engage in a performance which would create the impression that they are not mentally ill. If we translate our predictions in terms of analysis of variance, we would hypothesize that a significant interaction between groups and tests should occur, with no significant main effects occurring. Optimally, examination of the cells should show a reversal of scores between groups, with significant differences occurring between tests within each group and between groups on identical tests.

Subjects

All subjects in the study were hospitalized male patients. The mean age of the patients selected was 37.2 years with a standard deviation of 10.65. The mean educational level of the total group was 10.2 years of schooling with a standard deviation of 3.64. In terms of general diagnostic categories, we found that 68% of the sample were diagnosed as schizophrenic, an additional 20% were diagnosed as psychotic but not schizophrenic, and the remaining 12% as neurotic. If we compare subjects in the short-timers group with subjects in the old-timers group, we find, as should be expected, age and educational differences. The mean age and educational level for the short-timers was correspondingly 31.3 years and 11.0 years as compared to the old-timers means of 43.0 and 9.45 years. There were no differences between old-timers and short-timers in the distribution of diagnostic categories. In addition, a cell by cell comparison on the above variables showed the success of the randomization procedure in that no subgroup differences existed between the two experimental induction conditions within each of the experimental groups.

TABLE 1   MEAN NUMBER OF TRUE RESPONSES ENDORSED BY OLD- AND SHORT-
TIMERS

Groups	Mental Illness test	Self-Insight test
Old-timers	18.80	9.70
Short-timers	13.00	18.80
Old-timers (control)	14.60	14.30

The control group which consisted of 20 old-timers had a mean age of 38.9 years with an *SD* of 11.13. The mean educational level was 9.0 years with an SD of 3.23. Seventy percent were diagnosed as schizophrenic, 15% were diagnosed as psychotic, and the remaining 15% as neurotic.

Results and Discussion

Table 1 shows quite clearly that the old-timer group had a higher mean number of items endorsed as True on the Mental Illness Test than they did on the Self-Insight Test (which contains the identical items). The reverse effect occurred for the short-timers. They endorsed a significantly greater number of items as True on the Self-Insight Test than they did on the Mental Illness Test. Using the Newman-Keuls procedure (Winer, 1962) the differences between cells within experimental groups and between the experimental groups on identical tests are significant beyond the .01 level.

The analysis of variance based on the data in Table 1 presents the significant source of variation as due to the interaction between the Test-Induction Conditions and the Experimental Groups ($F = 15.61, p < .01$). The significant "balanced" reversal of mean scores between experimental groups allows for the significant interaction effect and disallows for either a simple Test-Induction effect or a Group effect. It is interesting to note that the sum of the means for each group approximately equals the total number of items of the test. One may attribute this to the equal effectiveness of the inductions in each condition. Thus no one condition seems more effective in producing the significant interaction, nor does the effect favor any particular experimental group. In summary, both old-timers and short-timers appear to engage in impression management on the tests. Old-timers present the group profile of being "ill" with the implications of their performance perceived as leading to a greater chance of remaining hospitalized. Short-timers present the group profile of being "healthy" with the implications of their performance perceived as allowing for only a short stay in the hospital.

A comparison of means between old-timers in the experimental and control condition was made to determine whether the effects obtained are due to the specific verbal induction presented by the experimenter or to the titles of the tests. It is clearly noted in Table 1 that the control group presents no mean differences between the Mental Illness and Self-Insight Tests. In the analysis of variance between experimental and control old-timers we find a significant source of variation due to tests ($p < .05$) and a tendency toward a significant interaction between groups and tests ($p < .10$). This can be attributed solely to the differences obtained between tests in the experimental old-timers group. The induction appears then as quite effective in structuring the testing situation by (a) making salient patient's motives of leaving or staying, (b) offering a script for "proper" or need appropriate performance, and (c) evoking impression management in patients.

With full cognizance of the cardinal error of surplus meaning, let us examine some of the implications of these results. Some readers may feel impelled to offer the interpretation that the study has demonstrated the phenomenon of impression management in the service of helplessness. That is, mental patients will attempt to maintain a mode of adaptation, in other words, staying in a hospital, that supports and reflects their helplessness and dependency.

We find it more plausible and parsimonious to view these findings in terms of the assumptions we hold about people in general. Thus the job applicant who attempts to control the impression the interviewer forms of him and the mental patient who engages in the same kind of manipulative behavior in order to stay or leave the hospital can be understood within a single conceptual framework. Both have strong desires, and both attempt to control the outcome of their interactions in a manner which maximizes the chances of fulfilling their desires.

One may argue that important differences exist in this analogy. First, the job applicant will probably be more effective than the mental patient in realizing his goals since the applicant is a "healthy" or at least a non-hospitalized citizen. The present study does not offer direct evidence to refute this argument. However, it offers information that makes the assumption of patient effectiveness quite plausible (i.e., the relationship between patient desires and discharge rates).

A second argument can be offered to the presented analogy. The job applicant has a "healthy" desire for employment while the patient who wishes to remain in the hospital has a "disturbed" and socially deviant desire. The patient must be basically a dependent, helpless, and ineffectual individual since he does not wish to join the outside community but rather wants to maintain the less socially competent role of being a patient. The above viewpoint appears quite sound but only if we use commonly held middle-class values as our frame of reference in interpreting this kind of behavior. If we make the assumptions that a good many patients do not subscribe to the sets of values incorporated by the hospital staff or society and in addition that they now lead a more comfortable life than they did prior to being hospitalized, wishing to remain in the hospital, then, is not necessarily an expression of helplessness, but rather one of a different set of values and goals.

It is even possible to view the patient who desires to remain in the hospital as placing himself in a challenging, and rather exciting, position. He is matching himself and his goals against the hospital's ideal of short-term stays and quick discharges. This would not appear then as the appropriate milieu for an overly dependent and ineffectual person, but rather a situation for only the manipulative, confident, and adept individual.

Thus far, our discussion has focused on the motivational basis of the manipulative behavior of mental patients. It seems appropriate at this point to present an alternative interpretation for the results of this study based upon cognitive dimensions, that is, the self-concepts of mental patients. One may argue that old-timers see themselves as being sick or ill, thus they will attempt to present an image of themselves in a manner congruent with their self-concept of illness. Conversely, short-timers may define themselves as essentially normal individuals. This definition suggests the kind of script appropriate to their performance. In no way do we have to infer desires to stay or leave as the basis for these two groups' performance on the "mental status" tests. Since we do not have an independent measure of the subject's motivations or self-concept, we cannot offer direct empirical evidence to refute this argument. However, data obtained from other studies (e.g., Joint Commission on Mental Illness and Health, 1961; Levinson, 1964) point to the fact that the majority of patients do not think of themselves as being mentally ill. If this is the case and old-timers were basing their test responses on their self-concept rather than on desires to stay, we would expect a test profile on the "mental status" tests similar to the ones obtained from short-timers. This, however, is not what we found.

Additionally, if we view acuteness of symptoms of felt mental distress or discomfort as an important basis in determining an individual's self-definition of relative normality, we would expect the short-timer (who is in the acute stages of his problems) to define himself as ill more readily than the old-timer (who for the most part is relatively free from acute and painful symptoms). Thus it would appear more plausible from this viewpoint to predict that short-timers should present themselves as being mentally ill and old-timers as being healthy. Again, this is not what we found.

Finally, one can argue that the very effectiveness of our induction suggests that patients are credulous and easily manipulated characteristics which would not be associated with relatively effective people. This argument implies that "seeing through" or being cynical of an induction is necessarily related to effectiveness. There is no empirical evidence to suggest that these two forms of behavior are related. To the contrary, Orne's (1962) studies have shown Harvard students to be quite believing of highly implausible experimental inductions. Yet we would not conclude from this that Harvard students are passive, easily manipulated, and ineffectual people. Additionally, one can assume that the patients may have been skeptical of the induction. However, since they could not be completely sure that the "tests" were not going to be used for the assessment of their mental status, it would seem intelligent to respond to the tests as if they were going to be used for this purpose. If by the slightest chance it would determine their status in the hospital, they will have protected their interests. If not, they will have lost nothing by following the induction and perhaps made a "friend" of the tester.

References

Crowne, D. P., & Marlowe, D. A new scale of social desirability independent of psychopathology. *Journal of Consulting Psychology,* 1960, *24*, 349–354.

Dahlstrom, W. G., & Welsh, G. S. *An MMPI handbook.* Minneapolis: University of Minnesota Press, 1960.

Davids, A., & Pildner, H. Comparison of direct and projective methods of personality assessment under different conditions of motivation. *Psychological Monographs,* 1958, 72 (11, Whole No. 464).

Downing, J. Chronic mental hospital dependency as a character defense. *Psychiatric Quarterly,* 1958, 32, 489–499.

Edwards, A. L. *The social desirability variable in personality assessment and research.* New York: Dryden Press, 1957.

Fairweather, G. W. *Social psychology in treating mental illness: An experimental approach.* New York: Wiley, 1964.

Getzels, J. W. The question answer process: A conceptualization and some derived hypotheses for empirical examination. *Public Opinion Quarterly,* 1954, 18, 80–90.

Goffman, E. *The presentation of self in everyday life.* New York: Doubleday, 1959.

Goffman, E. *Asylums.* New York: Doubleday, 1961.

Gordon, H. L., & Groth, L. Mental patients wanting to stay in the hospital. *American Medical Association Archives of General Psychiatry,* 1961, 4, 124–130.

Joint Commission on Mental Illness and Health. *Action for mental health.* New York: Basic Books, 1961.

Levinson, D. J., & Gallagher, E. B. *Patienthood in the mental hospital.* Boston: Houghton-Mifflin, 1964.

Orne, M. T. On the social psychology of the psychological experiment: with particular reference to demand characteristics and their implications. *American Psychologist,* 1962, 17, 776–783.

Winer, B. J. *Statistical principles in experimental designs.* New York: McGraw-Hill, 1962.

Schizophrenic Patients in the Psychiatric Interview: An Experimental Study of Their Effectiveness at Manipulation

Benjamin M. Braginsky and Dorothea D. Braginsky

The present investigation is concerned with the manipulative behavior of hospitalized schizophrenics in evaluative interview situations. More specifically, the study attempts to answer the question: Can schizophrenic patients effectively control the impressions (impression management, Goffman, 1959) they make on the professional hospital staff?

Typically, the mental patient has been viewed as an extremely ineffectual and helpless individual (e.g., Arieti, 1959; Becker, 1964; Bellak, 1958; Joint Commission on Mental Illness and Health, 1961; Redlich & Freedman, 1966; Schooler & Parkel, 1966; Searles, 1965). For example, Redlich and Freedman (1966) described the mental patient and his pathological status in the following manner: "There is a concomitant loss of focus and coherence and a profound shift in the meaning and value of social relationships and goal directed behavior. This is evident in the inability realistically to implement future goals and present satisfactions; they are achieved magically or through fantasy and delusion. . . [p. 463]." Schooler and Parkel (1966) similarly underline the mental patients' ineffectual status in this description: "the chronic schizophrenic is not Seneca's 'reasoning animal,' or Spinoza's 'social animal,' or even a reasonably efficient version of Cassirer's 'symbol using animal.' . . . Since he violates so many functional definitions of man, there is heuristic value in studying him with an approach like that which would be used to study an alien creature [p. 67]."

Thus, the most commonly held assumptions concerning the nature of the schizophrenic patient stress their ineffectuality and impotency. In this context one would expect schizophrenics to perform less than adequately in interpersonal situations, to be

Reprinted from the *Journal of Consulting Psychology*, vol. 31, 1967, pp. 543–547. Copyright 1967, by the American Psychological Association, and reproduced by permission. The authors would like to express appreciation to Doris Seiler and Dennis Ridley for assisting with the data collection.

unable to initiate manipulative tactics, and, certainly, to be incapable of successful manipulation of other people.[1]

In contrast to the above view of the schizophrenic, a less popular orientation has been expressed by Artiss (1959), Braginsky, Grosse, and Ring (1966), Goffman (1961), Levinson and Gallagher (1964), Rakusin and Fierman (1963), Szasz (1961, 1965), and Towbin (1966). Here schizophrenics are portrayed in terms usually reserved for neurotics and normal persons. Simply, the above authors subscribe to the beliefs that: (*a*) the typical schizophrenic patient, as compared to normals, is not deficient, defective, or dissimilar in intrapsychic functioning; (*b*) the typical schizophrenic patient is not a victim of his illness; that is, it is assumed that he is not helpless and unable to control his behavior or significantly determine life outcomes; (*c*) the differences that some schizophrenic patients manifest (as compared to normals) are assumed to be more accurately understood in terms of differences in belief systems, goals, hierarchy of needs, and interpersonal strategies, rather than in terms of illness, helplessness, and deficient intrapsychic functioning. This orientation leads to the expectation that schizophrenic patients do try to achieve particular goals and, in the process, effectively manipulate other people.

There is some evidence in support of this viewpoint (e.g., Artiss, 1959; Braginsky, Holzberg, Finison, & Ring, 1967; Levinson & Gallagher, 1964). Furthermore, a recent study (Braginsky et al., 1966) demonstrated that schizophrenic patients responded, on a paper-and-pencil "mental status" test, in a manner that would protect their self-interests. Those who wanted to remain in the hospital (chronic patients) presented themselves as "sick," whereas those who desired to be discharged (first admissions) presented themselves as "healthy." That is, they effectively controlled the impressions they wished to make on others. Their manipulative performance, however, was mediated by an impersonal test.

---

[1] This statement is explicitly derived from formal theories of schizophrenia and not from clinical observations. It is obvious to some observers, however, that schizophrenics do attempt to manipulate others. The discrepancy between these observations and traditional theoretical assumptions about the nature of schizophrenics is rarely, if ever, reconciled.

Therefore, the following question is asked: Can schizophrenics engage in similar manipulative behaviors in a "face-to-face" interview with a psychologist? That is, will chronic schizophrenics who desire to remain in the hospital and live on open wards present themselves in an interview situation when they perceive that their open ward status is being questioned as (*a*) "healthy" and, therefore, eligible for open ward living, and in another interview situation when their residential status is being questioned as (*b*) "sick" and, therefore, ineligible for discharge? If so, are their performances convincing to a professional audience (i.e., psychiatrists)?

Method

A sample of 30 long-term (more than 2 continuous years of hospitalization) male schizophrenics living on open wards was randomly selected from ward rosters. Two days prior to the experiment the patients were told that they were scheduled for an interview with a staff psychologist. Although each patient was to be interviewed individually, all 30 were brought simultaneously to a waiting room. Each patient interviewed was not allowed to return to this room, to insure that patients who had participated would not communicate with those who had not.

Each patient was escorted to the interview room by an assistant, who casually informed the patient in a tone of confidentiality about the purpose of the interview (preinterview induction). Patients were randomly assigned by the assistant to one of three induction conditions (10 to each condition). The interviewer was unaware of the induction to which the patients were assigned, thereby eliminating interviewer bias.

Induction Conditions

Discharge induction. Patients were told: "I think the person you are going to see is interested in examining patients to see whether they might be ready for discharge."

Open ward induction.[2] Patients were told: "I think that the

---

[2] It may be suggested that the open ward induction was meaningless, since no patient enjoying open ward status would believe that he could be

person you are going to see is interested in examining patients to see whether they should be on open or closed wards."

Mental status induction.[3]   Patients were told: "I think the person you are going to see is interested in how you are feeling and getting along in the hospital."

After greeting each patient the interviewer asked: "How are you feeling?" Patients who responded only with physical descriptions were also asked: "How do you feel mentally?" whereas those who only gave descriptions of their mental state were asked: "How are you feeling physically?" The patients' responses were tape-recorded. The interview was terminated after 2 minutes,[4] whereupon the purpose of the experiment was disclosed.

Three staff psychiatrists from the same hospital separately rated each of the 30 tape-recorded interviews during two 40-minute sessions. The psychiatrists had no knowledge of the experiment, and they were unfamiliar with the patients; they were told by the experimenter that these were mental patients residing in the hospital and that as a group they represented a wide range of diagnostic categories.

The psychiatrists rated the patients on the following dimensions: (*a*) the patient's degree of psychopathology, using a five-point scale ranging from "not at all ill" to "extremely ill"; (*b*) the amount of hospital control a patient needed, ranging on an eight-point scale from complete freedom ("discharge") to maximum control ("closed ward, continual observation"); and (*c*) the struc-

---

put on a closed ward on the basis of an interview. At the time this experiment was being conducted, however, this hospital was in the process of reorganization, and open and closed ward status was a salient and relevant issue.

[3] Mental status evaluation interviews are typically conducted yearly. Thus, patients who have been in the hospital for more than a year expect to be interviewed for the purposes of determining their residency status.

[4] Although, admittedly, psychiatrists would never base decisions concerning mental status and discharge on a 2-minute interview, it was adequate for the purposes of this study (namely, to determine if mental patients effectively engage in impression management). The 2-minute response to the single question provided sufficient information for psychiatrists to form reliable impressions of the patients. Interestingly, the typical mental status interview conducted by these psychiatrists is rarely longer than 30 minutes.

tural or qualitative aspects of the patient's speech, such as pressure of speech, affect, volume, etc. The score for each patient's speech characteristic was based on the sum of the psychiatrist's rating of 14 Lorr scale items (Lorr, 1953). Each item was rated on an eight-point scale ranging from not at all atypical to extremely atypical verbal behavior.

Predictions

If long-term patients are both motivated to live on open wards and to remain in the hospital and if, in addition, they effectively engage in impression management in order to realize these desires, then the following would be expected:

1. Psychiatrists will rate patients in the discharge and the mental status conditions as being similar with respect to psychopathology and need for hospital control. Mental status interviews are generally used by the hospital to evaluate patients for discharge; therefore, the mental status and discharge conditions offer the same potential consequences for patients. Thus, patients in both conditions will give the impression of being "sick" and in need of hospital control in order to decrease the probability of discharge. The purpose of including the discharge induction was to present the consequences of the interview as explicitly as in the open ward induction.

2. Psychiatrists will rate the patients in the open ward condition significantly less mentally ill and less in need of hospital control than patients in the discharge and mental status conditions. That is, patients in the open ward condition will give the impression of being "healthy" in order to maximize their chances of remaining on an open ward.

Subjects

The mean age of the patients was 47.4 years ($SD = 8.36$). The mean educational level of the group was 8.05 years of schooling ($SD = 3.44$). The median length of hospitalization was 10 years. In terms of diagnostic categories, 43% of the sample was diagnosed as chronic undifferentiated schizophrenic, 37% as paranoid schizophrenic, 10% as catatonic, and the remaining 10%

as simple schizophrenic. There were no differences between the three experimental groups on any of the above variables.

Results and Discussion

The reliability coefficients of the three psychiatrists' combined ratings of the patient interviews were as follows: (*a*) ratings of psychopathology—$r = .89$, $p < .01$; (*b*) need for hospital control—$r = .74$, $p < .01$; (*c*) normality of speech characteristics—$r = .65$, $p < .01$. Thus, it was concluded that there was significant agreement between the three psychiatrists.

The means of the psychopathology ratings by experimental condition are presented in Table 1. The ratings ranged 1–5. The analysis of variance of the data yielded a significant condition effect ($F = 9.38$, $p < .01$). The difference between the open ward and discharge conditions was statistically significant ($p < .01$; Tukey multiple-range test). In addition, the difference between the open ward and the mental status condition was significant ($p < .01$). As predicted, there was no significant difference between the discharge and mental status conditions.

The means of the ratings of need for hospital control are presented in Table 1. These ratings ranged 1–8. The analysis of these data indicated a significant difference between the means ($F = 3.85$, $p < .05$). Again, significant differences (beyond the .05 level) were obtained between the open ward and the discharge conditions, as well as between the open ward and mental status conditions. No difference was found between the discharge and mental status conditions.

On the basis of these analyses it is clear that patients in the open ward condition appear significantly less mentally ill and in less need of hospital control than patients in either the discharge or mental status conditions. Obviously the patients in these con-

TABLE 1   MEAN PSYCHOPATHOLOGY AND NEED-FOR-HOSPITAL-CONTROL RATINGS BY EXPERIMENTAL CONDITION

Rating	Open ward		Mental status		Discharge	
	M	SD	M	SD	M	SD
Psychopathology	2.63	.58	3.66	.65	3.70	.67
Need for hospital control	2.83	1.15	4.10	1.31	4.20	1.42

ditions convey different impressions in the interview situation. In order to ascertain the manner by which the patients conveyed these different impressions, the following three manipulative tactics were examined: (a) number of positive statements patients made about themselves, (b) number of negative statements made about themselves (these include both physical and mental referents), and (c) normality of speech characteristics (i.e., how "sick" they sounded, independent of the content of speech). The first two indexes were obtained by counting the number of positive or negative self-referent statements a patient made during the interview. These counts were done by three judges independently, and the reliability coefficient was .95. The third index was based on the psychiatrists' ratings on 14 Lorr scale items of the speech characteristics of patients. A score was obtained for each patient by summing the ratings for the 14 scales.

Ratings of psychopathology and need for hospital control were, in part, determined by the frequency of positive and negative self-referent statements. The greater the frequency of positive statements made by a patient, the less ill he was perceived ($r = -.58$, $p < .01$) and the less in need of hospital control ($r = -.41$, $p < .05$). Conversely, the greater the frequency of negative statements, the more ill a patient was perceived ($r = .53$, $p < .01$) and the more in need of hospital control ($r = .37$, $p < .05$). It is noteworthy that patients were consistent in their performances; that is, those who tended to say positive things about themselves tended not to say negative things ($r = -.55$, $p < .01$).

When self-referent statements were compared by condition, it was found that patients in the open ward condition presented themselves in a significantly more positive fashion than patients in the discharge and mental status conditions. Only 2 patients in the open ward condition reported having physical or mental problems, whereas 13 patients in the mental status and discharge conditions presented such complaints ($\chi^2 = 5.40$, $p < .05$).

The frequency of positive and negative self-referent statements, however, cannot account for important qualitative components of the impressions the patients attempted to convey. For example, a patient may give only one complaint, but it may be serious (e.g., he reports hallucinations), whereas another patient may state five complaints, all of which are relatively benign. In order to examine the severity of symptoms or complaints reported by patients, the number of "psychotic" complaints, namely, reports of hallucinations or bizarre delusions, was tallied. None of the patients in the open ward condition made reference to having had hallucinations or delusions, while nine patients in the discharge and mental status conditions spontaneously made such reference ($\chi^2 = 4.46$, $p < .05$).

In comparing the structural or qualitative aspects of patient speech no significant differences were obtained between experimental conditions. Patients "sounded" about the same in all three conditions. The majority of patients (80%) were rated as having relatively normal speech characteristics. Although there were no differences by condition, there was a significant inverse relationship ($r = -.35$, $p < .05$) between quality of speech and the number of positive statements made. That is, patients were consistent to the extent that those who sounded ill tended not to make positive self-referent statements.

In summary, then, the hypotheses were confirmed. It is clear that patients responded to the inductions in a manner which maximized the chances of fulfilling their needs and goals. When their self-interests were at stake patients could present themselves in a face-to-face interaction as either "sick" or "healthy," whichever was more appropriate to the situation. In the context of this experiment "sick" impressions were conveyed when the patients were faced with the possibility of discharge. On the other hand, impressions of "health" were conveyed when the patients' open ward status was questioned. Moreover, the impressions they conveyed were convincing to an audience of experienced psychiatrists.

One may argue, however, that the differences between the groups were a function of differential anxiety generated by the inductions rather than a function of the patients' needs, goals, and manipulative strategies. More specifically, the discharge and the mental status conditions would generate more anxiety and, therefore, more pathological behavior than the open ward condition. As a result, the psychiatrists rated the patients in the discharge and mental status conditions as "sicker" than patients in the open ward condition. According to this argument, then, the patients who were rated as sick were, in fact, more disturbed, and those rated healthy were, in fact, less disturbed.

No differences, however, were found between conditions in

terms of the amount of disturbed behavior during the interview. As was previously mentioned, the psychiatrists did not perceive any differences by condition in atypicality of verbal behavior. On the contrary, the patients were judged as sounding relatively normal. Thus, the psychiatrists' judgments of psychopathology were based primarily on the symptoms patients reported rather than on symptoms manifested. Patients did not behave in a disturbed manner; rather, they told the interviewer how disturbed they were.

The traditional set of assumptions concerning schizophrenics, which stresses their irrationality and interpersonal ineffectuality, would not only preclude the predictions made in this study, but would fail to explain parsimoniously the present observations. It is quite plausible and simple to view these findings in terms of the assumptions held about people in general; that is, schizophrenics, like normal persons, are goal-oriented and are able to control the outcomes of their social encounters in a manner which satisfies their goals.

References

Arieti, S. *American handbook of psychiatry.* New York: Basic Books, 1959.

Artiss, K. L. *The symptom as communication in schizophrenia.* New York: Grune & Stratton, 1959.

Becker, E. *The revolution in psychiatry.* London: Collier-Macmillan, 1964.

Bellak, C. *Schizophrenia: A review of the syndrome.* New York: Logos Press, 1958.

Braginsky, B., Grosse, M., & Ring, K. Controlling outcomes through impression-management: An experimental study of the manipulative tactics of mental patients. *Journal of Consulting Psychology,* 1966, *30,* 295–300.

Braginsky, B., Holzberg, J., Finison, L., & Ring, K. Correlates of the mental patient's acquisition of hospital information. *Journal of Personality,* 1967, *35,* 323–342.

Goffman, E. *The presentation of self in everyday life.* New York: Doubleday, 1959.

Goffman, E. *Asylums.* New York: Doubleday, 1961.

Joint Commission on Mental Illness and Health. *Action for mental health.* New York: Basic Books, 1961.

Levinson, D. S., & Gallagher, E. B. *Patienthood in the mental hospital.* Boston: Houghton-Mifflin, 1964.

Lorr, M. Multidimensional scale for rating psychiatric patients. *Veterans Administration Technical Bulletin,* 1953, *51,* 119–127 .

Rakusin, J. M., & Fierman, L. B. Five assumptions for treating chronic psychotics. *Mental Hospitals,* 1963, *14,* 140–148.

Redlich, F. C., & Freedman, D. T. *The theory and practice of psychiatry.* New York: Basic Books, 1966, *29,* 67–77.

Schooler, C., & Parkel, D. The overt behavior of chronic schizophrenics and its relationship to their internal state and personal history. *Psychiatry,* 1966, *29,* 67–77.

Searles, H. F. *Collected papers on schizophrenia and related subjects.* New York: International Universities Press, 1965.

Szasz, T. S. *The myth of mental illness.* New York: Hoeber-Harper, 1961.

Szasz, T. S. *Psychiatric justice.* New York: Macmillan, 1965.

Towbin, A. P. Understanding the mentally deranged. *Journal of Existentialism,* 1966, *7,* 63–83.

The Case for Impression Management in Schizophrenia: Another Look

Richard H. Price

Perhaps the most consistently obtained finding in research on schizophrenia is that, on the average, schizophrenics perform more poorly than nonschizophrenic control subects. Nearly all investigators agree on the universality of this empirical finding. However, here the agreement ends. Interpretations of these findings vary widely, but for the purposes of this review they may be grouped under two broad headings. The poorer performance of schizophrenics has been viewed (a) as a product of ability loss, and more recently, (b) as a product of impression management.

This research was supported by the United States Public Health Service Grant PHS SO5 FR7031. Thanks are due to Kenneth Heller, Alexander Buchwald, and Dennis Bouffard for their comments on the issues raised in this paper.

Schizophrenic Performance as Ability Loss

The term "psychological deficit" was originally used by Hunt and Cofer (1944) to describe the performance of an individual who showed a decrement in the efficiency of his psychological performance when compared with the behavior of other non-impaired individuals. In using the term "deficit" it was Hunt and Cofer's intention to introduce a term which was neutral with respect to the explanation for lowered performance. Deficit was intended only to describe the fact of lower task performance. The term continues to be widely used today, particularly to characterize the performance of individuals diagnosed as schizophrenic (Buss & Lang, 1965; Lang & Buss, 1965; Yates, 1966).

It should be noted that most if not all deficit-oriented studies imply that the performance decrement displayed by schizophenics involves some loss of ability. This is not surprising, since the concept of "deficit" does carry surplus meaning over and above that intended by Hunt and Cofer (1944). Furthermore, the almost uniformly poorer performance of schizophrenics obtained in a large number of studies (see Buss & Lang, 1965; Lang & Buss, 1965) leads quite naturally to the assumption that lower performance reflects lower ability. The lowered-ability assumption remains precisely that, however—an assumption potentially subject to empirical confirmation or disconfirmation.

Schizophrenic Performance as Impression Management

Recent evidence (Braginsky, Braginsky, & Ring, 1969; Fontana & Klein, 1968) suggests that the interpretation of deficit studies may have been too narrowly conceived. Typically, attempts to understand the meaning of lower performance scores among schizophrenics have focused exclusively on the formal demands of the experimental tasks themselves and have largely ignored a number of additional requirements made on the subject by the experimental setting and his adjustment to it. For example, the experimenter may present hospitalized schizophrenic subjects with a reaction-time task in the belief that he is measuring attentional and psychomotor performance. The subject, on the other hand, may be asking himself, "What will happen to me if I perform well or poorly? Will they think I am well enough to go home even though I don't want to leave?" Clearly the task requirements as seen by the *experimenter* and the task requirements as seen by the *subject* may be quite different.

Thus, until recently, deficit studies have not considered variables such as: (1) the patient's goals in the hospital setting (for example, discharge, transfer to another ward, retention in the protective hospital setting); (2) the contingency relations perceived by the patient between his goals and his task performance (for example, will good task performance result in a desired or in some cases an unwanted discharge?); and (3) management of task performance to fulfill these goals (such as deliberately poor performance in order to remain in the hospital). These considerations suggest that it is necessary to enumerate the experimental task requirements as the *subject* views them as well as those traditionally considered by the experimenter.

In an experiment derived from this line of thinking, Braginsky and Braginsky (1967) tested open-ward schizophrenic patients who were assumed to be motivated to remain on the open ward rather than be discharged or sent to a closed ward. Before being interviewed by the experimenter, subjects were randomly assigned to one of three experimental conditions manipulated by a confederate. In the Discharge condition, patients were told that the purpose of the interview was to see if the patient was ready for discharge. In the Open-Ward condition, patients were told that the interview was intended to determine whether they should remain on the open ward or be transferred to a (presumably less desirable) closed ward. In the Mental-Status condition patients were told that the purpose of the interview was simply to find out how they were getting along. Blind ratings of the interviews by staff psychiatrists indicated that patients in the Mental-Status and Discharge conditions produced significantly more psychopathology and appeared to need significantly more hospital control than did the Open-Ward group. These results suggest that hospitalized schizophrenics are capable of controlling symptom expression in order to manage the impressions they make on hospital staff and thereby control their hospital fate.

However, Elliott (1970) has performed a replication and extension of the Braginsky and Braginsky (1967) experiment that does not confirm these results and leads to some very different conclusions. Elliott tested open-ward schizophrenic subjects in a psychiatric interview situation, using the same experimental conditions as did Braginsky and Braginsky (1967). In addition, he tested a hospitalized nonschizophrenic control group. He found that nonschizophrenic subjects were rated as displaying significantly less psychopathology and less need for hospital control than the schizophrenic control group. This finding is consistent with the nearly universal finding, mentioned earlier, of performance decrements among schizophrenics when compared with nonschizophrenic controls.

In addition, schizophrenic subjects in the Open-Ward condition (who were told that the interview could result in closed-ward placement) were rated as displaying significantly more psychopathology and to be in need of more hospital control than the schizophrenic control Mental-Status group. This is precisely the *opposite* of the results obtained by Braginsky and Braginsky (1967).

Elliott (1970) points out that to explain his findings as goal-oriented impression management, one would have to assume that schizophrenic patients in the Open-Ward condition were actually motivated to live on a closed rather than an open ward. This seems implausible, and Elliott offers what appears to be a more plausible explanation of his findings. He suggests that the Open-Ward condition (which carries the threat of closed-ward placement) may have been quite anxiety provoking and that the arousal of anxiety may have disrupted interview performance.

These findings indicate that, within the context of the psychiatric interview used by Braginsky and Braginsky (1967), schizophrenics display a performance deficit when compared with nonschizophrenic hospitalized controls. This finding is of course consistent with the literature on schizophrenic deficit, but is difficult to interpret in the context of an impression-management paradigm. Thus, the experimental conditions used by Braginsky and Braginsky (1967) appear to be capable of producing results consistent with explanations very different from those suggested by the impression-management hypothesis. At the very least, Elliott's results suggest that the generality of the phenomenon of impression management is more limited than its advocates had suggested.

Fontana, Klein, Lewis, and Levine (1968), however, have elaborated the impression-management concept. They suggest that some patients may be motivated to present a healthy, competent impression (healthy presenters) while others may wish to present themselves as incompetent and sick (sick presenters). In order to distinguish patients as healthy or sick presenters, Fontana et al. (1968) constructed a scale that was assumed to measure differing degrees of self-attribution of pathology.

Fontana et al. (1968) suggest that extremes of the healthy-presenter–sick-presenter continuum represent different motivational orientations toward the presentation of symptoms rather than actual differences in degree of psychopathology or ability. It is at this point that the concept of impression management and the healthy-presenter–sick-presenter distinction in particular offer a direct challenge to the concept of schizophrenic deficit as loss of ability. The crucial question then may be stated as follows: Do sick presenters attribute psychopathology to themselves more than healthy presenters do simply because this is their chosen mode of impression management or because they are actually more severely disturbed?

However, experimental attempts to answer this question must deal with the following difficulty. It is quite likely that there is a positive relationship between the degree of self-attribution of psychopathology as measured by the Fontana et al. (1968) scale and the actual degree of psychopathology. Therefore, if one obtains results indicating that sick presenters produce poorer or more pathological performances on other independently obtained measures of psychopathology, such findings could be misinterpreted as merely additional instances of impression management —a finding consistent with the impression-management hypothesis. Since it is likely that these two variables are confounded, correlational studies can only produce findings consistent with the assumptions of impression management.

An experimental manipulation is therefore needed to answer this question, and it must meet four basic requirements: (1) It must serve to separate subjects on the basis of the degree to which they attribute pathology to themselves. (2) It must be capable of motivating subjects to perform in a manner they believe to be consistent with their chosen mode of impression management, if such motivations do, in fact, exist. (3) The subject's understanding of what constitutes "healthy" or "sick" performance on the task must be demonstrated. (4) Definition to the subject of performance as "healthy" or "sick" must be independent of actual task performance. That is, it must be possible to describe either high or low scores to the subject as either "sick" or "healthy." A failure to meet any one of these requirements will render the results of the experimental test ambiguous and open to alternative interpretations.

Price (1972) has conducted an experiment that provides a direct test of the theoretical question and that meets the experimental requirements listed above. The results indicated that healthy-presenter schizophrenics responded to the experimental instructions in the manner predicted by the impression-management hypothesis but that sick-presenter schizophrenics did not. That is, after receiving the false normative information concerning the meaning of their task performance, healthy-presenter schizophrenics appeared to be suppressing their initial responses and searching for responses that were consistent with their own motivations and the experimental instructions, but sick-presenter schizophrenics were unable to engage in any form of impression management.

These findings suggest a clear limitation on the generality of the impression-management hypothesis. Although impression management can and sometimes does occur among schizophrenics, the likelihood of its occurrence depends to an important degree on the degree of psychopathology and ability loss displayed by the subject.

Does Impression Management Have Implications for the Description of Schizophrenia?

If impression management has substantial importance for the description of schizophrenic behavior, then it should be possible to answer four questions in the affirmative: . (1) Is impression management as a phenomenon unique to schizophrenia? (2) Is impression management common to all schizophrenics? (3) Is impression management the only factor that produces schizophreniclike symptoms? (4) Do the variables involved in the production of impression management produce enduring changes in schizophrenic behavior?

Is Impression Management, as a Phenomenon, Unique to Schizophrenia?

The idea that symptom presentation may be goal directed is not a new one, as Holzberg (1969) has pointed out. Freud (1936) recognized that symptoms may persist because of their secondary gain value. Similarly, individuals who are motivated to appear incompetent have long been described as "malingerers." Other psychiatric populations for whom evidence of impression management has been reported include nonpsychotic psychiatric patients (Fontana & Gessner, 1969) and institutionalized retardates (Braginsky & Braginsky, 1971).

Moreover, impression management is not confined to psychiatric populations. Braginsky and Braginsky (1971) suggest that "When any person (P) has an important goal, is dependent upon others (O) for the realization of this goal; and O has clearly defined standards of conduct for P; then P will most likely engage in impression management" (p. 51). One qualification which should be added to the Braginsky and Braginsky formulation is that the ability to engage in impression management seems to be limited in schizophrenic patients who show marked degrees of psychopathology.

Thus, impression management is not unique to schizophrenics but is instead an interpersonal strategy that may be employed under certain motivational conditions by schizophrenics who are not severely disturbed.

Is Impression Management Common to All Schizophrenics?

The importance of impression management as a descriptive aspect of the behavior of schizophrenics would be greatly increased if it could be shown that all or nearly all persons diagnosed as schizophrenic engaged in impression management under the appropriate motivational conditions. However, Elliott's (1970) findings as well as those of Price (1972) suggest that impression management is not common to all schizophrenics. Elliott found results opposite to those obtained by Braginsky and Braginsky under the same motivational conditions. Furthermore, the results reported by Price (1972) suggest that ability loss or psychopathology is a limiting factor on schizophrenic subjects' ability to engage in impression management. Thus, it may be concluded that impression management is not common to all persons diagnosed as schizophrenic.

Is Impression Management the Only Factor That Produces Schizophreniclike Symptoms?

Chapman (1969) has pointed out that there are a variety of conditions which are schizomimetic. Among the conditions he lists are LSD and other drugs, sensory deprivation, sleep deprivation, hypnosis, speeded performance, distraction, relaxed attention, anoxia, brain damage, childhood, "primitive" racial development, and dreams and sleep. Chapman points out that researchers have erroneously concluded that since these states produce behavior which resembles schizophrenic thought disorder, they necessarily provide evidence concerning the nature of schizophrenia. However, Chapman suggests that "The diversity of such allegedly schizomimetic conditions cast doubt on the validity of interpreting schizophrenic symptoms on the basis of any one of them" (p. 646). Thus, impression management is not the only factor that is capable of producing schizophreniclike symptoms. Instead, it appears that impression management may be added to the rather lengthy list of conditions which produce schizophreniclike performance.

Do Variables Involved in Impression Management Produce Appreciable or Enduring Changes in Schizophrenic Behavior?

If the variables producing impression management were capable of accounting for large proportions of the performance variance among schizophrenic subjects, then one would have to acknowledge its potential importance for the description of schizophrenic behavior. However, the types of variables involved in the induction of impression management (for example, the use of motivating instructions and reinforcement) have been shown to have little enduring effect upon schizophrenic behavior. As Rosenbaum (1969) points out, "The theoretical problem of schizophrenia is the explanation of the failure of social instructions and reinforcement to appreciably modify symptomatic behavior in approximately one percent of the population" (p. 643). Buss and Lang (1965) have reviewed the literature on schizophrenic deficit and suggest that biologically noxious stimulation is one of the few conditions which has produced the complete elimination of schizophrenic deficit. A study by Rosenbaum (1967) produced such changes using biologically noxious stimuli, while, as Frankel and Buchwald (1969) point out, verbal reinforcement has been much less effective in changing the symptomatic behavior of schizophrenics.

A strong affirmative response cannot, therefore, be given to any of the questions posed above. Instead, impression management among other causal factors, and among some persons diagnosed as schizophrenic, may produce temporary symptomatic changes, but these changes are not unique to the schizophrenic population. We may ask, however, what the status of impression management, even under these limited conditions, is as a causal factor in symptom production among psychiatric patients.

Impression Management as a Determinant of Symptom Production

The finding that persons diagnosed as schizophrenic can, in some cases, manage the symptom picture they present (Braginsky & Braginsky, 1967) or that normal subjects can produce behavior characteristic of schizophrenics (Levitz & Ullmann, 1969) is frequently misinterpreted. The inference often drawn from such findings is that because a particular independent variable is capable of affecting the probability of occurrence of a particular symptom or symptom picture, it is also the case that the independent variable is causally related or has etiological significance for the origin of that symptom. This inference is clearly unwarranted. As Buchwald and Young (1969) suggest,

> It is important to remember that behavior is a final common pathway, that it is susceptible to a large number of influences. The way in which responses are changed need not parallel the way in which they were originally acquired. The asymmetry between

the course of a behavioral disorder and the method of treatment may be illustrated by the case of aphasic patients. They have lost the ability to speak as a result of a vascular accident or other brain lesion, but they can sometimes be taught to speak again. The behavioral loss is due to a physiological insult but there is no known physiological or medical technique for overcoming this handicap. That the only known successful treatment is a behavioral one implies nothing about the origin of the deficit. Similarly, if a mute schizophrenic can be taught to speak again by shaping and reinforcement (and such efforts have had some limited success), there is no implication that his speech was lost due to the operation of reinforcing factors in his social environment. (p. 618)

Thus, it should be clear that the ability to manipulate symptomatic behavior need not have implications for the origin of that symptomatic behavior.

A second and related distinction to be made in this context is between those factors that are responsible for the *origin* of a particular symptom or behavioral pattern and those factors that are capable of *maintaining* the behavior once it has occurred. It is very likely that factors which are involved in the production of impression management have considerable importance for the maintenance of symptomatic behavior, particularly in institutional settings. However, this does not suggest that these same factors were important in the origin of the symptomatic behavior. The findings reported by Braginsky, Braginsky, and Ring (1969), as well as those reported by Fontana and others, may tell us a great deal more about the situational determinants and conditions which maintain symptomatic behavior in institutional settings than they do about the original source of that behavior. Although the etiological significance of impression management for schizophrenia is uncertain at best, the fact that impression management can affect symptomatology which is already present does have clear methodological implications for etiological research. These implications will now be examined.

Methodological Implications for Etiological Research

Etiological research in schizophrenia most often begins with the observation of hospitalized individuals who have been already identified as schizophrenic (Mednick & McNeil, 1968). The basic requirement of this method is the selection of patient samples on the basis of presented symptomatology. The phenomenon of impression management can be a serious threat to valid inference in this case. Several examples should make this point clear.

First, situational variables may have substantial effects on the amount of pathological behavior displayed by patients. Zarlock (1966) has reported large increases in bizarre and pathological verbal and physical behavior among patients when confronted with a medical situation in which personnel wore white coats as compared with other nonmedical (recreational and social) situations. Zarlock (1966) suggests that the white coats actually "demanded" deviant behavior in schizophrenic patients.

Second, in the classic twin study method (Gottesman & Shields, 1966; Rosenthal, 1970) the obtained concordance rates for schizophrenia among index cases and co-twins depend heavily upon the reliable diagnostic differentiation of individuals as either schizophrenic or nonschizophrenic. To the degree that the behaviors which are identified as schizophrenic are situationally determined products of impression management, concordance rates may be systematically biased. This may not be a serious source of error when it can be argued that both monozygotic and dizygotic twin pairs are subject to similar situational variables. However, if for any reason it can be argued that situational variables may differentially affect the degree to which index cases and co-twins present or control their symptoms, then diagnoses —and consequently concordance rates—may be differentially affected as well.

Third, any study which compares hospitalized patients with nonhospitalized control groups is subject to error since both Braginsky and his co-workers (1969) and Fontana and Klein (1968) have shown that hospital environments themselves may produce much situationally determined symptomatology. However, using only hospitalized patients as subjects is not necessarily an adequate solution to this problem, since Braginsky, Grosse, and Ring (1966) have shown that "newcomers" and "old-timers" differ in their motivation to leave the hospital and will present symptomatology to fulfill their goals of staying or leaving the hospital as the case may be. This in turn would suggest that using only hospitalized patients equated for length of hospitalization would be adequate to control the hospitalization factor. However, Fontana and Klein (1968) have shown that background factors, such as residence on treatment or custodial wards, may also differentially affect symptom production. Thus, residence in a psychiatric hospital appears to produce a variety of situational variables that may lead patients to manage the impressions they make upon examiners by denying or displaying symptomatic complaints.

Finally, Dohrenwend and Dohrenwend (1969) have suggested that epidemiological data are difficult to interpret without knowledge of whether symptoms are persistent or situationally determined. Furthermore, they point out that even persistent symptoms may be the result of secondary gain. Impression management in the form of tendencies to minimize or maximize symptomatic complaints may significantly affect the true rates of psychological disorder in different populations. Since the total rates of disorder in various epidemiological studies range from less than 1 percent to a high of 64 percent, it is quite possible that some portion of this variance can be accounted for by impression management on the part of respondents.

Thus, situational variables and impression management may crucially affect the results of several research strategies commonly used in etiological research in schizophrenia. Continued research on the problem of impression management may provide useful information concerning the situational and/or personality variables most productive of symptom display or suppression. Researchers concerned with the etiology of schizophrenia, regardless of the nature of their etiological hypotheses, would do well to remember Buchwald and Young's (1969) comment that "behavior is a final common pathway."

References

Braginsky, B. M., & Braginsky, Dorothea D. Schizophrenic patients in the psychiatric interview: An experimental study of their effectiveness at manipulation. *Journal of Consulting Psychology*, 1967, *31*, 543–547.

Braginsky, B. M., Braginsky, Dorothea D., & Ring, K. *Methods of Madness: The mental hospital as a last resort.* New York: Holt, Rinehart and Winston, 1969.

Braginsky, B. M., Grosse, M., & Ring, K. Controlling outcomes through impression-management: An experimental study of the manipulative tactics of mental patients. *Journal of Consulting Psychology*, 1966, *30*, 295–300.

Braginsky, Dorothea D., & Braginsky, B. M. *Hansels and Gretels: Studies of children in institutions for the mentally retarded*. New York: Holt, Rinehart and Winston, 1971.

Buchwald, A. M., & Young, R. D. Some comments on the foundations of behavior therapy. In C. M. Franks (Ed.), *Behavior therapy: Appraisal and status*. New York: McGraw-Hill, 1969, pp. 607–624.

Buss, A. H., & Lang, P. J. Psychological deficit in schizophrenia: I. Affect, reinforcement, and concept attainment. *Journal of Abnormal Psychology*, 1965, *70*, 2–24.

Chapman, L. J. Schizomimetic conditions and schizophrenia. *Journal of Consulting and Clinical Psychology*, 1969, *33*, 646–650.

Dohrenwend, B. P., & Dohrenwend, B. S. *Social status and psychological disorder: A causal inquiry*. New York: Wiley & Sons, 1969.

Elliott, R. D. Effects of impression management and task requirements on schizophrenic performance. Unpublished Dissertation. Indiana University, Bloomington, Indiana, 1970.

Fontana, A. F., & Gessner, T. Patients' goals and the manifestation of psychopathology. *Journal of Consulting and Clinical Psychology*, 1969, *33*, 247–253.

Fontana, A. F., & Klein, E. B. Self-presentation and the schizophrenic "deficit." *Journal of Consulting and Clinical Psychology*, 1968, *32*, 250–256.

Fontana, A. F., Klein, E. G., Lewis, E., & Levine, L. Presentation of self in mental illness. *Journal of Consulting and Clinical Psychology*, 1968, *32*, 110–119.

Frankel, A. S., & Buchwald, A. M. Verbal conditioning of common associations in long-term schizophrenics: A failure. *Journal of Abnormal Psychology*, 1969, *74*, 372–374.

Freud, S. *The problem of anxiety*. New York: W. W. Norton & Co., 1936.

Gottesman, I. I., & Shields, J. Contributions of twin studies to perspectives in schizophrenia. In B. Mahers (Ed.), *Progress in experimental personality research*, Vol. 3. New York: Academic Press, 1966, pp. 1–84.

Holzberg, J. D. Introduction. In Braginsky, B. M., Braginsky, Dorothea D., & Ring, K. *Methods of Madness: The mental hospital as a last resort*. New York: Holt, Rinehart and Winston, 1969, pp. 1–12.

Hunt, J. McV., & Cofer, C. N. Psychological deficit. In J. McV. Hunt (Ed.), *Personality and the behavior disorders* Vol. 2. New York: Ronald Press, 1944, pp. 971–1032.

Lang, P. J., & Buss, A. H. Psychological deficit in schizophrenia: II.

Interference and activation. *Journal of Abnormal Psychology*, 1965, *70*, 77–106.

Levitz, L. S., & Ullmann, L. P. Manipulation of indications of disturbed thinking in normal subjects. *Journal of Consulting and Clinical Psychology*, 1969, *33*, 633–641.

Mednick, S. A., & McNeil, T. F. Current methodology on the etiology of schizophrenia: Serious difficulties which suggest the use of the high-risk-group method. *Psychological Bulletin*, 1968, *70*, 681–693.

Price, R. H. Psychological deficit vs. impression management in schizophrenic word association performance. *Journal of Abnormal Psychology*, 1972, *79*, 132–137.

Rosenbaum, G. Reaction time indices of schizophrenic motivation: A cross cultural replication. *British Journal of Psychiatry*, 1967, *113*, 537–541.

Rosenbaum, G. Schizophrenia as a "put-on." *Journal of Consulting and Clinical Psychology*, 1969, *33*, 642–645.

Rosenthal, D. *Genetic theory and abnormal behavior*. New York: Mc-Graw-Hill, 1970.

Yates, A. J. Psychological deficit. *Annual Review of Psychology*, 1966, *17*, 111–144.

Zarlock, S. P. Social expectations, language and schizophrenia. *Journal of Humanistic Psychology*, 1966, *6*, 68–74.

PART FIVE

The Mental Hospital: The Effects of Institutionalization

Patient counterpower has its limits. Large numbers of patients remain in psychiatric institutions for long periods of time; either for the lack of other alternatives, by their own choice, or because they have been committed. Once in the institution, they are likely to become institutionalized.

The disturbed and apathetic condition of mental patients who have remained in the hospital for long periods of time is often thought to be the result of the natural course of the illness. Consequently, staff attitudes and treatment practices reflect the view that they are dealing with hopeless cases. Ironically, these same attitudes and practices have had the effect of creating, to some degree, the hopeless cases that they assumed existed in the first place. Until recently, most large public psychiatric hospitals provided environments which, with their restraints and lack of opportunity for social activity, have markedly negative effects on the course of the patient's disorder.

As Zusman points out in his article, the belief that mental hospital environments may have actually produced many of the disabling symptoms observed in chronic mental patients first appeared in the psychiatric literature as early as the eighteenth century. However, since then, with the exception of a brief period of "moral treatment," the idea has won little acceptance.

In his review, Zusman describes the "social breakdown syndrome." He believes the syndrome is a result of the interaction between the particular personality characteristics of the disturbed individual and the environment in which he lives. Zusman views the syndrome as a complication of acute psychosis, but it is a syndrome that can also accompany other conditions. The individual who becomes institutionalized is a person who is deficient in self-concept and dependent on current cues for making judgments about himself and the world around him. Combined with these preconditions, the person may have been labeled as incompetent or dangerous, either explicitly or as an implicit result of the fact that he has been hospitalized. The person then is inducted into the "sick role" he learns in the hospital setting. As a result, his work and social skills begin to atrophy and he comes to identify with the "sick" community in the hospital. Thus, Zusman sees the social breakdown syndrome as a social phenomenon but as one that interacts with the initial disorder from which the patient suffers.

The social breakdown syndrome, or something very much like it, accounts for the fact that nearly two thirds of the resident hospital population in the United States consists of chronic patients. These people are seen as an important target population for resocialization and rehabilitation by a growing number of mental health workers. In his paper on the chronic mental patient, Paul reviews much of the recent literature on this problem. He also takes an important first step in conceptualizing an approach to rehabilitation. He specifies target areas for rehabilitation and reviews promising approaches to treatment. Paul emphasizes a social-learning approach to rehabilitation and specifies a set of procedures based on social-learning principles. Programs of this kind provide some hope that large numbers of people now languishing in mental hospitals may someday return to the community.

Some Explanations of the Changing Appearance of Psychotic Patients: Antecedents of the Social Breakdown Syndrome Concept

Jack Zusman

The Changing Clinical Picture of Psychoses

It seldom happens in any field of medicine that a disease suddenly and radically changes its characteristics so that what had been immutable truths at one moment within the space of a few years become just the discarded contents of old textbooks. This is happening today in psychiatry.[1]

Schizophrenia—still called dementia praecox by some older psychiatrists—once a label indicating a hopeless downhill course to mute withdrawal, incontinence, dangerous loss of self-control, and complete social disability requiring lifetime care, has come to represent a serious but treatable condition which can be handled in a day hospital or by outpatient treatment. It should be noted that although the majority of hospitalized mental patients are schizophrenics, the changes in appearance are not limited to patients in this category alone. Changes have occurred in all types of hospitalized patients. The accompanying remarkable change in mental hospitals—still our main resource in treating psychoses—must be seen to be believed. The barred windows, the heavy wooden furniture, the concrete floors designed for easy cleaning with a hose, the smell of urine, the straps and belts and sheets for restraint, have all been replaced by open doors, mod-

Reprinted from E. M. Gruenberg, ed., *Evaluating the effectiveness of community mental health services*, New York: Milbank Memorial Fund, 1966.

[1] The concept that much of the disability associated with psychotic illness can be prevented by integrated, comprehensive, and continuous treatment programs suggests that discontinuous rejecting treatment can add to this disability. Some of the ideas along this line, appearing in the English language since Pinel, are summarized in this paper. It is hoped that the reader will get a picture from them of the lines of reasoning which have led to the demonstration services discussed in this volume.

ern movable furniture, and a homelike atmosphere in which patients and staff are often indistinguishable.

The Types of Explanations

Simultaneously with these changes in the hospitalized patients' appearances and in the courses of their illnesses many new therapies have been introduced. Most conspicuous, of course, has been the use of the tranquilizing drugs. These are, undoubtedly, effective and powerful medications. It should be kept in mind, however, that the changes in patient behavior described above began to occur before the new tranquilizers were introduced and have occurred in situations where use of the tranquilizers was at a minimum.[2]

These changes in the manifestations of mental illness in hospitalized patients forcefully struck a committee of New York State hospital directors appointed by the late Commissioner Paul H. Hoch to visit England in 1956 and examine mental hospitals which had undergone radical changes in policy.[3,4]

These district mental hospitals had unlocked all ward doors and generally eliminated all forms of physical restraint. In order to accomplish this, a number of changes in traditional patient-staff relationships and divisions of responsibility had been necessary. By the time these changes were completed, the general appearance and behavior of the patients had moved considerably toward a more socially appropriate level, and their illnesses were no longer following the previously expected course of deterioration.

In other hospitals serving similar districts—and, therefore, presumably receiving similar patients, but where no changes from traditional practice had been made—the patients' appear-

---

[2] Smith, T. C., et al., Influence of Policy and Drugs on Colorado State Hospital Population, *Archives of General Psychiatry, 12,* 352, 1965.

[3] Hunt, Robert C., Summary of Findings, *Mental Hospitals, 8,* 6, 1957.

[4] Gruenberg, Ernest M., and Boudreau, Frank G., Preface to *An Approach to the Prevention of Disability from Chronic Psychoses: The Open Mental Hospital within the Community,* Proceedings of the Thirty-Fourth Annual Conference of the Milbank Memorial Fund, 1957, New York, Milbank Memorial Fund, 1958, Part 1, pp. 7–8.

ances and behavior were still deteriorated. These experiments seemed to demonstrate so clearly how the style of hospital treatment affected symptoms of mental illness that the Americans were greatly impressed.[5,6] They introduced many of the treatment innovations into American hospitals where the results were further substantiated. What remained to be discovered, however, was the process by which these occurred—the forces which could lead to such a major change in the course of serious mental illness.

The Social Breakdown Syndrome Concept

One explanation proposed is the concept of the social breakdown syndrome.[7] This concept relates many symptoms of chronic mental illness to the attiudes and actions of those who are around the mentally ill person. The picture presented by the mentally ill person is felt to be a result of the interaction between a person suffering from an illness and his current environment. This concept emphasizes that an adequate description of a mentally ill person requires a statement of the conditions under which he has been observed.

This explanation suggests that the hospitalized mentally ill repond to being crowded into locked, barred, unstimulating rooms by becoming deteriorated and animal-like. Staff attitudes which give little hope for recovery, combined with the patients' not being permitted to wear their own clothing, have clocks, calendars, or mirrors, and an unchanging daily routine, lead to lack of concern for personal appearance, present activities, or future prospects. The social breakdown syndrome concept assumes a

---

[5] It is interesting to note that similar visits by superintendents of American asylums were made to England and Scotland around 1880. The impressions regarding the deleterious effects of physical restraint and confinement of patients were the same. Despite arguments about the differences between American and British culture and American and British patients, many of which are current now, nonrestraint became popular in American asylums, only to be discarded later.

[6] Hurd, H. M. (editor), *The Institutional Care of the Insane in the United States and Canada*, Baltimore, The Johns Hopkins Press, 1916, Vol. 1, p. 226.

[7] Program Area Committee on Mental Health, American Public Health Association, *Mental Disorders: A Guide to Control Methods*, New York, American Public Health Association, 1962.

very direct relationship between the surroundings of a mentally ill person and the course of his illness. It explains why so many varied forms of treatment for acute and chronic psychosis— therapeutic community, remotivation, compensated work, open hospital, day care, patient government, etc.—have had striking successes. All of them involve humane treatment of the patient coupled with social pressure to act in a socially acceptable way. They permit and encourage the patient to make use of the normal social skills which he has and help him to develop new ones. They prepare him during all phases of treatment to return to his life as a functioning member of society.

The purpose of this paper is to examine some highlights of the development of the idea that many symptoms of mental illness are results of conditions under which the mentally ill are treated and not a part of the primary illness.

The Effects of Humane Care and "Moral" Treatment

The belief that treatment in mental hospitals produces many unpleasant and disabling symptoms first appeared in the literature as early as the eighteenth century. Since then there have been many ups-and-downs in its acceptance. The idea has not been demonstrated convincingly enough to make it completely and permanently accepted. Because our knowledge of the course of severe mental disorders is based almost exclusively on experience with hospitalized patients, such a demonstration is peculiarly difficult. Until recently one part of every accepted treatment for psychosis was immediate hospitalization. Almost every patient who came to the attention of a physician, and thus became accessible to study, was hospitalized. Under such conditions there was no way to distinguish the effects of the hospital treatment from the manifestations of the illness. Occasionally a physician had the courage to radically modify hospital treatment. When this occurred, comparison between patients receiving the previous form of treatment provided the opportunity to obtain some idea of the effects of hospital treatment on the patients.

Pinel[8] is often credited with being the first to make effective

---

[8] Pinel, Phillipe, *A Treatise on Insanity* (translated by D. D. Davis), New York, Hafner Publishing Company, Inc., 1962, pp. 67–68.

modifications in the treatment of hospitalized mental patients and thus demonstrate the relationship between the patients' symptoms and their environment. He changed the emphasis in treatment from confinement, physical methods, physical restraint and control by use of force to "moral treatment."[9] Pinel makes clear in his writing, however, that he had studied reports of English physicians who had worked before him and who had found that mental patients responded well to gentle and humane treatment. Pinel determined to try this approach himself and, when put in charge of a Paris mental hospital, the Bicêtre, he did so. He found, contrary to the predictions of many of his colleagues that he would be fiercely attacked by the wild lunatics when he released them from their chains, that there was an improvement in the behavior of the patients. Pinel did not believe however, that all restraints could be removed. He thought that subjugation of mental patients was of great importance, but that this should be accomplished by humane means. He removed the chains from his patients but took care to "render the effect of fear [in the patients] solid and durable," and noted that "straight waist coats, superior force and seclusion for a limited time are the only punishments inflicted [at the Bicêtre]."

Pinel does not distinguish sharply between the effects of moral treatments on the symptomatic behavior of psychotics and on the course of the primary illness. He did not, consequently, deal explicitly with the possibility of "secondary manifestations."

Following Pinel, a number of other workers began to use moral methods of treatment. They went further and further in eliminating force, fear and restraint. Tuke[10] at the York Retreat and Conolly[11] at Hanwell Asylum, both in England, are the men who have been acclaimed for these advances.

Conolly was able to abolish restraint completely at Hanwell and found, as he had predicted in advance, that rather than becoming dangerous and uncontrollable his patients developed

---

[9] The word "moral" has no exact modern equivalent. It referred in contrast to physical treatments, to psychological, relationship and milieu treatments, not excluding the use of authority, generally coupled with the concept of humaneness.

[10] Tuke, Samuel, *Description of the Retreat*, York, W. Alexander, 1813.

[11] Conolly, John, *Treatment of the Insane without Mechanical Restraints*, London, Smith Elder and Company, 1856.

more self control. Over the middle part of the nineteenth century, moral treatment gradually became the accepted mental hospital treatment in England. During this period, consideration for the human needs and comforts of the patients went so far that mental hospital superintendents and their families sometimes lived among the patients, ate with them, and spent as much time as possible with them. The superintendent treated the patients in many ways like his children, and his goal was to provide elements of a happy family life to assist in their recovery. When patients behaved inappropriately, the superintendent dealt with them by exhortation, rather than force or restraint.[12] Difficulties with this approach seemed to occur relatively infrequently, and the reported discharge rates from mental hospitals have never been equalled since. This seemed to represent a major change in the picture of mental illness from that typical in the eighteenth and early nineteenth centuries.

The implication of such changes was considered by John Reid in 1812. He recognized and discussed some questions which we are currently concerned with for an understanding of mental illness. He stated that it was not surprising that confinement to a mental hospital often led to a worsening and perpetuation of the mental disorder. A person's knowledge that others consider him insane "is almost of itself sufficient to make him so, and when such a mode of management is used with men, as ought to not be . . . applied even to brutes, can we wonder if it should often, in a person of more than ordinary irritability, produce, or at any rate accelerate the last and incurable form of . . . disease?"[13] Thus, in one rather long sentence, Reid raises questions still being considered but not yet satisfactorily anwered by modern workers: the effect upon the patient of knowing that he is considered and treated by others as mentally ill; the effect of inhumane treatment in the mental hospital; and the possibility that mental illness increases susceptibility to the disabling social pressures present within hospitals.

---

[12] Tuke, D. Hack, *Reform in the Treatment of the Insane*, London, J. & A. Churchill, 1892.

[13] Reid, John, *Essays on Insanity, Hypochondriasis and Other Nervous Affections*, 1812; reprinted in Hunter, R., and MacAlpine, I., *Three Hundred Years of Psychiatry*, 1535–1860, London, Oxford University Press, 1963, p. 724.

The Abandonment of Moral Treatment

Toward the end of the nineteenth century—for reasons which are not completely clear—moral treatment was gradually, yet almost completely, abandoned. There was a return to physical treatment methods as well as to severe confinement, restraint, and subjugation. These were accompanied by a resurgence of the feeling that mental illnesses had a hopeless prognosis, and it was during this period that the term "dementia praecox" was introduced by Morel. The symptoms of schizophrenia as well as of many other major mental illnesses could be seen in their most classic and florid forms in any mental hospital. This was the age of the catalogers of psychopathology, for psychiatrists were able to do little more than describe what they saw.

In a sense, this change in the course and appearance of the major mental illnesses which occurred was the converse of the experiment which had begun with Pinel and culminated with Conolly. Decreasing physical restraint and emphasis on self-control had resulted in one type of behavioral reactions and prognosis. Now, in countless hospitals, a return to severe restrictions and an emphasis on patient control by physical means was accompanied by a return to rapid deterioration and a generally deteriorating course. During this period, mental illnesses apparently were considered to consist of discrete syndromes whose course was inevitably downhill and unaffected by environment. Symptoms were believed to be an integral part of the illness, and study of them consisted merely of listing them with little consideration of the patient's previous history or, more important, the conditions under which he was being observed. Patients tended to be considered as helpless victims of their illness and completely without control over any of their actions. Textbooks stated that patients with certain mental illnesses, once admitted were only rarely discharged.[14]

---

[14] Kraepelin, Emil, *Clinical Psychiatry*, abstracted and adapted from the sixth German edition by A. Ross Defendorf, New York, The Macmillan Company, 1902.

Some Stepping Stones in Treatment Concepts

The return to moral treatment began around the turn of the century with the work of two giants of psychiatry—Freud and Bleuler. Freud was not primarily interested in the psychoses. However, his emphasis on the meaningfulness and treatability of the symptoms seen in neurotic patients led naturally to a similar consideration of psychosis. His famous discussion, in 1911, of the autobiographical description of a psychosis by Schreber described his new way of looking at symptoms.[15] Freud freed psychiatrists from their previous helpless and hopeless cataloging of symptoms to considering what led to the occurrence of each particular symptom in a patient and an understanding of the meaning of the symptom. He looked to early events in the patients' lives for this meaning and gave little weight to the patients' present circumstances. He did not make any direct contribution to effective methods of treating the psychoses but as will be seen, his followers did attempt to extend psychoanalytic treatment into this area.

Bleuler was also interested in the psychology of symptom formation and coined the concept of "the group of schizophrenias." Perhaps in reaction to Kraepelin's implication of inevitable deterioration in dementia praecox, he pointed out again and again that some cases of schizophrenia remit, some arrest at each stage and some remain asymptomatic and unrecognized for a life time. More important for our present purpose, he made the distinction between primary and secondary symptoms. Furthermore, he stated that the presence and severity of secondary symptoms depended on several factors, among them the patient's present situation, including his hospital environment.

"We can only understand a psychically determined psychosis if we distinguish the symptoms stemming directly from the disease process itself from those secondary symptoms which begin to operate only when the sick person reacts to some internal or external process.

"The primary symptoms are the necessary partial phenomena

---

[15] Freud, Sigmund, Psychoanalytic Notes upon an Autobiographical Account of a Case of Paranoia (Dementia Paranoides) in *The Collected Papers of Sigmund Freud*, New York, Basic Books, Inc., 1959, Vol. III.

of a disease; the secondary symptoms may be absent, at least potentially, or they may change without the disease process having to change at the same time.

"Almost the totality of the heretofore described symptomatology of dementia praecox is a secondary, in a certain sense, an accidental one. Therefore, the disease may remain symptomless for a long time. Whether a particularly chronic schizophrenic is able to work peacefully today or wanders about and quarrels with everyone, whether he is neat and clean or smears himself—that is, the nature of the symptoms—depends mainly on past or present events and not directly on the disease. Some affectively charged experience releases a hallucinatory agitated state. A transfer to another hospital may bring about the disappearance of the same hallucinations.[16]

Although it took many years to come to fruition, a major step toward our present understanding of the relationship of psychotic symptoms to treatment environment was clearly taken.

The next step in the rediscovery of the effectiveness of moral treatment came in 1929 when Hermann Simon published his new method for treating schizophrenia.[17] Similar work was later repeated and published in the U.S. by Meyerson who called it the "total push method."[18] It consisted of forcing regressed withdrawn chronic mental patients into many forms of activity. Every patient was pushed into every possible program to counteract the withdrawal and regression. The total push method was reported to be effective and useful. Meyerson recognized he was dealing with deterioration which is not "an entirely necessary product of the disease." He felt his method counteracted "a prison stupor or psychosis" which hospitalization produced in schizophrenics.

In 1929 Simmel reported his method of treatment for hospital-

---

[16] Bleuler, E., *Dementia Praecox or the Group of Schizophrenias*; translated by Joseph Zinkin, New York, International Universities Press, Inc., 1950, p. 349.

[17] Simon, Hermann, *Aktivere Krankenbehandlung in der Irrenanstalt*, Berlin, DeGruyter Co., 1929.

[18] Meyerson, Abraham, Theory and Principles of the "Total Push" Method in the Treatment of Chronic Schizophrenia, *American Journal of Psychiatry*, 95, 1197–1264, March, 1939.

ized neurotics and early psychotics.[19] Based upon psychoanalytic principles, it is noteworthy because it called attention to the ways in which symptoms could be modified by interactions between patients and hospital staff. Simmel assumed that the patient identified hospital life with the intra-uterine situation. The patient uses the protected hospital environment to regress in fantasy to the early stages of development while the therapist, by directing treatment "against the pleasure principle" to frustrate the "unconscious instinctual demands," hoped to modify the symptoms. Simmel also insisted that the patients "respect reality demands"; patients were "banished to their rooms" if they did not control their moods, and restrain "asocial and antisocial impulses."

In 1930, Sullivan reported on the work he had been doing for the previous 10 years with schizophrenics.[20] Using specially selected personnel, he had set up a six-bed ward at Shephard and Enoch Pratt Hospital, "in which it was proposed that a study be made of the therapeutic possibilities of carefully organized personal environments . . . the mental hospital became a school for personality growth rather than a custodian of personality failures." Combining his analytic background and his unique sociological approach Sullivan produced an environment which he reported was successful in leading to recovery from schizophrenia.

Sullivan's work differed from previous reports in several aspects. He did not attempt to deal directly with any intra-psychic configuration but rather emphasized relationships between patients and staff—a genuine, personal one. Sullivan treated the schizophrenic illness in a specially structured social environment, seeking first "social recovery" through improvement in social skills; he believed that under the right conditions this could lead to "personality reorganization in our special sense." This reorganization does not appear to have required a change in internal psychological structure.

---

[19] Simmel, E., Psychoanalytic Treatment in a Sanitarium, *International Journal of Psychoanalysis, 10,* 70–89, January, 1929.

[20] Sullivan, Harry S., Socio-Psychiatric Research; Its Implication for the Schizophrenia Problem and for Mental Hygiene, *American Journal of Psychiatry, 10,* 977–991 (May), 1931; reprinted in Sullivan, Harry S., *Schizophrenia as a Human Process,* New York, W. W. Norton & Company, Inc., 1962.

The Menninger Clinic carried Simmel's approach further by arranging for the physician to prescribe the emotional character of the hospital staff's approach to the patient.[21] The phyisican could indicate as part of his admission orders which of six approaches he wished the staff to take to meet the patients' unconscious needs: to afford an outlet for aggressions, to encourage advantageous identifications, to permit atonement of guilt, to afford a means of obtaining love, to encourage acting out of fantasies or to afford an opportunity to create. Although later investigations found it impossible to establish that the prescriptions made a difference in observed staff behavior, the scheme is noteworthy because it focused on patient-staff interaction as well as general hospital atmosphere as a means of treatment. It went further than Simmel in providing for variation depending upon the individual patient's needs.

Two more recent developments in England are also important. The first one began as an attempt to treat "effort syndrome" (breathlessness, palpitation, chest pain, giddiness, fainting attacks, and fatigue) in British military personnel during World War II by setting up a unit at Mill Hill Emergency Hospital under Jones and Wood. Several changes from standard hospital operations were introduced there fortuitously.[22] The available nurses were relatively untrained because of the war and lacked allegiance to the traditional nurse's "subservient and unquestioning role." They began to take a more active role in dealing with the patients and to share responsibility with the physician. At the same time, the doctors felt it was therapeutic to explain to the patients some of the anatomy and physiology of their symptoms. The doctors led group discussions on this subject, but the patients could take a major part. It was soon found that such changes from traditional roles of active, authoritarian physician, obedient, impersonal nurse, and passive patient changed the patients' attitudes toward their illnesses as well as the atmosphere on the ward. After a time other matters began to be brought up

[21] Menninger, William C., Psychiatric Hospital Therapy Designed to Meet Unconscious Needs, *American Journal of Psychiatry*, 93, 347–360, September, 1936.

[22] Jones, Maxwell, et al., *Social Psychiatry*, London, Tavistock Publications, 1952.

by the patients in their group meetings—incidents on the ward, personal problems, etc. It became clear that what happened throughout the day at the hospital was important to effective treatment, perhaps more important than individual interviews with the physician. Recovery seemed to occur most rapidly when traditional social barriers between doctors, nurses, and patients were lowered and social interaction was at a maximum. Simultaneous vocational preparation and hospital "penetration" into the community through vocational courses in the neighboring community were also found to be important. Possibly these emphasized to the patients the expectation that they were to return to normal social roles and become productive members of society.

Following World War II this treatment method was continued by Jones with ex-prisoners of war and then with the "chronic unemployed neurotic." It has now been used by Jones and many others in prisons, in mental hospitals, and in various other settings. The common elements in all of these "therapeutic communities," as the treatment has come to be called, seem to be increased freedom of communication among patients and staff, an attempt to reduce social distance among the participants, the use of social pressure to induce behavior conforming to set standards, and an emphasis on the expectation that patients will return to society in normal roles. Although the therapeutic community used alone has not been a major element in treatment of schizophrenics, it has been widely used in combination with other measures. Its success has served to call attention to the effectiveness of social pressure in influencing mental patients' behavior, even of patients who are very regressed and withdrawn.

The Open Hospital

Possibly the most significant development in the modern rediscovery of the influence of the hospital on mental illness occurred shortly after World War II. As has already been mentioned, three British mental hospital superintendents began to make major changes in their hospitals. In each case the crucial step was to unlock all doors in the hospital. Necessarily this measure was accompanied by many other elements of what had formerly been called "moral treatment." Bell[23] in Scotland may even have started before the war. Later Rees[24] and Macmillan[25] in England followed similar courses. Each began by placing the best integrated patients in one ward and unlocking it completely. They gradually extended this to the rest of each hospital until the hospitals were completely without locked doors. The guiding principle in each case seems to have been that mental patients are able to assume much more responsibility for themselves than had been believed possible. Perhaps in response to their doctors' belief, the patients did improve to the extent that they were able to take more responsibility for themselves.

What Conolly had said in 1856 was again proved by these men to be true. Mental patients need not be controlled by force. When exclusively psychological methods of control are used, many socially disabling symptoms do not appear or quickly disappear.

Theoretical Implications

Simultaneous with the proliferation of the therapies has been the proliferation of theories explaining the behavior seen in institutions. Barton,[26] Miller,[27] Wing,[28] Sommer and Witney,[29] Mar-

---

[23] Bell, G. M., A Mental Hospital with Open Doors, *International Journal of Social Psychiatry, 1*, 42, 1955.

[24] Rees, Thomas P., and Glatt, M. M., The Organization of a Mental Hospital on the Basis of Group Participation, *International Journal of Group Psychotherapy, 5*, 157, 1955.

[25] Macmillan, Duncan, Hospital-Community Relationships, in *An Approach to the Prevention of Disability from Chronic Psychoses: The Open Door Mental Hospital within the Community*, Proceedings of the Thirty-Fourth Annual Conference of the Milbank Memorial Fund, 1957, New York, Milbank Memorial Fund, 1958, Part 1, p. 29.

[26] Barton, Russell, *Institutional Neurosis*, Bristol, John Wright & Sons, 1959.

[27] Miller, D. H., Psycho-social Factors in the Aetiology of Disturbed Behaviour, *British Journal of Medical Psychology, 34*, 43–52, 1961.

[28] Wing, John K., Institutionalism in Mental Hospitals, *British Journal of Social and Clinical Psychology, 1*, 38–51, 1962.

[29] Sommer, Robert, and Witney, G., The Chain of Chronicity, *American Journal of Psychiatry, 118*, 111–117, August, 1961.

tin,[30] Goffman,[31] the American Public Health Association,[7] and Gruenberg,[32] are some of those who have been active in this field.

Barton

Russell Barton used the term *institutional neurosis* to describe a syndrome characterized by apathy, lack of initiative, loss of interest (more marked in things and events not immediately personal or present), submissiveness, lack of expression of feelings of resentment at harsh or unfair orders, lack of interest in the future, deterioration in personal habits, loss of individuality, and a resigned acceptance of things as they are.

The severity of the syndrome varies and the patient who is active and cheerful but has no interest in leaving the hospital is afflicted as definitely as the back-ward patients. Aggressive outbursts are part of the syndrome, and investigation of events preceding the outbursts usually reveals that the outbursts are not senseless but have been provoked. There is a characteristic posture and gait—hands held across the body, shoulders drooped, head forward, with shuffling restricted movements.

The syndrome may be confused with the end stages of schizophrenia, and the distinction between the two may become clear only after a course of rehabilitation eliminates the symptoms of institutional neurosis, leaving the schizophrenia unaffected. Organic dementias also may be confused with, or complicated by, institutional neurosis. Again, clearing of symptoms after intensive rehabilitation makes the distinction.

Institutional neurosis is felt to be associated with many environmental factors. But one over-all factor may be the "tendency, of most human beings, to modify ambition and establish a way of

[30] Martin, D. V., Institutionalisation, *Lancet*, 2, 1188–1190, December 3, 1955.

[31] Goffman, Erving, Characteristics of Total Institutions, in Walter Reed Army Institute of Research, Symposium on Preventive and Social Psychiatry, April 15–17, 1957, Washington, D.C.

[32] Gruenberg, Ernest M., Discussion of critical reviews of Pueblo, Western, and Denver Tri-County Divisions, in Stone, Bernard (editor), A Critical Review of Treatment Progress in a State Hospital Reorganized toward the Communities Served, Pueblo, Colorado, Pueblo Association for Mental Health, May 1963 (mimeographed).

life as trouble-free and secure as possible." Seven general areas are identified by Barton as important in genesis of the syndrome.

Loss of contact with the outside world is first. This results partly from locked doors and limited visiting in the mental hospital and partly from subtle rejection by others because of both stigmatization as a patient and strangeness of appearance. Enforced idleness, either as a routine program (confinement to a day room) or as a result of "kindness" of staff members, who perform all housekeeping and self-care functions for the patients, is the second.

Bossiness and an "unjust conviction of superiority" by the staff is the third. This results in such things as the physician's confidence that he knows how bad it would be for the patient to be subjected to stresses, such as news of family deaths and disasters or the need to make important personal decisions. The physician is consequently willing to lie to the patient about these matters "for his own good." The next factor is the loss of personal friends, possessions, and events. It has been common for patients entering the hospital to be required to leave behind all their belongings, including clothing—thus leaving behind them a part of their identities.

Loss of old friendships and meaningful occasions as a result of isolation from the community is another factor. Drugs are also a factor when used to enable the patient to adjust calmly to his unpleasant surroundings. Heavy sedation can lead to apathy and idleness, where active resistance and struggling would be more appropriate.

The general ward atmosphere is important as a factor. Atmosphere depends on the physical setting and also on the attitudes of staff. The final factor is loss of prospects outside the institution. A patient who has little to look forward to after discharge is not likely to work toward discharge.

Barton points out that institutional neurosis can occur in those not institutionalized—in hermits, housewives, and the aged. It is more common, however, in institutions and was first described there. Barton emphasizes factors in the institution in accounting for cases which develop. He recognizes that staff attitudes and behavior are major etiological factors, but does not discuss how these attitudes and behavior may reflect attitudes in society outside the hospital.

Barton recognizes the widely varying degrees of severity which institutional neurosis may take—from the mute, stuporous patient to the active, cheerful one who shows no desire to leave the hospital. He apparently does not believe there is necessarily a progression from the mild to the severe form in a single patient over a period of time.

The detailed description of the symptoms of institutional neurosis includes several points of differential diagnosis. Barton feels that in some cases definitive diagnosis can be made only in retrospect. After an intensive course of rehabilitation, institutional neurosis will be improved, but schizophrenia and organic psychosis will not. In this way, institutional neurosis and schizophrenia are simultaneously defined—the latter as untreatable and the former as treatable—by response to rehabilitation. Among present-day American psychiatrists, there must be few who would agree that schizophrenia never responds to rehabilitation. Even organic psychosis may conceivably improve to a limited extent with rehabilitation. It seems more reasonable to suppose that some improvement in rehabilitated patients may be due to response of the primary mental illness to treatment.

Of the seven specific etiological factors which Barton lists one is the use of drugs. Little attention has been devoted in the psychiatric literature to the use of psychotropic drugs primarily to help patients adjust to unpleasant hospital situations. Drugs can be used to produce co-operation where a more normal response would be rebellion. Drugs can also dull social needs and increase isolation. Barton points out that drugs can be used "to make [the patient] accept the unpleasantness of his surroundings, the injustice of his incarceration, and the terrible lack of care and foresight of doctors, committees, and legislative bodies."

Another of Barton's factors often neglected in accounting for the course of illness, is the nature of the patient's prospects outside the hospital. Barton emphasizes the importance of "the prospect of having a place to live in, a job to work at, and friends to stop loneliness. . . . It is not sufficient to tell him [the patient] that he might get a job and get out—he might as well fly or strike oil in the lavatories."

Finally, the aptness of one of Barton's phrases is very much worth noting. He calls institutional neurosis "a mental bedsore."

Miller

Miller discusses chronic institutional reactions and finds five main types of reaction may occur: 1. "a chronic paranoid response in which the individual is constantly at war with his environment and feels that it is against him and means to harm him"; 2. a "depressive reaction" in which "there tends to be a chronic change in the activity level of the patient, often his appearance is dilapidated and he shows an inadequate and inappropriate environmental response"; 3. "a chronic catatonic response" in which there is "a psychological and physical withdrawal with intermittent bursts of diffusely directed aggressive activity"; 4. "a psychopathic response in which the individual is constantly manipulating the external environment to obtain gratification for himself"; and 5. "a passive neurotic response in which the individual 'gives in' and willingly fulfills the infantilizing demands of the institution."

Except for catatonia all these responses occur independently of diagnostic categories. They also occur in custodial institution staff members who have been employed for long periods.

Miller notes that "all hospitals also tend to develop typical patient group reactions to stress which are special to the institution. Some have episodes of incontinence, others clothes-tearing, others running away, others property destruction or alcoholism." Thus, in one institution the patients may traditionally use one of these means of reacting at stressful times, while other means, although available, are never employed. In another institution some other means will be the accepted one. Customs and fashions in an institution greatly influence patients' actions.

When discussing etiology, Miller says that all of these reactions occur more frequently in institutions "in which, whatever the overt goal, ideologically the staff tend to be authoritarian and disciplinarian with a prime goal of having the institution run as peacefully as possible." These he calls custodial institutions as distinguished from therapeutic institutions.

Miller divides chronic antisocial reactions to institutionalization into types, each with a name suggestive of standard diagnostic categories. His description of each type is reminiscent of the corresponding diagnostic category. In this paper he deals in more detail with organized collective disturbances in institution-alized adolescents, but does not explain further the distinction between the type of chronic antisocial reaction exhibited by an individual and his underlying mental illness. The types of reac-tion Miller describes might be expected to occur in individuals who are predisposed to them under any sort of stressful situation. Previous paranoid, catatonic or psychopathic behavior presum-ably is what got the patient into the hospital. Such behavior when seen in the hospital may be simply part of the continuing process. The contribution of the hospital atmosphere to the frequency of each type of reaction is not specified. Miller's description of Chronic Antisocial Behavior and his assertion that its form varies from institution to institution may be seen as an indication that social pressures are effective in modifying symptomatic behavior in institutions; but there may be other explanations for this pat-tern such as selective admission policies.

Miller states that "chronic institutional reactions occur much more frequently in custodial institutions in which the therapeutic goal has become obscure." Whether or not this is true is open to study.

Wing

Wing discusses institutionalism. He feels that three types of variables are relevant in understanding institutionalism: 1. social pressures of an institution; 2. pattern of susceptibility or resistance to these pressures which an individual possesses when he is ad-mitted; and 3. length of time an individual is exposed to these pressures.

Two types of social pressures are exerted on mental hospital inmates. These are effects of the routines of general institutional living which, Wing thinks, have been adequately described by Goffman (*see* below), and effects of the special treatments offered in mental hospitals, e.g., physical treatments (leucotomy, drugs, etc.), and social treatments (psychotherapy, group therapy, therapeutic milieu, etc.). Dietary deficiency and underactivity have also been noted in mental hospital patients.

The second set of variables, those which influence susceptibil-ity to institutional pressures, includes a number of factors which are associated with a tendency to be admitted to mental hospitals—lack of ties to the community, poverty, age and social position, "those who have never been concerned with problems of personal liberty and decision-making" and "those in whom social relationships induce anxiety or discomfort and who prefer a social environment where interaction can be minimal." Wing states that these make up a "state of susceptibility to institutionalism"; patterns present before admission to the institution influence susceptibility so that "at its most extreme, a person may show dependence on the institution, and apathy about leaving, very shortly after admission." In the ". . . limiting case . . . such behavior is already present in embryo before admission."

The third variable is the length of time the patient has been institutionalized. A short stay in an institution is likely to affect only the most susceptible persons, while most people would probably be affected by a long stay in such a place.

Wing considers the effects of institutional pressure on the symptoms of schizophrenia to be a major question. The majority of long-term hospital patients are schizophrenics. Among non-hospitalized schizophrenics, shallowness of affect and lack of motivation (which might be considered to be symptoms of institutionalism) are typical symptoms. It is important to distinguish symptoms which are clearly characteristic of schizophrenic deterioration and which are inherent in the illness from those of institutionalism. Wing suggests that blunting of affect, disordered speech, delusions, and hallucinations are inherent in schizophrenia regardless of the setting. Dependency, apathy about leaving, lack of interest in outside events, and resignation result from being in an institution. He believes schizophrenic symptoms can be distinguished from institutional symptoms by lack of change over a long period of time in the former, while institutional symptoms continue to progress during hospitalization.

Sommer and Witney

Sommer and Witney discuss "Chronicity." They state that others have considered two years' residence in a mental hospital as the criterion for Chronicity. Once past this point, a patient's chances for discharge are poor. Sommer and Witney concentrate on the sequence of events which leads to Chronicity and feel that each one of a number of steps is necessary for the condition to develop. At each point there is an alternative which if taken, averts Chronicity.

The sequence begins when the patient falls ill and his illness is manifested by peculiar behavior. If it is not noted the behavior may eventually disappear. If the peculiar behavior is noted by those around him it may be brought to the attention of some official agency—clinic, police, etc.; alternatively, it may be "accepted by family and friends." If the behavior comes to the official agency's attention, the patient may be sent to a mental hospital; alternatively, he could be referred to outpatient treatment. When admitted to the hospital the patient is placed on an admission ward where he has a fairly good chance of being treated until discharged. Otherwise he will be transferred to a "continued treatment ward." This leads to "regular émployment at a hospital job, loss of contact with family and the outside, acquisition of institutional values."

Sommer and Witney devote major attention to this transfer from admitting ward to continued treatment ward which they state is a crucial link in "the chain of chronicity." They describe the symbolic meaning of this transfer to both patient and staff, but stress the importance of the objective differences between admission and continued treatment wards, including staff-patient ratios and physical surroundings. "It not only marks the patient as a 'failure,' in many cases it insures that he becomes one." As a "self fulfilling prophecy" this step "can include rejection of the patient by the staff, coupled with guilt at their inability to help him and loss of hope by the patient accompanied by acceptance of a passive institutional role."

In discussing "Chronicity," Sommer and Witney cite data to show that the longer a patient remains hospitalized, the fewer visits and letters he receives, the less he is in touch with developments on the outside, and the more his values differ from those of the outside community. Passivity, dependence, and blind acceptance of authority are other symptoms of prolonged care.

Sommer and Witney say some chronic patients function well in hospital society and are not withdrawn patients. Sommer and Witney distinguish chronic patients from chronic schizophrenics. A chronic schizophrenic is a person "whose illness and behavior have reached a stable level"; many of these people live outside of institutions. The chronic patient, on the other hand, "is a person unable to manage outside of an institution"; many no longer suffer from their mental illnesses. These are two separate problems even though chronic schizophrenics, once admitted, are especially likely to become chronic patients.

Martin

Martin describes "Institutionalisation" as a phase in a process through which the patient ceases to rebel against, or question his placement in, a mental hospital. The patient becomes resigned and "cooperative" and at the same time loses much of his individuality and initiative. Martin states that this condition may be a desirable adjustment for those patients who are beyond treatment but its effect upon newly admitted cases needs investigation. He notes that some feel this state is an end form of schizophrenia, but points out that since the condition is found among all diagnostic classes there must be something besides the illness which leads to Institutionalisation.

The factors in the patient which may predispose toward Institutionalisation are inadequate personality, unfavorable economic circumstances, and lack of satisfying interests and relationships. The process producing Institutionalisation begins prior to hospitalization when the patient is suffering considerably because of his illness, the distress he is causing others and material discomfort. Upon admission to the hospital, this suffering ceases or is considerably diminished, and the impetus for the patient to take responsibility for solving his own problems is diminished. This is the first step in the development of dependency leading to Institutionalisation. The patient "settles down," without any effort or planning on his own part. "Many patients get more positive pleasure out of life through the amenities of the hospitals than they obtain outside."

For those patients who criticize the staff or organization of the hospital or show dissatisfaction with the way their needs are met, there is the threat of transfer to "refractory ward." This is terrifying because of the fantasies which are common among mental hospital patients about this type of ward. The availability of such wards permits the staff to use them rather than inquire into what is upsetting the patients. The staff tends to fall into a pattern of avoiding questions of possible real faults of organization or personal relationships without being aware of what they are doing.

The doctors, overburdened as they tend to be, have an interest in keeping the patients "well institutionalized"—free of complaints. A doctor's personal insecurity may predispose him to fall in with this system. Close relationships with patients may face him with the dilemma of being loyal to the interests of the patient or of the institution: he tends to sacrifice his relationships with patients.

Nurses are in an even more difficult position since they work more closely with patients than do the doctors and their training is more destructive of personal individuality. Better training in human relations would help support them in the conflict between patient and institutional interests. They are expected to obey orders regardless of their own judgment of the effect on the patients. So long as their efficiency is judged by the quietness and tidiness of their wards rather than their relationships with the patients they will tend to remain unconscious of the conflict.

Martin concludes that the answer to the problem of Institutionalisation "would be to staff our mental hospitals only with men and women sufficiently independent and integrated to replace an authoritarian system by real human relationships."

Martin's description of the syndrome of Institutionalization is confined to "cooperativeness," lack of questioning of orders given, loss of individuality and initiative and surrender to institutional life.

Martin suggests that suffering prior to entering the hospital is the strongest force driving the patient to seek a solution to "the problem of his illness." When the institution relieves this suffering it lessens his drive to solve his difficulties. The acceptance of a dependent relationship to the institution and its tenacity presumably depends on the amount of suffering and the degree to which the hospital relieves it. This is worthy of consideration since traditionally it is assumed that the job of the hospital is to relieve suffering. Might effectiveness in this area interfere with recovery? Martin suggests rather that deliberate steps be taken to counteract the consequent dependency analogous to the excessive dependency seen in the first stages of individual psychotherapy.

Goffman

Goffman has brilliantly described the concept of the Total Institution. This is an institution which encompasses its inmates almost totally[33]—"symbolized by the barrier to social intercourse with the outside that is often built right into the physical plant: locked doors, high walls, barbed wire, cliffs and water, open terrain, and so forth."[34]

Goffman further explains "We tend to sleep, play and work in different places, in each case with a different set of co-participants under a different authority and without an overall rational plan. The central feature of Total Institutions can be described as a breakdown of the kinds of barriers ordinarily separating these three spheres of life. *First*, all aspects of life are conducted in the same place and under the same single authority. *Second*, each phase of the member's daily activity will be carried out in the immediate company of a large batch of others, all of whom are treated alike and required to do the same thing together. *Third*, all phases of the day's activities are tightly scheduled [and] imposed from above through a system of explicit formal rulings and a body of officials. Finally, the contents of the various enforced activities are brought together as parts of a single over-all rational plan purportedly designed to fulfill the official aims of the institution."[35]

Goffman emphasizes the experience and forces acting on an inmate of any total institution. Unlike other authors, he does not describe a syndrome in mental patients resulting from hospitalization. He describes characteristic inmate behavior which he feels results from adjustment to any total institution.

On entrance into the total institution, "the stripping processes [begin] through which mortification of the self occurs. Personal identity equipment is removed, as well as other possessions with which the inmate may have identified himself, there being a system of nonaccessible storage from which the inmate can only obtain his effects should he leave the institution. As a substitute

---

[33] Goffman, *op. cit.*, p. 43.
[34] *Ibid.*, p. 44.
[35] *Ibid.*, p. 45.

for what has been taken away, institutional issue is provided, but this will be the same for large categories of inmates and will be regularly repossessed by the institution. In brief, standardized defacements will occur. Family, occupational and educational career lines are chopped off and a stigmatized status is submitted. Sources of fantasy materials, which had meant momentary releases from stress in the home world, are denied. Areas of autonomous decision are eliminated through the process of collective scheduling of daily activity. Many channels of communication with the outside are restricted or closed off completely. Verbal discreditings occur in many forms as a matter of course. Expressive signs of respect to the staff are coercively and continuously demanded. And the effect of each of these conditions is multiplied by having to witness the mortification of one's fellow inmates."[36]

The mortification process may purposely be exaggerated during the first few days of an inmate's stay as a form of initiation. It commonly includes communication of several standard aspects —"the house rules—which lay out the main requirements of inmate conduct"; "rewards and privileges (which) are held out in exchange for obedience to staff in action and spirit" and "punishments (which) are designated as the consequence of breaking the rules." "An institutional arrangement which causes a small number of easily controlled privileges to have a massive significance is the same arrangement which lends a terrible significance to their withdrawal."[37]

Around the privilege system grows up a whole set of customs— adjustments which the inmates develop. These are unique to institutional life and set the inmate off from his previous world. These include such things as "release binge fantasy" (fantasy of what one will do on release or discharge), "institutional lingo," and "secondary adjustments" (means of obtaining forbidden satisfactions without directly challenging the staff).

Another influence on the inmate is the "fraternalization process" through which previously socially distant persons find themselves providing mutual support and developing common counter-mores in opposition to a system that has forced them into intimacy and

---

[36] *Ibid.,* p. 50.
[37] *Ibid.,* pp. 53–54.

into a single equalitarian community fate. Thus the new inmate starts out with the outside world's stereotyped view of inmates and does not consider himself typical. He comes to find that the other inmates "have all the properties of ordinary decent human beings," and eventually identifies as one of them.

The inmate may adapt to his new environment in several ways. *Situational withdrawal* involves withdrawing attention from everything except immediate events and seeing these in a perspective not used by others present. In mental hospitals, this is called regression; in prisons, prison psychosis or stir simpleness, and in concentration camps, acute depersonalization. The *rebellious line* involves challenging the institution in every way possible. This may result in high morale for the inmates involved. Interestingly, Goffman points out, complete rebellion requires an intimate knowledge of the intricacies of the rules and a need to examine every action with regard to them. The rebel is as committed to the rules as the conformist. The institution, in turn, may especially devote itself to the rebel in an attempt to change him. Rebellion is typically a temporary reaction leading to some other adaptations.

Colonization occurs when the inmate becomes contented with his existence and makes the most of his situation. He is no longer oriented toward the outside world and if discharge seems imminent may behave so as to prevent it. This is sometimes called "hospitalitis" or "institutional cure" in mental hospitals. Lastly, there is *conversion*. The inmate appears to take over the staff view of himself and tries to act out the role of the perfect inmate. This differs from colonization in that the colonizer tries to make the best of his position while the convert moralistically does what is expected of him. In mental hospitals conversion is possible to one of two points of view—that of the professional staff, or that of the attendants.

Goffman feels that the majority of inmates do not follow any one course of adjustment consistently, but rather "play it cool"— "a somewhat opportunistic combination of secondary adjustments, conversion, colonization, and loyalty to the inmate group." A small group of inmates comes from an outside world which is either similar to or worse than the institutional one. Those Goffman calls *immunized against the institution*. They need no particular scheme of adaptation, but live much as they did before admission.

Goffman then examines staff participation in the mortification process. The contradiction "between what the institution does and what its officials must say that it does, forms the central context of the staff's daily activity." There is a constant conflict between humane standards and institutional efficiency. For example, removal of personal possessions makes transfer of inmates from place to place easier. Shaven heads make it easier to keep inmates clean. Removal of teeth from certain aggressive patients prevents injuries to others. The staff is constantly faced with the dilemma of making things easier for themselves (and often gaining the approval of their supervisors for their efficiency) or treating the patients as human beings. One reason for the distance between staff and inmates is that in the face of this conflict close involvement by a staff member can lead to his being hurt by what inmates do and by the sufferings they undergo. It is thus safer for the staff members to avoid any sort of meaningful personal relationship, which lets them see inmates as human beings like themselves.

Goffman's concept of the total institution has been widely accepted and found useful. Although he developed it with a background of having studied a large public mental hospital, it obviously applies to many social agencies. Indeed, it probably is applicable, at least in part, whenever large numbers of people are dealt with by means of a bureaucratic organization. The bureaucracy inherently has a goal of efficient and impartial operation. Concern with individual differences and needs is antithetical to this goal. When this method of administration is applied to every facet of the inmate's life the total institution results.

Goffman seems to describe the mental hospital as essentially a culture separate from that of the outside world. Although he states it is not a separate culture but depends on tension between the inmates and the outside world, he treats it as an entity with its own philosophy of life, mores, and methods of communication. He does not discuss possible disability or difficulties when inmates of a total institution return to the outside world, except in terms of "stigmatization."

He does not seem to consider how the attitudes of the extra-institutional world may shape the institutional environment or even prepare the way for institutional adaptation before the patient is admitted. This is of particular importance in the mental hospital where the disruption of outside contacts and previous identity results not only from action of the institution but also from rejection by the outside world.

One of Goffman's contributions is his detailed but general description of how an individual's identity can be systematically removed to give him a new one. The mortification of the self and the stripping process can be used, as he points out, to develop army officers, nuns, or tractable mental patients. From his description, it seems clear that such a process must take place in mental patients as long as they are admitted into large self-sufficient, walled-off institutions which require styles of living completely different from those of the general community. If the goal in treating mental patients is return to the community, then treatment must consist in large part in living as the community does—self-mortification or stripping processes can only be a hindrance to recovery.

Goffman's work is a noteworthy theoretical advance for several reasons. It attempts to explain the behavior of patients in mental hospitals without reference to mental illness. The behavior is seen as normal adjustment to existing conditions. This provides an important clue as to how this behavior can be modified or avoided. It calls to attention the similarity in the behavior of mental hospital patients and other institutional inmates—a fact that others had noted but not attempted to explain. It points out that behavior of the staff in the hospital is also a rational result of the system of organization. Finally, where psychiatrists studying the same phenomenon had concentrated on the end results of hospitalization—the deteriorated patient—Goffman's presentation concentrates on the process which leads to deterioration. In specifying process, it simplifies attempts at prevention.

American Public Health Association

Social breakdown syndrome is the term used by the Program Area Committee on Mental Health of the American Public Health Association to name "a socially determined reaction pattern which the committee believes can be identified as a major target for community mental health programs today." The Committee describes the syndrome as consisting of withdrawal or anger and hostility, as well as combinations of these two, leading to more or less severe destruction of the affected person's relationships. Withdrawal is manifested as lost interest in social functions, such as work responsibilities, housekeeping, and ordinary social obligations. Loss of concern about personal appearance and cleanliness leads eventually to "the standard picture of the deteriorated, dilapidated, unresponsive, soiling, helpless, vegetative creature who in former times inhabited our mental hospitals' back wards."

Anger and hostility may consist of expressions of resentfulness, quarrelsomeness, and hostility, or may go so far as physical violence toward others or toward self. Also included is "a way of withdrawing aggressively" by such actions as echoing others' speech, assuming bizarre postures, etc.

Although the committee's conception of the etiology of the syndrome is not explicitly stated, a number of statements in the description provide some information about this:

"The frequency of the syndrome depends upon the social setting and the way other people and social institutions and medical facilities respond to the underlying disorders. Depersonalized institutionalization is considered to be capable of producing this syndrome.

"One of the primary factors in the process of deterioration has been the assumptions of the public, and to some extent of the medical profession, about the nature of the mental illness. Many people view mental disorders as conditions from which there is no recovery. Within the medical profession itself ideas of slow but inevitable deterioration in such conditions as schizophrenia and epilepsy have been remarkably tenacious. This assumption has made the staffs of large hospitals tolerate the very conditions which brought about deterioration. The realization that much of the disability seen in the mentally ill is neither inherent in the mental process as such nor an inevitable accompaniment of mental disorders is leading to a changed attitude towards mental disorders. While it is true that a schizophrenic disorder is probably never cured and that in some other underlying disorders treatment can only alleviate symptoms, experience has now shown that the amount and severity of associated disability can be very greatly reduced.

"It has been found that much of the antisocial and irresponsible behavior of mental patients disappears when they are treated as responsible human beings."[38]

The committee makes clear what they think the importance of the syndrome to be:

"It is responsible for much of the noisy violence associated with 'disturbed wards' in the hospitals and 'craziness' in the community. It produces a major health and welfare problem and a great deal of human distress. . . . It is responsible for a very large part of the institutionalized mentally disordered; it is responsible for much of the other forms of extreme social disability." And, most significantly, "the outstanding advances in the control of mental disorders in recent years derive from the gradual recognition that this syndrome can be prevented or modified."

The description of the social breakdown syndrome is notable, understandably enough, for its emphasis on the social importance of the syndrome and on the steps necessary to prevent it. The description is partly in terms of behavior seen in individual patients, and partly in terms of the kinds of behavior that experience has shown can be prevented by proper treatment of hospitalized patients. This resembles Barton's approach to "institutional neurosis"—i.e., behavior which disappears after a course of rehabilitation. In this case, social breakdown syndrome is behavior which no longer appears in modern, well-run mental hospitals but did appear in old-fashioned ones.

As an unambiguous definition, this is not quite satisfactory since it implies that modern hospitals are able to prevent a reaction to hospitalization—a questionable assumption. It makes the definition depend on the current state of hospital treatment as well as upon hospital to hospital variations.

The other part of the committee's description—the presence in individual patients of symptoms indicating anger or withdrawal —is more definite. However, it is not clear from the description whether the committee feels all such behavior seen in hospitalized patients is part of the social breakdown syndrome, or, if not,

---

[38] Program Area Committee on Mental Health, *op. cit.*

how much of such behavior can be attributed to social break-down syndrome and how much to the primary illness.

The committee does not state unequivocally, but seems to imply, that social breakdown syndrome leads eventually to deterioration. This is in contrast to most of the other authors who see patients adjusting in a number of different ways and at different stages of reaction.

The discussion of the etiology of social breakdown syndrome is notable in that the committee sees the attitude of society toward mental illness as a fundamental factor. Thus any person who comes to be classified as mentally ill, whether he is in or out of the hospital, will be regarded by those around him in a very special (and probably harmful) way. He will then be specially treated by others and may accept as justified the treatment and attitudes which lead to social breakdown syndrome. Because such treatment tends to be administered in hospitals, it is most common there. It can be seen outside hospitals as well. The important etiological factor is not the institution but rather those around the patient—whether they be hospital staff and other patients or parents and siblings.

Gruenberg

Gruenberg, speaking in 1963,[39] and Gruenberg and Zusman[40] in 1964 further specified the picture of social breakdown syndrome. The syndrome is a complication of acute psychosis, but can also be seen as a result of other conditions. Although it is similar to asylum lunacy and institutionalism, it is not exclusively a product of hospitalization. In mental hospitals it is often called "chronicity." It develops out of the interaction between a susceptible person and a particular kind of environment. Gruenberg[41] offered a tentative seven-stage formulation of the syndrome's pathogenesis.

1. Precondition or Susceptibility: Deficiency in Self-concept
The social breakdown syndrome will occur only in persons with

---

[39] Gruenberg, Ernest M., and Zusman, Jack, The Natural History of Schizophrenia, *International Psychiatry Clinics*, *1*, 699, 1964.

[40] Gruenberg and Zusman, *op. cit.*

[41] Gruenberg, *op. cit.*

weakened or deficient inner standards regarding interpersonal relations, rules of behavior, social obligations of themselves and others, and social roles. In other terms, these people have been described as having an identity problem or a lack of strong allegiance to a reference group, or poor ego strength. In any case, such a person's picture of who he is in relation to others, and how it is proper for him to act, is easily disturbed. In a person whose inner standards in this sense are not weak, social breakdown syndrome will not occur, even if the events described in the subsequent steps do occur.

This weakened self-concept may arise in several ways. It is always present in some people because of a physical handicap which has interfered with normal socialization experiences, or because of deficient or destructive socialization experiences.

More commonly in our state hospital population this weak state of inner standards and concepts regarding oneself and others results from an acute episode of mental turmoil in a person who has previously developed adequate standards for his own behavior and concepts of what is appropriate. An acute psychotic episode can do this and is a common cause. But acute social crises, disasters, acute physical illnesses, wars, and imprisonment can produce similar effects.

These acute episodes break the person's picture of himself from his past accumulated experience. This break can be due to disruption of memory systems but is more usually due to an overwhelming loss of confidence in his past patterns of thinking and feeling. The unquestioned standards of appropriate responses to people and situations by which we all live are precipitously thrown into a serious question. The individual has lost confidence in his own past modes of thought and response. Some might say it is a special form of "identity-crisis." Others might say there is a sudden loss of "reference groups."

A defect of grasp arising from an acute brain syndrome can leave similar effects.

2. Dependence on Current Cues　The person rendered susceptible, because frames of reference derived from past experience are not available, becomes unusually dependent on current stimuli for cues regarding appropriate behavior, determining what is right and wrong, true and false, and judging which impulses to obey and which to inhibit. This is an inevitable consequence of the preliminary condition.

3. *Social Labeling as Incompetent and Dangerous* The social environment defines the person as incompetent, dangerous, incapable of self-control. This is done variously by calling the person "crazy," by ridicule, by sending him into a mental hospital. The most authoritative social action is a public court certification.

The key to understanding the relationship between the second and third stages is the fact that a person who has lost confidence in his own judgments, and thus become excessively dependent on cues in his immediate environment, is told—directly and indirectly—that he is even more incompetent and dangerous than he had thought previously. This is a vicious circle in which the third step—defining the individual as unfit for life in ordinary society and for the responsibilities of an independent citizen—increases the preliminary condition.

4. *Induction into the Sick Role* The initiation into an institution which defines the person—who has now become a "patient" —as part of a social system which suggests to him that he adopt a passive, helpless—perhaps potentially dangerous—certainly "sick" role with little prospect of change, is a crucial moment in the pathogenesis: What the institution communicates to this fearful and self-distrusting person—by direct statements and implications contained in the "admission routine" (what Goffman calls "mortification" and "defacement")—can make an enormous difference. This induction into the patient role is a matter of hours, days, or weeks.

5. *Learning the Chronic Sick Role* Our institutions offer roles of chronic withdrawal, chronic or intermittent hostility and aggression, or chronic dependency without extreme withdrawal or aggressiveness (good working patients). As these roles are built, what was previously an acutely disrupted set of social identities and personal standards become chronically rejected and are replaced by the standards appropriate to the new state.

6. *Atrophy of Work and Social Skills* As a hospital patient there is no opportunity to use the previously acquired skills of

everyday living—cooking, sewing, driving, taking a train. Work skills are also unused. They atrophy from disuse. Even if some of these skills remain intact, changes in technology and customs are likely to make them obsolete and useless if the patient is discharged years later.

7. *Identification with the Sick*   The patient joins the sick community. At some point the chronic state of sick functioning is not only acepted by the patient but he comes to see himself as like the other sick people with whom he lives, and no longer looks on himself as exceptional. At first he gets his cues from staff and old patients, but later he becomes an old patient who knows the cues before they are given and can give them himself if another patient is lacking in adeptness at being in a chronic state. He has become a member of the team. Goffman says he has been "converted."

Separation of the pathogenesis into seven stages is important. Prevention and treatment of each stage may require approaches different from those appropriate to other stages. Even the best approach for a single stage may differ depending on where it takes place—a hospital or other setting.

The hypothesis embodied in the social breakdown concept suggests that those who develop social breakdown syndrome are extremely susceptible to the attitudes of others and to external cues. Commonly held attitudes toward the mentally ill include the feeling that they are wild, childlike, irresponsible, frightening, and hopeless. It is difficult to tell when such behavior does appear in hospitalized patients, how much of it is in response to these attitudes—acting as self-fulfilling prophecies. When even the best hospitals are examined from this point of view it is striking how little opportunity they provide for patients to exercise normal social skills, and how much pressure hospitals exert to make patients act in socially deviant ways and to carry out the popular expectations of "crazy" actions. Hospitals often seem to be designed to force communications into stylized staff-patient patterns, making use of symptoms and bizarre actions rather than direct person-to-person contact. Recognition of this tendency leads to the suggestion that the best institution for mental patients should resemble a hotel or a college more than a conventional hospital.

It is important to keep in mind the fact that social breakdown syndrome occurs outside of mental hospitals, not always in association with mental illness. It develops out of the interaction between a susceptible person and a particular kind of environment. Symptoms of social breakdown syndrome are seen outside of hospitals in people subjected to special circumstances. These circumstances also involve either a process which disrupted the person's relationship to a previous self-concept or prevented him from developing an adequate one, and then provided him with a new one. The new self-concept usually leads to behavior which is appropriate in many ways for the special situation but which disables the person for ordinary life in society at large.

The social breakdown syndrome concept seems to be a significant advance in theory for several reasons: It offers an explanation of the changing picture of the psychoses in recent decades and of the reported success of the varied forms of social therapy which have recently become popular. It explains how the symptoms usually considered characteristic of long-term mental hospitalization can be seen in those who have never been hospitalized and have never been mentally ill. The suggested pathogenesis suggests areas for research and offers opportunities to test the theory. Finally, it has already led to the development of a survey instrument which is easily used on a broad scale.

The Chronic Mental Patient:
Current Status—Future Directions

Gordon L. Paul

Since 1955, the total resident population in public mental hospitals has consistently decreased, in spite of increased admissions —thus indicating renewed effectiveness of institutional treatment programs. The basis of this encouraging trend appears to lie in

Reprinted from *Psychological Bulletin*, vol. 71, 1969, pp. 81–94. Copyright 1969 by the American Psychological Association, and reproduced by permission.

a number of progressive changes, including the introduction of psychoactive drugs, a return to "moral treatment" with open-door philosophies, unit decentralization, and increased focus on the community (Bellak, 1964; Gilligan, 1965; Pasamanick, Scarpitti, & Dinitz, 1967). A hidden feature of these release rates, however, is that the increased efficacy appears to relate to less than a third of the resident beds (Glass, 1965). Jones and Sidebothem (1962) go so far as to state that each hospital has really become "two hospitals"—one an acute, short-term, rapid-turnover facility, and the other a large, custodial facility with a static population. In the United States, this chronic population currently constitute approximately two-thirds of the resident hospital population, and will likely continue to increase, even with higher initial discharge rates, since the proportion of first-admission functional psychotics who never leave the hospital, combined with readmissions who become long term, still runs from 20% to 75% (Hassall, Spencer, & Cross, 1965; Hogarty & Gross, 1966; Person, 1965; Peterson & Olsen, 1964; Ullmann, 1967).

The purpose of the present paper is to review, from a social interaction frame of reference, potential factors which appear to contribute to the failure of current institutional programs with the "hard-core" chronic population, and to suggest areas of necessary focus for rehabilitation. To this end, the conclusions of recent studies of postrelease followups are reviewed. Subsequently, based upon the latter studies, target areas for attempted rehabilitation of long-stay mental patients are delineated, and the literature examined for promising treatment approaches within these target areas. The final section touches briefly on the implications of this review for future directions of treatment research and application with the chronic mental patient.

An Interactional Frame of Reference: Social Breakdown

Literally hundreds of prognostic studies have been undertaken relating individual patient characteristics to outcome, usually defined as length of hospitalization or early release (see Becker, 1956, 1959; Peretz, Alpert, & Friedhoff, 1964; Sherman, Ging, Moseley, & Bookbinder, 1964; Vaillant, 1966; Zubin, Sutton, Salzinger, Salzinger, Burdock, & Peretz, 1961). Even though the majority of such studies are retrospective in nature and lack cross-validation and demonstration of reliability of measurement, considerable agreement exists about significant factors, such as age, sex, marital status, education, socioeconomic class, and, most importantly, the presence of withdrawn, inadequate prehospital adjustment. However the degree of overlap between patients possessing negative prognostic indicators who do and do not become long-stay chronic hospital residents, combined with the fact that the majority of prognostic studies have been conducted in traditional hospital settings, precludes assignment of the major accountable variance to patient characteristics alone. This is particularly apparent in prognostic studies involving both traditional hospital programs and experimental treatments (see Sanders, Smith, & Weinman, 1967).

On the other hand, numerous writers have described the features of the custodial hospital itself which appear to result in the "typical institutionalization syndrome" of dependency, apathy or troublesome behavior, withdrawal, lack of responsibility, etc., over and above the problems which may have initially led to hospitalization (e.g., Bockoven, 1963; Goffman, 1961; Kahne, 1959; Kantor & Gelineau, 1965; Lehrman, 1961a; Sommer & Osmond, 1961; Ullmann, 1967). Gruenberg (1967) and Zusman (1966) have specifically focused on what appears to be the core problem in the chronic population and provide a convenient descriptive term in the "Social Breakdown Syndrome" (SBS). The latter authors further offer an appealing theoretical explanation for the development of SBS in terms of an *interaction* between patient characteristics and custodial hospital environments, and they review data which suggest that community-oriented treatment facilities can help prevent the development of such institutionalization.

Honigfeld and Gillis (1967) have recently found that time-in-hospital is linearly related to the development of social breakdown, when other variables are partialed-out of the relationship, and several studies show that the longer a person remains in the traditional mental hospital, the poorer are his chances of release (Dunham & Weinberg, 1960; Kramer, Goldstein, Isreal, & Johnson, 1956; Malzberg, 1958; Odegard, 1961; Wanklin, Fleming,

Buck, & Hobbs, 1956). In fact, the probability of release and community stay after 2 years continuous hospitalization is reported to be about 6%, without change in this century (Gurel, 1966; Hassall et al., 1965; Kramer, Pollack, & Redick, 1961; Morgen & Johnson, 1957; Ullmann, 1967). Even more disheartening are the conclusions of recent reviews, that no specific treatment has been shown to have any long-term effect on discharge and community stay of the chronic population (see Fairweather & Simon, 1963; Gurel, 1966; Piotrowski & Efron, 1966; Sanders et al., 1967; Vitale, 1964).

However, the interactional view of Gruenberg (1967) and Zusman (1966) regarding SBS suggests that much of the failure of past treatment attempts with the "hard-core" hospitalized group may lie with the restrictive view that the basis of their social breakdown was to be found entirely in the individuals themselves. In contrast, if the environment plays a major role in the development, and, more importantly, the maintenance of SBS, hope for the long-stay mental patient may still be found through changing this environment. Since the goal of mental health facilities, on both economic and humanitarian grounds, is not merely to improve patient functioning within institutions but to eventuate release to the community, the interaction between patient behavior and the postrelease environment would also be an important consideration in any attempt to bring about change.

Many theorists operating from a social interactional view have pointed to the complexity of the patient-community relationship in determining both the definition of "deviance" and hospitalization or rehospitalization (see H. S. Becker, 1963; Ferster, 1965; Goffman, 1961; Parsons, 1957; Paul, 1967; Peterson, 1968; Szasz, 1963; Ullmann, 1967; Ullmann & Krasner, 1969). Basically, this formulation views the labeling of a particular individual or act as "deviant," and the resulting social action of hospitalization or rehospitalization, *not* as an inherent characteristic of the person or his behavior but as the application by others of sanctions for behavior which was upsetting. Thus, the factors determining community stay for a released mental patient might be expected to reflect both the individual's behavior in important areas, and the degree of distress imposed upon significant-others in his postrelease environment, interacting with the expectations, tolerance, and support offered.

Postrelease Follow-up Studies

The above social interactional forumlation gains considerable empirical support from follow-up studies of released mental patients, even though the majority of these investigations, like the earlier prognostic studies, have been retrospective, correlational, and lacking demonstrated reliability of measurement and cross-validation. Although length of hospital stay (the longer the stay, the greater the readmission rate) is the most consistent factor identified in follow-up studies (Lehrman, 1961b), several other factors appear with regularity. The occurrence of bizarre behavior on the part of the patient in the community is identified as a major reason for rehospitalization in a series of papers from the Ohio State University Psychiatric Hospital acute patient follow-up program (see Pasamanick et al., 1967, for a summary), and in numerous other reports (e.g., Brown, Carstairs, & Topping, 1958; Forsyth & Fairweather, 1961; Greenblatt, Solomon, Evans, & Brooks, 1965; Lorei, 1967; Sanders et al., 1967; Wing, 1965). Additionally, the type of living arrangements (alone, parental vs. conjugal family, relatives, boarding house) and employment have been related to community stay in many reports (e.g., Brown et al., 1958; Forsyth & Fairweather, 1961; Lorei, 1967; Nameche, 1967; Sherman, Ging, Moseley, & Bookbinder, 1964; Vitale & Steinbach, 1965; Wohl, 1964).

Essential support and clarification of the above factors may be found in the series of studies carried out by Freeman and Simmons (1963). Early retrospective surveys, in which rehospitalization and performance were found to relate to the type of household to which patients were released, were taken as support for family "tolerance for deviance" as the major factor in posthospitalization outcome. "Tolerance for deviance" in these early studies was restricted to mean "the continued acceptance of the former patient by his family members, even when he fails to perform in instrumental roles." However, later prospective studies, which assessed the patient's behavior as well as attitudes of significant-others, produced results more in keeping with other reports and with an interactional view of post-release community stay. In essence, social class and significant-others' expectations regarding performance levels were significantly related to patient's performance but not to rehospitalization. Rather, four areas were significantly related to whether patients were rehospitalized or remained in the community at least a year: (*a*) work, (*b*) social participation, (*c*) the occurrence of bizarre behavior, (*d*) the degree to which patients presented a management problem for families. While work and social participation were significantly related to community tenure, there was more overlap between success and failure groups in these areas, which led Freeman and Simmons to recast their position on the "tolerance for deviance" hypothesis, as the original "deviance" was restricted to instrumental role deviance. However, work, management problems, and bizarre behavior were all interrelated, and all pose the general problem of distress for significant-others. Thus, the patients' behavior, the degree of distress imposed, and tolerance and support of significant others may all be viewed as important to community tenure.

Miller (1965, 1967) presented the most comprehensive analysis and summary of interacting factors and characteristics associated with community stay and rehospitalization in a retrospective study of over a thousand patients released to a California Bureau of Social Work. In addition to replicating others' findings with regard to significantly better prognosis for lower age, shorter hospitalization, higher social classes, and the currently married, Miller further found marriage to be a positive factor only in the absence of marital conflict. Sex, religion, race, and place of residence (urban-rural) were unrelated to success, as was official diagnosis. Unlike Freeman and Simmons, Miller found that patients returning to conjugal homes were rehospitalized less than patients returning to parental homes (although patients returning to other relatives did as well as those returning to spouses, and those living alone did as poorly as "adult-children"). The suggested basis for this one reversal was that inclusion of VA patients with pensions in the Freeman and Simmons sample increased the "tolerance" of deviant behavior for parents but reduced it for wives.

Except for the latter reversal, even stronger relationships were found for the factors identified earlier: Employment status was significantly related for males in all living conditions and for females living alone or with relatives; for wives returned to their conjugal home, employment status was unrelated, but perform-

ance of household responsibilities was related—that is, performance of instrumental roles in which financial support by self or
spouse was obtained. Those experiencing closer social relationships, regardless of sex or type of "family," were more likely to
remain in the community, while "isolates" were more likely to
return. Finally, the occurrence of bizarre behavior on the part
of the released patient was the most consistent variable related
to rehospitalization across all living conditions (excluding length
of hospitalization). However, Miller found a curvilinear relationship between the severity of distressing behaviors and the
reactions of family and community members: Relatively "mild"
behavior, such as, "always appeared nervous," "often appeared
in a daze," "drinks too much," etc., although out of the ordinary,
was tolerated by all, and was not associated with rehospitalization. Severe deviations which would appear to distress nearly
anyone, such as, "couldn't dress or take care of self," "made no
sense when they talked," "hurt someone else," "forgot to do important things," etc., were highly associated with rehospitalization
and independent of living arrangements. However, a middle-
range group of deviant behaviors, such as, "said they heard
voices," "got into debt with foolish buying," "do not want to talk
or be with anyone," were associated with "tolerance of deviance"
—that is to say, if significant-others were distressed, rehospitalization occurred, if significant-others were not overly distressed,
community stay continued.

Miller (1965) appropriately pointed out that care must be
taken not to overevaluate the explanatory power of data from
follow-up studies such as those reviewed above. First, since the
studies are necessarily correlational, specific causality remains a
"strengthened hypothesis." Second, the prognostic value of such
findings is quite limited in the traditional setting because hospital
release without rehospitalization is a statistically rare event—
even more rare when discussing the long-stay mental hospital
patient, since in Miller's sample of 546 patients released after
2 or more years hospitalization, only 39 (i.e., 7%) were *not*
rehospitalized during the 5-year follow-up period.

Target Areas for Rehabilitation

What the above follow-up studies do suggest, in combination
with the social interactional view of changing the treatment environment, is a demarcation of target areas for attempted rehabilitation for long-stay patients characterized by chronic social
breakdown (as well as control factors to be included in treatment evaluations). Thus, if the long-stay SBS patient is to have
any chance of return to the community with tenure, with even
a minimally independent existence, rehabilitation would necessarily focus upon: (*a*) *resocialization*, including the development
of self-maintenance, interpersonal interaction, and communications skills; (*b*) *instrumental role performance*, including the
provision of "salable" vocational skills, and "housekeeping" skills;
(*c*) *reduction or elimination of extreme bizarre behavior*, including appropriate changes in frequency, intensity, or timing of individual acts or mannerisms consensually identified as distressing;
(*d*) *provision of at least one supportive "roommate" in the community*, including either a spouse, relative, parent, or friend.
Additionally, both the social interactional view and follow-up
studies which have focused specifically on the long-stay patient
suggest that continuity of care through professional help would
be most important in the period immediately following release,
since the great majority of released chronic patients are rehospitalized within the first 6 months (Brown et al., 1958; Fairweather, Sanders, Maynard, & Cressler, 1969; Vitale, 1964; Vitale
& Steinbach, 1965; Wohl, 1964).

Promising Approaches to Treatment

Even though the reviewers previously mentioned consistently
conclude that no specific treatment has been found to produce
long-term effects with the chronic mental hospital group, it might
be asked if there is even suggestive evidence that changing the
usual custodial environment along the lines described has any
promise. Since instrumental role performance seems to be an
essential feature, and vocational retraining necessitates a change
from the traditional custodial environment by nature of intro-
ducing trainers, or sending patients to trainers, vocational re-

habilitation programs might offer some promise. Unfortunately, in a recent summary of the results of all vocational rehabilitation efforts with hospitalized mental patients in projects supported by the United States Vocational Rehabilitation Administration, Crisswell (1967) reported that no matter what retraining procedures have been tried, 59–80% return to the hospital, and two-thirds of those who remain out are maintained by continued professional contact. Similarly, Neff and Koltuv (1967) reported the results of a massive effort in a 5-year research and demonstration project including several different approaches to vocational training, with auxiliary individual and group psychotherapy available, and adequate control groups and statistical analyses: While a "quite moderate" increase in vocational success was obtained for experimental clients, no differences were obtained with regard to rehospitalization, or personal and social adjustment. It, then, appears that an attempt to increase instrumental role performance, alone, is not a very promising approach.

On the other hand, there are promising trends which have often included work and vocational training as a part of broader environmental changes with custodial patients. The two most promising trends which have come to focus upon resocialization and the reduction of extreme bizarre behavior have been derived from totally different backgrounds—"milieu therapy" or the "therapeutic community," derived from a return to moral treatment philosophy in the applied setting—and "social learning therapy," derived from basic laboratory research on the principles of learning, motivation, and social interaction.

The "Milieu" Approach

While the milieu therapy approach is becoming better articulated (e.g., Artiss, 1962; Cumming & Cumming, 1962; Edelson, 1967; Jones, 1953; Kraft, 1966; Wilmer, 1958), no well-controlled studies have yet evaluated the effectiveness of such specifically defined therapeutic communities with the "hard-core" chronic mental patient. However, a large literature exists concerning the general milieu therapy approach, which is characterized by increased social interaction and group activities, expectancies and group pressure directed toward "normal" functioning, more informal patient status, focus on goal-directed communication, freedom of movement, and treatment of patients as responsible human beings rather than custodial "cases." Gilligan (1965) reviewed the positive reports of improved behavior following the early "total push" projects, in which both somatic and milieu treatments were included. Since these early projects, numerous reports have appeared in which within-hospital improvements in socialization and bizarre behavior were observed in small groups of patients following the introduction of special milieu therapy programs (e.g., Barrett, Ellsworth, Clark, & Enniss, 1957; Martin, 1950; D. H. Miller & Clancy, 1952; Rashkis & Smarr, 1957). Other special milieu therapy programs have been reported to result in moderate, but increased discharge rates for chronic patient groups, in comparison to status prior to the introduction of special programs (e.g., Bartholow & Tunakan, 1967; Brooks, 1960; Ellsworth, Mead, & Clayton, 1958; D. H. Miller, 1954). Similar promising improvements in discharge rates of chronic patients have been reported for entire hospitals following a change to a therapeutic community operation (e.g., Clark, 1965; Clark & Oram, 1966; Cumming & Cumming, 1962; Ellsworth & Stokes, 1963; Galioni, 1960; Wing, 1965).

A few studies, more or less approaching adequate experimental design, have compared a special milieu therapy program with the traditional custodial treatment provided in large mental hospitals. Galioni, Adams, and Tallman (1953) reported an intensive milieu program of 18-months duration with a chronic population in which prior release rates had been less than 2%. At the completion of the project, the release rate for the experimental group was "two and a half times" that of controls (40 of 214 vs. 15 of 223). However, by an 18-month follow-up, because of rehospitalization rates, the net-release rates between the two groups did not differ. Moderate within-hospital improvement with chronic patients was reported by Appleby et al. (1960), although results are difficult to interpret since "controls" improved as well, and were housed within the same ward. In a pioneering project of the Dutchess County Unit of Hudson River State Hospital, Kasius (1966) found moderate within-hospital improvement for a group of "hard-core" chronic patients in the new unit in comparison to a similar group in the parent hospital; however, after 5 years of operation, 73% of males and 60% of females in residence still consisted of chronic patients transferred to the unit at its inception (Bennett, 1966).

In contrast, four projects, with smaller groups of patients, have found significantly better release rates for long-stay patients undergoing variations of milieu therapy in contrast to usual custodial care. The first series of studies were summarized by Wing (1965); however, the patients involved were selected from "moderately handicapped" long-stay patients who were prejudged to have rehabilitation potential. More impressive, because of unselected use of "hard-core" chronic patients with equated experimental and control groups, is a study by Ellsworth (1964). In this study, 142 male functional psychotics with at least 5 years continuous hospitalization were assigned to a milieu therapy unit or to regular chronic wards at the Fort Meade VA hospital. Following 30 months of treatment, the milieu program resulted in a 59% release rate, as compared to 25% on regular wards: Additionally, on 12-month follow-ups, 87% of milieu versus 64% of controls had *not* been rehospitalized. While over two-thirds of these patients were discharged to sheltered-care facilities, perhaps accounting for the very low rehospitalization rates, Ellsworth's results are most promising controlled findings. The third project was conducted at Philadelphia State Hospital and reported by Sanders et al. (1967). Three milieu programs, varying in the degree of social interaction required, were conducted for a 12-month period, along with a control treatment consisting of the usual hospital program, with a 36-month follow-up. A total of 278 patients were involved, ranging in age from 19 to 72 years, and length of hospitalization from 1 to 36 years; unfortunately, like the Wing studies, subjects were selected from "better-adjusted chronic patients" on clinical evaluation of ability to leave the hospital within 12 months, resulting in an unusually high release rate for all groups during the study period. Within-hospital improvements were found in socialization for the milieu patients, and significant differences in release rate were found over the entire study period (78% for the milieu program demanding most activity vs. 58% for controls); however, when rehospitalizations due to the occurrence of bizarre behavior were taken into account, the net-release rates over the 4-year period varied from 27% to 38% and did not differ between groups. It was found that older patients with greater length of hospitalization showed the greatest comparative response to the milieu programs. The fourth project was conducted by Gellman and Soloff at Chicago State Hospital (summarized in Neff & Koltuv, 1967). Three groups of "hard-core" chronic patients were involved, none of whom was exposed to a total therapeutic community. Rather, all groups continued to reside at the hospital, but two groups were bussed daily to another location where they were exposed to one of two variants of milieu therapy—one emphasizing vocational training at a sheltered workshop—the other emphasizing social and recreational activities at a Mental Health Center. While results were, again, modest and characterized by high readmission rates, both groups exposed to 3–6 hours per day milieu programs for 9–12 months showed higher discharge rates than patients continuing the regular hospital programs, and no significant differences between each other.

It should also be noted that several authors have reported a failure of milieu therapy to have a positive impact on long-stay mental patients (e.g., Durell et al., 1965; Greenblatt et al., 1965; Kraft, Binner, & Dickey, 1967; Rapaport, 1960; Wilensky & Herz, 1966). However, it is interesting that those providing adequate descriptive data appear to have violated some of the basic tenets of the milieu therapy approach (see Cumming & Cumming, 1962); specifically, group interaction was given less emphasis than individual, psychoanalytically oriented psychotherapy, and the "patient role" appeared to remain unmodified.

In summary, the general milieu therapy literature is characterized by a paucity of solid evidence and a plethora of equivocal results. However, the bulk of evidence suggests that when the principles of milieu therapy are applied with long-stay chronic mental patients, resocialization frequently results, and to a lesser extent, some reduction of extreme bizarre behavior. The few controlled studies which have appeared offer the promise of greater release rates than previously obtained with traditional treatment alternatives, although an adequate test of a well-articulated milieu therapy program has not yet appeared. The greatest weakness to date appears to lie in a failure to include systematically specific focus on instrumental role training, elimination of bizarre behavior, and provision of community support and follow-up within the milieu program.

The "Social Learning" Approach

The second promising approach for rehabilitating the chronic mental patient along the lines described earlier may be termed "social learning therapy." This essentially refers to the systematic extension of principles and techniques derived from basic research on learning to the clinical alteration of behavior—especially the principles of instrumental and associative learning, along with appropriate types and schedules of reinforcement. While a social learning approach shares much in common with milieu therapy, there are basic differences in the form of greater emphasis on response-contingent consequences, rather than group pressure and encouragement, as basic vehicles of change. Also, due to the differing historical bases from which the two approaches were derived, social learning therapy necessitates more systematic control of physical and social interchanges. Like the status of milieu therapy, no well-controlled studies have yet appeared which evaluate the specific effectiveness of a total learning therapy program for returning the "hard-core" chronic mental patient to a relatively independent existence. However, since this approach has grown from basic laboratory research, a large number of controlled investigations underlie the broader extensions and applications.

Many examples of the extrapolation and testing of principles and techniques of social influence and learning to the treatment context are summarized in recent books by Franks (1969), Goldstein, Heller, and Sechrest (1966), Krasner and Ullmann (1965), and Paul (1966). Ullmann and Krasner (1965) summarized the major principles and techniques, and presented several reports indicating highly promising results in the treatment of chronic hospital patients. In one comprehensive controlled study, Meichenbaum (1966a) has recently demonstrated remarkable changes in schizophrenic patients' pathognomic verbalizations and level of abstraction through the systematic application of social and token contingencies—in most cases, training these patients to even *surpass* the "normal" population in a total of eight sessions. Additional controlled experimental studies involving the contingent manipulation of reinforcement schedules through social attention, interest, and pleasure have effectively modified such modal problems of social breakdown and bizarre behavior as the expression of affect (Salzinger & Pisoni, 1958; Weiss, Krasner, & Ullman, 1963), "'sick" and "healthy" talk (Ullmann, Forsman, Kenny, McInnis, Unikel, & Zeisset, 1965), and delusions (Rickard, Digman, & Horner, 1960; Rickard & Dinoff, 1962). Effects of systematic learning procedures have similarly been shown on increasing social behavior (King, Armitage, & Tilton, 1960; Ullmann, Krasner, & Collins, 1961), perception (Ullmann, Weiss, & Krasner, 1963), abstraction level (Little, 1966; Meichenbaum, 1966b), and common associations (Sommer, Whitney, & Osmond, 1962; Ullmann, Krasner, & Edinger, 1964). Wagner and Paul,[1] in a pilot project with 19 totally incontinent male patients averaging 25 years continuous hospitalization, have reduced the number of soilings per day from an average of 19.5 to 3.5 in 17 weeks of treatment, using only contingent materials and social reinforcement through an understaffed group of aides. Several studies by Ayllon and colleagues (e.g., Ayllon, 1963; Ayllon & Haughton, 1964; Ayllon & Michael, 1959) investigated the utility of the procedures for instituting change in the behavior of chronic mental patients by identifying specific behaviors, recording their frequency of occurrence, and then reducing, increasing, and again reducing their frequency as a consequence of contingent token or social reinforcement. A wide range of bizarre verbal, motoric, and interpersonal behaviors characteristic of SBS were demonstrated to respond to such controlled contingencies. Thus, while none of the previously mentioned studies involved total treatment programs, the effectiveness of the extended procedures for changing specified bizarre behavior and increasing instrumental role performance within the hospital setting is well documented.

The extension of social learning therapy to a systematic wardwide or unit-wide treatment program is both relatively recent and, as yet, in the stages of infancy, even though many service programs for chronic patients have been initiated on the basis of the rather limited current literature (see Davison, 1969; Krasner & Atthowe, 1968). Teodoro Ayllon and his colleagues are responsible for formulating the initial procedures for extending the use of learning principles to complete ward programs. Ayllon

---

[1] Wagner, B. R., and Paul, G. L., Reduction of incontinence in chronic mental patients: A pilot project. *Journal of Behavior Therapy & Experimental Psychiatry* 1970, 1, 29–38.

christened the basic approach "token economy," since actual "tokens," such as special cards or chips, were vested with reward value to mediate control of behavior, much in the way that money does in a natural economy. Ayllon and Azrin (1965) reported several studies conducted at Anna State Hospital, within a closed-ward token economy. This report established the ability of a token-economy program to change chronic psychotic behavior within a highly controlled ward; however, this program was directed at the development of procedures and testing of principles, rather than with therapeutic goals.[2] Atthowe and Krasner (1968) reported the results of a token-economy program undertaken with a chronic brain-damaged and geriatric ward at Menlo Park VA Hospital which replicates Ayllon's findings. Quite dramatic results for increased in-hospital adjustment were seen in increased social responsiveness, attendance at group activities, number of passes, and responsible self-maintenance. Even though the nature of the population (brain damaged and geriatric) precluded hospital release as a major goal of the program, the release rate more than doubled during the first year of operation, in comparison to a base-line period with the same staff. Another token-economy program with therapeutic goals has been in operation at Patton State Hospital (Bruce, 1966) with two open wards of chronic patients. Although the service orientation of the Patton program has not provided an adequate design to evaluate the comparative effectiveness of the program, the impression of the hospital administration, supplemented with anecdotal evidence, has been quite favorable (Gericke, 1965). Controlled studies within the Patton program have, however, again replicated the findings of Ayllon and Azrin and Atthowe and Krasner on the effectiveness of contingent social and token reinforcement for changing behavior characteristic of SBS (Schaefer, 1966). Particularly impressive were the results of a recent controlled study by Schaefer and Martin (1966). Highly significant decreases in apathy and corresponding increases in responsibility and activity ‚were obtained through the token economy, over a 3-month period, with 20 chronic patients as compared to an equated group not receiving the token treatment. Finally, Steffy, Torney, Hart, Craw,

---

[2] Since the present article was completed, an excellent book on principles of token economics has appeared: Ayllon, T., & Azrin, N. *The token economy.* New York: Appleton-Century-Crofts, 1969.

and Marlett (1966) reported a token economy program at Lakeshore Psychiatric Hospital with a female population of chronic schizophrenics and mental defectives. Like the other token programs, the latter project has its main focus on increasing adaptive behavior within the hospital and does not include a control sample for evaluating effectiveness in terms of release. Steffy has, however, included a continuing assessment battery. Again, the results of the Anna State, Patton State, and Menlo VA programs have been replicated in Steffy's program in showing effective within-hospital change for SBS and such bizarre behaviors as refusal to eat, withdrawal, violent acts, delusional and incoherent talk, mutism, inappropriate affect, and meaningless, repetitious activities.

At the time of this writing, no negative reports have appeared concerning the effectiveness of token-economy programs, even though some 22 separate institutions have such programs in varying stages of development with chronic mental patients (Krasner & Atthowe, 1968). However, at least two well-planned token-economy programs had to be abandoned after early starts. Hughes (1965) attempted to establish a token-economy program on a service basis without external support at Anna State Hospital; and Hallsten and Fletcher (1966), after winning the Francis F. Gerty Award for their proposal, attempted to establish a program at Galesburg State Research Hospital. In both instances, the programs were abandoned due to administrative obstruction which prevented adequate training, control, and retention of staff.[3] Similar verbal reports have been obtained regarding both milieu therapy and token-economy programs in several parts of the country.

In summary, the literature on social learning therapy with the "hard-core" chronic mental hospital population has established its efficacy for improving socialization, reducing extreme bizarre behavior, and improving instrumental role performance within the institution. The bulk of evidence further suggests that a comprehensive social learning program, focused upon returning the chronic patient to a relatively independent role in society, could be quite successful; however, such a program has not yet

---

[3] Hallsten, E. A., and Fletcher, S., personal communication, 1967. Hughes, H., personal communication, 1967.

been undertaken for evaluation. Like milieu therapy, the greatest weakness to date has been in the failure to include provision for community support and follow-up.

"Bridging the Gap"

One last research program should be noted, as it shared some characteristics of both milieu and learning approaches described above, and further contributes suggestive evidence regarding the problem of rehospitalization. Fairweather (1964) first reported the results of a program which was focused upon resocialization and instrumental role performance, involved the establishment of problem-solving patient groups and the use of group pressure, and combined these with a step-system in which responsibilities, passes, and funds were contingent upon appropriate behavior. A traditional ward program served as a control, and staff were equated by switching midway through the experimental period. A total of 195 patients were randomly assigned to the two wards. As the patients were previously housed in VA open wards, none was the severe social breakdown problem seen on state hospital "back wards" or in the Atthowe and Krasner study conducted at the same hospital; although, about half of the patients had accumulated 2 or more years hospitalization. Highly significant differences were obtained in favor of improved within-hospital performance for the experimental program. However, significant effects were found between the two *staff* groups, indicating that transfers, attention, and bizarre behavior were more a function of the particular staff involved than of treatment programs. Additionally, while the experimental program resulted in more earlier releases, no systematic aftercare was included; by the time of a 6-month postrelease follow-up, rehospitalizations were sufficient that no difference in net release existed between the experimental and control groups. Like previous follow-up studies, supportive living situations were more related to community stay than were treatment programs in the institution, and the institutional treatment made no specific contribution in bridging the gap to the community.

However, Fairweather et al. (1969) have recently completed an extension of the Fairweather (1964) program which compared the follow-up status of patients released from the experimental treatment programs in two different ways: One group was released to the community with the regularly available extramural care, such as outpatient care, home care, etc. The other group was released to a "community lodge," supported by the mental health facility, where the *patients* continued to function as a "family," providing mutual support for one another. The lodge group was initially followed by professional staff, with contact gradually reduced until the "subsociety" became completely autonomous. By the end of 6 months, 65% of the lodge group had been in the community over three-quarters of the time, as compared to 24% of the control group. Similarly, 50% of the lodge group had been employed over three-quarters of the time compared to 3% of the control group. Significant differences between the two groups continued for the 30-month study period. While the number of patients to leave the lodge for independent living arrangements was negligible, Fairweather notes that the cost of maintaining a patient in the lodge with employment was $3.90 per day, as compared to the hospital cost of $14.34.

Although Fairweather is not the first to find that groups of chronic patients can be moved to "hospital extensions" in the community, successfully and at lower cost (e.g., Berrington, 1966; Vitale & Steinbach, 1965; Wing, 1965), the finding that released patients can be taught to live together in mutual support after a declining-contact period of professional direction is most important. Pasamanick et al. (1967) similarly found that new hospitalizations could be effectively prevented by providing drugs, advice, and reassurance to patients and relatives in their homes on a declining-contact basis. Combining these two findings suggests a promising addition to the attempt at community-return of the long-term hospital patient, which has not been systematically dealt with by either the milieu or social learning approaches—namely, the provision of a supportive "roommate" in the community for those who have either undesirable relatives or those who have none. By providing declining contact in the living situation from the time of release, support of the released patient by significant-others may be taught and maintained—when no appropriate significant-others exist before release, patients may be taught to be significant-others themselves, released as a "family," and similarly treated in the community.

Summary and Conclusions

The "hard-core" refractory group of chronic mental patients is clearly one of the most difficult problems facing the mental health field today. The central problem for these individuals may best be described as "social breakdown," which appears to result from an interaction of patient characteristics and traditional hospital environments. Similarly, the results of follow-up studies suggest that the likelihood of a patient remaining in the community after release is a joint function of patient behavior, environmental factors, and the interaction between the two. Considerable agreement on these latter factors, from both empirical studies and social interaction theory, suggests the necessary focus of rehabilitation efforts to lie in the areas of resocialization, instrumental role performance, extreme bizarre behavior, and community social support. Milieu therapy and social learning therapy both appear to offer promise, but neither has yet been carefully evaluated with the longstay chronic population. Current evidence suggests that both milieu and social learning approaches may be effective in resocialization, and the social learning approach appears to be quite effective in reducing or eliminating bizarre behavior and increasing instrumental role performance. While neither milieu nor social learning programs has systematically included direct provision for community social support, recent research results offer direct suggestions for "bridging the gap" from institution to community by training "families" to live together in mutual support, starting in the institution and extending maintenance into the community on a declining-contact basis. An additional feature which appears necessary to all focal areas of rehabilitation with the chronic mental patient is the inclusion of clear and explicit "steps," which successively approximate "normal" behavior, through which patients progress. While this feature is not a typical part of milieu therapy with acute patients, it was a major part of Fairweather's (1964) program, and identifiable steps explicitly related to increased levels of responsibility and functioning have been common to the more promising programs with chronic patients—both milieu (Cumming & Cumming, 1962; Ellsworth, 1964), and social learning (Atthowe & Krasner, 1968; Steffy et al., 1966).

Due to the paucity of well-controlled investigations in the institutional treatment area, it appears that the major focus for future research regarding the chronic mental patient would be best directed to outcome studies following sound and rigorous experimental principles (see Paul, 1969). On the basis of current evidence, both milieu and social learning approaches seem sufficiently promising to undertake controlled comparative studies to clearly determine overall and differential degrees of success in the chronic population.[4]

Until data are available from controlled empirical studies, current treatment programs might best follow procedures shared in common by the most promising approaches, plus those suggestions regarding program structure and aftercare derived from recent research. Specifically suggested are those procedures which:

1. Emphasize a "resident" rather than "patient" status through informal dress of staff, open channels of communication in all directions, and broad (but clear) authority structure.

2. Make clear, through a set of rules and attitudes, that the residents are responsible human beings; are expected to follow certain minimal rules of group living; and are expected to do their share in participating in self-care, work, recreational, and social activities.

3. Utilize step systems which gradually increase the expectations placed on the residents in terms of their degree of independence and level of responsibility, with community return emphasized from the outset.

4. Encourage social interactions and skills and provide a range of activities as well as regular large and small group meetings.

5. Emphasize clarity of communication, with concrete instruction in appropriate behavior and focus on utilitarian "action" rather than ad hominum "explanation."

6. Provide opportunity to practice vocational and housekeeping skills, with feedback, and specific training in marketable skills when needed.

7. Reacquaint residents with the "outside world" by exposing them to the community and bringing in community volunteers for discussions.

---

[4] Such a comparative study is currently in preparation at the Adolf Meyer Zone Center, Decatur, Illinois.

8. Identify the specific unique areas for change and support in concrete terms for each individual.

9. Prepare residents and significant-others to live in mutually supportive ways in the community through prerelease training and scheduled aftercare.

10. When no significant-other exists, follow Point 9 above, by training and releasing residents in groups of 2–3 as a "family" to provide significant-others for one another.

References

Appleby, L., Proano, A., & Perry, R. Theoretical vs. empirical treatment models: An exploratory investigation. In L. Appleby, J. M. Scher, & J. Cumming (Eds.), *Chronic schizophrenia*. Glencoe: Free Press, 1960.

Artiss, K. L. *Milieu therapy in schizophrenia*. New York: Grune & Stratton, 1962.

Atthowe, J. M., & Krasner, L. A preliminary report on the application of contingent reinforcement procedures (token economy) on a "chronic" psychiatric ward. *Journal of Abnormal Psychology*, 1968, *73*, 37–43.

Ayllon, T. Intensive treatment of psychotic behaviors by stimulus satiation and food reinforcement. *Behavior Research and Therapy*, 1963, *1*, 53–61.

Ayllon, T., & Azrin, N. H. The measurement and reinforcement of behavior of psychotics. *Journal of the Experimental Analysis of Behavior*, 1965, *8*, 357–383.

Ayllon, T., & Haughton, E. Modification of symptomatic verbal behavior of mental patients. *Behavior Research and Therapy*, 1964, *2*, 87–97.

Ayllon, T., & Michael, J. The psychiatric nurse as a behavioral engineer. *Journal of the Experimental Analysis of Behavior*, 1959, *2*, 323–334.

Barrett, W. W., Ellsworth, R. B., Clark, L. D., & Enniss, J. Study of the differential behavioral effects of reserpine, chlorpromazine and a combination of these drugs in chronic schizophrenia. *Diseases of the Nervous System*, 1957, *18*, 209–215.

Bartholow, G. W., & Tunakan, B. Role of the community mental health center in the rehabilitation of the long-hospitalized psychiatric patient. In J. H. Masserman (Ed.), *Current psychiatric therapies*. New York: Grune & Stratton, 1967.

Becker, H. S. *Outsiders*. Glencoe: Free Press, 1963.

Becker, W. C. A genetic approach to the interpretation and evaluation of the process-reactive distinction in schizophrenia. *Journal of Abnormal and Social Psychology*, 1956, *53*, 229–336.

Becker, W. C. The process-reactive distinction—A key to the problem of schizophrenia? *Journal of Nervous and Mental Disease*, 1959, *129*, 442–449.

Bellak, L. (Ed.), *Handbook of community psychiatry and community mental health*. New York: Grune & Stratton, 1964.

Bennett, C. L. The Dutchess County Project. In E. M. Gruneberg (Ed.), *Evaluating the effectiveness of community mental health services*. New York: Milbank, 1966.

Berrington, W. P. Resocialization: Undoing the damage. *International Journal of Social Psychiatry*, 1966, *12*, 85–97.

Bockoven, J. S. *Moral treatment in American psychiatry*. New York: Spring, 1963.

Brooks, G. W. Rehabilitation of hospitalized chronic schizophrenic patients. In L. Appleby, J. M. Scher, & J. Cumming (Eds.), *Chronic schizophrenia*. Glencoe: Free Press, 1960.

Brown, G. W., Carstairs, G. M., Topping, G. Post-hospital adjustment of chronic mental patients. *Lancet*, 1958, *7048*, 685–689.

Bruce, M. Tokens for recovery. *American Journal of Nursing*, 1966, *66*, 1799–1802.

Clark, D. H. The ward therapeutic community and its effects on the hospital. In H. Freeman (Ed.), *Psychiatric hospital care*. London: Bailliere, 1965.

Clark, D. H., & Oram, E. G. Reform in the mental hospital: An eight year follow-up. *International Journal of Social Psychiatry*, 1966, *12*, 98–108.

Crisswell, J. H. Considerations on the permanence of rehabilitation. Paper presented at the meeting of the American Psychological Association, Washington, D.C., September 1967.

Cumming, J., & Cumming, E. *Ego and milieu*. New York: Atherton, 1962.

Davison, G. C. Appraisal of behavior modification techniques with adults in institutional settings. In C. M. Franks (Ed.), *Assessment and status of the behavioral therapies and associated developments*. New York: McGraw-Hill, 1969.

Dunham, H. W., & Weinberg, S. K. *The culture of the state mental hospital*. Detroit: Wayne State University Press, 1960.

Durell, J., Arnson, A., & Kellam, S. G. A community-oriented therapeutic milieu. *Medical Annals, D. C.*, 1965, *34*, 468–474.

Edelson, M. The sociotherapeutic function in a psychiatric hospital. *Journal of the Fort Logan Mental Health Center*, 1967, *4*, 1–45.

Ellsworth, R. B. The psychiatric aide as rehabilitation therapist. *Rehabilitation Counseling Bulletin*, 1964, *7*, 81–86.

Ellsworth, R. B., Mead, B. T., & Clayton, W. H. The rehabilitation and disposition of chronically hospitalized schizophrenic patients. *Mental Hygiene*, 1958, *42*, 343–348.

Ellsworth, R. B., & Stokes, H. A. Staff attitudes and patient release. *Psychiatric Studies and Projects*, 1963, 7, 1–6.

Fairweather, G. W. (Ed.), *Social psychology in treating mental illness: Experimental approach.* New York: Wiley, 1964.

Fairweather, G. W., Sanders, D. H., Maynard, H., & Cressler, D. L. *Community life for the mentally ill: An alternative to institutional care.* New York: Aldine, 1969.

Fairweather, G. W., & Simon, R. A further follow-up of psychotherapeutic programs. *Journal of Consulting Psychology*, 1963, *27*, 186.

Ferster, C. B. Classification of behavioral pathology. In L. Krasner & L. P. Ullmann (Eds.), *Research in behavior modification.* New York: Holt, 1965.

Forsyth, R. P., & Fairweather, G. W. Psychotherapeutic and other hospital treatment criteria: The dilemma. *Journal of Abnormal and Social Psychology*, 1961, *62*, 598–604.

Franks, C. M. (Ed.), *Assessment and status of the behavioral therapies and related developments.* New York: McGraw-Hill, 1969.

Freeman, H. E., & Simmons, O. G. *The mental patient comes home.* New York: Wiley, 1963.

Galioni, E. G. Evaluation of a treatment program for chronically ill schizophrenic patients—a six year program. In L. Appleby, J. M. Scher, & J. Cumming (Eds.), *Chronic schizophrenia.* Glencoe: Free Press, 1960.

Galioni, E. G., Adams, F. H., & Tallman, F. F. Intensive treatment of backward patients—a controlled pilot study. *American Journal of Psychiatry*, 1953, *109*, 576–583.

Gericke, O. L. Practical use of operant conditioning procedures in a mental hospital. *Psychiatric Studies and Projects*, 1965, *3*, 1–10.

Gilligan, J. Review of the literature. In M. Greenblatt, M. H. Soloman, A. S. Evans, & G. W. Brooks (Eds.), *Drug and social therapy in chronic schizophrenia.* Springfield, Ill.: Charles C Thomas, 1965.

Glass, A. J. The future of large public mental hospitals. *Mental Hospitals*, 1965, Jan., 9–22.

Goffman, E. *Asylums.* Garden City, N.Y.: Doubleday, 1961.

Goldstein, A. P., Heller, K., & Sechrest, L. B. *Psychotherapy and the psychology of behavior change.* New York: Wiley, 1966.

Greenblatt, M., Soloman, M. H., Evans, A. S., & Brooks, G. W. (Eds.), *Drug and social therapy in chronic schizophrenia.* Springfield, Ill.: Charles C Thomas, 1965.

Gruenberg, E. M. The social breakdown syndrome—some origins. *American Journal of Psychiatry*, 1967, *123*, 12–20.

Gurel, L. Release and community stay in chronic schizophrenia. *American Journal of Psychiatry*, 1966, *122*, 892–899.

Hallsten, E. A., & Fletcher, S. *Toward the systematic use of rewards.* Galesburg, Ill.: Galesburg State Research Hospital, 1966.

Hassall, C., Spencer, A. M., & Cross, K. W. Some changes in the composition of a mental hospital population. *British Journal of Psychiatry*, 1965, *111*, 420–428.

Hogarty, G. E., & Gross, M. Preadmission symptom differences between first-admitted schizophrenics in the predrug and postdrug era. *Comprehensive Psychiatry*, 1966, 7, 134–140.

Honigfeld, G., & Gillis, R. The role of institutionalization in the natural history of schizophrenia. *Diseases of the Nervous System*, 1967, *28*, 660–663.

Hughes, H. B. *2-B's credit system.* Anna, Ill.: Anna State Hospital, 1965.

Jones, K., & Sidebotham, R. *Mental hospitals at work.* London: Routledge & Kegan Paul, 1962.

Jones, M. *The therapeutic community.* New York: Basic Books, 1953.

Kahne, M. J. Bureaucratic structure and impersonal experience in mental hospitals. *Psychiatry*, 1959, *363*, 375.

Kantor, D., & Gelineau, V. Social processes in support of chronic deviance. *International Journal of Social Psychiatry*, 1965, *11*, 280–289.

Kasius, R. V. The social breakdown syndrome in a cohort of long-stay patients in the Dutchess County Unit, 1960–1963. In E. M. Gruenberg (Ed.), *Evaluating the effectiveness of community mental health services.* New York: Milbank, 1966.

King, G. F., Armitage, S. G., & Tilton, J. R. A therapeutic approach to schizophrenics of extreme pathology: An operant-interpersonal method. *Journal of Abnormal and Social Psychology*, 1960, *61*, 276–286.

Kraft, A. M. The therapeutic community. In S. Arieti (Ed.), *American handbook of psychiatry.* Vol. 3. New York: Basic Books, 1966.

Kraft, A. M., Binner, P. R., & Dickey, B. A. The community mental health program and the longer-stay patient. *Archives of General Psychiatry*, 1967, *16*, 64–70.

Kramer, M., Goldstein, H., Israel, R. H., & Johnson, N. A. Application of life table methodology to the study of mental hospital populations. *Psychiatric Research Reports*, 1956, 5, 49–76.

Kramer, M., Pollack, E. S., & Redick, R. W. Studies of the incidence and prevalance of hospitalized mental disorders in the United States: Current status and future goals. In: P. H. Hoch & J. Zubin (Eds.), *Comparative epidemiology of the mental disorders.* New York: Grune & Stratton, 1961.

Krasner, L., & Atthowe, J., Jr. *Token economy bibliography*. State University of New York at Stony Brook, 1968. (Mimeo)

Krasner, L., & Ullmann, L. P. (Eds.), *Research in behavior modification*. New York: Holt, 1965.

Lehrman, N. S. Do our hospitals help make acute schizophrenia chronic? *Diseases of the Nervous System*, 1961, *22*, 489–493. (a)

Lehrman, N. S. Follow-up of brief and prolonged psychiatric hospitalization. *Comprehensive Psychiatry*, 1961, *4*, 227–240. (b)

Little, L. K. Effects of the interpersonal interaction on abstract thinking performance in schizophrenics. *Journal of Consulting Psychology*, 1966, *30*, 158–164.

Lorei, T. W. Prediction of community stay and employment for released psychiatric patients. *Journal of Consulting Psychology*, 1967, *31*, 349–357.

Malzberg, B. *Cohort studies of mental disease in New York State: 1943–1949*. New York: National Association for Mental Health, 1958.

Martin, M. A practical treatment program for a mental hospital "back" ward. *American Journal of Psychiatry*, 1950, *10*, 758–760.

Meichenbaum, D. H. The effects of instructions and reinforcement on thinking and language behaviors of schizophrenics. Unpublished doctoral dissertation, University of Illinois, 1966. (a)

Meichenbaum, D. H. The effects of social reinforcement on the level of abstraction in schizophrenics. *Journal of Abnormal Psychology*, 1966, *71*, 354–362. (b)

Miller, D. Worlds that fail: Part I, Retrospective analysis of mental patients' careers. *California Mental Health Research Monograph*, 1965, No. 6.

Miller, D. Retrospective analysis of posthospital mental patients' worlds. *Journal of Health and Social Behavior*, 1967, *8*, 136–140.

Miller, D., & Dawson, W. Worlds that fail: Part II, Disbanded worlds: A study of returns to the mental hospital. *California Mental Health Research Monograph*, 1965, No. 7.

Miller, D. H. The rehabilitation of chronic open-ward neuro-psychiatric patients. *Psychiatry*, 1954, *17*, 347–358.

Miller, D. H., & Clancy, J. An approach to the social rehabilitation of chronic psychotic patients. *Psychiatry*, 1952, *15*, 435–443.

Morgan, N. C., & Johnson, N. A. The chronic hospital patient. *American Journal of Psychiatry*, 1957, *113*, 824–830.

Nameche, L. F. Life histories of schizophrenics before and after hospitalization. Paper presented at the meeting of the American Psychological Association, Washington, D.C., September 1967.

Neff, W. S., & Koltuv, M. *Work and mental disorder*. New York: Institute for the Crippled and Disabled, 1967.

Odegard, O. Pattern of discharge and readmission in psychiatric hospitals in Norway, 1926 to 1955. *Mental Hygiene*, 1961, *45*, 185–193.

Parsons, T. The mental hospital as a type of organization. In M. Greenblatt, D. J. Levinson, & R. H. Williams (Eds.), *The patient and the mental hospital*. Glencoe: Free Press, 1957.

Pasamanick, B., Scarpitti, F. R., & Dinitz, S. *Schizophrenics in the community*. New York: Appleton, 1967.

Paul, G. L. *Insight vs. Desensitization in Psychotherapy: An Experiment in Anxiety Reduction*. Stanford, Calif.: Stanford University Press, 1966.

Paul, G. L. The strategy of outcome research in psychotherapy. *Journal of Consulting Psychology*, 1967, *31*, 109–118.

Paul, G. L. Behavior modification research: Design and tactics. In: C. M. Franks (Ed.), *Assessment and status of the behavioral therapies and associated developments*. New York: McGraw-Hill, 1969.

Peretz, D., Alpert, M., & Friedhoff, A. Prognostic factors in the evaluation of therapy. In P. H. Hoch & J. Zubin (Eds.), *Evaluation of psychiatric treatment*. New York: Grune & Stratton, 1964.

Person, P. H., Jr. *The relationship between selected social and demographic characteristics of hospitalized mental patients and the outcome of hospitalization*. Washington, D.C.: United States Government Printing Office, 1965.

Peterson, D. R. *The clinical study of social behavior*. New York: Appleton, 1968.

Peterson, P. B., & Olsen, G. W. First admitted schizophrenics in the drug era. *Archives of General Psychiatry*, 1964, *11*, 137–144.

Piotrowski, Z. A., & Efron, H. V. Evaluation of outcome in schizophrenia. In P. H. Hoch & J. Zubin (Eds.), *Psychopathology of schizophrenia*. New York: Grune & Stratton, 1966.

Rapaport, R. N. *Community as doctor*. Springfield, Ill.: Charles C Thomas, 1960.

Rashkis, H. A., & Smarr, E. R. Drug and milieu effects with chronic schizophrenics. *Archives of Neurology and Psychiatry*, 1957, *78*, 89–94.

Rickard, H. C., Digman, P. J., & Horner, R. F. Verbal manipulation in a psychotherapeutic relationship. *Journal of Clinical Psychology*, 1960, *16*, 364–367.

Rickard, H. C., & Dinoff, M. A follow-up note on "verbal manipulation in a psychotherapeutic relationship." *Psychological Reports*, 1962, *11*, 506.

Salzinger, K., & Pisoni, S. Reinforcement of affect responses of schizophrenics during the clinical interview. *Journal of Abnormal and Social Psychology*, 1958, *57*, 84–90.

Sanders, R., Smith, R. S., & Weinman, B. S. *Chronic psychosis and recovery.* San Francisco: Jossey-Bass, 1967.

Schaefer, H. H. Investigations on operant conditioning procedures in a mental hospital. *California Mental Health Research Monograph,* 1966, *8,* 25–39.

Schaefer, H. H., & Martin, P. L. Behavior therapy for "apathy" of hospitalized schizophrenics. *California Department of Mental Hygiene Research Report,* 1966, August, No. 379.

Sherman, L. J., Ging, R., Moseley, E. C., & Bookbinder, L. J. Prognosis in schizophrenia: A follow-up of 588 patients. *Archives of General Psychiatry,* 1964, *10,* 123–130.

Sommer, R., & Osmond, H. Symptoms of institutional care. *Social Problems,* 1961, *8,* 254–263.

Sommer, R., Witney, G., & Osmond, H. Teaching common associations to schizophrenics. *Journal of Abnormal and Social Psychology,* 1962, *65,* 58–61.

Steffy, R. A., Torney, D., Hart, J., Craw, M., & Martlett, N. An application of learning techniques to the management and rehabilitation of severely regressed, chronically ill patients: Preliminary findings. Paper presented at the meeting of the Ontario Psychiatric Association, Ottawa, Canada, February 1966.

Szasz, T. S. *Law, liberty, and psychiatry.* New York: Macmillan, 1963.

Ullmann, L. P. *Institution and outcome: A comparative study of psychiatric hospitals.* New York: Pergamon, 1967.

Ullmann, L. P., Forsman, R. G., Kenny, J. W., McInnis, T. L., Unikel, I. P., & Zeisset, R. M. Selective reinforcement of schizophrenics' interview responses. *Behavior Research and Therapy,* 1965, *2,* 205–212.

Ullmann, L. P., & Krasner, L. (Eds.), *Case studies in behavior modification.* New York: Holt, 1965.

Ullmann, L. P., & Krasner, L. *A psychological approach to abnormal behavior.* Englewood Cliffs, N.J.: Prentice-Hall, 1969.

Ullmann, L. P., Krasner, L., & Collins, B. J. Modification of behavior through verbal conditioning: Effects in group therapy. *Journal of Abnormal and Social Psychology,* 1961, *62,* 128–132.

Ullmann, L. P., Krasner, L., & Edinger, R. L. Verbal conditioning of common associations in long-term schizophrenic patients. *Behavior Research and Therapy,* 1964, *2,* 15–18.

Ullmann, L. P., Weiss, R. L., & Krasner, L. The effect of verbal conditioning of emotional words on recognition of threatening stimuli. *Journal of Clinical Psychology,* 1963, *19,* 182–183.

Vaillant, G. E. The prediction of recovery in schizophrenia. *International Journal of Psychiatry,* 1966, *2,* 617–627.

Vitale, J. H. The emergence of mental hospital field research. In G. W. Fairweather (Ed.), *Social psychology in treating mental illness.* New York: Wiley, 1964.

Vitale, J. H., & Steinbach, M. The prevention of relapse of chronic mental patients. *International Journal of Social Psychiatry,* 1965, *11,* 85–95.

Wanklin, J. M., Fleming, D. F., Buck, C., & Hobbs, G. E. Discharge and readmissions among mental hospital patients. *Archives of Neurology and Psychiatry,* 1956, *76,* 660–669.

Weiss, R. L., Krasner, L., & Ullmann, L. P. Responsivity of psychiatric patients to verbal conditioning: "Success" and "failure" conditions and pattern of reinforced trials. *Psychological Reports,* 1963, *12,* 423–426.

Wilensky, H., & Herz, M. I. Problem areas in the development of a therapeutic community. *International Journal of Social Psychiatry,* 1966, *12,* 299–308.

Wilmer, H. A. Toward a definition of the therapeutic community. *American Journal of Psychiatry,* 1958, *114,* 824–834.

Wing, J. K. Long-stay schizophrenic patients and results of rehabilitation. In H. Freeman (Ed.), *Psychiatric hospital care.* London: Bailliere, 1965.

Wohl, S. A. Follow-up community adjustment. In G. W. Fairweather (Ed.), *Social psychology in treating mental illness.* New York: Wiley, 1964.

Zubin, J., Sutton, S., Salzinger, K., Salzinger, S., Burdock, E. I., & Peretz, D. A biometric approach to prognosis in schizophrenia. In P. H. Hoch & J. Zubin (Eds.), *Comparative epidemiology of the mental disorders.* New York: Grune & Stratton, 1961.

Zusman, J. Some explanations of the changing appearance of psychotic patients. In E. M. Gruenberg (Ed.), *Evaluating the effectiveness of community mental health services.* New York: Milbank, 1966.

PART SIX

Living on the Outside: Stigma and Passing

The ex-mental patient's difficulties are far from ended when he leaves the mental hospital. As the person returns to the community he must face the attitudes of the general public toward ex-mental patients. The social stigma attached to having been a mental patient is, as Lamy points out in his article, widely shared, negative, and distinguishable from other forms of negative social sanction. Lamy's research indicates that public reaction to ex-mental hospital patients is a mixture of fear, sympathy, and contempt.

The paper by Farina and Ring suggests that our interpersonal relations with ex-mental patients are clearly affected by our attitudes. In a cleverly contrived laboratory situation, Farina and Ring demonstrate that, when asked to work with a person who is described as having suffered from mental illness, people prefer to work alone rather than with him. In addition, the ex-mental patient is blamed for inadequacies in their joint performance, even when there is no objective basis for such blame.

In the final paper in this section, Miller and Dawson make it clear that the effects of the stigma of mental illness are not confined to laboratory settings. Their large-scale survey of the employment patterns of ex-mental patients after release from the hospital indicate that, not only do ex-mental patients feel inferior and, therefore, reluctant to seek employment, but also that their actual employment rate is significantly reduced after hospitalization. Furthermore, even when ex-mental patients do gain employment, there is a marked downward shift in the patient's occupational level following release from the mental hospital.

It is possible that the results reported by Miller and Dawson are a result of the subjectively felt stigma of being an ex-mental patient. On the other hand, they may be partly a result of the debilitating conditions of long-term hospitalization or of a severe psychiatric disorder. Whatever the cause, the apparent inability of ex-mental patients to regain their original employment status is almost certain to increase the chances of being hospitalized again. Thus, the self-perpetuating, vicious circle of the mental patient's career is assured.

Social Consequences of Mental Illness

Richard E. Lamy

Although the term "mental illness" is being increasingly condemned as a term unacceptable to science, for example, by Adams (1964), Hoffman (1960), Leifer (1962–1963), and Szasz (1960), the term nonetheless seems to be taken quite seriously by the general public (and perhaps by a large share of psychiatrists and psychologists), and public notions of "mental illness" may have significant implications for persons who have been mental hospital patients. The present paper is especially concerned with the public social evaluation of the person who is publicly known to have been officially "diagnosed" as having a "mental illness," has received "treatment" at a mental hospital, has been officially discharged from hospital care, and now is to return to life in the community.

A number of investigators (Cumming & Cumming, 1956, 1957; Nunnally, 1957; Woodward, 1951) have concluded that the general public does not share the frame of reference of the psychiatrist or psychologist for judging mental illness. Wrench (1958) concluded that attitudes toward mental illness were not similar to those toward child socialization. Social class level has been asserted to relate both to agreement with mental health experts, and educability in that direction (Hollingshead & Redlich, 1958; Ramsey & Seipp, 1948; Redlich, 1950; Redlich, Hollingshead, & Bellis, 1955). Freeman (1961), however, concluded that social class variables are not related to lay attitudes toward mental illness when the factor of level of education is controlled. Dohrenwend (1962) decided that community leadership manifested through an educational role had more of a psychiatric orientation toward mental illness than did leadership of a religious, political-legal, or economic type.

Woodward (1951), Lystad (1958), and Lemkau and Crocetti (1962) inferred that the public was rapidly becoming desensitized toward mental illness, but their views are at variance with those of a number of investigators who inferred a distinctly nega-

Reprinted from the *Journal of Consulting Psychology*, vol. 30, no. 5, 1966, pp. 450–455. Copyright 1966 by the American Psychological Association and reproduced by permission.

tive public reaction (Clausen, Yarrow, Deasy, & Schwartz, 1955; Crawford, Rollins, & Sutherland, 1960; Eisdorfer & Altrocchi, 1961; Lamy, 1961; Nunnally & Bobren, 1959; Nunnally & Kittross, 1958; Whatley, 1959; Yarrow, Schwartz, Murphy, & Deasy, 1955). Whatley (1959) inferred that primary-group intimacy was denied the ex-mental patient. Gursslin, Hunt, and Roach (1960) cautioned that "Lower-class people who take on forms of behavior implicit in the mental health model are apt to find themselves alienated from lower-class society. . . ."

Rothaus and Morton (1962) and Rothaus, Hanson, Cleveland, and Johnson (1963) concluded that a mental hospital patient will be more employable if he explains his hospitalization in terms of interpersonal problems rather than mental illness. Landy and Griffith (1958) reported that employers indicated an unexpected willingness to hire ex-mental hospital patients; Olshansky, Grob, and Malamud (1958), however, who had face-to-face interviews with large-scale employers in the same metropolitan area, inferred that employers had serious misgivings about such ex-patients and that a sharp discrepancy existed between employers' expressed willingness to hire and the low level of actual hirings. Pindell (1958) elucidated employers' devious rejection strategies toward ex-mental patients.

Problem

Three questions seem basic in regard to the frame of reference or system of values used to evaluate persons who have had hospitalization for mental illness:

1. How *general* is the evaluative complex in a particular subculture or segment of the public: that is, what proportion of the population shares a common value system?

2. How *specific* an evaluative complex is present: that is, does the complex of ideas, beliefs, attitudes, etc., toward the ex-mental hospital patient overlap with other complexes, or is a distinction made?

3. What are the salient aspects that may be inferred to underlie the judgmental pattern used in regard to persons who have had mental illness?

The experimental method involved the gathering of data relevant to the role of "ex-mental patient." In order to show specificity as well as generality for judging the person who had had a hospitalization for mental illness, it was deemed necessary to have a "control" negative role; it seemed possible that subjects, when evaluating ex-mental hospital patients, could respond on the basis of social approval or social disapproval, and their consensuality in this area be mistaken for a consensus in relation to ex-patients. It was desired that a control role should have certain negative aspects which were assumed to be potentially prominent in the students' evaluation of an ex-mental hospital patient —strongly negative social evaluation, power to evoke fearful or anxious reactions in persons, and handicapping stigma in a wide range of life situations. The control role selected was that of "ex-convict." The ex-convict role was considered to be a possible point of reference as to the depth of aversion toward the ex-patient.

Subjects

Students enrolled in lower division undergraduate liberal arts courses at state-supported universities were considered to represent a lay segment of the public who had little or no formal knowledge of psychiatry or psychology and who would function importantly in the future social action. Two samples were used. The first consisted of 80 students (34 male, 46 female) spread among various sections of a sophomore level introductory general psychology course at the University of Oregon in 1960; these 80 subjects were part of a total population of 322 subjects, the other 242 of whom simultaneously performed tasks for another experiment. The second group was composed of 78 students (30 male, 48 female) spread among a number of lower division liberal arts courses at the University of Missouri at Kansas City in 1964; these 78 subjects were part of a total population of 197 subjects, the other 121 of whom simultaneously performed tasks for another experiment. The median age for both groups was approximately 19–20 years; the students contributed anonymously and gave no personal data other than their sex.

Procedure

The experiment employed a forced-choice technique. For each of the 30 situations of Table 1 the subject chose "The man who has been in a mental hospital," or "The man who has served a prison sentence."

Directions for the subjects were as follows:

Whenever it is possible, we like to make any important decision only after we have carefully considered a good deal of information about the problem. Sometimes, however, we have to make quick decisions or "snap judgments" on the basis of very little information.

You are to give your opinions as to the "snap judgment" that people (or you yourself) might make in different circumstances. Of course, with more information these judgments could very well be different—but this is not important here, for we are interested particularly in these *first, unthinking* reactions or "snap judgments."

You will find below a series of situations to be faced by two young men who are about equal in intelligence, education, and appearance. Each one, however, has had some special problems. One man had a serious mental illness and had to spend considerable time as a patient in a mental hospital. The other man was guilty of a serious criminal offense and had to spend considerable time serving a prison sentence. Now they are to return to ordinary life.

This is all we know. We do not know enough to be able to guess what final decision might be made in each case. We can, however, indicate which information—mental patient or prisoner —does more to "push" a decision one way or the other.

You may sometimes feel you can't decide, but in each case make a choice—for these choices, no matter how they are arrived at, represent the information that is important.

TABLE 1   FREQUENCIES OF CHOICES AND RELATED LEVELS OF SIGNIFICANCE FOR A (EX-MENTAL PATIENT) AND B (EX-CONVICT)

Item (numbered as in experimental format)	fA	fB	P[a]
3. An employer seeking a man for a job involving minor responsibilities but the handling of large sums of money would be *less* likely to consider	8	150	a
5. Most people feel that the man *more* responsible for his own troubles is	9	149	a
30. If parents would pay more attention to disciplining their children, we would have *less* men in the predicament of	18	140	a
13. Most people in the community feel that the parents *more* responsible for their son's trouble are the parents of	20	138	a

29.	The man who would be helped *more* by joining the Army is	22	136	a
22.	If we had a better economic system, we would have less people in the predicament of	23	135	a
20.	The man who could be *more* successful in seeing that his children did not have to go to an institution such as his, is	29	129	a
28.	The man whom most people would place *more* confidence in, in an emergency, is	37	121	a
25.	If he could find a good, steady job, the man *more* likely *not* to return to the institution is	39	119	a
15.	The man who would worry *more* about his children's having to go to the same institution as he did, is	111	47	a
16.	A lady having one single room for rent would *less* want to have for a roomer	48	110	a
7.	The man who is *more* likely to return to the institution is	51	107	a
27.	The man who would be helped *more* by being trusted with responsibbility on the job is	52	106	a
11.	If they had to choose, most men would rather be	53	105	a
26.	Should the same life situations appear again, the man *less* able to keep from going back into the same type of institution is	105	53	a
14.	The man who is *more* worried about his future is	104	54	a
2.	A mother who is very solicitous of her children would be *less* willing to have them go on a weekend camping trip in the sole care of	101	57	a
21.	The man about whom people could later say, "You'd never know he'd been in an institution," is *more* likely to be	101	57	a
9.	An employer seeking a permanent member for his business, who would be supervising many other people and handling a great deal of responsibility, would be *less* likely to hire	98	60	b
24.	The man who would benefit *more* from trying to help others to keep out of the institution he was in is	61	97	b
8.	The mother who would be *less* worried about .her children's having to spend time in the same institution as their father is the wife of	96	62	b
12.	The man whom a woman, by her love, is *more* likely to feel she can keep from returning to the institution is	64	94	c
18.	The man around whom his children would feel *more* relaxed is	65	93	d

ᵃ a = $p \leq .001$; b = $p \leq .01$; c = $p \leq .02$; d = $p \leq .05$; n.s. = $p > .05$.

TABLE 1   (continued)

Item (numbered as in experimental format)	fA	fB	Pa
4. A wife can feel *more* confident of the family future if her husband is	91	67	n.s.
23. The man who will be *less* likely to give unselfish devotion to his wife and children is	69	89	n.s.
1. A young lady about to be married would be *more* upset to learn that her fiance is	87	71	n.s.
10. Most people would feel *more* comfortable if assigned to share an office with	87	71	n.s.
17. After he had had five years of good work on the job, an employer would be *more* inclined to give an important promotion to	73	85	n.s.
19. Kind, loving parents would have been of *more* help in preventing the problem of	75	83	n.s.
6. The man who would feel *more* embarrassed about telling a potential employer of his stay in an institution is	79	79	n.s.

[a] $a = p \leq .001$; $b = p \leq .01$; $c = p \leq .02$; $d = p \leq .05$; n.s. $= p > .05$.

Results

The Missouri students were used to test whether the Oregon findings were generalizable across geographically separate student samples, and across time. In statistical analyses, two-tailed reasoning was used in both studies, rather than using the Oregon results to predict the Missouri results with a one-tailed statistical logic. Each of the 30 situations was examined by means of the chi-square test, two-tailed with alpha at .05, to see if males and females differed in their choices. For the Oregon students, one situation only showed a difference, and one situation only for the Missouri students; this was well within chance limits. The 34 males and 46 females of the Oregon group were hence pooled into a sample of 80 subjects, and the 30 males and 48 females of the Missouri group constituted a sample 78 subjects.

For each of the 30 situations the binomial test, corrected for continuity (Siegel, 1956, p. 46), two-tailed with alpha at .05, was used to test for a differential choice. The Oregon sample made differential choices in 23 situations, the Missouri sample in 18.

TABLE 2   THE RELATIONSHIP BETWEEN THE LEVELS OF SIGNIFICANCE WITH
WHICH THE OREGON AND THE MISSOURI SUBJECTS ENDORSED THE
THIRTY ITEMS OF TABLE 1

Missouri	*Oregon*				
	$p > .05$	$.02 < p < .05$	$.01 < p < .02$	$.001 < p < .01$	$p < .001$
$p < .001$	0	0	0	1	9
$.001 < p < .01$	0	1	1	1	1
$.01 < p < .02$	2	0	0	0	0
$.02 < p < .05$	0	1	0	0	1
$p > .05$	5	0	2	3	2

Table 2 shows the agreement between the Oregon and Missouri
groups: for example, of the 13 items judged as significant beyond
the .001 level by the Oregon students, 9 of these 13 were also
discriminated beyond the .001 level by the Missouri students,
1 between .001 and .01, 1 between .02 and .05, and 2 not significantly discriminated. When the 16 situations which had a statistically significant choice by both groups (see Table 2) are ranked
in order of definitiveness of choice for each group, the Spearman
rank coefficient of correlation is .94; over the 30 items the rank
order coefficient is .91. The Oregon and Missouri samples were
hence pooled; the binomial test, as above, was used with the 158
subjects and revealed 23 significantly discriminated items. Table 1
gives the frequencies and minimum significance levels for each
of the 30 situations.

Discussion

The results indicate that the students did share a *general* frame
of reference or value system relative to ex-mental hospital patients, inasmuch as 18 of the 23 significant choices are beyond
the .001 level and the statistical significance of a choice is a direct
function of the number of students who chose a particular alternative. A *specific* evaluative pattern is also indicated, in that the
ex-mental hospital patient role was differentiated from another
social role presumably having somewhat similar negative aspects.
The content of the differentially discriminated items suggests
some possible aspects of the students' evaluative complex relative
to persons who have had a mental illness.

The role of ex-mental hospital patient was viewed as less desirable even than the highly negative role of ex-convict (Item 11), and a very solicitous mother was judged more likely to trust the care of her children to the ex-convict (Item 2).

The ex-patients seemed to be viewed as rather permanently susceptible to breakdown under stress. The ex-convict was heavily endorsed as more reliable in an emergency (Item 28). Items 7 and 26 show that while the ex-convict was judged more likely to be reinstitutionalized, the ex-patient was judged less able to deter reinstitutionalization. Employers were judged to strongly prefer the ex-patient for a job requiring minor responsibility and great honesty (Item 3), but to prefer the ex-convict for a permanent position entailing high responsibility (Item 9)—and even after years of good service not to prefer the ex-patient for an important promotion (Item 17).

The ex-convict was considered the more responsible for his own troubles (Item 5), and parental responsibility for their son's trouble was more direct in the ex-convict's case (Item 13).

While more consistent parental discipline was considered more likely to reduce criminality than mental illness (Item 30), kindly parental love was not seen as more effective in preventing mental illness (Item 19). Item 20 gives a heavy majority to the ex-convict in the ability to prevent his children's having an institutionalization similar to his. A better economic system was considered more likely to reduce criminality than mental illness (Item 22). In every situation suggesting remediation for one's problems—being loved by a woman (Item 12), trying to help others avoid misfortunes similar to one's own (Item 24), finding a good steady job (Item 25), being trusted with responsibility on the job (Item 27), joining the Army (Item 29)—the remedy was judged more efficacious for the ex-convict.

The ex-mental hospital patient was judged to worry more about his future (Item 14) and about his children's having to go to an institution similar to his (Item 15); the students perhaps responded less to the content of the items than to the "worry" component—for the ex-patient's wife was judged at least as confident as the ex-convict's in regard to the family future (Item 4), and less worried than the ex-convict's about her children's following their father's path to institutionalization (Item 8). The author is at a loss to hypothesize why, in Item 21, the ex-patient was chosen as the one who would show fewer traces of institutionalization. The ex-patient was deemed the more likely to give unselfish devotion to his wife and children (Item 23), but to generate more anxiety or tension in his children (Item 16).

No statistically significant choice was given as to the shock of a young lady upon learning of her fiance's institutionalization (Item 1), the embarrassment of revealing one's institutionalization to a potential employer (Item 6), or acceptability to share an office (Item 10).

Moving somewhat farther from the literal content of the items, the data seem to indicate that the person who has had a mental hospitalization suffers a depreciation of social esteem in a wide range of social roles. He was judged to be permanently vulnerable to further episodes—and, perhaps of even greater significance, not able to forestall such recurrences either through his own efforts or by means of good medical advice. He was perceived as liable to "go to pieces" under stress, to have diminished self-control, and to be a source of anxiety to those in his presence. It was felt that employers would not trust him with responsibility. Even the stigma of a prison record was preferred to that of mental hospitalization.

The preceding inferences seem consonant with those of other investigators cited earlier, who dealt with different segments of the lay public and used different methodologies. The present investigator infers two broad dimensions in the negative evaluation of the ex-mental hospital patient—an "anxiety-fear" dimension in that the mysticism, strangeness, and unpredictable behavioral peculiarities attributed to the "mentally ill" are thought to be latent indefinitely in any person who has ever been so diagnosed —and a "sympathy-contempt" dimension in that the person who has been a mental hospital patient is thought to possess attributes which are in direct conflict with the cherished American ideal of "rugged individualism." It is predicted that the discharged mental patient will find the social community nonhostile, but unaccepting.

References

Adams, N. B. "Mental illness" or interpersonal behavior. *American Psychologist*, 1964, *19*, 191–197.

Clausen, J. A., Yarrow, M. R., Deasy, L. C., & Schwartz, C. G. The impact of mental illness: Research formulation. *Journal of Social Issues*, 1955, *11* (4), 3–6.

Crawford, F. R., Rollins, G. W., & Sutherland, R. L. Variations in the evaluation of the mentally ill. *Journal of Health and Human Behavior*, 1960, *1*, 211–219.

Cumming, J., & Cumming, E. Affective symbolism, social norms and mental illness. *Psychiatry*, 1956, *19*, 77–85.

Cumming, J., & Cumming, E. *Closed ranks: An experiment in mental health education.* Cambridge: Harvard University Press, 1957.

Dohrenwend, B. P. Some aspects of the appraisal of abnormal behavior by leaders in an urban area. *American Psychologist*, 1962, *17*, 190–198.

Eisdorfer, C., & Altrocchi, J. A comparison of attitudes toward old age and mental illness. *Journal of Gerontology*, 1961, *16*, 340–343.

Freeman, H. R. Attitudes toward mental illness among relatives of former patients. *American Sociological Review*, 1961, *26*, 59–66.

Gursslin, O. R., Hunt, H. C., & Roach, J. L. Social class and the mental health movement. *Social Problems*, Winter 1959–60, *7*, No. 3, 210–218.

Hoffman, M. Psychiatry, nature and science, *American Journal of Psychiatry*, 1960, *117*, 205–210.

Hollingshead, A. B., & Redlich, F. C. *Social class and mental illness.* New York: Wiley, 1958.

Lamy, R. E. Conceptions of maladjustment and mental illness among college undergraduate students. Unpublished doctoral dissertation, University of Oregon, 1961.

Landy, D., & Griffith, W. D. Employer receptivity toward hiring psychiatric patients. *Mental Hygiene*, 1958, *42*, 383–390.

Leifer, R. The competence of the psychiatrist to assist in the determination of incompetency: A sceptical inquiry into the courtroom functions of psychiatrists. *Syracuse Law Review*, 1962–63, *14*, 564–575.

Lemkau, P. B., & Crocetti, G. M. An urban population's opinion and knowledge about mental illness, *American Journal of Psychiatry*, 1962, *118*, 692–700.

Lystad, M. Day hospital care and changing family attitudes toward the mentally ill. *Journal of Nervous and Mental Disease*, 1958, *127*, 145–152.

Nunnally, J. C. The communication of mental health information: A comparison of the opinions of experts and the public with mass media presentations. *Behavioral Science*, 1957, *3*, 220–230.

Nunnally, J. C., & Bobren, H. M. Variables governing the willingness to receive communications on mental health. *Journal of Personality*, 1959, *27*, 30–46.

Nunnally, J. C., & Kittross, J. M. Public attitudes toward mental health professions. *American Psychologist*, 1958, *13*, 589–594.

Olshansky, S., Grob, S., & Malamud, I. Employers' attitudes and practices in the hiring of ex-mental patients. *Mental Hygiene*, 1958, *42*, 391–401.

Pindell, H. D. Employer attitudes about psychiatric patients. *Journal of Rehabilitation*, 1958, *24*, 6–7.

Ramsey, G. V., & Seipp, M. Attitudes and opinions concerning mental illness. *Psychiatric Quarterly*, 1948, *22*, 429–444.

Redlich, F. C. What the citizen knows about psychiatry. *Mental Hygiene*, 1950, *34*, 64–79.

Redlich, F. C., Hollingshead, A. B., & Bellis, E. Social class differences in attitudes toward psychiatry. *American Journal of Orthopsychiatry*, 1955, *25*, 60–70.

Rothaus, P., Hanson, P. G., Cleveland, S. E., & Johnson, D. L. Describing psychiatric hospitalization: A dilemma. *American Psychologist*, 1963, *18*, 85–89.

Rothaus, P., & Morton, R. B. Problem-centered vs. mental illness self descriptions. *Journal of Health and Human Behavior*, 1962, *3*, 198–203.

Siegel, S. *Non-parametric statistics*. New York: McGraw-Hill, 1956.

Szasz, T. S. The myth of mental illness. *American Psychologist*, 1960, *15*, 113–118.

Whatley, C. D. Social attitudes toward discharged mental patients. *Social Problems*, 1959, *6*, 313–320.

Woodward, J. L. Changing ideas on mental illness and its treatment. *American Sociological Review*, 1951, *16*, 443–454.

Wrench, D. F. Attitudes toward child socialization and attitudes toward mental health. Unpublished master's dissertation, University of Oregon, 1958.

Yarrow, M. R., Schwartz, C. G., Murphy, H. S., & Deasy, L. C. The psychological meaning of mental illness in the family. *Journal of Social Issues*, *11* (4), 1955, 12–24.

The Influence of Perceived Mental Illness on Interpersonal Relations

Amerigo Farina and Kenneth Ring

It seems clear that, in America at least, there is a generalized highly unfavorable attitude toward the mentally ill (Nunnally,

Reprinted from the *Journal of Abnormal Psychology*, vol. 70, 1965, pp. 47–51. Copyright 1965 by the American Psychological Association, and reproduced by permission. This study was, in part, financed by a research grant (M-6167) from the National Institute of Mental Health, United States Public Health Service.

1961; Nunnally & Kittross, 1958). Evidence suggests that such a pandemic attitude can color the perception of a person believed to be mentally ill even when his behavior is, by all objective standards, "normal." For example, it has been found (Jones, Hester, Farina, & Davis, 1959) that subjects listening to standardized taped "interviews," dislike the speaker more when they are told (by the experimenter) that she is maladjusted than when they believe she is well adjusted.

Interesting as such studies are, in general they provide no more than a glimpse into prevalent American attitudes and stereotypes about the mentally ill. Conceivably, such attitudes are maintained through what Newcomb (1947) has called "autistic hostility." That is, these attitudes resist change because an individual holding them ceases to communicate with the class of persons unfavorably evaluated. Certainly, most Americans have very limited face-to-face contact with the mentally ill. The situation is reminiscent of the early studies on stereotypes (e.g., Katz & Braly, 1933) where it was shown that, in the main, Turks were strongly disliked in spite of the fact that few of the respondents had ever known one.

In the present study we are concerned with the modifiability of such stereotypes as a function of face-to-face interaction with a "mentally ill" person whose behavior in no way supports the common attitude toward him. We are asking, in effect, if the mentally ill person is a prisoner of his own reputation. In this, the present research is relevant to certain hypotheses recently suggested by Goffman (1963) regarding the stigma attached to the ex-mental patient.

In addition to studying the effect of direct interaction (something that earlier studies lacked) on the perception of a person believed to be mentally ill, the effects of such a belief on the performance of a dyadic cooperative task is also of interest. If, as the previously cited research would suggest, unfavorable attitudes toward the mentally ill are highly generalized, one would expect them to influence behaviors over a wide variety of interpersonal contexts. For this reason, in the interaction studied, a motor task which seems completely unrelated to mental illness was deliberately chosen.

The question now arises: what is likely to be the effect of believing a co-worker to be mentally ill on the performance of a cooperative task? There seem to be several possibilities. First of all, on the basis of an anxiety-performance decrement hypothesis, it might be expected that perceiving the co-worker as emotionally disturbed would lead to decreased adequacy of performance. This would occur if the perceiver's level of anxiety were raised by the belief that the co-worker was, because mentally ill, unpredictable, tense, and dangerous. This increased anxiety should interfere with the performance on the very difficult task used.

On the other hand, two other possibilities suggest that seeing the co-worker as mentally ill would increase performance adequacy. It might be *less* threatening to work with someone who is seriously maladjusted and consequently in a poor position to evaluate others than to work with a normal person who might be more justifiably critical and judgmental. In this case, anxiety should be higher and, therefore, the performance lower when the co-worker is perceived as normal than when he is perceived as mentally ill. The same relationship is suggested by the very different possibility that when the co-worker is perceived as mentally ill, he is thought to be less competent to perform the task. The subject may compensate for the imagined inadequacy of his co-worker by trying harder. Therefore, better performance would be associated with the perception of the partner as mentally ill. In view of the seeming reasonableness of these contradictory alternatives and the absence of any guiding data, no predictions were made. It was thought, however, that if differences in adequacy of performance in fact emerged, their meaning would be clear when examined in the light of measures of perception of the co-worker.[1]

Method

Subjects. The subjects of this study were 60 male undergraduate students enrolled in psychology classes at the University of Connecticut. They were all volunteers and were given no pay for participating in the experiment. The subjects participated in pairs

---

[1] It is of course conceivable that two of these processes might counterbalance each other in which case no differences would emerge in spite of the presence of these processes.

composed in all cases of 2 students who were unacquainted with each other.

Procedure. After the subjects were introduced, they were asked to sit at two desks facing each other. However, a partition was placed between the desks in such a way that the students could not see each other but could at all times be seen by the experimenter. They were then told that this study sought to determine how much a person could tell about another from certain standard cues and were instructed to refrain from talking to each other. It was explained that the experimenter wanted them to know some specific things about each other and that they were to write that information on blank sheets of paper which would subsequently be exchanged. They were asked to list three kinds of information: (*a*) the sort of person they were, (*b*) anything unusual about themselves, and (*c*) something about their plans for the future. They were urged to be as candid as possible inasmuch as it would be very important to the study.

When a student indicated he was finished (generally 5 to 15 minutes) his background information sheet was picked up by the experimenter and the subject was given a brief one-page questionnaire about his school and family. The sole purpose of this questionnaire was to facilitate the substitution of faked background information sheets for the real ones. These fake sheets, which described the writer either as normal or maladjusted, were placed on the students' desks while they were engaged in completing the questionnaire. They were then told that, as soon as they had completed the questionnaire, they were to read their co-worker's information sheet very carefully.

The normal information sheet was as follows:

> I tend to think of myself as a relatively normal person; at least I don't have what you could call any "problems." I enjoy going to college, but like to have my fun, too. I think I'm pretty popular with my group, am engaged, and am doing pretty well (29 QPR)[2] in school.
>
> Frankly, I can't think of anything that's "unusual" about myself.
>
> As for my goals for the future, after graduating from college, I plan to get married and hope to go to graduate school.

---

[2] About a B average.

The "sick" one, on the other hand, read:

> You asked us to be candid, so here goes: I have certain prob-
> lems in adjustment which I first noticed in high school and which
> still bother me quite a bit. I guess I am somewhat different from
> most people. I tend to keep pretty much to myself and, frankly,
> I don't really have any close friends. At school I am doing pretty
> well (29 QPR).
>
> I suppose what's most unusual about me is that twice (once
> in my senior year in high school and once in college), I have
> been placed in a mental institution when I had a kind of nervous
> breakdown.
>
> As for my goals for the future, after graduating from college,
> I hope to go to graduate school.

When both subjects had finished, they were taken to another
section of the room where a toy manufactured in Sweden and
sold under the brand name *Labyrintspel* (Labyrinth Game) was
on top of a table. Subjects were asked to sit on chairs in front of
the *Labyrintspel*, their chairs were drawn up against each other,
and they were asked to examine the toy. It resembles a box,
measuring 13×11 inches, it is approximately 4¾ inches high,
and there is a knob at each of two sides. Each knob controls an
angle of the plane at the top of the box so that a small steel ball
on it can be made to follow any path desired by appropriate and
simultaneous manipulation of the two knobs. The movable plane
is a maze formed by raised wooden partitions and a series of
40 holes. There is only one possible path from the starting point
to the goal and that is indicated by a black line. There are 59
points at which the ball can fall into a hole and these are num-
bered from 1, which is the first pitfall, to 59, which is the last,
before the goal.

The subjects were each assigned a knob and they were told
to make the ball go as far as possible on each trial and when the
ball fell in a hole they were to pick it up as it emerged, place it
in the starting box, and begin another trial.[3] They were given
three practice trials and told that they were free to talk about
the task at any time. The performance consisted of 50 consecutive

---

[3] A small percentage of subjects (15% overall) had had some prior experience with the toy but the percentage did not differ across groups.

trials with a 1-minute rest period after Trial 25. For each trial the hole in which the ball fell was noted and the time required was also recorded. The latter variable was not analyzed and served primarily to reduce the time the experiment required by causing the subjects to work more rapidly.

At the termination of the maze performance subjects returned to their desks and were given a final questionnaire to complete. They were told that the questionnaire was strictly confidential and would not be seen by their co-worker. It consisted of 14 statements which subjects could answer by placing a check mark at the appropriate place and a fifteenth statement which called for a free description of the co-worker. After the questionnaire, a discussion was held with the subjects in order to determine if any were suspicious and, subsequently, to reveal the true nature of the study to them. Two subjects guessed the real intent of the study and were discarded.

Experimental design. The subjects were randomly assigned to one of three groups, each group being composed of 10 pairs of subjects for a total of 30 pairs. The groups differed only with respect to the information sheet received. In the normal-normal (N-N) group, both subjects received a normal information sheet. For the normal-sick (N-S) group one student received the normal information sheet but the other received the sick one. The last group was the sick-sick (S-S) group and each student in the group received the sick background information sheet. For the analysis of the performance measures, these three groups are compared. However, for measures of perception only two groups of 30 subjects each were compared. Those who received the sick background information sheet comprised one while those receiving the normal sheet formed the other group. The three groups were combined into two after it was determined that the perception of the co-worker was not influenced by the background information sheet the co-worker received.

Results

An important fact to determine at the outset is how successful the manipulation was in inducing the subjects to perceive their co-worker in line with experimental intentions. On the final ques-

TABLE 1 MEANS AND STANDARD DEVIATIONS OF TOTAL SCORE OBTAINED FOR 50 TRIALS ON THE LABYRINTSPEL

Group	M	SD
N-N	252.3	71.8
N-S	275.5	101.8
S-S	334.8	94.6

tionnaire there were four items which are relevant to this question. Those who received the sick sheet, in comparison to those who received the normal one, described their co-worker as: less able to get along with others, less able to understand others, less able to understand himself, and more unpredictable. For these four items the differences reached significance levels ranging from $p < .01$ to $p < .0001$. These results indicate that the manipulation was completely successful and, in addition, confirm Nunnally's (1961) findings that mentally ill persons are perceived as unpredictable.

The results of the performance on the *Labyrintspel* are presented in Table 1. The numbers in this table represent sums of scores obtained for the 50 trials. The N-N group was least adequate while the S-S group performed best, suggesting that perceiving the co-worker as mentally ill enhances performance. These results were analyzed by means of a trend analysis (Edwards, 1960) which showed that only the trials main effect reached a statistically significant level. Neither the groups main effect nor the Groups $\times$ Trials interaction was found to be statistically significant. Since it had been expected that the N-N and S-S group scores would be most disparate (whatever the effect of perceived mental illness), an additional analysis was carried out. Here the performance of the N-N and S-S groups was compared by means of a t test. The results indicate that the S-S group performance was reliably better than that of the N-N group ($t = 2.2$, $df = 18$, $p < .05$) and suggest that perceiving the co-worker as mentally ill facilitates performance.

Analysis of questionnaire items concerned with social perception (other than those mentioned at the beginning of this section) revealed that the background information sheet had a significant influence on the perception of the co-worker in spite of the opportunity the students had of interacting with him. The results from one item which required the subjects to state whether they

TABLE 2   NUMBERS OF SUBJECTS DESCRIBED AS HELPING OR HINDERING PER-
FORMANCE AS A FUNCTION OF BACKGROUND INFORMATION SHEET
RECEIVED

| | | Co-worker described as: | | χ^2 | df | p |
		Helping	Hindering			
Background information	normal	27	3	5.7	1	.02
sheet received	sick	18	12			

thought their co-worker helped or hindered in the performance
of the task are presented in Table 2. Subjects who received the
sick information sheet, more often than those receiving the normal sheet, reported their co-worker hindered the joint performance. This occurred *in spite of the fact* that the former group did
objectively better on the task than the latter. Subjects were also
asked to indicate whether they preferred working on the task by
themselves (controlling both knobs) or with their partner. The
relevant data are presented in Table 3. They clearly support the
idea that believing an individual to be mentally ill reduces the
perceiver's willingness to work with him. A third item of this kind
was in the same direction as the preceding two in that the sick
co-worker tended to be held more responsible for causing the
ball to drop into a hole. However, the difference between the
groups did not reach statistical significance.

Of the remaining items on the questionnaire, those concerned
with estimates of the co-worker's intelligence and his ability to
perform well on similar motor tasks showed no difference between groups. While sick co-workers were judged to be less
liked by *others* than normals ($p < .01$), subjects themselves did
not rate a sick co-worker any less likable than a normal one.
Neither did subjects feel any less "comfortable" working with a
sick co-worker compared to a normal one. These two findings

TABLE 3   NUMBERS OF SUBJECTS CHOOSING TO WORK WITH PARTNER OR
ALONE AS A FUNCTION OF BACKGROUND INFORMATION SHEET RE-
CEIVED

| | | Choice to work with: | | χ^2 | df | p |
		Partner	Alone			
Background information	normal	17	13	7.1	1	.01
sheet received	sick	6	24			

seem to be at variance with the data already presented which would lead one plausibly, if not logically, to expect differences on these items. Also somewhat surprising is the absence of any difference between groups on questions dealing with how much attention the co-worker gave to the task and how willing the subject would be to work with his partner on a future, similar task.

Discussion

The most important conclusion of this study is that believing an individual to be mentally ill strongly influences the perception of that individual; this is true in spite of the fact that his behavior in no way justifies these perceptions. When a co-worker is viewed as mentally ill, subjects prefer to work alone rather than with him on a task and also blame him for inadequacies in perform-ance. Since objective measures of performance do not warrant such responses, these findings attest to the importance of believ-ing another to be mentally ill as a factor in interpersonal rela-tionships.

The significance of this variable is further emphasized by sev-eral considerations. The subjects of this study were young and well educated, characteristics shown to be associated with rela-tively favorable attitudes toward the mentally ill (Nunnally, 1961). Also, it seems very likely from the data referred to at the end of the Results section that the sick sheet either created a rather strong sympathy reaction in the subjects or made them less willing to say anything unfavorable about the co-worker. In spite of these counteracting factors it was still found that the generalized negative attitude had a strong effect on interpersonal relationships.

The finding of a difference in performance on the *Labyrintspel* suggests that perceiving someone as mentally ill affects a very broad spectrum of interpersonal behaviors. That is, while it might be expected that such a perception would influence a person's decision to hire someone as a baby sitter, the behavior measured in this study seems quite peripheral to mental illness. What fac-tors may account for this finding?

It will be remembered that two possibilities were suggested for anticipating the finding obtained: (*a*) one was based on the hypothesis that a normal and successful peer would be threatening and (*b*) another assumed that compensation for perceived inadequacy would occur. If the first hypothesis were true, it would imply a decrement in performance in the N-N group while the second would suggest a facilitation of performance in the S-S group. Obviously these two hypotheses are not mutually exclusive.

It was decided to test the second of these hypotheses by running an additional group of 10 pairs of students. In this group, the clumsy-clumsy (Cl-Cl) group, each student received a background information sheet which was identical to the normal one except for the addition of one phrase: "About the only thing I can think of is that "I'm 'all thumbs'; I don't learn to do things with my hands very well." The success of the manipulation was checked by comparing the N-N to the Cl-Cl group on the item which asked for an estimation of the co-worker's dexterity at motor tasks such as the one they had just completed. The z score yielded by the Mann-Whitney U test was 4.1 which is highly significant and in the expected direction. However, the task performance of the group was not different from that of the N-N group nor were the groups different with respect to their perception of the co-worker. These results are inconsistent with the compensation hypothesis, leaving the threat hypothesis as a possibility.

Of course, it could well be that the list of alternative hypotheses which could explain the original S-S—N-N difference has not been exhausted. For example, Ghiselli and Brown (1955, pp. 293–294) cite evidence indicating that performance on certain tasks is improved by distracting influences such as noise. Perceiving the co-worker as mentally ill may constitute a distracting influence and may have enhanced performance. Such hypotheses, clearly, may be subjected to direct test.

It has been demonstrated that, under certain circumstances, what a person reportedly says about himself significantly influences the interpretation of his behavior by another even though the behavior does not justify that interpretation. But, it might be argued, the type of encounter studied here was brief and superficial. If contact had been prolonged and intimate, isn't it reasonable to suppose that one's interpretation of another's behavior would be based less on stereotypes and more on the behavior itself? This is possible. Insofar as stereotypes about mental illness are concerned, however, this objection can be answered by submitting that it is precisely because of these stereotypes that distortions in perception are likely to occur in the *initial* phases of interaction and thus reduce the likelihood of further interaction of the kind necessary to eradicate such stereotypes.

References

Edwards, A. L. *Experimental design in psychological research.* New York: Rinehart, 1960.

Ghiselli, E. E., & Brown, C. W. *Personnel and industrial psychology.* New York: McGraw-Hill, 1955.

Goffman, E. *Stigma.* Englewood Cliffs, N.J.: Prentice-Hall, 1963.

Jones, E. E., Hester, S. L., Farina, A., & Davis, K. E. Reactions to unfavorable personal evaluations as a function of the evaluator's perceived adjustment. *Journal of Abnormal and Social Psychology,* 1959, *59,* 363–370.

Katz, D., & Braly, K. Racial stereotypes of 100 college students. *Journal of Abnormal and Social Psychology,* 1933, *28,* 280–290.

Newcomb, T. M. Autistic hostility and social reality. *Human Relations,* 1947, *1,* 69–86.

Nunnally, J. C., Jr. *Popular conceptions of mental health.* New York: Holt, Rinehart and Winston, 1961.

Nunnally, J. C., Jr., & Kittross, J. M. Public attitudes toward mental health professions. *American Psychologist,* 1958, *13,* 589–594.

Effects of Stigma on Re-employment of Ex-mental Patients

Dorothy Miller and William H. Dawson

The Greeks used the word *stigma* to denote bodily signs designed to expose something unusual or bad about the moral status of the subject. Today the term refers to the disgrace itself rather than to the bodily evidence of it. The post-hospital mental patient is thought to be stigmatized in varying degrees. In a way, all mental patients are potentially stigmatized since, even when the

Reprinted from *Mental Hygiene,* vol. 49, 1965, pp. 281–287.

background of mental illness is not known at first glance, there is the ever-present possibility that it will become known.

Goffman[1] has discussed the effects of "discrediting information" upon the social identity of a person who is then reduced in the eyes of others, by virtue of the knowledge of his past mental illness, from a "whole and usual person to a tainted, discounted one."

The shadow of disclosure, as well as the post-hospital status itself, gives rise to the stigma felt by the patient as he experiences it in the psychologic and social realities of his everyday life. Goffman[2] has stated:

> By definition, of course, we believe the person with a stigma is not quite human. On this assumption we exercise varieties of discrimination, through which we effectively, if often unthinkingly, reduce his life chances.

Goffman goes on to propose[3] that the stigmatized person has the same beliefs about himself that others do. This causes shame to become a . . .

> central possibility arising from the individual's perception of one of his own attributes as being a defiling thing to possess, and one he can readily see himself as not possessing.

Assuming that alumni of public mental hospitals constitute one category of persons in our society who are likely to be viewed by others as having a "stigma," i.e. being less than human, undesirable, dangerous or weak, it would seem necessary to study the awareness of "stigma" the former patient feels in his own life and the effects it has upon his re-employment.

In the California State Department of Mental Hygiene about one-half of all released mental patients are placed on "indefinite leave of absence" under the supervision of the Bureau of Social Work, which is staffed by trained psychiatric social workers who aid these patients with their problems of social adjustment.

---

[1] Goffman, Erving, Stigma, Prentice-Hall, Inc., Englewood Cliffs, New Jersey, 1963, p. 3.

[2] *Ibid.*, p. 5.

[3] *Ibid.*, p. 7.

TABLE 1   EMPLOYMENT STATUS OF PATIENTS PRIOR TO AND AFTER HOSPITAL-
              IZATION

STATUS	Prior to admission		After release	
	NUMBER	PER CENT	NUMBER	PER CENT
Employed, full time	209	19	133	12
Employed, part time	180	17	77	7
Psych. or phys. disabled	82	8	219	20
Seeking employment	29	2	94	9
Not in the labor market	582	54	559	52
Total	1,082	100	1,082	100

A longitudinal study of 1,082 leave patients has recently been completed.[4] One of the variables studied was the employment status of patients both prior to admission and at the point of leave-of-absence. Twelve months after their release, only 12 per cent of these former patients were employed full time. Another 8 per cent were employed part time or intermittently. This finding contrasts with employment status at admission, when 19 per cent were employed full time and 17 per cent part time. Of those who were working after release, two-thirds had low status jobs in unskilled labor, e.g., domestics, janitors, "shoe-shine boys," and the like. These gross figures tell us little about the problem as it was faced by each individual. However, they do give us a background for further examining the effects of stigma upon the re-employment problems of former mental patients. Table 1 shows employment after a twelve-month period following release from a mental hospital contrasted with pre-hospitalization employment status.

Twenty per cent of the released mental patients were classified by their social workers as unemployable due to a psychiatric or physical disability at the termination of leave; only 8 per cent were so classified at the time of admission. (This category excluded aged patients and housewives, and included only patients

---

[4] This study was based on data collected on all patients released to the Northern Region Bureau of Social Work (BSW) April to June, 1962. It comprised data obtained from the Basic Leave Document designed by Layle Weeks, Research Section, California Department of Mental Hygiene, and from BSW psychiatric social workers who dealt with each of the 1,082 leave patients. These were followed through the termination of their leave period, July 1, 1963. The study was done under the jurisdiction of J. J. Ploscowe, Regional Supervisor.

who would normally be expected to be in the labor market.) These presumably incapacitated ex-patients would be likely candidates for some form of job training, retraining, or sheltered workshop activity. This finding raises provocative questions about the size of the population possibly needing some type of vocational rehabilitation. If 20 per cent of all released state hospital patients are "incapacitated" and likely to need vocational guidance services of some sort, we obviously face challenging problems in planning the rehabilitation of posthospital mental patients. Consider as a reasonable goal the return of the ex-patient to his former employment status. On this basis, figures show that while 36 per cent had some form of employment *prior* to their admission to the hospital, fewer than 20 per cent were able to find any kind of work by the end of the twelve-month period following their release. This points up the re-employment needs of an additional 17 per cent of the released population who would appear to require some form of employment services. *A third of all released patients seem to have some form of employment problem.*

We need much further research on this question. Considering all available studies, it seems that fewer than one per cent of the total leave population is now actively engaged in some form of vocational rehabilitation project. Harvie[5] found that only a few of these potentially rehabilitative patients could meet the criteria of training for the competitive labor market. She posits the need for focusing on the long-term problem of the chronic mental patient in a sheltered workshop program. Selkin[6] describes the types of chronic schizophrenic patients served in such a workshop. He feels that these programs are both workable and essential in helping such patients live outside the mental hospital.

One additional factor our employment research has uncovered is the likelihood that mental patients will experience a lowering of their position on the occupational ladder, both in degree and kind, perhaps as a result of their hospitalization. More were working prior to admission than were working twelve months

[5] Harvie, Barbara, "Employment Status of Patients on Leave of Absence in San Francisco," Bureau of Social Work paper, San Francisco, March, 1964.

[6] Selkin, James, "The Treatment of Ambulatory Schizophrenia in a Rehabilitation Workshop," Rehabilitation Counseling Bulletin, Vol. 5, No. 1, pp. 22–29.

TABLE 2   OCCUPATIONAL IDENTITY OF PATIENTS PRIOR TO AND AFTER RE-
LEASE FROM A MENTAL HOSPITAL

	Prior to admission		After release	
OCCUPATION	NUMBER	PER CENT	NUMBER	PER CENT
White collar	174	22	83	10
Blue collar	292	36	235	30
No occupation	326	42	474	60
Total	792	100	792	100

N = 792

after release, as shown in Table 1. These patients tended to go from higher to lower skilled jobs, from full to marginal employment, and from higher to lower paying jobs in the course of their mental illness. We do not know, however, what part stigma has played in this downward mobility. Table 2 shows the patients' drastic occupational downgrading, both in type and amount of re-employment.

Such a major shift offers substantial and shocking evidence of work role deterioration. One could conjecture that such a change is an indication of the lowering of the patient's sense of identity. Not only are patients likely to be under-employed after hospitalization; they are also likely to *classify themselves* in a lower occupational status. Certainly such a downward shift in work role identity provides a favorable climate for the further development of subjective feelings of stigma.

How is stigma related to the re-employment problems of released mental patients? To study the possible relationship, we interviewed (as part of an on-going research project[7]) 156 mental patients who returned to the mental hospital and inquired about their experiences in the labor market. We asked this question: "Did it seem to you that being a mental patient made any difference in getting along outside the hospital? If so, in what ways?"

[7] This datum is part of a preliminary report of a larger study of 250 patients interviewed as they return to the mental hospital from leave of absence. This project, financed by the National Institute of Mental Health, is being carried out at the State Hospital, Stockton, California, under the direction of D. Miller and J. J. Ploscowe, investigators of "Reasons for Return to the Mental Hospital," (NIMH 1269-1). Research Interviewer is William H. Dawson, M.S.W.

TABLE 3   PATIENTS' OPINIONS ABOUT THEIR ABILITY TO WORK

Responses	Number	Per cent
Able to work	74	45
Not able to work	84	52
No response	5	3
Total	163	100

N = 163

These patients were returning to the mental hospital after being in the community for an average of ten months They were also asked about their alignment to the labor market. We found out, also, how many of them considered themselves able to work. While 45 per cent felt that they had been able to work while on leave, only one-fourth of these had been able to obtain any kind of work. Very few had been fully and competitively employed and able to support themselves during the leave period. We then asked if they had attempted to seek work or not, and if not, why not.

Tables 3 and 4 show how these ex-patients sought work during their stay in the community. We found that those who secured jobs generally worked only part time or intermittently as domestics or field hands, or at other menial or marginal jobs. Almost all were financially dependent, at least in part, upon their families or public welfare agencies. Many indicated that this support had been inadequate to their needs.

These findings suggest that while many of the returning patients felt they had been able to work while out of the mental hospital, hardly any had been able to find or hold adequate employment. Are these findings evidence of the effects of stigma?

TABLE 4   PATIENTS' RESPONSES REGARDING ATTEMPTS TO FIND WORK (LABOR MARKET PROSPECTS ONLY*)

Job attempts	Number	Per cent
Tried, successful	18	24
Tried, unsuccessful	28	38
Did not try	28	38
Total	74	100

N = 74

* Housewives and the aged eliminated from sample

Feelings of shame and stigma, being highly subjective, cannot be studied directly. Our interviews indicated that being a mental patient had been hard on them while they were in the community. Of those who answered "no" to our question, many qualified their answer by stating that it had *not* been hard because they had managed to keep their status a secret. This certainly meant that they were acutely aware of the effects of stigma.

Using the Berelson[8] method of content-analysis, we developed four types of stigma effects. Perhaps the most serious of these was shown by those who indicated that the fact of their mental illness was used as a threat or a "club over their heads." Sixteen per cent of the returning patients (largely middle-aged wives) indicated that they had felt stigma in this form. While this group was for the most part not actively engaged in the employment market, it gave evidence that experiencing the effects of stigma is a destructive element within the family.

The second group involved 16 per cent of the respondents who indicated that their status as former mental patients had seriously blocked communication with friends and family and had brought about a destructive change in self attitudes. This group too was primarily one of women, largely living in a dependency relationship with others. They seemed to experience the effects of stigma on a subjective or an affective level and felt that stigma resulted in a change in their attitudes and in the quality of their communications with others.

The next two types of stigma effect are most pertinent to our inquiry about re-employment. Both types of response indicated difficulty in re-entering the labor market. A group of 35 per cent of the returning patients had experienced stigma in the form of self-derogation, i.e. a lack of confidence in themselves or feelings of low self-esteem. Many were females or dependent males who had considered themselves able to work, but felt such a lowering of self-esteem that they made little or no effort to seek employment or re-employment while on leave. This seems to indicate the need of both psychiatric therapy and vocational guidance to help self-disparaging patients restore sufficient ego-strength to take up productive adult work roles in the community.

[8] Berelson, B., "Content Analysis," in Lindsey, G., ed., Handbook of Social Psychology, Vol. 1. Addison-Wesley, Mass., 1954.

The fourth type of response (given by 33 per cent of the subjects, mostly males) indicated that being a former mental patient had directly affected the search for, the procurement of or the holding of employment during the subjects' stay in the community. For example, one said: "When they found out I was a mental patient, they turned me down." While such feelings may be a part of a delusional system, it does appear that stigma is a factor in the re-employment of former mental patients.

In another study of stigma problems, Freeman and Simmons[9] asked relatives of mental patients about their attitudes. They reported that relatives' feelings of "shame or disgrace with concomitant withdrawal and concealment were probably less prevalent than has been commonly assumed." In our study of returning mental patients and their families, we sought information about the relatives' feelings of stigma by asking them if having a mental patient in the home had been hard on them. Seventy-one per cent indicated that it had. Of these, 52 per cent indicated that they were afraid or uncertain regarding the patient's social behavior, 33 per cent felt nervous, embarrassed or concerned about the effect of the patient's interpersonal behavior, while 15 per cent complained about the patient's excessive dependency, that is, requiring "too much care" in the home. These responses may not indicate stigma *per se*, but rather may refer to a cluster of feelings—rejection, exhaustion, depletion of resources and so forth—in families who were returning the patient to the hospital. Therefore, since we do not have such data from all patients' relatives, it may not be possible to compare our findings with Freeman and Simmons' findings on stigma.

Stigma must be clearly defined before findings can be meaningful. We studied patients' statements about their feelings, took these as our operational definition of stigma, and then investigated their association with the released mental patients' employment status.

Vocational counselors are aware of the negative or ambivalent feelings of employers in accepting former mental patients into their work force, but little is known of the effects of stigma upon some ex-patients' seeming "lack of motivation" or the low self-

---

[9] Freeman, Howard and Ozzie G. Simmons, *The Mental Patient Comes Home*, John Wiley and Sons, Inc., New York, 1963, p. 162.

esteem which often seems to hamper retraining or successful vocational development. It would seem, from these findings, that attention needs to be focused upon the patient's own definition of his status in considering his vocational counseling needs. As Sullivan[10] put it:

> The awareness of inferiority means that one is unable to keep out of consciousness the formulation of some chronic feeling of the worst sort of insecurity, and this means that one suffers anxiety and perhaps even something worse . . . if others can disrespect a person because of something he·shows, this means that he is always insecure in his contact with other people; and this insecurity arises, not from mysterious and somewhat disguised sources, as a great deal of our anxiety does, but from something which he knows he cannot fix. Now that represents an almost fatal deficiency of the self-system, since the self is unable to disguise or exclude a definite formulation that reads, 'I am inferior. Therefore people will dislike me and I cannot be secure with them.'

These feelings may be kept within the patient or projected onto others. Their importance and their relationship to "reality" needs further attention and study. However dismal the re-employment picture seems for most ex-patients, it can only be further complicated by powerful feelings of shame and stigma experienced by them in their relationships with prospective employers and others.

Summary

Stigma is a subjective feeling, arising from a person's perception of himself as possessing a defiling attribute. Freeman and Simmons based their study of stigma on data received from relatives of mental patients. In our study we defined stigma operationally as the returning patient's own answers to a question about his experiences in the community. To relate the effects of stigma to re-employment problems of post-hospital patients, we first

---

[10] Sullivan, Harry Stack, Clinical Studies in Psychiatry. H. S. Perry, M. L. Gawel and M. Gibbons, eds., W. W. Norton and Co., New York, 1956, p. 145.

studied the prior- and post-employment situations of a large, representative sample of released mental patients. It was found that:

(1) While 36 per cent of these patients had some type of employment prior to their admission to the mental hospital, fewer than 20 per cent were employed in any way a year after their release.

(2) While only 8 per cent had been judged to be psychiatrically or physically disabled prior to admission, 20 per cent were so classified after release.

(3) Sixteen per cent of the released patients have a re-employment problem, and another 20 per cent have a rehabilitative problem insofar as their being able to take on an adult work role is concerned.

(4) We noted a severe downward shift in patients' occupational identities following their release from a mental hospital. For example, while 22 per cent were white collar workers prior to admission, only 10 per cent were so classified at the time of leave-of-absence termination.

(5) We interviewed patients returning to a mental hospital and found that 45 per cent had felt able to work while they were in the community, but fewer than 25 per cent were able to find any kind of work during their time out of the hospital.

(6) Of these returning patients, one-half indicated that their status as ex-mental patients had created a hardship for them in the community. We took this as an operative definition of stigma.

(7) Of those patients who felt stigma, 16 per cent characterized this ex-patient status as "a club held over their heads" by relatives and others; 16 per cent felt they suffered blocked or distorted communications with others; 35 per cent experienced severe feelings of self-derogation and loss of self confidence; and 33 per cent indicated that being a former mental patient had directly prevented them from seeking, obtaining, or holding a job.

(8) Our data indicated that nearly three-quarters of the patients' relatives felt that having a mental patient in the home had created a hardship for them. While such data may indicate generalized attitudes of rejection in the families of returning patients and exhaustion of their social and personal resources, it also seems to point to some feelings of shame and stigma as well. Among this group at least, such feelings seem to play an important role in the patient's post-hospital adjustment.

We report here on two studies: (1) the longitudinal study of 1,082 released patients; and (2) interviews with 163 returning patients and their families. We conclude that feelings of stigma are a factor in the re-employment problems facing the ex-mental patient. However, exact amount, extent, and type of stigma effects cannot be fully documented. Further research is needed. There can be no doubt, however, that the problems of employment and re-employment faced by post-hospital mental patients are extensive indeed. Evidence indicates the need for vocational services of many kinds.

INDEX